BROKERS, BAGMEN, AND MOLES

BROKERS, BAGMEN, AND MOLES

□□□

*Fraud and Corruption
in the Chicago Futures Markets*

DAVID GREISING
LAURIE MORSE

John Wiley & Sons, Inc.

New York   Chichester   Brisbane   Toronto   Singapore

Recognizing the importance of preserving what has been written,
it is a policy of John Wiley & Sons, Inc.,
to have books of enduring value printed on acid-free paper,
and we exert our best efforts to that end.

LIBRARY OF CONGRESS CATALOGING-IN-PUBLICATION DATA

Greising, David, 1960–
    Brokers, bagman, and moles : fraud and corruption in the Chicago futures
markets / David Greising and Laurie Morse.
        p.   cm.
    Includes bibliographical references (p.   ) and index.
    ISBN 0-471-53057-3 (cloth)
    1. Chicago Board of Trade—Corrupt practices. 2. Chicago Mercantile
Exchange—Corrupt practices. 3. Futures market—Illinois—Chicago—Corrupt
practices. I. Morse, Laurie. II. Title.
    HG6049.G74   1991
    364.1'68—dc20   91-6413

Printed in the United States of America

91 92   10 9 8 7 6 5 4 3 2 1

For Cindy, for everything

—DG

To Christopher, who was a student of ethics and who understood the conflicts between public and private interests.

—LAM

--- □□□ ---

Acknowledgments

THIS BOOK TELLS THE STORY of the federal government's four-year investigation of the Chicago futures markets, and the frantic six months leading up to the August 2, 1989, indictment of 45 Chicago traders and a trader's clerk. It also seeks to put the investigation into a historical context, and, finally, outlines changes we believe should be undertaken to help make the markets a fairer, more efficient place for the world's business.

Telling a story like this is never simple. As with all journalistic endeavors, it relies on the varying recollections of numerous people. But through hundreds of interviews with scores of subjects, as well as days of reading transcripts and attending trials, we have assembled a mosaic that we think accurately reflects events as they happened. When we have reconstructed dialogue during private meetings, we have done so according to the best recollections of as many of those present who would comment on the matter. Most reconstruction of dialogue in the pits comes directly from transcripts of FBI tapes or testimony at trial. However, some individuals did not testify or agree to be interviewed. As we went to press, trials of Swiss franc and soybean traders were complete, and a jury was weighing evidence in the trial of Japanese yen traders.

We wish to thank the dozens of people who graciously took time to grant us interviews and to return our numerous follow-up telephone calls. We particularly want to acknowledge those government sources who lowered the veil of secrecy enough for us to gain new insights into this unique and far-reaching operation. In many instances, they risked career consequences by talking, and we are grateful to them for doing so.

We also would like to thank the exchange executives and staff members who answered our questions, despite their occasional distaste for the topic of this book. And, of course, the many traders and exchange members on and off the trading floor who shared their experiences and insights with us.

Numerous people offered help, advice and encouragement during the sixteen months during which this project moved from idea to execution. Owen Gregory helped orient us to the history of the markets and guided us through the Chicago Board of Trade's archives. John H. Stassen offered a helpful orientation toward legislative history. The staffs at the Chicago Board of Trade and Chicago Mercantile Exchange libraries were always helpful, as were the people at the Chicago Historical Society, the Commodity Futures Trading Commission, and the National Futures Association.

In keeping tabs on the traders' trials and other legal maneuverings, we received assistance from numerous defense and government lawyers. We would particularly like to thank Harvey Silets of Silets & Martin and Eddie Genson of Genson, Steinback & Gillespie, for allowing us into their firms' offices to review trial and audiotape transcripts. Cheri Lundi was remarkably helpful and gracious in this regard, as were Julie DeMatteo and James Dailydis. At the U.S. Attorney's office, Barbara Lazarus pitched in with some last-minute fact checking.

Our colleagues in the press corps offered invaluable help. As credited in the Notes to the book, we drew on numerous publications to help flesh out our reporting. And we particularly benefited from reading the coverage and listening to the advice of Greg Burns of the *Chicago Sun-Times* and Dan Weir of Knight-Ridder Financial News. At the *Chicago Sun-Times*, editors Dennis Britton and Larry Green kindly allowed us access to the newspaper's library, and librarian Judith Halper provided invaluable assistance. Tom Sheridan came through, on short notice, to provide key photographs.

We could not have completed this project without the patience, understanding, and support of our colleagues at work. At *Business Week*, Steve Shepard, Keith Felcyn, and Jim Ellis granted the time away from work and abided the many distractions during the weeks and months that were consumed by this project. Julia Flynn Siler helped persuade us there was a book in this story. The executives at Knight-Ridder Financial News, Angus Robertson, Sally Heinemann, Robert Bogda, and Suzanne Cosgrove were similarly kind. And numerous colleagues at *Business Week*, Knight-Ridder, and the *Chicago Sun-Times* were of immeasurable aid, both personal and professional.

We benefited from the legal advice of two sage counselors: Joel Weisman, who helped get the project off the ground, and Robert A. Greising, who weighed in with some wrap-up work.

We also wish to thank the people at John Wiley & Sons, who were always helpful and remarkably patient. Without our publisher, Karl Weber, we would never have begun this project, and without his firm yet pleasant prodding, we would still not be finished. In between, Karl offered important criticism of the work in progress. Judith Aisen's careful reading immeasurably improved our manuscript.

Most of all, we wish to thank our families and friends, who lived through this project with us and, sometimes, without us. Brian Homans offered both technical assistance and moral support. And Cindy and Wesley Greising remained ever happy to see Daddy whenever he found time to climb out of the study.

DAVID GREISING
LAURIE MORSE

Chicago, Illinois
June 1991

Contents

PART III

Hog Butcher for the World,
Tool Maker, Stacker of Wheat,
Player with Railroads and the Nation's Freight Handler;
Stormy, husky, brawling,
City of the Big Shoulders

—Carl Sandburg
"Chicago"

Mountain grog seller and river gambler, Generous Sport and border jackal, blackleg braggart and coonskin roisterer, Long Knives from Kentucky and hatchet-men from New York, bondsmen, brokers and bounty jumpers—right from the go it was a broker's town and the brokers run it yet.

—Nelson Algren
Chicago, City on the Make

PART I

PROLOGUE

□□□

Secrets of the Pit

SHE STANDS 51 FEET HIGH, brushed aluminum outlining the contours of her body—Ceres, the goddess of grain. From every approach to the Chicago Board of Trade building atop which she stands—down the canyon of LaSalle Street ending in its polished granite facade, by el train clacking along the south end of Chicago's Loop, from Lake Michigan to the east, the gritty tenements to the west, the working-class neighborhoods to the southwest, or the yuppie ghetto of Lincoln Park to the north—her simple, shapely figure commands attention. Ceres's face, a convex unadorned sheet of aluminum, is as mysterious as it is plain. She has no mouth to tell us what her eyes have not seen: a fitting icon of the closed, clubby society she symbolizes.

Ceres delicately grasps a sheaf of wheat in her left hand, a bag of corn in her right. And she's got the financial world by the throat.

No ear of corn, no pound of pork, no U.S. government bond, no share of stock, no deutsche mark, no yen, no pound, no franc—no nothing—is priced around the world without Chicago's trading pits having their say. New York stock traders, Iowa farmers, Montana ranchers, London gold bugs, Tokyo bankers, Saudi oil barons: They all come to Chicago to do business in a market that can swallow billions with barely a burp. Contracts worth more than $61.5 trillion pass each year through the hands of traders at the Board of Trade and its cousin, the Chicago Mercantile Exchange. That's 60 times the value of all the shares traded on the New York Stock Exchange. The trades made in Chicago's futures pits have their impact on the economies of every nation in the world.

This is an overwhelming responsibility to put in the hands of some 6,000 traders on two trading floors in downtown Chicago. But it's inevitable. The world's banks, its brokerage firms, its grain merchants, its corporations of every sort, even its small investors—all need a place where market forces can discover the fair prices, the proper interest rates, the appropriate rates of exchange. To protect the integrity of these markets, the system is run by a strict set of rules and a historic code of honor. Experienced traders staff the exchanges' boards of directors and enforce the regulations; a government agency, the Commodity Futures Trading Commission, looks over their shoulders; Congress keeps tabs on the commission. The system isn't simple, but it works. At least, that's what the public has been told.

Appearance and reality: They're quite different in Chicago's commodities pits. There are exchange rules, CFTC rules, and federal laws, all of them part of an intricately woven system that gives the futures markets the appearance of fairness and a patina of respectability. Then there are floor rules, the kind that help traders fit the caveman methods of the trading pits to the computer age of today. Floor rules have one common element: They are all violations of official rules. Everyone knows the floor rules, though they're not written down. Even those who insist on trading by official rules still must know the laws of the floor. Sometimes they hurt the customer, sometimes they help. But to many traders in the pits, floor rules are the ones that make the system work.

Making the markets work is the bottom line in Chicago, where the markets are the masters of their own fate. Ceres has stood 45 stories above LaSalle Street since 1930, when the Union Stock Yards still used everything in the pig but the squeal, when the city's rail yards were still the commercial crossroads of the nation. Others in the saga of Chicago have come and gone. First the railroad barons of the 1880s shipped in enough cheap labor to build a metropolis. Next came the grain elevators, the lumberyards, and the meatpackers; the stench from the stockyards filled the summer air. Architects Burnham, Sullivan, and Adler created an unprecedented builders' salon on the Chicago streets. Gangsters made the twenties roar. The Manhattan Project, born under a grandstand at the University of Chicago, created the nuclear age. Mayor Richard J. Daley was Boss. Harold Washington, the first black mayor, was here "For All of Chicago." And now Richard II, Daley's son, reigns. Through it all, the futures markets persist.

Like the city that spawned them, Chicago's two exchanges are both clannish and conflict-ridden. When threatened by outsiders from New York, Tokyo, or Washington, D.C., they band and fight together. But left to themselves, they bicker and bluster like feuding cousins. The Board is Irish; the Merc, Jewish. The Board is fourth-generation grain traders from the lakefront suburbs; the Merc, hustlers from the city streets. The Board is tradition-bound; the Merc, nimble and opportunistic. Even their buildings are different. The Board of Trade's is an art-deco masterpiece, its grand location at the foot of LaSalle Street a testament to the Board's political clout. The Merc, its serrated twin granite towers cutting into the Chicago sky, is modern and on the move.

Whatever their differences, the exchanges have a common philosophy: "Free Markets for Free Men." It's the gospel of the Chicago markets, the battle hymn of the trading pits. Money is the religion, and contract prices are its holy texts, spelled out for the congregation of traders on one-story-high electronic quote boards that track the trading, moment by moment, through the day. But there is more to free markets than unobstructed price changes. Freedom, for members of the exchanges, means freedom from outside interference, freedom from regulators, freedom most particularly from Washington. And if ever there was a group of willing and well-armed freedom fighters, the Chicago exchanges are they. Laden with buckets of cash—together their political contributions dwarf those of most other interest groups in the nation—they take their fight to Washington.

With that money, they purchase one simple, vital right: self-regulation. Let us run our own markets, they say. And they justify the demand with arguments both simple and condescending. Futures markets are too complex for anyone but us to understand, they say. What is a "future"? It's the obligation to buy or sell a given quantity of a particular commodity at a specified price, a defined location, and an exact time. If that's a complicated concept (and it is), they say, then how could any outsider ever hope to run our markets without mucking them up? If the regulators cramp our style, the markets will lose their agility, their power to innovate and compete, as other American industries have. Don't let the foreigners take our business, just as they did in steel and cars and electronics. So the arguments run. And, encouraged by generous donations, the legislators who oversee Chicago's commodities pits have swallowed the arguments and let the markets run free.

Freedom from interference has paid off for the traders and their markets, particularly in their remarkable expansion period that began in the 1970s. Though Ceres has reigned over the downtown skyline for years—the Board of Trade building was long the city's tallest— only in the last 15 years has her industry truly dominated Chicago business. A single innovation, the creation of financial futures, made the Board and the Merc the city's most important industry almost overnight. The steelworks and other heavy manufacturers were tired and ready to give way when financial futures were introduced in 1972. But even in their heartiest days those hulking old industries would have been hard-pressed to match the staggering growth of the futures markets during the past two decades.

When the Chicago Mercantile Exchange introduced trading in foreign currency futures on May 16, 1972, a new era was born. The traditional pork bellies and corn futures were giving way to new ideas that would turn the Chicago exchanges from farmers' markets to global capital centers. Futures contracts, which allow people to set a price today for something they will not actually buy or sell until a future time, would revolutionize the way financial institutions world- wide do business. The success of currency futures led to futures on U.S. Treasury bonds, which enable banks and other institutions to hedge against changes in long-term interest rates. The bonds would become the world's most actively traded futures contract. The Merc's Eurodollar futures meant funds on deposit overseas could be protected against rate changes. And the Standard & Poor's 500 future, launched in 1982 as a five-year bull market was reaching stride, quickly became the Merc's biggest trading arena. It spawned mini-industries of its own, known by such names as "program trading" and "portfolio in- surance," which soared until the contract's image and growth were damaged by the 1987 stock market crash.

When the 6,500-pound statue of Ceres was first raised in 44 sep- arate pieces to her perch, telephones were still a relative novelty. Trolleys trundled down the city's main thoroughfares. Today, just yards away from Ceres stand three roof-mounted radar dishes that continually send price quotes to New York, London, Tokyo, and Syd- ney. Fully one-third of the capital flowing through Chicago comes from overseas, much of it from Japan, some from London, and grow- ing sums from the European continent. Barely had Berliners stepped through holes in the wall when Eastern European leaders made their first pilgrimages to the Chicago markets. Now, even the Soviets have opened a commodities exchange in Moscow.

No place in the world is more important to prices anywhere than the square block of real estate below Ceres's pedestal, and similar footage beneath the Chicago Mercantile Exchange complex a few blocks away. But it's not the real estate that matters. It's not the warrens of cramped offices stuffed with computers, trading clerks, and brokers, the mahogany-paneled board rooms, or the vaults in the basements. It's one simple element: the pit.

The Chicago trading pit has an aura almost mythical. But the pit itself is rather plain. Different pits vary in size depending on their trading volume, but all fit the same description. Three steps up from outside the ring brings the trader to the top step, the most important tier on the trading floor. From there, traders can see all they need to do business—the price boards, the telephones, the other pits on the floor. On one side of the octagonal pit is a kind of pulpit, from which exchange employees report prices via radio wave to keypunch operators, who relay the prices to the outside world. From the top, four steps descend into the center of the pit, generally the least desirable location for traders. For traction, the steps are covered with a knobby rubber surface. The larger pits have bannisters, padded to prevent injury as traders jostle for position. Surrounding the pits are huge banks of telephones, staffed by trading clerks from the great firms like Prudential-Bache Securities, Merrill Lynch Futures, Refco, and Lind-Waldock. Some big-time traders can phone their orders directly to the floor, but most customers' orders are relayed from brokers' offices around the world.

The pits are strewn like independent pods across the trading floors of the exchanges. The Merc's floor is one vast room, about the size of a football field. Directly below the windows of the fourth floor visitors' gallery is the Standard & Poor's 500 pit. Behind the S&P is the Eurodollar pit, today the Merc's biggest and fastest growing. To the left, along the back wall, is the foreign-currency complex. Also to the left, but nearest the visitors' gallery, comes the meats complex, where futures on live cattle, hogs, and pork bellies are traded.

The floor of the Board of Trade is split into two rooms, one for agricultural commodities, the other for financials. The ag floor, named for Eddie Mansfield, a security guard who for decades remembered the name of every trader, clerk, and reporter who ever crossed the threshold, is dominated by the corn and soybean pits in its center. The financial floor is dominated by the Treasury-bond pit, which on a busy day is crowded with nearly 500 traders. It is encircled by pits for trading other debt-related instruments.

Each of the big pits is paired with an options pit, where traders with brains like slide rules swap options on futures. (Briefly, an option gives the investor the right, but not the obligation, to buy a futures contract at a specific price at any time before the option expires. Options trading is governed by mathematical rules that make college calculus look like tic-tac-toe.)

Not that any kind of futures trading is easy. It's not. The risks are tremendous, and the markets unforgiving. In the stock market, rising prices can benefit both buyer and seller. But futures is a zero-sum game. For every dollar made, a dollar is lost. And with the tiniest price movement on a single contract generally worth $12.50, the dollars move fast, especially since traders routinely swap hundreds of contracts at a crack.

What's more, with up-front margin payments of only four percent, the leverage on a trader's position is both powerful and dangerous. Tales of quick fortunes made, and lost, are legion. For every Richard Dennis or Tom Baldwin, two rags-to-riches stories of recent years, there are dozens who watch horrified as the market changes direction and wipes out their capital. Roughly a third of the membership of the Chicago exchanges turns over every year—the "bust out" rate is high, indeed.

But there's always a new body to fill the space on the floor. Traders come from all walks of life: They are former cops, lawyers, grammar school teachers, philosophy majors, and high school dropouts, as well as the sons and grandsons of traders. There are a handful of women, but the trading floors are predominantly a man's world with a locker-room atmosphere to match. Most are lured by hopes of striking it rich. The trader's life-style, seemingly made up of short hours, flashy cars, and fast times, is a lure. Few novices realize at the start how much work, and how much stress, is really involved. But they all learn.

Traders are split into two groups, "locals" and "brokers." Locals are independent speculators who trade for their own accounts. The money they make or lose is their own. Most jump quickly in and out of the market, "scalping" their positions as prices move. Brokers do some of their own trading, but the great bulk of their work is filling customer orders, for which they are paid about $1.25 per contract. Good brokers, those who can fill orders quickly and accurately, trade thousands of contracts a day. They don't take the market risk locals do, but their business does have a downside. When brokers make mistakes, the lost money comes out of their own pockets, not the customers'. At least, that's what the rules say.

The trading day begins in Chicago at 7:20 A.M., when currency and interest-rate futures open on the Merc. But the floors of both exchanges are active well before any traders arrive. Green-jacketed outtrade clerks turn up as early as 4:00 A.M. to check for their bosses' names on the list of outtrades—discrepancies between buyers and sellers about price and quantity, or even about the parties to a trade. The two sides are supposed to split the difference on an outtrade, meaning that one trader must write a check to the other. But in real life, under floor rules, the debt owed by one trader to another is commonly cancelled by pre-arranged trading in the market. It's illegal, but no customers are involved, so nobody gets hurt, or so the thinking goes.

Next to fill the floor are brokers' clerks, the worker ants of the trading pits, kids in their teens and twenties who hope someday to be able to pay a clerk to hold a trading spot for them. Arriving about an hour before trading begins, the tan-jacketed clerks mark time in the most active pits, reading newspapers or working crossword puzzles, occupying favorite spots until traders arrive just moments before the bell signals the day's opening.

By 7:15 A.M., the traders have taken their places in the currency pits, adhering to a dress code that makes the floor riotously colorful. Traders must wear neckties and jackets, but they are hardly dressed in business suits. The ties range from tired rags supposed to carry good luck to colorful handpainted prints of dollar signs, wild animals, even naked women. The jackets are loose-fitting, with wide, open pockets to hold a stack of the 3½″ × 5½″ cardboard trading cards on which traders pen the details of their buying and selling activity. Many coats have perforated jersey material running down the sides and backs for ventilation. And without exception, the jackets are in bold colors, normally chosen by the clearing firms with which the traders do business. The clearing firms guarantee that traders on the floor will meet their financial obligations and also ensure that all buys and sells are matched against opposite transactions each day. On the Merc, for example, traders cleared by Merrill Lynch wear forest green; First Boston, dark blue; Dellsher, slate blue; Shearson, black and white stripes. Locals can choose their own colors, which makes for some eye-catching, though unstylish, tailoring.

By the time the opening bell actually rings, it is redundant. Moments before the 7:20 A.M. bell, the pits are a swirl of motion and sound as traders shoulder against one another, readying for the start. A few voices call out, hoarsely quoting prices that will become actual bids or offers once trading begins. From the visitors' gallery, the pits look like shoals of choppy water, waves of traders heaving to and fro, crashing into one another, then buffeting in another direction. An occasional fistfight flares and dies. As the digital clock suspended over the pits ticks off the last few moments before 7:20, the lonely shouts become a chorus, the waves crash, arms fly, and the din of a trading day begins.

The trading method used in Chicago is called "open outcry." It means that any bid or offer on a futures exchange must be offered to the entire pit. Normally that means trades are made by shouting. Veteran traders develop raspy voices, years of screaming working like an abrasive on their vocal cords. But the commotion can drown out even the strongest voices, so traders also use hand signals. Trades sometimes are made by signals alone, when noise or trading volume stymie oral communication. Arms raised, palms facing out means selling; palms in, buying. Fingers upright signal quantity of contracts; fingers sideways, price. Those are the very basics. The details of the shorthand differ by pit and exchange and can be as complex and varied as the dialects of a language.

During the opening flurry, which usually lasts from two to ten minutes, prices are so volatile that they are reported to the public as an "opening range" rather than a single price. For unscrupulous traders, the opening range is an opportunity to steal, taking advantage of the difference between the best and worst prices in the range by giving customers the worst and taking the best for themselves. Customers have no way of knowing the difference. After the opening, prices are noted moment by moment as traders report their activity to the exchange-employed price reporters. Then, a few minutes before the close, a "closing range" emerges.

During trading, the floor resembles an anthill. The narrow aisles between the pits fill with a heel-to-toe traffic of runners, hired by clearing firms to take orders from the telephones to the pit. The busiest brokers hire clerks just to hold and organize their "decks" of orders. "Stop" orders must be exercised after the market reaches a specified price; an "MOC," or market on close, must be executed at market price at the close of trading. Good brokers have dozens of orders in their decks at any time, with dozens coming in and out during the trading day. Many brokers band together into groups, splitting the work load and the commissions and elbowing out competitors by cutting the costs they charge customers.

Local traders fight to stay as close as possible to the biggest brokers. The flow of "paper," trader parlance for customer orders, keeps the pit alive. If the local can't handle 100 contracts when a change of $.0001 in the dollar's value against the yen or the franc means a gain or loss of $1,250 at a crack, he won't last the day trying to mark time near a busy broker. Bigger locals will chase him away. The paper flow makes big brokers powerful people. Simply by looking one way or another in the pit, a broker can make a local rich or poor. So when brokers make mistakes on customer orders, locals offer to help out. They willingly take a loss, knowing they'll get repaid at some later time, at some other customer's expense. It's a violation of law and exchange rules, but many traders consider such accommodations necessary to keep the market going. Those who don't help can find themselves frozen out, particularly by the big broker groups that dominate the pits.

Some locals go beyond just helping out. In the trade, they're called "bagmen." And they make out big. For a crooked broker, the temptation of handling so much money while getting only a buck or so a contract is just too great—all those greenbacks slip through their hands, and so few stick. It doesn't take a genius to pinch a tick here or a tick there from a customer trade, or, when an order comes in that will move the market once it hits the pit—say, a big buy order that will make prices jump—maybe to step in beforehand. It may not take big brains, but it does take a friend, an accommodating local—in short, a bagman. Ripping off a customer is difficult without a bagman's help. Trading ahead is possible, but foolhardy, because it's so easily detected by exchange surveillance. That's what bagmen are for—to help out with a little scam for a slice of the action, to always have a bag ready to catch the cash that spins out of the system.

Bagmen, in reality, don't act much differently than honest locals. Nor do the crooked brokers appear any different than the straight. They all go through the same routines, just with different motives. Within minutes of each trade, locals and brokers meet to double-check their information. Price, quantity, time of trade, clearing firm, and trader identification—all are confirmed on each trader's cardboard tally card. To save time, traders are identified by acronyms of two to four letters, embossed on the heavy plastic badges pinned to the chests of their coats. Trade checking is the best opportunity to make certain that buyer and seller agree on particulars. For some, it's also a chance to make extra money by rewriting history. As long as they don't do anything stupid—say, agree on a price that never actually traded in the pit in a given time bracket—the exchange's surveillance system will not detect the illegal alteration.

For surveillance purposes, the trading day is divided into half-hour brackets marked by letters on traders' cards. After the opening range, these periods take on their own character, depending on events in the world. Any release of government information—deficit figures, trade numbers, unemployment rates—often means unpredictable, heavy action until currency futures stop trading at 2:00 P.M. Capital flows and trading often adjust as the other big markets open—cash government securities trading at 8:00 A.M., and the S&P's open at 8:30. But there are quiet days, too, when the pits all but empty after the open and don't pick up again until just before the close.

By law, trading must stop when the final bell sounds. By floor rules, it halts some five to ten minutes later, when the after-hours market called the "curb" finally quiets down. Prices can't change much there, but the curb gives brokers a chance to fill their last MOC orders. And it enables locals to buy or sell enough contracts to go home "flat"—with no open positions that can wipe them out if some unforeseen overnight event makes the next day's market a killer. Within minutes, the final trades are checked and the floor empties. Traders hurry to the clearing firms to reconcile the day's activities, check their books, perhaps even look at price charts that can tip them to the next opening. Some repair to the local bars—the Limit Up at the Merc and the Ceres Cafe at the Board are among the most popular. Others travel a half-mile north to the East Bank Club, a tony health spa frequented by the wealthy, the powerful, and the many who want to rub sweaty shoulders with them. Others just go home.

For nearly two years, there were four traders in the Chicago markets whose working day was only half over with the closing bell. For Richard Carlson in the Board's soybean pit, Michael McLoughlin in the bonds, Peter Vogel in the Merc's yen pit, and Randy Jackson in the Swiss franc, the end of trading marked the start of the swing shift. These four were special. They dressed like traders, they talked like traders, they acted and lived like traders, but they weren't traders— or not *just* traders. They were FBI agents working undercover in the commodity pits. When trading ended, they went back to their offices or to their apartments at a trader-populated complex known as Presidential Towers. In privacy, they doffed their trading jackets, ejected microcassettes from tape recorders concealed inside, and began transcribing tapes and making notes of conversations. To the government, they were heroes. To the traders, when their secret identities and missions were ultimately revealed, they would be known forever as "moles."

The tapes and the agents' notes would become the key evidence in the most ambitious and most expensive government undercover investigation ever undertaken. The dual probes—Operation Sourmash at the Board of Trade and Operation Hedgeclipper at the Merc—were designed to root out corruption on the trading floors and as far up into the hierarchy of the exchanges as possible. The investigation went public late in the evening of January 17, 1989, when the undercover agents, teamed with government lawyers, fanned out across the Chicago area and paid the first of many surprise visits at traders' homes. From that moment on, the industry would never be the same. The private club of the trading floor would be open to public scrutiny as never before.

This is the story of the investigation—where it succeeded, where it failed, and why. It is the story of government investigators misjudging their approach to a private domain where the normal investigative tactics do not apply. It is the story of a system of self-regulation that has become simply a system of self-protection. It is the story of a commodities industry obsessed with writing its own rules, but not recognizing that those rules may in the end spell its own doom.

This is the story of how faceless Ceres was forced to open her eyes, and her mouth. And when she did, she had quite a tale to tell.

CHAPTER ONE

□□□

The Knock at the Door

THIS WAS THE WORST DAY of Jimmy Sledz's life.

Perhaps that's not saying much for a kid who grew up in the privileged North Shore suburbs of Chicago and, at age 25, already owned a seat on the Chicago Mercantile Exchange worth nearly $500,000. A life like that doesn't have many really bad days.

By all outside appearances, Wednesday, January 18, 1989, looked no different from any other work day. Jimmy had just left his condo in Presidential Towers, the four-building complex favored by Merc traders for its two-block walk from work, its running track, its officious security system, shiny lobby, and Porsche-filled indoor parking lot. He was hustling through the cold wind on his way to the Merc's twin-towered red granite building across the Chicago River on Wacker Drive.

If this were a normal day, Jimmy would be on his way to trade in the Japanese yen futures pit. He would worry about what had happened to the yen in Tokyo overnight and how the London currency markets were trading as he walked. President-elect Bush's inauguration on Friday might possibly affect the markets.

But the future course of the yen was the last thing on Jimmy Sledz's mind this day. Instead, he could not take his thoughts off the tiny tape recorder stowed in the right pocket of his blue cotton-blend trader's jacket. That recorder, placed there at 6:30 that morning by two FBI agents, was part of a trap. And now Jimmy Sledz was under orders to spring it on his friends on the trading floor.

Jimmy's job was to approach Sam Cali, his brother Brian's best friend, and persuade Sam to come back to Jimmy and Brian's apartment. Waiting for him there would be the same surprise Jimmy had had the night before—a couple of government lawyers, an anonymous-looking FBI agent, and another FBI agent named Dietrich Volk.

Cali would recognize the short, silver-haired Volk immediately. Jimmy Sledz certainly had. Until just before Christmas, Volk had been a trader in the yen pit answering to the name Peter Vogel. He was the kind of guy who was happy to break the rules to help out a friend. As it turned out, he was also an undercover agent about to cause Sledz, Cali, and more than a dozen other yen traders a bunch of trouble.

As he forced one foot in front of another, Sledz could not believe what happened next. He cried. Real tears were streaming down his cheeks as he made his way toward the Merc to save his own skin by giving the government the hide of a friend. But he kept walking, and before he knew it, Jimmy was on the trading floor, bumping his way into the yen pit.

Shaking and pale, a lump filling his throat, Jimmy went through the motions of trading. Buying and selling yen contracts was the last thing he wanted to do. But the government agents had told him to trade, so trade he did.

Jimmy caught Sam's eye just as Cali saw him. Tall, rail-thin, his gray-flecked hair and mustache conspicuous among the youthful traders, Sam Cali had no way of knowing what was about to happen. And Jimmy was surprised at what did. Despite the drilling from the government agents—engage Sam, they had said, talk to him about trading, invite him to the apartment—Jimmy lost his nerve. He grabbed a trading card from his chest pocket and printed very clearly with his pencil: "Don't say anything."

Sam would call later, but they said little else. Sam could see there was a problem. And a cryptic note from Brian Sledz later in the morning made matters clearer. "The house may be bugged," it said. "Sam, I can't answer any questions." Suddenly, whispers about an investigation rippled across the floor, where news travels faster than light.

Before Jimmy Sledz could think, he was practically running off the trading floor. Crossing the river, he again surprised himself by what he did next. He ripped the tape recorder from his trading jacket, yanked out the microcassette, and tossed it off the bridge. He knew there'd be hell to pay, but it was better than causing more trouble for Sam.

Already, Jimmy had a good read on the government boys. As he expected, they were angry. Dan Gillogly, a quick-tempered career prosecutor with red hair combed across a balding pate, practically jumped when Jimmy broke the news about the tape and the note to Sam. After giving Sledz an abrupt dressing-down, Gillogly warned him, "You tell the truth all the time, and stop the nonsense with the notes," he said. "Don't make us look like fools."

Exhausted, Jimmy could barely respond. "That's one of the most difficult things I've ever had to do," he told Volk. "And I don't want to have to do it anymore."

Back at the Merc that afternoon, Sam Cali rushed to a telephone. David Horberg, another yen trader, had just explained the riddle that had been presented by the Sledz brothers' odd performance in the morning: The FBI had put undercover agents on the floor. Peter Vogel was a fed. Subpoenas had gone out.

When Jimmy answered the phone, Sam spoke immediately. "I don't want to come up to your apartment," he said. "The fucking guy lives in your building." Sam paused. "You know who I'm talking about."

Sam's voice was panicky, and Jimmy understood why. But with a little convincing, Sam agreed to come to the Presidential Towers lobby, just to talk. When they met, Sam looked ashen. He refused to go upstairs. He wanted to get a read on Brian Sledz's predicament. He wanted to see his friend. "Get Brian down here," Cali demanded. "But I'm not going to go up there."

Jimmy phoned up to the apartment while Sam waited by the fountain in the lobby. When he hung up, Jimmy tried to impress Sam with the gravity of the situation. "Listen, Sam," Jimmy explained in a low voice. "We were wired on the floor. Everybody's been wired. It's all over."

As they talked, they rode up the escalator toward the security entrance to the apartment elevators. On the down escalator coming toward them was a frightening sight: Brian Sledz and the once friendly seeming Peter Vogel. "Why didn't you tell me they were up there?" Sam muttered to Jimmy as they approached the pair.

Then, as the escalators brought the duos face to face, Cali hailed Vogel: "Hi Peter. Or whoever you are."

It took little to get Sam to come to the apartment now. Few people would want to discuss a possible indictment in the lobby of an apartment tower. But when the three traders and the fed reached the Sledz apartment, it was worse than Sam had expected. They sat him in a chair in the middle of the room, facing two government lawyers and an unfamiliar-looking FBI agent. Volk sat between Cali and the door.

Brian and Jimmy were in the entrance hall, though within a few minutes they quit the apartment, leaving Sam alone with the feds.

Gillogly started by telling Sam there was an investigation under way at the Merc. "It's a big deal. There are a lot of people involved," he explained. Then Volk advised Sam to cooperate, in the same tone of voice he would have used in tipping him to a trade. Volk listed some of the possible criminal charges Sam might be facing: wire fraud, mail fraud, racketeering—serious stuff. The racketeering count could mean jail time and the loss of Sam's Merc seat and other property, even his house.

Then Gillogly said something that seemed utterly preposterous to Sam under the circumstances: "You're free to come and go if you please."

Almost interrupting, Volk talked again, assuring Sam that traders who cooperated probably would not be charged with racketeering.

Instinctively, Sam knew he should ask the next question: "Do you think I should get a lawyer?"

And just as quickly, Gillogly offered a half-answer. "We can't advise you on that."

Sam decided to talk. An hour, then two went by. They wanted to know everything. Whom he traded with. Where he stood in the pit. Whose orders he filled. How much volume he did. Who he knew. Sam got dizzy with the details. Finally, the G-men seemed satisfied with what they had. They asked Sam to be available for more questions later.

Cali promised he'd have more to say, especially if he could review some trading records. He was a member of ABS Partners, the most powerful group of brokers on the floor. The feds wanted anything they could get on ABS and on the men who ran it, Maury Kravitz and Jimmy Kaulentis, some of the Merc's most powerful and controversial traders.

Sam asked a question that seemed bizarre in retrospect: "Is it okay if I continue trading?" The answer, briefly, was no.

As Sam was leaving the apartment, Volk offered what was almost an apology. Volk said he was just doing his job, and at times like this, the job wasn't easy.

Sam's thoughts were reeling—this normal-seeming day had gotten twisted out of shape. He wanted to express his befuddlement and to somehow let Volk know that he was a good, law-abiding guy. "I'm not a criminal," Sam said. "I mean, I am, but I'm not."

□ □ □

ERNEST B. LOCKER, JR., never got more excited than this. Tonight was the biggest event in the four-year undercover investigation of Chicago's commodity markets, and Locker was in control. He headed a command center set up in the FBI's conference room on the eighth floor of the Dirksen federal building, a black monolith in the city's central business district. Eight temporary telephone lines snaked out of the wall, ready for the hectic activity to come. Agents and government lawyers were milling around, the tension mounting as the time approached when Operation Sourmash and Operation Hedgeclipper would be unveiled to surprised traders at their lush homes throughout Chicago and its suburbs.

Locker sat at a conference table, filling in a massive grid pattern. The light reflected from his bald forehead, his thick glasses focused directly on the work in front of him, his long, thin hands methodically inked names into squares of the grid. Locker worked with the concentration of a child laboring over a coloring book, making certain the crayon doesn't cross the black lines.

But this was not child's play. It was the culmination of four years of work and the biggest project in Locker's 27 years as a career FBI man. In each square of the grid appeared the name of a subject, a trader who had attracted the attention of the four undercover FBI agents posing as traders on the two Chicago exchanges.

With help from Jeffrey Frank, the FBI case agent who had worked under Locker in carrying out the commodities probe, it was Locker's job this night to plan the movements of six teams of FBI agents and Assistant U.S. Attorneys. Locker and Frank had organized the teams with help from Assistant U.S. Attorney Ira Raphaelson, who headed the probe for U.S. Attorney Anton Valukas.

The plan was as simple as a postman's route. Teams would spread across the city, quietly knocking on traders' doors and identifying themselves as government agents. They would talk for as long as the traders were willing, urging them to cooperate. Many of the subjects would recognize at least one of the late-night visitors, because four of the teams included an FBI agent who had worked undercover in the pits. When one conversation ended, the team would move on to its next stop.

The trap that had yawned quietly and inconspicuously in the commodities markets since early 1986 was about to be sprung. Locker would have preferred it if the undercover phase of the operation had not ended so soon. But by mid-December of 1988, the cover was starting to blow. There were occasional rumors on the trading floors about undercover agents, and the U.S. Attorney's office was starting to get telephone calls. The agents had to be recalled. Before and after Christmas, one by one they had turned in their trading jackets and started the full-time paperwork needed to prepare the subpoenas that would go out this night.

Violence against the agents could not be ruled out. In mid-1988, a suspicious Merc trader had threatened the lives of agents Dietrich Volk and Randall Jannett, accusing them of being G-men. That scare had blown over. The trader never mentioned his seemingly wild notion again. But still, the fear of violence was there. "There have been hundreds of gangland slayings in Chicago, and there's lots of people down on the exchanges whose names end in *a, e, i, o,* and *u,*" an FBI agent said later, indifferent to the implied ethnic slur.

Gathering quietly in the Dirksen building nerve center, Locker and the rest of the agents were not yet congratulating themselves on the success of the mission. There would be no backslapping, no dramatic speeches. Instead, Locker's briefing was simple and to the point. "If they agree to cooperate, call in and let us know. We might send you somewhere else," Locker advised. "If they don't, just move on to your next assignment."

With Locker and Frank manning telephones at headquarters, the operation proceeded as planned. Until after midnight Wednesday night, and as early as 6:30 the next morning, the teams knocked on traders' doors, and at each delivered the same news: "We've got you on tape." They asked the same questions: "Who did you trade with? How much did you steal?" They offered the same deal: "If you cooperate now, you won't be charged with racketeering." And they delivered the same threat involving RICO, the infamous Racketeer Influenced Corrupt Organizations Act: "If you are charged with RICO, you'll lose your house, your seat on the exchange, all your property. And you'll go away to jail for a good long time."

This was hardball enforcement work. Melanie Kosar, a 25-year-old Treasury-bond trader, answered the front door of her suburban apartment at 10:30 Wednesday night dressed only in a bathrobe. The four government agents introduced themselves and began a four-hour interrogation during which Kosar never got dressed. Robert Mosky's two-year-old daughter watched as the feds interviewed her daddy about trades in the Swiss franc pit. The visits would last through the weekend, and follow-ups would extend into the next week. Traders would begin swapping hard-luck stories of overzealous government agents trampling into their once-cloistered lives.

Not that Locker, or Raphaelson, or Valukas would care. In their view, wealthy traders who had stolen from customers should be treated the same as bank robbers or gangsters. "The only reason you're hearing these complaints is because these guys are rich enough to pay for lawyers," Valukas would say later. "This is standard operating procedure, and it's not going to change just because the guy is stealing on the exchange and not in the streets."

One of the FBI agents in charge of the probe explained the strategy simply. "You want to be the one to break the news to them," the agent said. "Your chances of cooperation are a lot greater if the first time they hear about it, it's from you."

The late-night offensive was the first that large numbers of traders would hear of a top-secret probe of Chicago's commodities markets. But for traders, lawyers, the press, and the public, this much was clear: It certainly would not be the last.

□ □ □

To JOHN BAKER, the comfortable brick-and-cedar two-story house in suburban LaGrange represented success. He, his wife, Sally, and their two children had moved in seven years earlier, when the house was brand-new. It had been a big step up, part of a life-style made possible by Baker's growing success as a commodities broker in the Chicago Mercantile Exchange's Japanese yen pit. It was a life that had not been attainable during Baker's earlier careers as a short-haul truck driver, postal carrier, and children's book salesman. The house wasn't flamboyant, but it was comfortable.

It was the house, and the security it represented to his family, that allowed John Baker to endure the turmoil of the futures pits and the inevitable ups and downs of trading. He had taken his share of losses, and on this January day in 1989, he was just beginning to feel financially secure again after eating a big loss on a bad customer "fill" more than a year earlier.

Wednesday, January 18, was "trade figure day," when the monthly release of U.S. Commerce Department statistics on the country's trade balance meant at least an hour of hell in the yen futures pit. Baker left home early enough to reach the Chicago Mercantile Exchange well in advance of the opening, check his account balances, and make sure his customers were squared away after Tuesday's session.

His route in the pre-dawn chill was familiar. He had taken this commute since 1976, when a neighbor introduced him to the business and found him a job as a floor clerk. Baker started trading in the arcane egg futures pit, then made a successful transition into foreign currency futures. Barely ten years later, he owned his own seat, had built up a substantial deck of customers, and had recently formed CSI Brokerage of Chicago. He hoped the firm would be his ticket out of the pit and off the trading floor, where life is best for the fit and the under-30.

The city was still dark as Baker walked through the Merc Center's revolving doors and rode up the escalators. He knew the trading floor would be buzzing by the time he arrived. Baker's head was also buzzing. A heavy drinker, he had lived it up the previous evening. Some mornings Baker would meet other traders in the Merc's bar for a breakfast drink after the openings, a nip to steady his hands and head. But this morning would be too busy for such an interlude.

As usual, the yen pit was jammed with traders jostling for position. Baker and his partner, Tom Crouch, had long-established spots with good sightlines to their customers, who worked from booths on the sidelines. Youthful for his 51 years, Baker was tall and broad-shouldered, and had an easy smile. He good-naturedly nudged himself into his pit position well ahead of the bell, while checking the opening orders with his clerk. He knew these were the last minutes of calm before the opening downburst of orders.

Baker was older than most of the traders surrounding him and had lived hard. But the drinking had not put him so far out of shape that he couldn't still move fast in the pit. His hair was thinning and nearly all white; in an effort to preserve an image of vitality, Baker had attempted to color it, with limited success. "Old Bluehair," some of the younger traders called him behind his back.

The bell rang, and by 8:00 A.M., Baker's fading blue, pink, and orange tropical-print trading jacket streamed with sweat. The trade data showed another big deficit. In response, March yen futures first rallied, then collapsed, fueling chaos in the pit.

Baker finally got a break from trading about 10:00 A.M., glad to divert his attention from his deck and the pit. Traders often get headaches from the intense concentration and the din of trading, and today was a headache day for Baker. Hurriedly swigging coffee in the break room, he saw fellow yen broker Dave Horberg approach. What Horberg told him sparked a pang of fear. The government had caught wind of something. There was an investigation. No one knew exactly what was involved, but it could be the feds were looking for gambling violations. They were definitely targeting the currencies, and particularly the yen pit. Baker began to worry. "If the FBI calls you, don't talk to them," Horberg advised.

Back in the pit, Baker's mind was anywhere but on the market. He noticed that Sam Cali, another yen broker and a frequent competitor for his business, had left. By the 2:00 P.M. close Baker's head hurt, his feet hurt, and he was overdue for a beer. One drink led to another, and Baker didn't leave downtown until 5:00 P.M. By the time he pulled into the driveway, the streetlights were on again. His son Mark, who also worked at the Merc, was already home.

When Baker walked in the door, Sally was angry, as Baker expected. After 29 years of marriage, Sally could handle the mood swings of trading, but she hated when John came home four sheets to the wind. She had not bothered to cook dinner. Baker slumped at the kitchen table with his coat still on, and they argued. In a sour mood, they drove to the local Burger King to grab a take-out order.

By 7:30 P.M., the Bakers had each popped open an Old Style and started to relax. Bags of fries and hamburger cartons littered the kitchen table, smelling of grease and onions. When the doorbell rang, Baker thought it might be one of Mark's friends. Instead, Pete Vogel, a drinking buddy and local trader in the yen pit, was standing in the porch light. He was flanked by three other men, two of them wearing suits and topcoats and looking nothing like traders. No one was smiling.

Despite the hints Baker had heard in the break room that day, he was not prepared for this doorstep visit. Pete Vogel's light-colored eyes were colder than usual, and his voice tough. "John," Pete said, brandishing some kind of badge, "you know who I am. We have you on tape. I think it would be a good idea if you listened to what we have to say."

Fear rose in Baker's throat as he tried to grasp Vogel's words. He heard Vogel say "trouble" and "on tape" again. Vogel reintroduced himself as "FBI special agent Dietrich Volk." The four men stood in the January chill as Baker, in a fleeting thought, recalled meeting Pete. Was it a year ago? Vogel had limped into the yen pit sometime after the 1987 stock market crash, complaining about big losses in the S&P's, and about needing to make the money back. Traders in the yen pit were a tight-knit group. The gregarious Baker had gone out of his way to help Vogel break in. They made a routine, with a few other traders, of going to breakfast, having drinks. The drinking, Baker reflected briefly, may have gotten him into trouble.

Vogel was a great listener, always interested in floor gossip and Baker's stories of big wins and losses. Vogel was a bit of a bumbler in the pits, and Baker had spent a lot of time with him, usually in the Merc Club bar, trying to get Vogel used to the business, the people— telling him stories. They had gotten close enough to do a few deals, often at Vogel's suggestion. In one barroom conversation, Vogel offered Baker the chance to pass him some trades on the floor in order to generate a few extra bucks for himself and give Baker a tax shelter. Vogel had been an accountant, and the tax deal looked pretty sweet at the time. It sheltered $4,750.00 of income

That was a few days before Christmas. Now, Vogel was standing on Baker's doorstep flashing the FBI badge, talking trouble. Baker, stunned, forgot Dave Horberg's warning and stood aside to let Vogel and his group in. As the men walked through the house to the kitchen, Baker noticed that Vogel—or Volk, or whoever the bastard was—was wearing a revolver under his short ski jacket.

Sally was even more startled than Baker had been when the four strangers walked into her kitchen. Introductions all around hardly broke the ice. The thin, pale, colorless man in the suit and topcoat introduced himself as Daniel Gillogly, an Assistant U.S. Attorney. Mark Pollack, handsome, dark, clean-shaven, was also a government prosecutor. The other two men said they were FBI. One of them Sally recognized. Vogel had stood in her kitchen barely three weeks earlier, a friendly guest at the Baker's annual Christmas party. Had he been an FBI agent then?

From John's voice and face, Sally could tell there was trouble. Still, when one of the prosecutors, surveying the living room, complimented her on her "nice house," she relaxed for a brief second. The next instant, there was malice in his words. "Too bad you'll have to lose it," he said.

"We're considering indicting your husband on federal racketeering and conspiracy charges. We have evidence—we have him on tape, breaking the law. If he doesn't cooperate, we'll charge him," said Gillogly. "You could lose your house, your jewels, everything you own. We have enough evidence to convict him for mail fraud, wire fraud, and conspiracy. He could be facing 20 years in prison, and he will never trade again." The voice of the prosecutor droned on, detailing a frightening array of possibilities: prison, huge fines, the word RICO.

Baker looked at his wife's face and crumbled. He backpedaled fast—he was not sure whether the men intended to arrest him. If they had videotaped the tax deal he'd made in Vogel's office, it could mean trouble. Baker considered his options and made an offer. "Look, if I can help, I will. But you have to give me some guarantees. Can you arrange to protect my family, keep the house out of it?" Baker pleaded.

Gillogly had the upper hand on this one, and he sensed Baker would talk if he kept the pressure on. "No deals at this time," he said, his voice terse and unyielding. Baker, after all, was one of Gillogly's biggest fish in this investigation. He intended to keep the pressure on until Baker cooperated and led him to even bigger catches, perhaps in the Merc's tight-knit circle of leadership.

It looked to Gillogly like he wouldn't have to use his trump card: Waiting just down the block in a government car was Brian Sledz, another Japanese yen trader who was already cooperating. Gillogly was prepared to use Sledz to shake up Baker if he balked at their questions.

Obtaining no concessions, Baker still agreed to talk. Trying to lighten the atmosphere, he offered the prosecutors a beer. When they refused, he popped open another Old Style for himself. Gillogly, Pollack, and Volk began a rapid three-on-one volley of questions. They asked Baker about Horberg, Cali, and other brokers in the yen pit. Volk asked for details of specific trades. Volk was forceful, persistent, hardly the way he had acted at the Merc Club or on the floor. Baker listened to him drag up trades and details of their conversations, and his mood became black. The second FBI agent, Mark Bargmann, busily wrote down everything Baker said.

By the time the questioning danced directly into Baker's own conduct, the four men had been in Baker's house more than an hour. The turn of the conversation alarmed Baker. "I need an attorney. Shouldn't I have an attorney here?" he asked. It was the second time that evening he had asked about a lawyer, but he did it with more conviction this time. Pollack said, "You don't qualify for a public defender because of your income." Gillogly said he didn't give legal advice.

They started in on the tax trade. "We taped all that," Gillogly said. "We taped Dietrich handing you the cash in his office. We have you nailed." Volk had asked Baker to do that deal. He claimed he had a customer with big losses for the year who could afford to take some winning trades. If Baker wanted to hand him a winner in the pit, Volk would gladly repay him 90 percent under the table. Baker had agreed.

"That was a good scheme, and you thought it up," Baker said to Volk angrily. He turned to Gillogly and said, "Isn't that entrapment? He suggested I do it."

Gillogly laughed. "Please John, let that be your defense," he jibed. "Let us hear that in court."

Baker felt worn down. He had another beer and asked to talk to Sally privately in the dining room. Pollack used the phone in the kitchen. When Baker returned, the four men asked him to leave the room for a while so they could discuss the case. By this time, Baker was foggy. It was late. He'd been up since 5:00 A.M. He accepted being banished to his own living room without protest.

The questioning resumed, but Baker's increasingly convoluted responses frustrated the prosecutors. "You're talking in circles," Gillogly said curtly. "We're getting confused here. Maybe we've had enough for one night." Gillogly knew he had another round of visits scheduled for early Thursday morning. And it looked as though they had obtained all they could use from Baker.

As the prosecutors prepared to leave, Baker worried aloud whether he'd be too upset to trade on Thursday. Gillogly and Volk were startled by his comment. "You hadn't better say a word to anybody on the floor about this," Gillogly warned. "If you go to work, if you intend to trade, you'd better be squeaky clean."

□ □ □

OUT-OF-TOWN CORRESPONDENTS come to Tribune Tower in Chicago all the time. Work brings them there, career necessity brings them there. But for Washington correspondent Christopher Drew, the *Chicago Tribune*'s Justice Department reporter, this January visit was anything but routine. Drew had in his notebooks the makings of the biggest story of his career, and he knew it.

A week earlier, Drew had phoned William B. Crawford, Jr., the *Trib*'s chief commodities reporter. Drew had heard that Anton Valukas, the U.S. Attorney from Chicago, was in Washington to visit with Attorney General Dick Thornburgh, and a Justice Department source said it had something to do with commodities trading but offered no details. Maybe Chicago would have some answers.

"Have you heard anything about anything going on at the exchanges?" Drew asked Crawford in the vague yet pointed manner reporters use when working a hot tip. He wanted some help, but would give details only if his colleague could offer something in return.

Crawford had something, but not much. As the *Trib*'s longtime Chicago federal courts reporter transferred to the commodities beat in one of editor James Squires's many staff reshufflings, Crawford knew about almost everything that happened at the Dirksen federal building. Crawford had picked up a rumor nearly a year earlier, just before he left the courts to work under William Neikirk on the business section. A lawyer departing the U.S. Attorney's staff had said there was an undercover operation going on at the Chicago futures exchanges. Crawford even asked Valukas about it once, but got only the kind of non-denial "No comment" that such questions usually elicited.

Other than that lead, Crawford could add no details for Drew. "Well, keep your ear to the ground," Drew said, his voice quieting. "But don't tell anyone about this conversation. Not Neikirk, not anyone."

Now Drew was in Chicago, and the story was about to blow open. He had confirmed that there was an undercover investigation, and his source said it was about to go public. Reporters in the cubicled burrows of the *Trib*'s business section could see through the glass doors into Neikirk's office, where the gaunt former Washington business columnist weighed the arguments spelled out by Crawford over when to run Drew's story.

Crawford wanted to hold the story for the Sunday paper. His raspy voice methodically laid out his reasons. It would have the most impact on a Sunday, when the *Tribune* sold more than a million newspapers. It would give them more time to ferret out the details. They knew there were undercover agents, but not exactly how many. They knew the agents were looking for "bucketing," the practice of matching customer orders away from the trading pits, but they knew little else about the scope of the investigation—how high up in the exchange it went, and what the feds had found.

Neikirk agreed to wait until Sunday, but only if the story would definitely hold. Drew clearly had a big scoop, and he would not tolerate getting beat. If *The Wall Street Journal* or the *Chicago Sun-Times* printed the story first, no amount of detail on a follow-up article would save face for the *Tribune*.

There was only one way to safely hold the story, and that was to go to prosecutor Valukas himself. He alone would control when the news broke. Once government agents went knocking on traders' doors, even the sleepy *New York Times* would hear about it, probably from the Knight-Ridder or Reuters wire services.

At 2:00 P.M. on Wednesday, January 18, Drew was ushered into Valukas's office on the 15th floor of the Dirksen building. Except for a stuffed bald eagle, the place displayed few of the trappings of power, few signs that this was where the federal government kept its prosecutorial sword sheathed. Valukas, dark haired, his expressive eyebrows arching behind designer eyeglasses, greeted Drew for the first time. Although Drew had worked in Chicago on the *Trib*'s business staff for several years, they never had sat for a one-on-one interview before.

This particular interview would be rather short. Drew laid out for Valukas what he knew. He recognized that a *Tribune* story the next day might prematurely blow the government's cover. He told Valukas that the *Trib* would hold the story, but only in exchange for detailed information about the probe.

No deal. "I've always enjoyed a good relationship with the *Tribune*, and I hope that won't stop," Valukas told Drew. "If you have a story, go ahead and print it."

Back at Tribune Tower, Drew was a flurry of activity. Stationed at a computer terminal in the middle of the *Trib*'s metro desk, he banged out the details of what his Washington source had told him, and what Crawford had been able to dig up during the day. Crawford played backup, checking facts, making certain nothing slowed down Drew's work. When he wanted coffee, Crawford ran for it. Drew still didn't have a clear fix on how "bucketing" worked in practice, so Crawford nailed that down. He came up with some other crucial trading terms, as well: "trading ahead," "kerb trading," "pre-arranged trading."

Whenever Crawford developed new tips that had to be checked with someone inside the investigation, Drew would move to verify or reject the information. A single telephone call to Washington always provided the answer. As deadline approached, Drew began sending the story in brief takes to Washington for editing by his bureau chief, Nicholas Horrock, who wasn't about to let go of this story just because his reporter had traveled to Chicago to write it. Only after Horrock's once-over would Neikirk get a look. Then Drew and Crawford would double-check the text before it went to the copy desk en route to the *Trib*'s printing plant located on the outskirts of the city's business district.

By the time the presses at Freedom Center started rolling, the paper carried on its front page a banner headline: "U.S. Probes Futures Exchanges." The story, a clean scoop of all other media, was about to be told. The battle for the headlines, which would keep the story on the front pages of the nation's newspapers for days, was on.

□ □ □

OUTTRADE CLERKS, the early-rising soldiers who sweep up trading errors in the dawn hours before the trading day begins, huddled in small groups on the cavernous floor of the Chicago Mercantile Exchange, poring over copies of the January 19 edition of the *Chicago Tribune*.

"U.S. Probes Futures Exchanges," the front-page headline trumpeted. "FBI Tapes Key to Fraud Investigation." The feeling of shock was palpable. In a world where rumors are relished, where knowing who you're trading with is the first principle of business, and where floor business is nobody else's business, it seemed incredible that the *Tribune* could deliver such dramatic news with so little warning.

One or two of the green-jacketed clerks went to the phones to rouse the brokers they worked for, telling them to buy the *Trib* on the way to the train. The clerks who had bought the *Sun-Times* that morning were shut out. The story was a *Tribune* exclusive. Copies of the paper would disappear from the Merc's newsstand by nine o'clock that morning.

The news was astounding—the FBI had planted an undetermined number of "moles" on the trading floors, secretly recording trades and conversations, maintaining their cover for more than two years. If it hadn't been printed in black and white, the folks on the floor would never have believed it.

As the regular cadre of traders and brokers began to trickle in for the 7:20 A.M. opening of the currency and Eurodollar pits, the floor buzzed about the story. Traders clustered in small groups, discussing first the article and then the rumors of FBI "raids" the previous night. In the break rooms, amid swirls of cigarette smoke and the smell of coffee dregs, people discussed which of their colleagues were absent that day, which might be "moles," and which targets.

At the Board of Trade, the scene was much the same. In the soybean pit, the mood was one more of fear than of shock—three of the pit's major brokers hadn't shown up for the opening. And tales of late-night FBI visits at the homes of at least a half-dozen bean traders left the whole pit cold. Some big locals left the pit early, taking their business with them.

There had been hints of trouble by midday Wednesday, when the first rumors of subpoenas had hit the exchange floors. But most traders had assumed that the probe focused on either gambling or drugs: With the Super Bowl pool topping $500,000, it wouldn't be surprising for the feds to crack down. Either that, or a drug sweep like the one at the Chicago Board Options Exchange a few years earlier would hardly be a shock. Everyone assumed that cocaine figured in the life-styles of at least one group of high-flying brokers.

As it turned out, cocaine would have been better news. The *Tribune's* contention that the FBI was investigating widespread cheating on the futures exchanges, and that as many as a hundred traders might be implicated, clouded the whole industry.

If the FBI was looking for crooked traders, it seemed to have missed its target. The traders who received the late-night visits were mostly ordinary Joes or complete unknowns—guys who might bag a trade now and then, but were not major players. The floor's true "slimeballs," who systematically cheated on orders but seemed to escape exchange scrutiny because of their rumored ties to the powers that be, apparently had been left untouched. Those traders were well known and conspicuously present on the trading floor on January 19.

Traders mentally worked back through the two years of the supposed inquiry, trying to remember when they'd said or done anything that might have attracted the FBI's attention. Two years was a long time. Many had bent the rules at least once to accommodate a customer or bail out of an expensive error. Had there been an FBI agent standing nearby wearing a tape recorder?

Worse, there might still be agents on the floor. The *Tribune* article left open that possibility. And some traders who had received subpoenas Tuesday had agreed to cooperate by wearing recorders in the pits. Rumors circulated of Jimmy Sledz's strange behavior Wednesday morning. To break the tension, phone clerks and runners began to make jokes, talking into make-believe microphones in the lapels of their tan jackets and pulling off their shoes in a parody of the shoe phone worn by secret agent Maxwell Smart in the old "Get Smart" TV series.

By the time the 8:30 A.M. bell opened trading in the S&P 500 futures pit, traders in the mainline of the rumor network had worked out who the moles had been. Randy Jackson from the Swiss franc pit and Peter Vogel from the yen had been among the midnight raiders.

They had accompanied federal prosecutors to Merc traders' homes Wednesday evening. On the Board, Rick Carlson had traded in the soybeans, and a fourth agent, Michael McLoughlin, was rumored to have staked out the Board's T-bond pit.

At the Merc, traders recalled, Jackson and Vogel were clean-cut and rather bumbling locals who had washed out of the S&P's after the October 1987 stock market crash and were trying a comeback in the currencies. S&P traders shook their heads and grinned. They laughed at the idea of the feds standing in the pit during the crash, trying to trade. It was no wonder they'd bailed out and moved into the currencies. Traders guessed the FBI's losses in the crash topped $5,200,000. "Shit," one trader exclaimed, "*I* should have taxpayers' money to trade with."

At the Board, Carlson had a slightly better pedigree. He was a working stiff who had climbed the ladder filling orders in the bean pit for the huge grain trading firm of Archer Daniels Midland. He had unexpectedly scraped enough cash together to buy his own seat. He was an ordinary guy, stocky, blond, and balding—few would have guessed where he got the dough.

The rumor mill also identified traders who were cooperating. Jimmy Sledz had disappeared after an incident in the yen pit Wednesday. His brother Brian was gone, too. Was it true that they had been wearing hidden tape recorders?

By lunchtime, traders eyed their pit mates. Who were the more recent arrivals? Who was suspiciously clean-cut, and new enough that you didn't know his father? Hell, nowadays everyone at the Merc was a newcomer. How about the guy you traded with last week who hadn't shown up in three days? Was he at the federal building making a case against you? And what about that tax deal that might look bad if the feds got interested?

By early afternoon, paranoia drove traders to leave the pits to make appointments with lawyers. The Merc paging system worked overtime, calling traders to their telephones. Reporters from across the country tried reaching anybody on the trading floor who would pick up a phone and make a comment. Managers for some of the larger clearing firms issued blanket orders: Under no circumstances should employees speak to the press. Floor managers for the big brokerage houses with retail clients quickly formulated an acceptable public line: "There are a few bad apples in every business. If some bad traders have been uncovered, it will be good for everyone. If they are guilty, they should be thrown out." Privately, the same managers were puzzling over why the names of the floor's really bad apples had not surfaced on the growing list of traders who had received subpoenas.

At the Board, press manager Ray Carmichael considered limiting press access to the trading floor. His office was swamped with inquiries, and traders were complaining of being badgered by reporters. His only response to the press was still, "No comment." Reporters also began calling traders' homes. Those phoning John Baker, one of the subpoenaed yen traders, were greeted by an answering machine recording in the voice of Daffy Duck.

Currency traders who knew Randy Jackson well enough to have his Presidential Towers phone number took turns calling his answering machine. The message was ironic: "Hello, sweetheart," Jackson's Bogart-toned voice said on the recording, "I'll take your case, but remember, I stick my neck out for no one. Now spill the beans or I'll come over and slap you in the mouth. Here's listening to you, kid . . ."

Enterprising back-office employees began designing a new generation of lapel buttons to reflect the mood on the trading floors. "Feds: 150, Locals: 0" one read, a reference to the rumored number of subpoenas. Another, in black gothic letters printed on a caution-yellow background, said, "Trust no one." Another was simply the graphic of a black microphone on a white background, canceled by a red slash. One trader made his own version of a protest button, "No Dwaynes." Dwayne Andreas, chairman of ADM, was already suspected of helping to launch the investigation against the Board and planting Carlson in the soybean pit.

Late in the afternoon, another blow fell: The U.S. Attorney's office had subpoenaed five years' worth of trading records from the clearing houses of the Board and the Merc. The feds meant business, and it didn't have anything to do with drugs or the Super Bowl pool. This was not something that would go away soon.

Merc traders stopped by the membership office after their markets closed. Seat prices were already falling. Some targeted traders had sold their seats, hoping to keep the assets out of the government's hands in case of RICO convictions. Other traders instinctively sold seats on the bad news, planning to buy them back cheaper. Thirty-five memberships, an unusually high number, changed hands that day as traders speculated on the price of the scandal. In the Chicago markets everything has a price, and selling on bad news is almost always a good trade.

□ □ □

AS WORD OF THE PROBE SPREAD, the telephones of Chicago's top criminal defense attorneys rang off their hooks.

Jim Streicker, a partner in Cotsirilos, Crowley, Stephenson, Tighe & Streicker, a prominent downtown law firm, was among the first to get a call. Arriving at his office on Wednesday, January 18, at about eight o'clock in the morning, his partner, Bob Stephenson, was already in his office, counseling a new client. Soybean trader Marty Dempsey was explaining that the U.S. Attorney's office had just blown open a case that promised to be as big as the much-publicized Greylord probe of judicial corruption in Chicago.

Dempsey, a beefy, balding soybean broker, had been visited by an Assistant U.S. Attorney and two FBI agents the night before. He had spent the night calling friends and tracking down the names of defense lawyers, and had arrived at Stephenson's office early, agitated and sweating.

Dempsey told the lawyers a tale that was to become familiar: He had submitted to a nearly three-hour evening interview with U.S. prosecutors and FBI agents at his lavish suburban home, during which he was repeatedly threatened with ruin by RICO. His visit to the Cotsirilos and Crowley offices the next morning could not undo the damage of that visit. Some of his statements to the agents would form the basis for charges in a 122-count indictment to be handed down August 2, more than seven months after that evening visit.

As the government made round after round of surprise visits, even through the weekend, lawyers' phones rang urgently. Former U.S. Attorney Dan Webb had calls from ten traders waiting for him when he returned from court on Thursday. Traders who had much to fear went from lawyer to lawyer, often using lists provided by the exchanges, until they found one without a prior client who would take their case. The competition for top legal help intensified as even traders who had not received subpoenas, but had stood within earshot of an undercover FBI agent, began calling lawyers.

The attorneys knew the commodities cases could be more lucrative than Greylord. Some joked about "The Defense Lawyers' Relief Act of 1989" as they sorted through potential clients. Some defense attorneys began turning down traders who wanted to plead guilty and cooperate, preferring to wait for the big client who would stand trial. Many of the traders, after all, had pockets deep enough to afford the biggest legal bills in town.

The traders found some of the best and brightest in Chicago's defense business, many of them former federal prosecutors. Yen trader Sam Cali landed Thomas A. Durkin fresh from victory in a highly publicized bankruptcy fraud case. Lead yen defendant Robert Bailin hired Eddie Genson, a courtroom magician specializing in politicians. Robert Mosky, a big Swiss franc broker, hired the sonorous Harvey Silets, a dean of the defense corps. Tom Sullivan, a former U.S. Attorney, performed initial defense work for yen broker John Baker. And bean trader Edward Cox landed Matthias A. Lydon, one of prosecutor Tony Valukas's closest friends.

In consultations with their distraught new clients, attorneys found that Raphaelson's home-ambush technique, while not unusual, was especially well organized and effective. With surprising frequency, traders had invited federal agents into their homes, even at odd hours, after being being shown an FBI badge. Many hoped to deflect suspicion, but wound up damaging themselves.

Commodities lawyers and defense attorneys also began calling their regular clients. Don't talk to anyone, they counseled. Trust no one, talk to no one. "Assume that every time anyone says 'Hello, how are you?' the person may be wearing a wire," lawyer Robert Byman told one client. After at least two years in the pits, the government already had plenty of evidence. There was no reason to give any more.

□ □ □

THERE WAS NO SENSE IN CALLING the meeting to order Thursday morning. Under the circumstances, there would be no order. The Board of Trade's executive committee was meeting, as usual, in president Thomas Donovan's office at 6:00 A.M. sharp. A copy of the *Chicago Tribune* lay on Donovan's desk. And on this morning, everybody at the meeting most definitely had read the day's paper. "U.S. Probes Futures Exchanges: FBI Tapes Key to Fraud Investigation," the front-page headline shouted.

For Donovan, it had been a long night. First had come the false hope, a call from the Board of Trade's public relations chief Ray Carmichael after the ten o'clock news. The story that had ricocheted around the Board that day, a sketchy rumor about FBI agents wired with tape recorders infiltrating the trading floor, had not made the TV news. The wire services—the AP, the Dow, Reuters, Knight-Ridder—all were clean. The phone in Carmichael's office had not rung since business hours ended. "Maybe there's nothing to it," Carmichael had said. "I'm going home."

But after Carmichael's call, Donovan's phone would not stop ringing. Trader after trader phoned. The stories they told were all the same: the knock on the door; the production of badges; the mention of the racketeering laws; the threats of losing homes, cars, and exchange memberships; and the inevitable, forceful requests for cooperation.

Now even in the middle of the executive committee meeting, Donovan was working the phones again. Most of his calls were going to Washington. The wall in Donovan's office was a photo gallery of Donovan with some of the most powerful politicians in the land. From Ronald Reagan to Representative Dan Rostenkowski to the late Mayor Richard J. Daley of Chicago, they were all up there grinning and grasping his hand. And Donovan's goal at the moment was to reach as many of the pols as he could, to try to put the Board's own spin on the news before faxes of the *Tribune* story got to them. Besides, the Board and Merc were cohosting a Washington, D.C., pre-inauguration party for legislators, all of whom would want advance warning of the crisis.

What Donovan and the others could not know was that Wednesday night was just the beginning. Even as the executive committee met, the terrible scene was being reenacted. Lawyers from the U.S. Attorney's office, teamed with FBI agents, were fanning out around the city and the suburbs. They were out there while Donovan was trying in vain to bring the meeting to order, to ascertain exactly how bad the situation was.

Scott Early, the Board's excitable general counsel, his six-foot-eight-inch frame folded onto a chair in front of Donovan's desk, was red-faced, table-thumping mad. He could not believe that the *Tribune* had run the story. "It's not legal. They can't get away with this," he steamed.

No one disagreed, but no one could do anything about it, either. The story had run. Based on the volume of calls Wednesday night, it was true. Now the only question was what to do about it.

Karsten "Cash" Mahlmann, the unflappable German who only two days before had been reelected to his third term as exchange chairman, reviewed the Board's predicament. Of the people in this room, the people who were supposed to know everything needed to run the exchange, not a one had heard in advance about the investigation. The *Tribune* sure seemed to know. There had been moles, they had been on the floor, they had now subpoenaed traders. But how many moles? Nobody knew. How many subpoenas? Nobody knew. What kinds of crimes were involved? Nobody knew. Were any traders cooperating? Nobody knew.

When the list of unknowns dwarfs the list of knowns, options are limited. "We're not going to say anything," Mahlmann stated in his clipped, deep Teutonic voice. "We don't know anything, and we're sure as hell not going to try to act like we do."

He looked to Ray Carmichael, who had handled the press throughout the case of a wig-wearing phony trader, through the great 1987 crash, through several farmers' marches on the Board when tractors had blocked LaSalle Street, "Ray, what do you expect?" Mahlmann asked.

"If we don't say anything, we're going to look uncooperative. We're going to look like we've got something to hide," Carmichael reasoned. "It's not going to be easy. We're going to look bad, but we don't have any choice. Long-term, no-commenting it is the right thing to do."

"You know what Leo's going to do," Donovan blurted. As usual, he was trying to anticipate the moves of Leo Melamed, the savvy chieftain of the rival Chicago Mercantile Exchange. Donovan, the old pol, had a grudging respect for Melamed's political acumen. "You know what he's gonna do. He's going to come out with both guns blazing."

Donovan's phone rang, and he snatched it to his ear. The voice on the other end was unmistakable. "This is Tony Valukas returning your call."

"Tony," Donovan said, his voice slipping into the familiar tones of an old friend—he had attended Valukas's second wedding and known Valukas's father, a circuit court judge, since the days when Richard J. Daley was mayor. "What can you tell me about this investigation?"

Valukas's next sentence neither surprised Donovan nor upset him. In a way, he had hoped it would come out this way, because it would fit into the Board's developing game plan. Dispassionately, Valukas offered only the old boilerplate: "Tom, I'm afraid I can't confirm or deny anything."

There was nothing to say but goodbye. "He's not telling us anything," Donovan said.

"We'll stick with the plan," Mahlmann said. "Ray, we don't say anything. When the reporters call, just tell them we don't know anything. We're not going to comment on something we don't know."

The session was breaking up. "And let's find out whatever the hell we can about what's going on here," Donovan commanded. "We've got the party in Washington tonight. Cash and I have got to go to that party. But I don't want to go there naked."

□ □ □

SPURIOUS RUMORS—IT SEEMED TO ANDY YEMMA, the Merc's media relations director, that he spent too much of his time checking them out and extinguishing them. The phone call early Wednesday afternoon from Knight-Ridder Financial News was asking him to confirm or deny one rumor that was as wild as they came.

The wire-service reporter had heard that the government was delivering subpoenas on the trading floor, and wanted confirmation. Knight-Ridder was well connected all across the floor and was usually not far off base. But this sounded bogus, and after a check, Yemma reported back that it obviously wasn't true. He returned to his desk, which overflowed with the aftermath of the exchange's annual election and a pile of phone messages.

Later, as Yemma wound down and was heading home, he took a final phone call. It was the *Tribune*'s Bill Crawford, who'd transferred to the futures beat about the same time Yemma joined the Merc after working as business editor of the *Chicago Sun-Times*. Crawford chatted, then asked how he could arrange to get in touch with Merc president William Brodsky and executive committee chairman Leo Melamed later that evening.

Curious, Yemma asked what he was up to. "I can't tell you, but it ain't cool," Crawford replied, exasperating Yemma. Melamed had already left for Washington to attend George Bush's inauguration, so Yemma gave Crawford Brodsky's home phone number. That evening, Yemma stayed home and close to his phone, half expecting to hear that Crawford had called Brodsky. The phone never rang.

Early Thursday morning, Yemma stepped out on the porch of his Evanston home and retrieved the newspaper. He cursed softly. "U.S. Probes Futures Exchanges," the front-page headline on the *Tribune* screamed. For a seasoned press man, particularly one working for the image-sensitive Merc, the story was a nightmare. By the time Yemma had finished his coffee and read through the story—full of details, but based solely on unnamed sources—his phone was ringing. The Merc's outside counsel, Jerrold Salzman, wanted to talk.

Yemma would have called the office, but there were few people to call. Nearly everyone authorized to speak authoritatively for the exchange was out of town—Melamed, former Merc chairman Jack Sandner, the newly elected chairman John Geldermann, and Bill Brodsky. They had all either left or were leaving early that morning to attend the inauguration.

The day was already shaping up as a replay of October 19, 1987, the day the stock market crashed and with it the Merc's S&P 500 stock-index futures contract. A big, negative story. Yemma braced for the pack of reporters who would be sent to cover the Merc, all of them wanting a story, and most desperately needing an education on how the Merc worked. When he arrived at the Chicago Mercantile Exhange Center, newspaper and wire service reporters were already camped out in the Merc's cramped media relations office. They wanted confirmation, details, names of traders to interview. Those who did not have floor passes demanded permission to go on the trading floor. He told them that he knew little more than what was in the *Tribune*. By 10:00 A.M., his office was mobbed with television cameras and the on-air talent that traveled with them.

Trying to placate the media monster, Yemma organized an impromptu press conference. He called Salzman, who had taken up interim command in Brodsky's office, to face reporters. Auburn-haired and fiftyish, Salzman was an inside man at the Merc, despite his title of outside counsel. He was a close compatriot of Melamed and the "young turks" who had rewritten the rules of the exchange in the early 1970s. But to most of the reporters hounding the FBI story, he was an unknown.

Yemma assembled the reporters in a corner of the Merc's fourth-floor boardroom. The large, formal room had housed press conferences before, but they were usually carefully orchestrated, with Leo Melamed and other Merc officers arranged photogenically at the foot of the massive mahogany conference table and reporters lounging tamely along its length.

Today, the reporters were in a froth, too agitated to sit down. Despite less than a half-hour's notice of the event, journalists had arrived from every major media outlet in Chicago. Cameras for the local business news programs and network television affiliates were set up in a semicircle in the one small corner of the boardroom that was not filled with furniture. The print reporters milled around, agitated and tense, bumping camera crews out of the way.

Salzman arrived, rumpled but calm. He took a place in front of the reporters, standing with his back to the wall. The television cameras crowded in, and he began to sweat in his tweed sportcoat. Yes, he explained, the Merc was aware of an ongoing FBI investigation involving some Merc floor traders. Yes, traders had called him to say FBI agents had served subpoenas the previous evening.

For the reporters, it was the first confirmation from a quotable source that there was an investigation. Salzman quickly added that neither the FBI nor the U.S. Attorney's office had notified the Merc of the investigation, and both still refused to acknowledge one. Anton Valukas was telling the Merc no more than he was telling reporters: no comment.

Then, Salzman sought to minimize the damage. The *Tribune* story, he suspected, had overblown the extent of the investigation. From what he could tell, it involved just a few individuals, and while he did not know what the FBI was looking for, he presumed they were after "minor trading infractions," like trading after the closing bell. The Merc would cooperate with authorities. Salzman could answer few questions seeking further details.

The reporters, relieved to have on-the-record confirmation of the probe, rushed back to their offices in time to meet their afternoon deadlines. All except *The Wall Street Journal* would offer little more than weak rehashes of the *Trib* story.

For the Merc, the press conference had provided temporary relief from the crush of reporters. The respite allowed Salzman to return to Brodsky's office and marshall the exchange staff. They had to get a grasp on what really had happened.

In the days to come, the facts about the government probe and the FBI's case against fraudulent dealings in the futures exchanges would slowly emerge. And as they did, they would make Salzman's comments about a minor investigation involving a few individuals look like a desperate, wishful dream.

PART II

———————— □□□ ————————

CHAPTER TWO

Manias, Bucket Shops, and Corners

WHEN 82 GRAIN MERCHANTS met on South Water Street along the bank of the Chicago River in 1848 to organize the Chicago Board of Trade, few, if any, had heard of the Tokugawa era in Japanese history. Fewer still would have known that, in forming the nation's first commodity exchange, they were repeating what their Japanese predecessors had done two centuries earlier. Like the Japanese rice merchants of the mid-1600s, the Chicago grain merchants were hoping to alleviate the economic havoc that resulted from the wild booms and busts of the agricultural production cycle.

By buying and selling forward contracts, which eventually were standardized as "futures," the merchants could lock in prices and reduce the dramatic swings between winter shortages, when cold weather blocked waterways to and from Chicago's grain elevators, and summer harvests, when so much corn, oats, and wheat flooded the market that boxcar loads of the suddenly worthless grain often were dumped into the waters of Lake Michigan. The merchants also learned quickly that the futures markets were naturally suited to yet another activity: speculation on price changes themselves.

The Board of Trade may have been conceived as little more than a stop-gap way station for handling market risks, but it has become far more than that. The futures markets—the Board and the Chicago Mercantile Exchange—have become engines driving Chicago's growth. They are major innovative forces in national and international financial trading, working together now on computerized trading systems that could revolutionize the world's capital markets. They form a locus of international finance on a par with New York, London, or Tokyo—a place where banks, insurance companies, pension funds, and agricultural giants all protect themselves against risks ranging from rising interest rates to hurricane damage to stock market crashes to summer droughts.

Much has changed in the nearly 150 years since a group of merchants, entrepreneurs, and hustlers meeting above an old flour store created the system that gave rise to the sophisticated high-tech wizardry of today's trading floor. But nearly as much has remained unchanged. In an age of computers, buy and sell orders are still shouted and conveyed by gesture in crowded trading pits. Brokers still record their deals in pencil on pocket-sized cardboard trading cards. The officials who run the exchanges are still mostly floor traders, leaving the pits just long enough to make multimillion-dollar decisions about the future of their industry. Pit traders still get by mostly on quickness and street smarts, making deals on the fly, running the markets by their own rules. In their cloistered world, people still like to believe that a trader's word is a trader's bond.

Look beyond today's computerized price quotes, the radiophonic headsets in the pits, the satellite dishes on the roof: The Board of Trade is still the Board of Trade; the Merc, still the Merc. The issues facing the exchanges today—trading scandals, meddling regulators, intermarket rivalries—have been with them since their start. And largely, the absence of change is a matter of choice. The Chicago exchanges adjust to the world only at their own pace. Whatever the pressures from Washington, outside investors, or even certain groups of members, reform is done the exchanges' way or not at all. That is the primary lesson of the nearly 350-year history of futures trading.

□ □ □

THE JAPANESE MARKET formed in Osaka in 1650, the forerunner of all futures markets, owed its birthright to the decrees of the Tokugawa shogunate. To keep feudal lords from becoming too powerful in their own districts and threatening the shogun's military and economic power, the ruler required his titled nobility to spend half a year in Tokyo, then known as Edo. These absentee landlords collected rent in payment of rice produced on their lands. In order to raise the baskets of cash needed to support their lavish lifestyles, the lords would sell their rice to the merchants of Edo and Osaka. But just as corn and oats are seasonal crops in North America, so is rice in Japan, and the regular influx of huge stores of rice from the countryside created a buyers' market that disadvantaged the nobles to the benefit of the rice merchants.

And the nobles needed all the money they could get for their rice. Their demands for cash went far beyond the sizable expense of living the plush life of the upper class occupying Japan's capital city. To collect rents, the landlords traveled each year to their estates, but by decree of the shogunate they had to travel with an elaborate and costly entourage that included a large number of samurai warriors. What's more, the shogun also required that his lords contribute heavily to extensive public works projects.

With no means of raising cash except for the seasonal collection of rents, the nobles began selling warehouse receipts that gave the holder rights to rice supplies in storage, either in the country or in city elevators. This was the first formal system of "hedging" against deliverable supply. As the rice tickets became common, they served as currency bought and sold by the merchant class. Eventually, merchants extended credit to the nobility based on their expected production of receipts: the concept of future delivery was introduced. One particularly successful merchant, Yodoya of Osaka, so dominated trade that his house in 1650 became the first commodity exchange organized in Japan. "The price at Yodoya's" was widely quoted as the prevailing rate in the city.

The commodity trading of the feudal Osaka, as described by historian Henry Bakken, bears a striking resemblance to the contracts traded on the computerized commodities exchanges of today. Transactions had to be made at recognized marketplaces. Contract terms were set in four-month intervals, and grain qualities were closely regulated. When a contract period expired, cash settlement was required rather than physical delivery—a feature that would not be introduced in the United States until the creation of the live cattle contract on the Chicago Mercantile Exchange in 1964. Trades were cleared through a clearinghouse, no open accounts could be carried past a contract's expiration date, and the clearinghouse was responsible for any defaults by individual traders. There was even an arbitration committee to settle disputes.

The Osaka market was a model for those that opened in several other Japanese cities. Over time, speculation became so widespread that prices in the commodities markets bore little resemblance to those in the cash market. The Meiji regime, which succeeded the Tokugawa dynasty in 1868, closed the markets because it considered futures trading nothing more than gambling. Two years later, as chaos gripped the rice market, the Meiji government reopened the exchanges, and eventually it promulgated a series of laws that led to the passage of Japan's Commodity Exchange Act of 1893, which the modern-day U.S. commodities code resembles.

If Japan is the cradle of organized commodities trading, then Holland is the place where wild and reckless speculation was conceived. Nowhere in the annals of markets is there an incident to match the tulip-bulb bubble that entranced the Dutch economy from 1634 until it burst spectacularly in November of 1636.

Tulipomania bloomed only half a century after the bulbs, imported from Constantinople to Augsburg, were first seen in Europe in 1559. By 1634, ownership of such prized bulbs as an Admiral Liejken or an Admiral Van der Eyck was a measure of one's standing in society. A single root of a rare species called the Viceroy once fetched the following articles in exchange: two lasts of wheat, four lasts of rye, four fat oxen, eight fat swine, twelve fat sheep, two hogsheads of wine, four tuns—large casks—of beer, two tuns of butter, one thousand pounds of cheese, a complete bed, a suit of clothes and, of course, a silver drinking cup. Total value: 2,500 florins. Bulbs were sold by the perit, a weight less than a grain.

The mania spread to all classes of society, although there were still a few who did not follow the tulip trade closely. A sailor, given a herring sandwich by a wealthy Dutch merchant he patronized, once pocketed what he thought was an onion to garnish his meal. Before the frantic merchant could find the rogue, the seaman had inadvertently eaten a Semper Augustus bulb worth 3,000 florins—enough to feed a ship's crew for a year. The Dutchman with the unwittingly expensive tastebuds was jailed on a felony charge of theft.

As happens with any commodity of value, markets for trade grew up around the tulip on the stock exchanges of Amsterdam, Rotterdam, and more than half a dozen Dutch cities, as well as London and Paris. And trading in forward contracts, whereby the buyer paid in advance for delivery at a later date, became common. When the tulip euphoria suddenly cooled, the bulbs lost three-quarters of their value in a few short weeks. The forward contracts left many traders, of both noble and lowly origin, florinless.

□ □ □

HOLLAND'S TULIPOMANIA and the orderly and rational futures markets in Japan provide fitting twin backdrops for the introduction of commodities trading in Chicago. For, rational as they may be in their structure and intent, the Chicago markets have been the scene of some of the wildest bare-knuckles brawls in the history of U.S. commerce. Unlike the stock exchange in New York, where membership is passed along as if by blue-blood pedigree, the Chicago futures markets always have been a place where street-smart ruffians with a flair for trading can make and lose fortunes. The list of occupations held by the Chicago Board of Trade's first 25 directors is telling: Besides the grain merchants of various means were a druggist, a bookseller, a tanner, a grocer, a coal dealer, a hardware merchant, and a banker.

The creation of the Board of Trade in 1848 was one of several events that would help make Chicago the commercial hub of the Midwest. That same year marked the opening of the Galena and Chicago Union Railroad, the first of many rail spokes out of the city. Within a decade, 10 major railroads would emanate from the city, with over 100 trains arriving or departing daily. Completion of a shipping canal through an old Indian portage linked the Chicago and Illinois rivers, opening river traffic directly from Chicago to the mighty Mississippi River. The new transit routes made Chicago the Midwest's most important city and enabled it to attract the livestock traffic that would make it meatpacker to the world. Within a decade, the great Union Stock Yards would open, attracting thousands of immigrant laborers and eventually creating a natural demand for the Chicago Mercantile Exchange to trade in futures on commodities like frozen pork bellies.

Ultimately, the Board of Trade proved a successful undertaking. But to its founders, survival was by no means guaranteed. Attendance was sparse. The exchange often attracted only two or three traders, prompting boosters to serve a sumptuous free lunch of cheese, cakes, and beer to attract grain merchants to the trading floor. But business did improve. In 1858, the Board introduced standards for grain quality that gave traders increased confidence. Trading began on a new invention, "to arrive" contracts, also called futures. The Board would not establish official rules of trading for futures until after the Civil War, but the new contracts were still an important breakthrough. For those in the grain trade, they helped stabilize prices by allowing the market to anticipate the harvest. They also lured speculative capital.

During this formative period the Board also scored its first legislative victory, convincing the Illinois legislature to grant a charter that gave the exchange virtually unfettered power to run business as it saw fit. The most important codicil of the 1859 Illinois charter endowed the Board of Trade's arbitration process with the same authority "as if it were a judgment rendered in Circuit Court." Thus empowered, the Board took two bold actions—eliminating "privilege," or options, trading in 1865, and creating regular trading hours in 1873. By refusing to stand behind any options deals or off-hour trades, the Board virtually eliminated those practices while still claiming to let the "free market" decide whether or not they should exist.

The free-market approach served the Board well during the Civil War years, a period when the exchange cemented its place as the nation's central grain marketplace. As the oats needed to feed horses and the corn and wheat needed for food became scarce, grain trading migrated to Chicago from river towns throughout the Midwest. Even a severe shortage of cash, caused as the money issued by individual states fell into irretrievable disrepute, did not slow the brisk trade. There was a food shortage in the Northeast, but high prices in Chicago attracted enough grain to keep the city's warehouses groaning full.

The insatiable need to trade foodstuffs led to the Board's first nighttime trading sessions some 125 years before the globalized economy would again create such a need. Traders worked madly from dawn to dusk—from the opening of the "First Board" at Clark and Randolph streets to the closing of the "Fourth Board" at the Tremont Hotel on the city's North Side—trying to let the markets respond to every bit of news about weather, the war, currency values, or grain quality. The secretary of the Board of Trade, Seth Catlin, understated affairs when he wrote in the exchange's annual report for 1863: "It is generally conceded that we are the gainers by the internal troubles that affect the country." Much of the increased trade came from growth in speculation. At first, Catlin and others at the Board did not know what to think of this new type of business. "It is to be hoped that with the return to peace this fever of speculation will abate, and trade will be conducted on a more thoroughly legitimate basis," he wrote to members in the 1864 report.

Over time, the Board recognized speculation as a necessary component of a liquid market. But the speculative urge that the Civil War years first loosed brought with it some unfortunate by-products. Foremost among them were repeated attempts to "corner" a market—in other words, to control all the deliverable supply of a given commodity at a given time. In the aftermath of the Board's explosive wartime growth, such actions brought disrepute on the exchange that colors its image even to the present day.

With farmers restive about the crash in grain prices following the Civil War, the manipulative practice of cornering would raise the ire of farmers' groups, led chiefly by the Grange movement that was flexing its political power through the plains states. Under Grange pressure, the Illinois legislature in 1866 prohibited short selling—selling grain one does not own, expecting to purchase it back later at a profit if prices decline. The law lasted only one year, but during its brief life spawned a farcical incident in which a number of prominent traders were dragged from the Board in horse-drawn paddy wagons, only to be returned to a heroes' welcome when charges were dropped.

The state made a more direct attack on cornering in 1874, even as exchange member William "Black Jack" Sturges was in the midst of a spectacular but unsuccessful attempt to corner the September corn market. The Board's directors, holding Sturges responsible for contributing to its legislative troubles, expelled him. But after Sturges appealed two Illinois Supreme Court rulings that acknowledged the Board's expulsion right, the exchange grudgingly readmitted him.

In the Board's early years, threats from the occasional corner were outweighed by a far more worrisome concern: the all-too-common bucket shop. Bucket shops are little more than gambling dens that run numbers games, using price tallies from legitimate markets like the Board of Trade as tote boards. In its less pernicious form—more common during the early years of the exchange—all parties at the bucket shop know they are gaming in off-market transactions. But in modern times, customers at the bucket shop normally are led to believe they're dealing with a legitimate commodities firm. The sham shops pretend customer orders are traveling to and from the exchange floor, when in truth the orders stay put. They are matched—or "bucketed"—illegally against other orders or against the house account. Bucket shops siphon potential business away from the exchange, diminish the exchange's ability to reflect true supply and demand, and tarnish the legitimate trading activity that occurs on the floor.

Today, when the Board does billions of dollars in business each year, bucket shops are little more than a pesky public relations problem for futures markets. Customer rip-offs, whether on or off the exchange floor, are not good for business, but the exchanges and their regulators seem more concerned with expanding their reach into new markets than protecting the integrity of the old. The Board did not always have that luxury. During their heyday, bucket shops represented a very real financial threat to the still-maturing Board of Trade.

Its early bucket shop battles were heated and frequent. The bucket shops struck at the Board's effort to build respectability. With anti-

Board sentiment already high among populist politicians and farmers, the Board could not risk having its image linked with that of the fraud-filled fake markets. Besides, every dollar that went to a bucket house was one dollar less that traveled to the trading floor.

Because the house played against the customer, and because most retail customers, then as now, were buyers in the market, bucket shops often would stage "bear raids" on the Board to drive down prices. If the market did go against the bucket shop, there was nothing to stop the firm from declaring bankruptcy, closing down, and then opening up under a different name at another spot.

Bucket shops were not immediately perceived as a threat. A newspaper advertisement of January 1878 sounded innocuous enough: "Every man is his own broker; middlemen abolished and each operator to conduct his own transactions on accurate information . . . . No deal over 5000 bushels." By 1879, the image had changed forever. The *Chicago Daily Tribune* wrote of the bucket shops: "The fraud, cheat and swindle are so transparent that it seems to be a libel on common intelligence to admit that these establishments do an immense business every day."

Once fully aware of the bucket shop threat, the Chicago Board of Trade engaged in pitched battles to wipe them out. The chosen tactic: attempting to disconnect the bucket shops from the Western Union wires that provided the market information they needed to survive. By 1882, the Board threatened to ban telegraph employees from the exchange floor if the bucket shops continued to obtain price quotes. In 1887, Abner "Charlie" Wright, president of the Board, carried an axe to the exchange's basement and chopped through any wires he found. During one period while the telegraph wires were shut down, the Board soaped its windows to stop trading-floor clerks from flashing price signals to bucket-shop clerks outside. Still, the bucket shops got their quotes and stayed in business.

A court battle over the legitimacy of bucket shops made its way to the U.S. Supreme Court in 1904. The Court ruled that the Board of Trade had the right to control access to information created on its exchanges. But Justice Oliver Wendell Holmes's opinion went a step further, giving legitimacy to the trading of futures contracts with the following words:

> Of course in a modern market contracts are not confined to sales for immediate delivery. People will endeavor to forecast the future and to make arrangements according to their prophecy.

Speculation of this kind is the self-adjustment of society to the probable. Its value is well known as a means of avoiding or mitigating catastrophes, equalizing prices and providing for periods of want.

The Holmes opinion was music to the Board, which in 1888 had seen anti-futures sentiment run high enough in Congress that separate bills sponsored by Senator William Drew Washburn, a Republican from Minnesota, and William Henry Hatch, a congressman from Missouri, nearly became law. With the welcome imprimatur of the U.S. Supreme Court, the Board's directors could now realistically consider themselves stewards of a national financial interest. The victorious battle against the bucket shops was the first time, but certainly not the last, that the exchange would wrap its self-interest in the cloaks of free trade, market stability, and fair business.

The high court's 1904 decision was a much-needed boost after a period of rocky public relations for the Board. In 1885, the exchange had moved from rented, cramped quarters at the city's Chamber of Commerce Building to a castlelike headquarters at the foot of LaSalle Street at Jackson Boulevard. The city fathers had gladly allowed the Board to block off LaSalle, a main thoroughfare, so the exchange could anchor a growing financial district. But their enthusiasm was not shared by the city's laborers and anarchists. On the night of the building's inaugural banquet, protesters tried to march on what they called "the board of thieves" and were cut short by a phalanx of Chicago police. The ten-story building would last the Board until 1928, when it was torn down to make way for the new, 45-story art deco building that opened in 1930.

While the Board had grown in stature, its rank-and-file members still considered themselves part of a privileged club and acted accordingly. One of the most noteworthy events was a raucous reception the Board held for King Kalakaus of the Hawaiian Islands in 1875. Members on the floor regaled the king with an impromptu verse of a popular song, "King of the Cannibal Islands." Confused, Mayor Calvin of Chicago then rose to introduce the city's guest, saying, "I have the honor of escorting into your midst the King of the Can . . ."

On another occasion, in 1888, veteran market cornerer Benjamin Hutchinson, or "Old Hutch" as he was known, was bemused by efforts of his son Charles, then president of the Board, to clean up the exchange's image by extolling its benefits to farmers. "Did you hear what Charlie said? Charlie said we were philanthropists," Old Hutch told a group of traders talking on the floor. "Why bless my buttons, we're gamblers. You're a gambler! You're a gambler! And I'm a gambler!" To the Board's leadership, Hutch's words were no more welcome in his day than was the dark humor that ran across trading floors in Chicago once the FBI sting became known in late January of 1989.

But Old Hutch was right. His was the day of the gambler at the Board of Trade. And as long as the occasional corners remained largely self-contained events played out among the boys on the trading floor, few people outside the exchange seemed to care. That would change for good in 1897. To the Board came Joseph Leiter, a man whose outrageous and ultimately unsuccessful attempt to corner the wheat market lasted more than a year and captivated the world's attention. Leiter's battle with P. D. Armour over the 1887 wheat crop was a clash of titans the likes of which would never be seen again. It would even be memorialized by Frank Norris in *The Pit*, a naturalistic novel that is practically required reading for literate traders at the Board.

□ □ □

LEITER WAS PART OF A NEW BREED of trader attracted to the Board: sons of successful businessmen willing to risk piles of the old man's cash to try their luck in the commodities markets. And Joseph's father was not just any sugar daddy. Levi Z. Leiter was a founding partner of the Marshall Field & Co. dry goods business who later turned to banking, real estate, and land development. Like his contemporaries Potter Palmer and Marshall Field, Leiter also was a noted philanthropist. Men like Levi Leiter do not risk their hard-earned fortunes foolishly; they leave that to their sons. And in his boy Joseph, Levi found one willing to take his dad's money for a wild ride.

Born to high station and educated at Harvard, Leiter had started in business with $1 million from his old man, money he was supposed to use to start a real-estate firm. But land speculation was too much work and too slow for the young Leiter, a protégé of the Board's John "Bet-a-Million" Gates—a man who earned his nickname when he once saw a fly on a pane of glass, drew a line on the glass, and offered to wager $1 million that the bug would not cross the line. (Leiter didn't take that bet, but did once lose $250,000 to Gates in a single night of card playing.)

In his trademark white waistcoat and pearl-gray stovepipe hat, the peripatetic Leiter was a latter-day Lord Byron, one of the most flamboyant figures of his day. The New York Supreme Court once declared him a "nomad" rather than try to list his place of domicile. Federal agents raiding his Washington, D.C., vault during prohibition found $300,000 worth of wine and liquor. Leiter once offered to buy the Great Wall of China; sought to form trusts to control milk, meat, and wheat; and founded the town of Zeigler, Illinois, which he said would one day be a major population center of the Midwest. (Today its population is 1,858.)

When his sister, Lady Marguerite Hyde, Countess of Suffolk and Berkshire, sued to remove Leiter as trustee of his father's $30 million estate, the eight-year court fight titillated the nation. Leiter ultimately prevailed, costing the estate $1.012 million in legal fees. Smaller matters also would bring him to court: Leiter once was sued for refusing to pay $1,332 for 111 pairs of $12 socks that he found unacceptable. At age 68, despite a severe cold that confined him to a wheelchair, Leiter insisted on staying outdoors to watch all the horse races on a spring trip to New Orleans. After returning to Chicago, he died of pneumonia.

Unfortunately for Leiter, the person on the other side of his wheat corner was the redoubtable P. D. Armour, a self-made man who was not amused by this upstart's brazen efforts. In trading, as in life, "Peedee" Armour was the young Leiter's opposite. Born fourth of ten children to middle-class parents in upstate New York in 1832, Armour never attended school after he was booted from the Cazenovia Academy for taking an unescorted buggy ride with a young lady late at night. Instead, he followed gold fever to California, where in four years he prospected and saved a small fortune.

Working as a Milwaukee meat packer during the height of the Civil War, at age 31, Peedee made his first large fortune by contracting to deliver then-scarce pork to New York at a bargain price of $40 a barrel. But before the contract came due, a series of Union victories sent pork down to $18 a barrel. Armour earned $1.8 million when he delivered the meat to the unhappy New Yorkers.

In 1875, the 43-year-old Armour moved to Chicago, where he became the city's largest owner of grain elevators, an investor in railroads and banks, and founder of Armour & Co., which would become the biggest meatpacking firm in a city of meatpackers. His wife was a noted socialite, but Armour cared little for the high life, choosing instead to work from 5:00 A.M. to 6:00 P.M., eat dinner at home, and find his mattress by nine o'clock each night.

Before he died in 1901, from pneumonia contracted while playing with his grandchildren in the season's first snow, Armour would spend $1.5 million to found the Armour Institute of Technology near his vast meatpacking operations on Chicago's South Side. His fortune would not last beyond the next generation, however. J. Ogden Armour, Peedee's son, guessed wrong on the duration of World War I, overstocked supplies of meat, and lost $31.7 million for Armour & Co. in 1921. He fell into disrepute for Armour Grain Co.'s handling of grain grading, and when he died, his estate was nearly $2 million in the red.

No battle in the Board of Trade's history has matched such notable opposites in so noble a fight. For all his flamboyance, Leiter is best remembered for his reckless attempt, at age 28, to corner the world supply of wheat from 1897 to 1898 and Armour, though he had other more important accomplishments, played the part of spoiler like the veteran trader he was.

The corner began in April of 1897, when Leiter's floor broker George B. French began buying September wheat at 67 cents a bushel. Other traders suspected Leiter was cornering wheat, but were placated when French claimed he was buying for New York investors, not the mercurial and well-capitalized Leiter. By the time the September contract came due, wheat had risen to 96 cents, and Leiter was still buying. When a group of short sellers came to ask him what it would take to buy him out of his position, Leiter replied, "I have bought your wheat, and I am ready to pay for it. I don't want your money, but I do want your grain." As grain did arrive, Leiter immediately shipped it out of Chicago, thereby maintaining the short supplies that would enable his corner to succeed.

For a time, the corner was working. But Armour had not yet gone to work. By early December, Armour was "short"—that is, he had sold—nine million bushels of December wheat, and thanks largely to Leiter's aggressive exporting, Armour had less than 350,000 bushels in his Chicago grain elevators. But that would change. Anticipating the onset of winter—if the northern rivers froze, he would be unable to ship wheat to Chicago—Armour sent men throughout the Northwest, encouraging farmers to sweep their barns to find every last kernel. With wheat trading at $1.07 a bushel by December 8, the farmers gladly complied. Finally, thanks in large part to the help of Minneapolis elevator king Frank Peavey, Armour had enough wheat, and now beating the weather was his main challenge. He chartered an armada of ice breakers and lake barges to sail to Duluth and bring in his wheat. By the time the December contract expired, Armour was able to present Leiter with receipts for his nine million bushels of wheat and to deliver an extra nine million bushels to his own elevators. The corner, at least for the time being, was broken.

Leiter wasn't broken, though. To forestall disaster, Leiter had to keep buying, and this he did. The news of the day helped him: The explosion of the battleship *Maine* in Havana harbor on February 15 meant war with Spain and therefore higher wheat prices, because soldiers would have to be fed. In the early spring, as rumors circulated that Leiter was facing a credit crunch, his position reached its peak: 18 million bushels of cash wheat and 22 million bushels owed him in futures contracts. Leiter traveled to Minneapolis and struck a deal with Peavey and C. A. Pillsbury to keep their wheat in the Northwest— an effort to avoid a repeat of Armour's December triumph. Wheat peaked at $1.85 a bushel on May 10, but by then Leiter quietly was selling, thanks in no small part to his father's sudden appearance in Chicago.

Events turned against Leiter. The first carload of winter wheat from Texas arrived June 2, the earliest first delivery on record. Then, on June 12, Marines landed in Cuba, meaning that the Spanish-American war would soon end. Leiter, seeing no escape, struck a deal to let Armour market some 15 million bushels of wheat. Leiter believed Peavey had double-crossed him by delivering wheat to Chicago despite their agreement and cut Peavey out of the deal he reached with Armour. Although Leiter at one point could have turned a profit of some $5 million on his corner, years later he would estimate his losses at $20 million. He never traded in the futures markets again.

□ □ □

IF A MAN OF LEITER'S MEANS could not make a corner work, who could? Why, James A. Patten, who successfully cornered the wheat crop in 1909, perhaps the only successful major corner in the Board of Trade's history. The son of a politically well-connected family in Chicago's far south suburb of Sandwich, Illinois. Patten was one of the most prominent traders on the Board. He had run a corner on July oats in 1902, prompting several bills in Congress to outlaw short selling and other speculative practices. But the 1909 wheat corner made Patten a household name, vilified in sermons and caricatured in newspaper cartoons.

The corner began in June of 1908, with wheat trading at 89.75 cents a bushel. Before the deal was done, Patten would buy ten million bushels and drive the price of wheat to $1.34 at the end of May 1909, the highest price since Leiter's corner. Patten's profits were estimated at more than $1 million. Whatever the profit, the corner extracted a price. The pressure from Washington was intense. Representative Charles F. Scott of Kansas introduced a bill to prohibit futures trading; Attorney General Wickersham launched an investigation of Patten's dealings; and Secretary of Agriculture Wilson blamed Patten for artificially raising the price of wheat when he claimed supplies were plentiful.

No legislation resulted directly from the Patten corner, but Patten's name would come up more than a decade later when Congress discussed the need for an agency to ride herd on the wild Chicago futures markets. And when the U.S. Supreme Court upheld the Futures Trading Act of 1922 as constitutional, Chief Justice William H. Taft would single out the Patten case as one that pointed up the need for government regulation of the markets.

At the height of the Patten panic, the newspapers brooded over fears of bread riots in Chicago's immigrant neighborhoods. Patten's Evanston house was targeted by a bomb scare, and he had to hire a second bodyguard. "Why, a woman can't fill a pincushion with bran without taking Jim Patten into account," wrote *Worker's Magazine*. A Chicago preacher labeled him "The God of Get."

To escape the pressure, and perhaps avoid an incipient nervous breakdown, Patten during the middle of the corner took a trip to Colorado, then to New Mexico. Prices eased to about $1.18 a bushel after Patten left town on April 24, but bumped right back to $1.25 upon his return in May. Perhaps feeling some sense of social responsibility, on expiration day, when he could have squeezed prices much higher, Patten pushed them up only a penny, to $1.34 a bushel. "That extra cent was just a tag on the deal to certify that I had been right," Patten wrote in a lengthy *Saturday Evening Post* article a few years later. "It was the confirmation of my judgment."

□ □ □

PATTEN'S CORNER was just a memory when the Board of Trade faced its next great test: the First World War, when the government got its first shot at futures markets regulation. While the war was still contained in Europe, grain prices shifted as expected while supply ebbed and flowed. Germany's declaration of unrestricted submarine warfare on February 1, 1917, caused a selling panic, but wheat quickly recovered a few days later when President Wilson announced the severance of diplomatic relations. Then came news from the Agriculture Department that the winter wheat crop would be the lowest on record, only 430 million bushels. A subsequent report put the forecast some 70 million bushels lower still, and May wheat, which had sold for $1.68 a bushel in February, suddenly fetched a record $3.25. Knowing runaway prices would bring calls for more Washington control over the Chicago markets, the Board formed a three-man commission, which immediately halted trading of May wheat and set a settlement price of $3.18.

The responsible Board action succeeded only in delaying the inevitable. With passage of the Lever Act on August 10, the new food administrator, Herbert Hoover, asked grain exchanges to stop trading wheat futures as of September 1, and the Board complied. The brief ban on futures trading did not hurt the Board nearly as much as did the resumption of trading after the war ended. In May 1919, with European demand still high, May wheat had sold at $3.45 a bushel. By the time the U.S. Grain Corporation dissolved itself in July, however, grain was headed down, and prices dropped dramatically just as futures trading resumed.

The price collapse was just the ammunition Populist politicians from the midwestern grain states needed. At the request of Kansas governor Henry Allen, President Wilson ordered the Federal Trade Commission to investigate grain trading. Senator Arthur Capper of Kansas and Congressman Jasper Tincher, also a Kansan, both headed inquiries that rivaled the Salem witch hunts for objectivity. Senator Capper's remarks were typical. "Today, under the cloak of business respectability, we are permitting the biggest gambling hell in the world to be operated on the Chicago Board of Trade," he said during the brief debate over what would become the Futures Trading Act of 1921. "The grain gamblers have made the exchange building in Chicago the world's greatest gambling house. Monte Carlo or the Casino at Habana are not to be compared with it."

Passed under such cool-headed guidance, it is no wonder that the Grain Futures Act was a draconian measure. It required "licensed contract markets" to admit farmer cooperatives as members, enabling them to trade without commissions. It ordered records kept so price manipulation could be reined in. And, to add punch to its powers, the law stipulated a 20-cents-per-bushel tax on every contract traded in markets found to be in noncompliance.

The Supreme Court found that the Act exceeded Congress's taxing powers. But Chief Justice Taft gave the Populists a road map to reform by observing that Congress could regulate the markets if futures trading was "directly interfering with interstate commerce so as to be an obstruction or a burden thereon." Capper and Tincher took the hint and dutifully pushed through the Grain Futures Act of 1922. The new law was similar to the 1921 Act, except that it eliminated the 20 cents tax and relied on Congress' power to regulate interstate trade.

If the underlying purpose of the law was to keep prices high—and it was—it fell far short. On July 11, 1923, wheat sold below $1 a bushel for the first time since before the war. The new Grain Futures Act also proved unable to stop manipulative practices like corners. Arthur Cutten, who was so indifferent to government regulation that he ran a corner during the interregnum between the Futures Acts of 1921 and 1922, would try to run a series of corners during the mid-1920s. With a keen ability to read weather maps, Cutten was a frequent corner man, but it was the wheat corner of 1924 that aroused the most interest. Even as Progressive party presidential candidate Robert LaFollette of Wisconsin called for an end to "gambling" in grain futures, Cutten was busily buying wheat, driving prices from $1.05 in 1924 to more than $2.05 in early 1925. But as lower-priced wheat from Argentina flooded the export markets, Cutten's corner began to collapse. He paid nearly $2 million in margin calls when wheat dropped more than 15 cents a bushel on March 13, and claimed to be selling all his wheat. But within weeks Cutten was buying again.

News that Cutten was back at it was too much for the new agriculture secretary, W. M. Jardine, who warned the Board of Trade to clean up its house before he did it for them. The regulation-wary Board promptly created the Business Conduct Committee to investigate the Cutten matter. In a face-off with Cutten, the committee convinced the speculator to trim his position "for the good of the Board of Trade." It is an argument used by the BCC—the Board's most powerful enforcement panel—to this day.

Walking away from the 1924 corner probably hurt Cutten's pride more than his pocketbook. His $540,000 income tax bill for 1925 was the largest ever recorded in northern Illinois. But the experience soured the mercenary Cutten on futures trading. He turned to the stock market, where he became a major holder of such firms as Continental Oil, Montgomery Ward & Co., and Radio Corp. of America. Not one to abandon the tricks he had mastered at the Chicago Board of Trade, Cutten began buying the stock of Baldwin Locomotive Works, running the share price up from $100 to $265 and getting himself a seat on its board of directors.

The 1929 stock market crash sizably reduced his fortune, and Cutten's attempts to lower his income tax burden that year and the next led the government to sue him for $644,469 in back taxes owed. When he did return to the futures markets in 1930, Cutten again played his old games. But this time, there were more serious consequences. In 1935, irritated by his repeated attempts to manipulate grain prices and his efforts to avoid detection by splitting his holdings among 32 different accounts, the Grain Futures Administration barred Cutten from the markets for two years, a ban that eventually was vacated by the U.S. Court of Appeals.

The Cutten corner of 1925 was the last great market adventure before the Board entered the darkest period in its history. The ravages of the Great Depression, followed by the price controls that nearly killed the exchange during World War II, threatened the Board of Trade's very existence as no events before or afterward have done. The market problems were bad enough, but political dissatisfaction of the Depression followed by the aggressive government mood of the Roosevelt era would mean troublesome regulatory challenges. Few traders would have guessed it at the time, but for years they would look back on the Cutten and Leiter corners, and the adventures of Old Hutch and Sturges, as the good old days at the Board of Trade.

CHAPTER THREE

□□□

Stumbling Toward Reform

IF THE GREAT DEPRESSION was a trying time for the Board of Trade, at least the exchange entered that era on a healthy note. After nearly two years in temporary quarters on Clark Street, the Board in 1930 moved back to its old site at LaSalle at Jackson, where a new 45-story building was ready. Atop this building, the city's tallest edifice, stood a statue of Ceres, the Roman goddess of grain, cast by sculptor John Storrs. The inauguration of the new building couldn't quite match the opening of the original Board of Trade building for drama—anarchism and Grangerism were both passé—but President Herbert Hoover was on hand to press a button that signaled the start of trading. After several trading sessions, when electronic bells on the floor to signal the opening and close of trading could not be heard above the din, they were replaced by an 800-pound gong, which had hung over City Hall before the great fire of 1871 and was recast for the Board's use.

The move into new quarters did not mean an end to the Board's age-old problems, however. With an increasingly aggressive legion of critics in Washington, each new attempt at a corner marked an invitation for more government control. One of the most notorious cases during this period was that of E. A. Crawford, a doctor from Jacksonville, Florida who traveled, first to New Orleans, then to New York, to make—and lose—several fortunes trading in cotton. In 1933, he turned his attention to the grains traded on the Chicago Board of Trade, and by the time wheat reached its peak of $1.27 in late July, he was said to be long 20 million bushels of various grains, primarily corn and wheat.

Crawford's huge positions, held partly in the form of "indemnity contracts" that were essentially options to buy wheat, were gross violations of a gentleman's agreement between the Board and the Depression-era Agriculture Adjustment Administration that no single trader would hold a position larger than five million bushels in any one contract. With a huge speculative long interest built up in the contract, the Board in late July voted to increase margins. Crawford could not meet the margin calls, a flood of selling followed, and wheat prices collapsed 26 cents in two days. Ominously, on each of those two days the drop in wheat prices more than doubled the single-day limit of five cents that had been suggested only a few weeks earlier by none other than President Franklin D. Roosevelt. The president was busy creating the Securities and Exchange Commission, en route to his reform of commodities regulation.

Ignoring the president of the United States' suggestions was bad enough. But the Board's Crawford headaches grew worse. The AAA, which was charged with keeping farm prices at 1914 levels, jumped on the incident. Rumors flew that members of the exchange's business conduct committee had served as Crawford's brokers even as the speculator built his huge position. AAA Administrator George N. Peek called an emergency meeting in Washington at which he lambasted the exchange. "I want to emphasize to everyone concerned with the grain trades the necessity that you put your house in order," he warned. The same day, Crawford was suspended indefinitely from the Board for "inability to meet obligations." It was never proven whether any Business Conduct Committee members had filled Crawford's orders, but Peek suggested at the time, "The personnel of their business conduct committee should not be made up of active traders or speculators, but that they should be selected as to warrant public confidence."

With public confidence a big issue, one would think that decorum on the exchange floor would be of paramount importance. But the average floor trader is often indifferent to the outside world, so despite the close attention the Board was receiving from Washington and elsewhere, the wheat pit was a scene of chaos on a slow December 26, 1933, when one unfortunate broker wore a pair of conspicuous new spats onto the trading floor. "To a crowd that in former years often amused itself in the holidays throwing sample packages till the place was bedlam, the broker with spats was like a red flag in a herd of bulls," observed the *New York Times*. "He was grabbed by the neck and heels, his spats twisted off in a twinkling, and thrown gayly at the ceiling as he beat a hasty exit." No matter how hard regulators and Board officials may try, some things about the markets will never change.

Lingering suspicions in Washington such as those evidenced during the Crawford case marked the atmosphere during the reworking of commodities regulation by President Roosevelt. The Commodity Exchange Act of 1936, a replacement for the 1922 Grain Futures Act, dumped the unenforceable gentleman's agreement and placed binding limits on the number of contracts speculators could hold. It also banned agricultural options, which had been the seeds of Crawford's undoing. For the exchanges trying to salvage what they could in a volatile atmosphere, sacrificing options was a necessary evil.

Except for the ban on options, the Board otherwise emerged with its autonomy mostly intact. The new law added provisions protecting traders against fraud by grain dealers, requiring trader registration, and introducing criminal sanctions for price manipulation. But no mention was made of Peek's pet objective—an independent Business Conduct Committee. To this day, the BCC is still comprised of active traders, and concerns about the potential conflicts of interest remain.

□ □ □

DESPITE THE NEW AND IMPROVED Commodity Exchange Act and the Board's greater vigilance, there were still some players who considered themselves bigger than the markets. The giant Cargill Grain Co. of Minneapolis was one such entity, and that firm's bid to turn a corner in the September 1937 corn contract set off a battle that ultimately led to expulsion of Cargill, one of the Board's biggest member firms. When Cargill later appealed the action to the new Commodity Exchange Authority, it tested the Board's ability to regulate its own market. The Cargill affair also was an interesting prelude to troubles between the Board and another major grain firm—Archer Daniels Midland, the firm that started the government investigation.

Cargill in 1937 was at the peak of a recovery from two trips to the brink of bankruptcy: one in 1909 after ill-considered railroad and irrigation investments by William Cargill, the founder's son, and another after the 1929 stock market crash. But by 1937, under the leadership of John MacMillan, who had married Will Cargill's daughter Edna, Cargill Grain was on a roll. Investments in transport and storage, including a new ten-million-bushel depot in Omaha and another built for Cargill by the Port Authority of Albany, New York, were turning big profits and reviving Cargill's adventurous streak. Under the guidance of Julius Hendel—a Jewish immigrant from Belorussia in the staunchly Protestant city of Minneapolis—Cargill saw in the failure of the 1936 corn crop an opportunity to run a corner in the September 1937 contract before any new crop appeared and pushed prices down.

By early August 1937, Cargill controlled 8.5 million bushels of September corn, just over 40 percent of the total contracts held overnight on the Board. Two weeks later, the firm controlled more than 50 percent of the open interest. By the time the contract expired in September, Cargill would hold more than 80 percent of the open interest. But to maintain the corner, Cargill had to control deliveries of corn to Chicago—and that it set out to do.

A subsequent Board of Trade investigation showed that Cargill brokers in Texas paid above-market prices to stop grain from being shipped to Chicago. In St. Louis, Cargill purchased ten boxcars of grain from the Terminal Grain Co. for as much as $1.16 a bushel, then resold it a few days later to Ralston Purina at $1 a bushel. The firm willingly lost on the trade in order to tie up the grain during a critical period. Meanwhile, Cargill disguised the size of its position by concealing holdings in accounts held at Continental Grain Co. and Uhlmann Grain Co. When a suspicious Richard F. Uhlmann asked whether Cargill's actions were legitimate, a Cargill employee claimed that the company was acting under instructions from authorities in Washington, an assertion the Board found to be false.

With prices peaking or plummeting with each new rumor about Cargill—fluctuations between August 21 and September 17 would increase the value of Cargill's holdings by $2 million—the Board took action. The Business Conduct Committee on September 2 demanded an explanation from Cargill and asked the firm to liquidate its position. Although Cargill at first appeared willing to do so, it sold no contracts. Then, when corn prices dropped on word of the Board's demands, Cargill on September 21 complained of a "bear raid" orchestrated by shorts who knew the Board was putting the screws to Cargill. A series of emergency nighttime negotiations in the staid University Club broke down. The Board ordered Cargill to liquidate its holdings; Cargill refused. On September 24, the Board halted all trading in September corn, set a settlement price (costing Cargill about $500,000), and began proceedings that led to Cargill's expulsion from the exchange.

Cargill took its case to the Commodity Exchange Authority. But the Board still expelled Cargill when Macmillan and other Cargill brass refused to appear before the Board's hearings. Then the CEA refused to overturn or even review the expulsion. The scars ran deep. Despite several invitations to Cargill to return to the Board, the firm refused until after MacMillan's death. Cargill today is a major firm, with one official, Hal Hansen, holding a seat on the board of directors.

□ □ □

DESPITE ITS VICTORY OVER CARGILL, the Board of Trade was headed for a difficult period, one of the worst in the exchange's history. Most Americans preferred to ignore the outbreak of a new war in Europe, but for the Board that was impossible. Not since the dark days of World War I, when the Secretary of Agriculture had given orders that eliminated most trading activities on the Board for nearly three years, had the exchange seen such slack trading volume. In December of 1940, a Board seat sold for $450, the lowest price since 1895. Two years later, the price dropped to an all-time low of $24. Everette Harris, secretary of the Board of Trade at the time, remembers when the famed meatpacker Oscar Mayer tried unsuccessfully to give one of his seats away to a longtime employee. "The old employee declined the offer," Harris recalls. "He didn't want to pay the dues."

Seat prices had collapsed when the government commandeered the important corn and wheat crops. Trading volume was almost nil. The one exception was the only grain that remained free from price control: rye. As the trade focused on this normally quiet seed, intrigue followed. In 1944 and again in 1945, corners were attempted on the May rye contracts, arousing the rhetoric of anti-Board legislators like Frank B. Keefe of Wisconsin. He attributed the latest scandal to "a group of manipulators . . . with tentacles reaching into Washington."

The 1944 corner was attempted by one of the Board's most successful and flamboyant members, Daniel F. Rice. It set the stage for a bitter, lengthy feud between Rice and the Board, and for continuing friction with Washington. Rice headed a group including the General Foods Corp. that eventually controlled 12 million bushels, or 89 percent of the deliverable supply of rye. The ill-timed adventurism brought the wrath of the War Food Administration, which charged the group with cornering the market and eventually suspended all participants from commodities trading, Rice and his firm for six months.

Irritated by the Rice corner and the 1945 squeeze on rye, the Secretary of Agriculture in 1947 released a list of 711 "big traders." The implication was that these men, Rice among them, were market manipulators with ill-gotten inside information about crop supplies, who made fortunes at the expense of farmers. The stunt excited a Congress that loved to vilify the Chicago exchanges. But Rice, with his usual churlishness, jabbed back. "We have no access to confidential information, and we don't want any," he told the *Chicago Sun-Times*. "If we have to trade on government information, we don't want to trade."

Indignation over the Secretary's action was characteristic of Rice, who would spend a great part of his life in highly publicized battles, such as the vitriolic fight to wrest control of Balmoral Park racetrack near Chicago from his co-investors. Tired of having the Board bust up his corner attempts, Rice charged that the Board's directors favored short sellers to the detriment of longs, and that they were far too submissive to government regulators. Rice was censured in 1959 for criticizing the board of directors, in his *Rice Commodity Letter* and then in the daily newspapers, for favoring shorts.

Rice was not finished. In November, he liquidated Daniel F. Rice & Co. so he could concentrate on his fight with the Board of Trade without jeopardizing his firm or customers. When the Board asked for an explanation, Rice responded with a six-page poison-pen letter, criticizing the Board and particularly its president. "Our president has taken himself over the country, delivering speeches that have been inimical to the best interests of the American farmers and have brought disrepute on the Board of Trade," Rice wrote in his confidential response to the directors. "A strong control should be exercised over this incompetent officer to avoid repetition of incidents which can only be construed as attempts at self-advancement to the prejudice and detriment of the association."

Rice also lashed out against his favorite whipping horse, the Commodity Credit Corp. Charging the government agency with "improper barter transactions and illegal sales," Rice said the CCC had been "used as a means of wrecking the market itself." Rice's diatribes against the CCC, and against Board policies for warehousing grain, lost some of their bite a few months later, however. That's because Board of Trade chairman Clarence Rowland Jr., returning tit for tat, revealed that Rice's Rice Grain Corp. was a major storer of CCC grain, and noted that Rice Grain's president, Ben Raskin, chaired the Board's warehouse and transportation committees. After this loss of face, Rice's feuding with the Board quieted considerably.

□ □ □

DURING THE POST-WAR YEARS, the Board of Trade was dragged into one of the biggest swindles in the history of the agricultural markets. In this case, the Board's antagonist would not have the opportunity to quit the exchange: He was thrown off. And this matter could not be controlled in-house; rather, it became the subject of grand jury proceedings.

Anthony "Tino" DeAngeles, a trader in soybean oil from Bayonne, New Jersey, had big ideas when the Agricultural Department in 1961 inked a major wheat sale to the Soviet Union. DeAngeles figured that deals in soybeans and soybean oil could not be far behind and began aggressively accumulating soybean oil via purchases on the Board of Trade. By 1963, he was said to control 90 percent of the soybean contracts traded on the Board of Trade. But just as his holdings peaked, the deals with the Soviets began falling apart. The price tanked. And DeAngeles was left with a huge market loss, estimated by the Board at $24 million.

That was just the beginning of DeAngeles's troubles. When two brokerage firms demanded nearly $19 million in margin payments, DeAngeles's firm, Allied Crude Vegetable Oil Refining Co., was forced into bankruptcy and lenders soon found that millions of pounds of soybean oil were missing from Allied's huge storage tanks in New Jersey—some were empty, some half full, and others filled with oil mixed with water. Taking full advantage of the Board's low margin requirements, DeAngeles had wildly exceeded his capital. Claims from domestic and international creditors eventually exceeded DeAngeles's supply of soybean oil by more than a billion pounds.

Unhappily caught up in the controversy, the Board on November 18 summoned DeAngeles before its Business Conduct Committee. When DeAngeles refused, he was expelled. The next year, he pleaded guilty to fraud and conspiracy and was sentenced to ten years in prison. The Board sought to cleanse its image by noting that no member firms had lost money and claiming that "existing margins were and are sufficient to protect others dealing in these commodity futures contracts." But the assertion rang hollow. For the first time, the nation's attention was focused on the difference between the five percent margins in the commodities markets and the 70 percent margins required on the New York Stock Exchange. And the issue could not be forced to go away by pronouncements from the pulpit of the Board of Trade.

□ □ □

THE DEANGELES CAPER also showed many in Washington and New York what people at the Board had long known: The futures markets were an integral part of the nation's economy that could not be written off as gambling dens run by and for Chicago cowboys. Welcome as it was, that realization also yielded another push for more regulation. In 1968 the federal government set minimum capital standards for futures brokerage firms and for the first time claimed authority to shut down markets if the Commodity Exchange Act was being violated. The move was only the preamble to another major revision of regulation in 1974.

This was a time of immense change for the Board and the industry. In 1970, as a result of President Nixon's imposition of wage and price controls, the exchange adopted its first self-imposed limits on one-day price movements for commodities like soybean oil and plywood. In 1972, recognizing the demand for trading options on securities, and also aware that its long-dormant registration as a securities exchange would soon lapse, the Board introduced a new market for the trading of options on securities. To mollify members concerned about the expense and financial risk of joining a new exchange, the Board granted each member automatic membership rights in the independent Chicago Board Options Exchange. The new focus on securities products marked a broadening of the Board's self-image. By 1975, the exchange would introduce trading in futures on Government National Mortgage Association certificates, better known as Ginnie Mae's. In 1977, the exchange opened trading in futures on U.S. government Bonds, and T-bonds over time would replace soybeans and corn as the exchange's most actively traded contract.

The exchange also had to be careful not to let its attention on internal change blind it to the many external forces coming into play. In 1973, Chicago's City Council dropped a bomb, proposing a transaction tax on the city's exchanges. Under pressure from the Board and the Merc that included direct threats to move out of the city, Mayor Richard J. Daley abandoned the transaction tax proposal. The threat of a transaction tax caused the markets such a fright that the Board and the Merc worked steadily behind the scenes in Springfield until 1982, when they convinced the Illinois state legislature to legally prohibit the city from ever passing a transaction tax.

There was also action in Washington that demanded the Board's attention. Extensive new regulation of the commodities markets was on its way to becoming law. The brainchild of liberal farm state legislators in both the House and the Senate, the Commodity Futures Trading Act of 1974 was the most aggressive regulatory effort yet. Driving the action on the Senate side were two former Democratic presidential contenders, George McGovern (of South Dakota) and Hubert H. Humphrey (of Minnesota). "Consumers, farmers and, in some instances, large commodity traders and brokers have lost confidence in the government's ability to regulate commodity exchanges," McGovern declared. The new bill established the first futures commission independent from the Secretary of Agriculture. It brought such non-tangible items as currency futures and mortgage futures under regulatory purview, and added silver, pork belly, and lumber futures as well. The Act also provided for the introduction of a voluntary futures association to regulate members. And by 1981, the National Futures Association was created as an industry-funded "watchdog"—although to this day the NFA is more poodle than doberman.

The new commodities legislation passed only after headline-making inquiries in the House and Senate turned up allegations that commodity traders were manipulating prices for their own benefit. There were charges that the exchanges and the CEA were not enforcing rules even when they knew about wrongdoing. Cargill, the Board's old nemesis, was named as one such example. The House investigation determined that even though a U.S. appeals court found that Cargill had illegally driven up the price of wheat in 1965, the CEA took no action for more than seven years. The CEA countered that it had waited for the Board of Trade to act.

In the Senate, the highlight of testimony was Bernhard Rosee, a 76-year-old former member embittered by a 13-year court battle with the Board, which he sued after he was expelled for refusing to pay a $27,000 claim by a member firm. A CEA investigation showed that the firm had commingled customer funds and actually owed Rosee money, and by the time he testified, Rosee had won a $700,000 award in his Cook County court suit against the Board. Ironically, Rosee's award was reversed in 1976 by a higher state court, but by then the new commodities bill was law. Rosee, who had lived on welfare while conducting his court campaign, unsuccessfully argued that the new Commodity Futures Trading Commission should refuse to designate the Board of Trade as a contract market. Judiciously, the CFTC found fit to ignore Mr. Rosee's advice.

The new agency could not escape the hangdog image it had inherited from the CEA; Senator Adlai Stevenson III of Illinois aptly described it as "a stepchild among regulatory agencies." Then as now, the CFTC was politically far weaker than the Securities and Exchange Commission, which enjoys a longer history and regulates the more widely respected markets of Wall Street. But the CFTC's problems are bigger than just its weak image. The agency appears to be endowed with virtually unlimited powers—the ability to take any "market neutral" actions during times of market emergencies. But because the 1974 Commodity Futures Trading Commission Act does not define events like "corners," "squeezes," or "manipulation," the agency has been reluctant to exercise these powers.

□ □ □

THE EXCHANGES AND THE NEW CFTC understandably were wary of each other from the start. But a common threat from outside, in the form of the wealthy Hunt brothers of Texas, showed the industry and its regulators the benefit of working together. The heirs to the H. L. Hunt oil fortune, the brothers Nelson Bunker and William Herbert Hunt had an appetite for Texas-sized plays in commodities. In early 1977, the brothers Hunt accumulated a 24-million bushel soybean position on the Board of Trade, eight times larger than position limits imposed by the CFTC.

The Hunts tried to skirt the limits by splitting their soybean holdings among sons and daughters, but the CFTC was not fooled and filed suit in a Chicago federal court to force the Hunts to liquidate most of their holdings. The agency earned a mixed victory—a finding by the court that the Hunts had indeed exceeded position limits, but a ruling that the agency, and not the courts, should have imposed sanctions for market manipulation. An appeal followed, the CFTC began its own administrative hearing, and eventually it fined the Hunts $500,000 and obtained a promise that they would stay out of the bean market for two years.

The soybean skirmish was only a preliminary to the 1979 silver war, which has become perhaps the most celebrated market manipulation scheme in the history of the Board. Dubbed "Silvergate" (every scandal in those post-Watergate days was dubbed "something-gate"), the battle pitted the wealthy Hunt family against the powerful Board of Trade and the then little-known CFTC. The Hunt adventures would also call attention to the differing approaches to market regulation by the Board and the Commodity Exchange of New York (COMEX). The wreckage from the unsuccessful corner of the world-wide supply of silver would lead the Hunts eventually to file for bankruptcy and liquidate their estate. The CFTC and the Board of Trade emerged from the fiasco battered and bruised, but with their authority to regulate markets largely intact.

Late in 1979, with silver climbing to $9 an ounce, there was little doubt that the Hunts were up to something big in silver. Not only were they taking delivery on every contract they held, but companies affiliated with them, such as the secretive International Minerals Investment Co., were doing so as well. The CFTC discussed taking action but could not agree on whether this was a "market emergency" under the 1974 Act's definition.

By early January of 1980, the situation was growing critical. The Hunts had ignored pleas from Board of Trade president Robert Wilmouth and continued accumulating silver. A CFTC staff study figured the Hunts and their partners had accumulated a position in excess of 200 million ounces. They controlled half of the supply for delivery on the Comex, and 70 percent in Chicago. The price of silver had run up to $37.50 an ounce. But still, CFTC chairman James Stone, who thought the agency should intervene in what he considered a clear "market emergency," could not get the votes necessary for the commission to act.

The Comex at last was spurred to action. Following in the tracks of the Board of Trade, the Comex imposed position limits of 500 contracts in each delivery month, effective in February. As the January contract approached expiration, the price of silver climbed precipitously, topping out in Chicago on January 18 at $52.50. Traders started talking about the possibility of $85 silver. But, $50-per-ounce silver was as much as the Comex's directors could stomach. On January 21, the Comex ordered that trading in silver would be for liquidation only—in other words, it would allow no one to buy silver. The price dropped to $44 that day, and to $34 the next, which was the day the Board of Trade also imposed a liquidation-only order.

The CFTC had demonstrated an acute inability to act even in the most extreme crisis. The Board of Trade and the Comex had shown they would jump in during an emergency in order to save their markets, even when immensely wealthy and powerful adversaries were involved. And they had left the Hunts and their banks to clean up the mess, and prepare for years of litigation.

□ □ □

WITH THE HUNT DEBACLE fresh on the minds of its regulators and overseers in Congress, there was little surprise when the industry became the target of a major new effort to change the way futures investments are taxed. By 1980, with Ronald Reagan in the White House, new taxes were taboo, unless of course those taxes could be inflicted on a group that had lots of money and little public sympathy— a group like commodities traders. So the Reagan administration suggested that "tax straddles" should be eliminated by law. Straddles were a technique by which traders took their losses at the end of the year, but deferred their profits until the next year—or, if they were smart, deferred taking profits in perpetuity.

The Board and the Merc went berserk over the Reagan proposal. They put their sizable Political Action Committees to work preaching the gospel of free market entrepreneurism in the corridors and, more importantly, the private offices of the Capitol. Through Representative Tony Coelho (D-California), the head of the fundraising Democratic Congressional Campaign Committee, the exchanges put out word that contributions from their powerful PACs would be commensurate with any lawmaker's support on the straddle issue.

Suddenly, thanks to the intervention of Representative Marty Russo (D-Illinois), a protégé of House Ways and Means Committee chairman Dan Rostenkowski, the committee presented a bill that parroted the industry's position in favor of continuing straddles. But this was Reagan's year as the Great Communicator, and the industry would not get in the way of his landmark Tax Recovery Act of 1981. Just as the Republican-controlled Senate had wanted all along, the law required that commodities positions would be marked to market at year end. Gains and losses would be figured as if the positions were closed that day, and taxed appropriately.

□ □ □

NOT ALL OF THE BOARD'S ENERGIES were directed against Washington. The Board in the mid-1980s was playing a pivotal role in blowing the first fatal holes in one of the most notorious bucket shops ever, First Commodity Corp. of Boston. For years, commodities regulators had kept their eyes on FCCB, which had a history of overly aggressive sales practices and excessive trading, or "churning," of customers' accounts. But enforcement against FCCB had been piecemeal at best.

Enter the tiny MidAmerica Commodity Exchange. This was the only exchange where FCCB was a member, primarily so it could keep costs low for those few orders it did send to the trading floor. Based on customer complaints about churning, the MidAm in 1985 expelled FCCB, initiating a regulatory review that eventually led the CFTC to ban First Commodity Corp. and its owners, Donald and Richard Schleicher. For the thinly capitalized MidAm, the expulsion of FCCB was a heroic but suicidal act. Legal bills exceeding $1 million forced the tiny exchange into a merger with the Board of Trade. John Gilmore, chairman of the Board at the time, marvelled at the MidAm's mettle. "FCCB made one mistake, and that was joining the MidAm," Gilmore said. "It was the least among us, the MidAm, that did the most."

The First Commodity case was a triumph for the Board and for the CFTC, giving both an opportunity to showcase their enforcement prowess and assure the public that they were protected against market fraud. But the glow from victory would not last long. This was the go-go 1980s, the age of the quick buck, the entrepreneur, and the leveraged buyout on Wall Street. And, after nearly a decade of capitalist excess, the government was starting to take notice. The surprise $100 million fine and criminal prosecution of Ivan Boesky in 1986 was a signal to the financial community that the "Greed is Good" decade was coming to an end. The feds were starting to attack insider trading in New York. And, though it wasn't known publicly at the time, a crackdown on commodities trading in Chicago was underway.

In Chicago, the Boesky episode had little direct effect, except perhaps in the offices of the U.S. Attorney for the Northern District of Illinois, Anton Valukas, and in the FBI offices at the Dirksen federal building, several blocks from the Board in downtown Chicago. The headline-making successes (and some would say excesses) of Rudolph Giuliani, the U.S. Attorney for the Southern District of New York, did not go unnoticed. And while Valukas apparently did not harbor the transparent political ambitions of Giuliani, the longstanding rivalry between the two districts continued. New York's insider trading success was putting on the heat in Chicago.

Rather than return fire for fire, Chicago came up with an entertaining but somewhat trivial matter: the famous wig case. Valukas in 1988 charged Thompson B. Sanders, a former Board member, with masterminding one of the most flamboyant frauds in the history of the markets. It was Sanders's plan in 1986 to send two confederates— one dressed in wig, phony reading glasses, and fake trader's garb, the other posing as his clerk—to trade in the frenetic Treasury bond pit. The scheme, worked out and rehearsed in the Blackstone Hotel downtown, was to walk away from losing trades and claim the winners for accounts set up by Sanders. Profits from the plan ran well above $200,000. But the scheme came crashing to a halt after David Pelleu, one of Sanders's boys, broke down and contacted the Justice Department. The Pelleu breakthrough was a godsend for Valukas, who had come up with nothing in the months since the Board of Trade in early 1987 had turned over its internal investigation of a series of mysterious unclaimed trades.

The Board's embarrassment over the wig case was compounded when Marvin Aspen, the federal judge who sentenced Sanders, launched a polemic against the Board. Expressing amazement at the "cesspool" at the Board of Trade, Aspen wondered at the "disgraceful manner" in which trading is conducted. The crimes of Sanders and his group were "the tip of the iceberg" at an exchange where an "insider entourage" runs affairs, "sham trades" are commonplace, and traders "change the history of what occurs with pencil and paper." Winding up for a big finish, Aspen told a packed courtroom, "It boggles the mind that in this computer age we live in that trading is conducted at the Board of Trade in the same way as in the horse and buggy era, with pits that can be turned into cesspools, with hand trades, with manipulation of bookkeeping in restaurants at the Board of Trade."

Not surprisingly, the Board took umbrage at Aspen's vitriol and defended its self-enforcement record. The exchange claimed that its computerized trade auditing system was without peer. In a tartly worded statement, Board president Thomas Donovan and chairman Karsten "Cash" Mahlmann compared Aspen's blanket indictment of the Board to "impugning the integrity of the entire U.S. judicial system for the corruption of a few judges." In the city of the Greylord judicial corruption probe—which until the commodities probe was the most famous FBI scam in Chicago—the Board's retort was pointed, indeed.

A few months later, when the pit probe became public knowledge, Aspen's attack would read like a rough draft of the daily front-page headlines. Though his timing and observations were astute, Aspen said he had no idea that, even as he spoke, disguises were again being worn on the floor, but this time by agents of the FBI.

□ □ □

THE BOARD HAD COME A LONG WAY from its humble beginnings beside the Chicago River. From the struggle for survival, to the bucket shop battles, to the corner crises, to the creation and evolution of its regulatory structure, the exchange had survived, and mostly thrived. In battling the bucket shops, the exchange's leaders had discovered the importance of a favorable public image. Fighting corner attempts from the likes of Patten and Leiter, the Board had managed market emergencies under great stress. Fending off major institutional challenges like those of the Cargill and Hunt corners, the exchange had overcome powerful interests with almost limitless resources. In influencing the constant evolution of its regulatory structure, the Board had learned the ropes of Washington intrigue and how to string a few strands of its own.

The history of scandal, corruption, high jinks, and politics had hardened the Board's leaders to take charge and fight when under attack, and to set policy when they had a chance. All of these experiences would come into play in the Board's next and most remarkable episode—the aftermath of an FBI sting conducted in its very midst. The closed society of the Board of Trade was about to be blown open. Every lesson from its checkered past would be called into play as the exchange battled to preserve its image, its way of doing business, its members, and its stature in the world of finance.

□□□

CHAPTER FOUR

Scrappy Survivor:
The Early Years of the Merc

WHILE THE CHICAGO BOARD OF TRADE was building its strength and stature at the juncture of LaSalle and Jackson streets, another young market with less-auspicious origins but an equally great destiny was in its infancy. The same conveniences of transportation that made Chicago a terminal market for the Board of Trade's wheat, corn, and other grain contracts also attracted commerce in other commodities—produce, eggs, lumber, and livestock. Trading sprang up throughout Chicago's downtown and along its riverfront, with merchants gathering to buy farm produce to meet the provisioning needs of the growing city, and laying the foundation for a market that one day would rival the Board for leadership in the international financial markets.

The most significant of these local markets, the Chicago Produce Exchange, opened in 1874 on the northeast corner of Clark and Lake streets. As many as 300 grocery dealers gathered there to buy and sell vegetables, butter, eggs, and other assorted dairy products. The Chicago Board of Trade already was trading forward or "to arrive" contracts for future delivery, but the Produce Exchange merchants traded only for "spot," or immediate delivery, and used the exchange as a handy place to meet colleagues and gather market information. In its earliest form, the exchange was more a club for produce traders than a place of business.

Interest in a formal marketplace waned, and the Produce Exchange became inactive in 1876. Competition from a couple of Chicago taverns, which were popular gathering places for the produce traders, diverted business from the exchange, which also suffered from the informal merchandising style of the times. The produce business was merely a kitchen-garden offshoot of the mighty midwestern grain machine. Produce by nature was perishable and, with the exception of eggs, was not storable or suitable for future delivery. The merchants who dealt in produce were not the robber barons of the grain exchanges. They were more likely to be newly arrived immigrants, speaking in the thick accents of their native countries, struggling to build family businesses.

Chicago's produce business probably would have remained a local market if not for the role played by eggs. As with grain, Chicago had become a transit point for eggs. Nearly every midwestern farm had a few laying hens, and farmers' wives carried their production into the nearest town to barter for other merchandise. Local merchants often accepted the eggs as a convenience to the farm wives, then packed the eggs off to Chicago, where dealers sold them to restaurateurs and wholesale grocers or arranged transit to egg-consuming markets in the Northeast or the South.

Eggs at the time were a highly seasonal crop, with most of the production in the early spring. For Chicago dealers, arranging year-round contracts in the country was important business. Each February, "the Big Butter and Egg Men" of Chicago (as they were called in a Broadway show of the times) would invite their country suppliers to a dinner at the downtown Chicago Sherman Hotel. After priming the rubes with lavish amounts of food and spirits, the city brokers would haul out contracts that committed the country folks to deliver set numbers of carloads of eggs at particular times through the year.

These forward contracts, like the rice certificates of feudal Japan, were traded year-round and fluctuated in value. However, they were a faulty currency. Delivery on the agreements was dismal, with country suppliers often refusing to ship if the price had risen in the intervening period and Chicago dealers refusing to pay when spot prices dropped below the forward price. There was no clearinghouse for the contracts and no way to enforce delivery.

These chronic problems contributed to the revival of the Chicago Produce Exchange in 1884. The born-again Exchange—an agglomeration of produce dealers, egg traders, and oleomargarine dealers—published a set price for butter and eggs at the end of each day. It was a modest endeavor with only fragmented rules and could not cure the forward-contract delivery problems. By 1895, a handful of dissenting members formed a splinter group that became known as the

Produce Exchange Butter and Egg Board. They sought to enforce stricter rules and post more realistic prices on the commodities they traded.

A controversy over oleomargarine was finally responsible for the Butter and Egg Board's permanent split from the Produce Exchange in 1898. Butter dealers, a major force on the new Board, were pressuring Illinois legislators to ban oleomargarine production—a position obviously not shared by the oleo traders who made up a strong faction on the Produce Exchange. The result of the clash was a permanent breach between the two groups.

□ □ □

THE NEW BUTTER AND EGG BOARD attracted little public notice. Its membership was a relatively unknown and insular group of staid, middle-class businessmen given to heavy wool suits, wire-frame glasses, and buttoned vests, who no doubt would be shocked by their disheveled professional offspring in the Merc's pits today.

Some of the Butter and Egg Board's most prominent members supplied eggs to the world, but unlike their successful counterparts at the Board of Trade, they rarely earned a mention in Chicago's social register. There is little doubt of their commitment to the new enterprise, however. Nearly all of the seven men who signed the Butter and Egg Board charter would participate in the organization's transformation into the Chicago Mercantile Exchange 21 years later.

The public looked on the Egg Board with suspicion. The same Populism that vexed the Board of Trade during this time haunted the Butter and Egg Board, with writers of the day championing the cause of farmers against the evil "middlemen." Even the Chicago Post Office took sides in the late 1890s, issuing circulars that listed the addresses of farmers who would bypass the new exchange and ship their produce directly to consumers.

With the memory of the 1919 New York and Philadelphia food riots still fresh, the Chicago exchanges were handy targets for demagogues who complained that farmers shared little in prosperity but lost dearly during hard times. This popular discontent with brokers and traders would persist, and it became one element in the forces drawing federal agents into undercover assignments on Chicago's trading floors.

At the turn of the century, the producers' resentment was, in some cases, well placed. Edwin Nourse, a student of the Chicago produce markets of the time, questioned the economic justification for the butter market at the Butter and Egg Board. "As a matter of fact, the Board makes a convenient place where fictitious or 'wash' sales may be made and the prices so established given considerable prominence," he wrote in his book on Chicago markets.

Nourse even claimed traders for the Butter and Egg Board would spend their weekends traveling to outlying markets like Elgin, Illinois, 30 miles from Chicago, to make certain the prices they fixed in the city would stick in the countryside. "Elgin is no longer a bona fide butter market," Nourse lamented. "And the only reason that Chicago dealers should keep up the absurd practice of going out there each Saturday to go through the forms of a 'call' would seem to be because it gives them some control over prices."

Despite the criticism, the exchange prospered through the turn of the century, testing its own limits and the rules. In 1917, the United States' entry into World War I caused egg prices to shoot up, and many forward contracts went unfulfilled, causing a scandal in the industry and with the public. Even as the Agriculture Department, shocked at the rapid rise in grain prices, shut down wheat futures trading on the Board of Trade, the tiny Butter and Egg Board's 1917 incident escaped government notice. But after witnessing the shutdown at the Board of Trade, Butter and Egg Board leaders decided to revise their trading practices, lest inaction invite government constraints.

□ □ □

THE DECISION TO REORGANIZE under the broader and more modern name of the Chicago Mercantile Exchange, with tougher rules and grading standards and a new clearinghouse, was made by a member referendum in September 1919. The directors of the Merc studied the futures markets at the Board of Trade and decided to initiate this method of trading at the new exchange. On opening day, some 100 people had each paid $100 for membership in the new Chicago Mercantile Exchange. The new Merc offered futures and forward contracts in eggs and butter only. But in 1929, cheese futures were added, and potato futures were launched two years later.

The birth of the new exchange incited controversy. Some members bristled at the demands of the clearinghouse, where trades were reported and margin payments required to ensure that traders met their obligations. Although the Board of Trade years earlier had realized that standardized rules and financial requirements promoted trade, some of the Merc's hardscrabble produce merchants considered the reporting and margining rules a threat to their businesses. Some of the same arguments 60 years later would form the kernel of the Merc's 20th-century crusade for "Free Markets for Free Men." Member resentment of the clearinghouse grew until 1922, when exchange officers quelled the unrest and prevented a membership split. By 1925, the clearinghouse was accepted as a means of guaranteeing business and was delivering significant income to the exchange.

The new exchange prospered, even though the egg business was in a slump. By 1923 the Merc's executive secretary, S. Edward Davis, complained that the set price for a new membership had risen so high that it discouraged membership expansion. At the time, an unlimited number of seats were offered, but at a prohibitive price of $1,500. "This $1,500 embargo should be removed and the price lowered to $850," Davis wrote in a members report. "New blood, new business, and healthy growth needed by the exchange would be the result." Heeding Davis's call, the directors in 1925 capped exchange membership at 500 seats and set $500 as the price for new seat sales. As Davis predicted, turnover of exchange seats began to rise.

When exchange volume reached a record 98,125 contracts in 1925, the Merc began planning for a new landmark building. Optimism was robust. The Merc boasted that land it had acquired at 110 North Franklin Street was worth $1 million. An enthusiastic Davis told members that bank support for the building project was so high that the $2.6 million construction bond in 1926 fetched "the highest price . . . that has ever been paid for any building project in the Loop." The new building had a 5,000-square-foot trading floor, unobstructed by columns, that was reached by six elevators and a marble staircase. While blackboard "call market" trading remained, there also were three pits for futures trading. The 17-story edifice featured a frieze carved with images of farm animals and bountiful baskets of eggs. Its style was monolithic and resembled that of the nearby Merchandise Mart, the largest building in the world at the time, built the same year.

Almost immediately after moving into the new building, the Merc was beset by the same hard times that plagued the country. Trading volume fell almost 20 percent in 1928. In 1929, after the stock market crash, the Merc's annual accounting reflected the toll: a net profit of only $12,000. That year the exchange absorbed big losses when two clearing firms failed, a distressing start to the long slide into the depths of the Depression. By the middle of the decade, the optimism that underpinned the Merc's ambitious construction project had vanished. Unable to meet its mortgage, the demoralized exchange sold its new building. The Merc continued to reside at 110 North Franklin, paying rent to landlord Colonel Henry Crown, the prominent Chicago real estate and construction tycoon.

The hard times brought with them government price support programs that further eroded the Merc's financial health. Empowered by the Agricultural Marketing Act of 1929 to subsidize crop prices, the government by 1932 had such a firm grip on prices that private dealers and commodities traders had dropped out of the market, nearly killing the futures trade. Meanwhile, the Merc leadership was in disarray. Davis had departed as secretary in 1928, and was not replaced until 1930, when a new business manager, Lloyd Tenny, was hired.

Tenny's first annual report to members summarized the dismal tenor of the times. Acknowledging that most members expected a down year in 1931, Tenny exhorted them to do something to ameliorate the troubles. "The hens are going to lay the eggs in 1931 just as they did in 1930. The cows are going to produce milk and the butter will be made," Tenny wrote. He exhorted Merc members to meet with the people who had those commodities in storage and persuade them to trade at the exchange. If any such meetings did take place, Merc volume did not benefit, and by 1932, it was about half of the 1925 peak.

To make matters worse, the sad condition of American agriculture had revived popular dissatisfaction with Chicago commodities traders. Farm organizations and farm-state legislators began launching fierce anti-futures attacks. "It is especially true that after two or more years of falling prices, the public generally begins to lay the blame on this or that, and with commodities that have the facilities of futures trading, the easiest thing is to blame this method of selling," Tenny wrote. Hoping to learn from the Board of Trade's long experience in this regard, the Merc in 1932 invited the president of the Board of Trade to speak at its annual meeting and rally his trading brethren at the struggling Merc. The Board, Tenny said in a flattering introduction, "has had a long and successful period of operation and has had many periods of depression to weather and much criticism to live through."

Conditions at the Merc improved slightly in the late 1930s, but the recovery was brief. The onset of World War II revived the economy but brought price controls to the commodities markets, and it very nearly wiped out Chicago's futures exchanges. Just as the Board's seat price dropped to an all-time low of $24, so did the Merc's. Trading volume at the Merc skidded to just 3,223 contracts in 1943, and half of that was in onion futures, introduced out of desperation in 1942.

Because onions did not fall under price controls or within the regulatory realm of the Commodity Exchange Act, they offered a refreshingly free market to traders. But even though onion trading brought new business to the exchange, the Merc probably would have folded if not for the strong connection most members still had to the cash markets for butter, eggs, and produce. While the war nearly snuffed out futures trading, supplying the war effort with foodstuffs kept many Merc member firms in business.

After the war, the economy revived briskly; the exchange, somewhat laggardly. Butter futures never recovered from price controls, and that pit died. The Merc survived on egg, onion, and potato futures. Attempts to trade commodities like apples and scrap iron were short-lived. Compared with its mighty neighbor on LaSalle Street, the Merc was floundering. Most Merc members were businessmen who traded only part time, coming to the exchange from their offices in the morning, trading in their business suits. Given the slow pace of trading, such gentlemanly attire was not a hindrance. Of 500 members, fewer than 150 came to the trading floor on a regular basis. But the established LaSalle Street brokerage houses at least had confidence in the exchange. Cross membership between the Chicago Mercantile Exchange and the Board of Trade became common for big securities and commodities trading firms during the postwar period. By the late 1970s the big firms comprised the majority of clearing members on each exchange, and 80 percent of the membership of the Merc also held seats on the Board of Trade.

□ □ □

RECOGNIZING THAT THE EXCHANGE needed more professional leadership in the postwar period, the Merc's business manager, Oscar Olson, began searching for his own replacement. Olson, the Merc's first chairman back in 1919, had returned as paid manager in the early 1940s. This was the time that the paid presidents of the Chicago exchanges became powerful men, principally responsible for rule enforcement and business development. They were given particular stature after the 1929 stock market crash and were meant to instill a public image of market integrity.

Olson mentioned his search to the head of the Chicago office of the Commodity Exchange Authority, who approached Everette "E. B." Harris, then secretary of the Board of Trade. "The gentleman who headed them [the CEA] up in Chicago and I had coffee every morning over at the Board of Trade, and later at the Merc," Harris recalls. "It was he who suggested that Mr. Olson wanted me to come over to the Merc and asked if would I meet with him." A surprised Harris at first suggested that perhaps the two exchanges should consider merging, but when that idea got a cool reception from the Board of Trade, he moved to the Merc as its president in 1953. Except for a short hiatus in the early 1960s, Harris would remain president of the Merc until 1977.

Harris found the Merc quite different from the Board. "It was dwarfed by the Board of Trade at that time . . . . I won't say I was disappointed, but I found it very different," Harris recalls. Much as they do to this day, members of the Merc's powerful board of governors treated each other as family, socializing together and joining each other on family outings.

When Harris arrived, eggs and onions were the Merc's primary markets, since the New York Mercantile Exchange had already captured potato futures. The egg contract sustained the exchange through the war years, but by 1950 eggs had ceased to need a futures market. Changes in production and transportation methods assured year-round egg supplies, smoothing out the seasonal cycles that generated forward contracts and the need for futures. Of the Merc's record 500,000 contracts traded in 1955, about 100,000 were onion futures, making the malodorous bulb the exchange's fastest-growing product.

Then the Merc lost the onion contract. It was an event that would send the starveling exchange into a near-terminal state and galvanize a set of Merc members into seeking fresh leadership. Dominated by a few dealers and growers, and with virtually inelastic demand, onions were a market waiting for trouble. Like egg futures before it, the onion contract had been the arena for multiple garden-variety cornering attempts and price manipulations over the years. And the Merc's onion crowd apparently saw no reason to curb their activities just because the Commodity Exchange Authority in 1955 for the first time claimed oversight of the onion market.

Once it gained jurisdiction, the CEA promptly investigated a $1.5 million price-rigging scheme in the onion pit that would be one of the most spectacular market-fixing incidents in the history of the Chicago markets. The corner—as it turned out, the last one for onions—centered on Sam S. Siegel, a Merc onion trader who owned a suburban Chicago produce company; Vincent Kosuga, a New York-based onion dealer; and a handful of unfortunate Michigan onion growers. Through aggressive selling on the Merc, the Siegel group between August 1955 and March 1956 pushed down the price of a 50-pound bag of onions from $2.55 to ten cents. At that level, the onions were worth less than the string bags in which they were shipped.

The abrupt price decline was hardly a result of free-market forces. A CEA investigation found that the collapse resulted from a traders' shoot-out in the onion market. In the fall of 1955, Kosuga had bought large quantities of November onion futures, causing the "shorts" in those contracts to ship 28 million pounds of onions into Chicago to deliver against Kosuga's long position. Meanwhile, Siegel and his produce company were also acquiring onions. By early December, Kosuga and Siegel had teamed together and had 1,000 carloads of onions stored in Chicago—a total of 30 million pounds, worth about $1.5 million.

In a year of onion scarcity, the accumulation of such large stocks in the hands of one or two traders might have constituted a corner that would have driven onion prices higher. But Siegel and Kosuga were done with their long position and wanted to start selling. They advised 13 big Michigan onion growers that the onions would be dumped on the market if the growers did not step in and buy out the dealers' stocks. Fearing they would be clobbered by a price slump, the growers reluctantly took title to 265 carloads of onions, worth about $168,000—a sizable amount, but far less than the $500,000 that Siegel and Kosuga had hoped to unload.

As part of the deal, Kosuga and Siegel had promised the growers they would keep buying enough onions on the cash market to support futures prices on the Merc. But that wasn't the real plan. Instead, Siegel and Kosuga began shorting onion futures almost immediately after the growers bought the onions. By February 6, the two men had sold 1,148 carloads of onion futures at a price of $1.02 per bag. The short position had one problem: The onions Kosuga and Siegel held in Chicago warehouses were starting to spoil. To make them suitable for delivery in Chicago the two dealers shipped the onions out of the city to have them cleaned and reconditioned. Seeing the carloads of onions return to Chicago, futures traders got the mistaken impression that new deliveries were heavy. The resultant selling depressed prices even further and added to the Siegel group's profits. As the March contract neared expiration, onions had skidded to ten cents a bag.

The enraged and double-crossed onion growers appealed to Congress, which opened hearings on a bill to outlaw onion futures trading even before the CEA started its investigation. Despite a strenuous outcry by the Merc and a public relations effort aimed at showcasing the benefits of onion futures, Congress in August 1958 amended the Commodity Exchange Act to abolish the onion market. Trading onion futures became a misdemeanor under federal law.

With its most dynamic market killed with the stroke of a pen, the Merc mustered its nascent political and legal resources, obtained an injunction, and sought to repeal the law by claiming unconstitutional restraint of trade. In November 1959, a three-judge federal court panel disagreed, ended the injunction, and upheld the new law, which remains in force to this day. Some 65 Merc onion traders went looking for a new commodity to trade. The demoralizing political loss in the battle to save the onion market would teach the Merc a valuable lesson. In the fight to save stock-index futures in the wake of the 1987 stock market crash, and the system of self-regulation after the FBI investigation became known in 1989, the Merc employed a powerful propaganda apparatus to battle the forces arrayed against the exchange.

□ □ □

WITH THE ONION MARKET GONE, the Merc was forced to reexamine its viability as an exchange. Potato futures, while a relatively small part of the Merc's business, were also under attack, with several congressmen eager to outlaw them along with onions. Butter trading was dormant, leaving Merc members to survive on the dregs of egg futures. That market also had a dastardly reputation. Egg corners and squeezes were a way of life, and the egg market was prone to the regular muscling of produce traders who controlled deliverable supplies. "I used to say three housewives could get together on the weekend and corner the egg market," a later Merc chairman, Leo Melamed, recalls.

In the midst of the onion brouhaha in 1956, the Department of Agriculture revoked the registration of Merc firm G. H. Miller and Co. for its role in a 1952 egg price manipulation scheme. The firm's principal partner, Gilbert H. Miller, also had his broker registration revoked, and nine egg dealers from Texas and Iowa were suspended from egg futures trading for six months to a year. The incident further undermined the Merc's last remaining market.

The exchange fell into another period of decline. Harris, discouraged, left the Merc in the early 1960s to try running a brokerage house. Merc seats were sold for about $3,000, and the exchange, in an attempt to limit the price slide, repurchased 45 memberships.

Desperately trying to forestall the exchange's collapse, a hardcore group of members, some of them on the board of governors, banded together to look at their options. They created the New Commodities Committee and named Glenn Andersen, a livestock and dairy man who had joined the exchange in 1952, as chairman. "We were hungry and aggressive," Andersen recalls. "We looked at all kinds of things, and listed them according to potential." Meats, orange juice, and oil looked like the strongest possibilities, but Andersen's expertise was in meats, and that's where he focused his attention.

Chicago had always been a big meat-packing town, but most of the trading was done in the cash markets of the sprawling Union Stock Yards on Chicago's Southwest Side. Modern marketing concepts like futures had not arrived in that putrid, primitive domain. "They had a Friday call market for hogs on the top floor of the stockyards," Andersen recalls. "It wasn't a futures market."

A short, cigar-smoking old-timer named Elmer Faulkner suggested that the Merc committee consider trading pork bellies—sides of frozen, uncured bacon. Faulkner remembered that pork bellies had traded at the Chicago Board of Trade during the Civil War when pig meat in the form of salt pork or so-called "sow bellies" was a soldier's main provision. Pork bellies had strong seasonal price changes, dipping in the fall during slaughtering season and then rising sharply in late winter as supplies thinned. With the advent of refrigeration, pork bellies were frozen and stored in warehouses, making the commodity suitable for delivery year-round. Besides, Andersen knew that a few heavily capitalized speculators already were trading bellies, buying warehouse receipts cheap and selling them rich, riding out sharp seasonal price volatility. It was a market waiting to be exploited.

Excited about the prospects, the committee built a pork belly futures contract from scratch. They drew up trading specifications, including grading standards, and taught Agriculture Department inspectors to grade bellies for weight and quality. Andersen claims bacon standards improved as a result. The group certified deliverable warehouses, talked up futures trading with the major meat packers, and taught the fundamentals of the seasonal pork belly trade to their fellow members and the brokerage houses.

Despite the efforts, pork bellies were not an immediate success after their September 1961 launch. The major packers, afraid of being forced to accept delivery of a competitor's meat, were leery of the market. Since quality was their only brand distinction, packers looked with skepticism on the futures market and its assumption of uniform quality standards. Only 561 pork belly contracts traded during the first full year, and 1,728 the second year. But that changed after the 1964 introduction of live cattle futures. With traders able to speculate on the relative price changes of bellies and beef, the belly market began to thrive.

To this day, some critics still say the Merc's pork belly contract lacks fundamental economic justification: The market should really consist of just a few meat packers trading bellies back and forth. But the contract proved a boon to the exchange. The cyclical nature of belly prices provided ample speculative opportunities and brought in a new crowd of commercial interests. By 1964, belly volume ballooned to 715,000 contracts, and by 1967 bellies became the exchange's first million-contract commodity.

The Merc capitalized on the success of pork bellies, selling the 45 memberships it had repurchased in 1960. For the first time, meat packing firms joined the exchange as clearing members. "I got 18 in that first year, including Wilson and Armour," Andersen boasts. Suddenly, meat was the wave of the future. Even Chicago bankers, normally wary of any new action at the hurly-burly futures exchanges, suddenly wanted in, clearing trades for meat brokers who until then had dealt only with the stockyards.

The striking success earned pork bellies a reputation as "the contract that built the Chicago Mercantile Exchange." But the belly contract could not have been a winner without the live cattle contract, which then-president E. B. Harris calls "my monument." Live cattle was the first futures contract based on a commodity that could not be stored like grain, eggs, or even bellies. "I argued that cattle in a feedlot of uniform quality were just as much in storage as graded cotton in a mill or wheat in an elevator," Harris recalls. "There was inventory risk that had to be protected." Harris secured quick approval for live cattle futures from his buddies at the CEA, and they were an immediate success. Fifty-nine thousand contracts traded in 1965, and 300,000 two years later.

The Merc built ambitiously on the success of bellies and cattle. Live hog futures debuted in 1966, feeder cattle in 1971. Forest products were launched in 1969, with random lengths lumber the most successful of the offerings. By then, the Merc's volume had reached 3.8 million contracts, and memberships were trading for $43,500, a healthy jump from $500 a seat during the starveling days.

Success in the meat markets brought a new set of complaints about price manipulation to the Merc, most notably from western livestock producers. Charges of speculative short-selling and market manipulation began almost with the first shouts in the belly pit but became louder when cattle futures started trading. To this day, cattle producers suspect that the large commodities speculators are in cahoots with the giant meat packers to keep prices under pressure. The National Cattlemen's Association at one point fought to have cattle trading banned. When the Merc awarded a member of the Cattlemen's Association a token seat on its board of governors in 1984, the anti-futures campaign withered. Still, distrust runs high among the cattlemen's rank and file: A 1986 poll found that 69 percent of NCA members favored discontinuing futures on live cattle and feeder cattle.

The livestock successes also invited competition with the Board of Trade, which for the first time saw the possibility of a challenge from the crosstown upstart. Noting the Merc's breakthroughs with the meat contracts, the Board scurried to launch its own live cattle contract. The Board's futures on dressed beef failed miserably, demonstrating the axiom that the exchange first and fastest with a new product always wins the largest market share. In the midst of their first competitive feud, the Merc's Harris met Board president Warren Lebeck for drinks. The two placed a bet on which exchange would win the battle for the beef. Harris says he can't recall whether Lebeck ever paid up.

□ □ □

WITH THE MERC EMERGING from 50 years of obscurity, the meat contracts had expanded the exchange's financial and customer bases. But they had done nothing to change the Merc's internal structure. Its rules were in disarray, with both the letter of the regulations and the means of enforcing them obscure. The old-line members were satisfied with clubby business practices that tolerated price manipulation and eroded public confidence in the market.

The Merc, always viewed as insignificant in relation to the Board, had felt little public pressure to clean up its image. Administrative power was concentrated in the hands of a few families that had controlled the exchange from its early days. With staff and membership lacking the will to police themselves, corners and other shady trade practices—particularly the Siegel onion corner—threatened the life of the exchange.

The Board of Trade had learned early that strong self-policing made a stronger exchange. But the Merc's members, after struggling so long simply to survive, had grown defensive about any restraints on their business. "Free markets" to some members meant freedom from even the mildest exchange surveillance. Not until a decade after the first pork belly future traded would the Merc finally begin to come to grips with these core weaknesses.

CHAPTER FIVE

□□□

Years of Plenty:
The Young Turks Take Charge

BOLSTERED BY THE SUCCESS of the pork belly and cattle markets and populated by rebellious traders anxious to challenge tradition with their new-found wealth, the Merc took on the character of an aggressive adolescent. By 1969, the produce dealers in their business suits had been replaced by full-time futures traders carrying the needs of their business in the pockets of their colorful trading jackets. But the Merc was still little more than an agricultural backwater, a nonfactor in international finance, and for the new breed of Merc trader heading into the tumultuous 1970s that was not nearly enough.

The character of the exchange had changed appreciably. In the Merc of the 1970s, the floor traders were more cowboys than onion peddlers, and the customers were big businessmen who used the Merc to hedge their huge risks in raising commercial livestock. In the United States at large, it was a time of protest and change. With the Vietnam conflict heating up, the national debt and global economic imbalances began to strain the economy. Lyndon Johnson's guns-and-butter economic policies—military buildup and social spending—inflated the economy, creating investor demand for hard commodities rather than financial assets. That climate created a bonanza for commodities traders, and stories of 24-year-old taxi-drivers-turned-belly-traders making a million dollars during their first year in the pits were the honey that drew more and more new traders.

At the same time, a young Chicago lawyer was demonstrating his talent for being in the right place at the right time, rising to the ranks of the Merc's board of governors just as the exchange was reaching its new bloom. Leo Melamed, the son of a refugee Hebrew teacher from Poland, had come to the Merc in 1954, working as a runner to finance his law studies. He continued as a part-time trader while pursuing a law practice in the early 1960s. During his time as a runner at the exchange, he worked for Joe Sieger at Merrill Lynch. A former chairman of the Merc during the early 1950s, Sieger taught Melamed the ropes of exchange politics. Melamed turned to trading full-time in 1966 and, running on a populist platform, was first elected to the Merc's board of governors in 1967, at age 35.

The Merc at the time was run by a tight clique of old-timers who dominated the executive committee and, to a lesser extent, the board of governors. Then, as now, exchange members elected the board members, and then the board—in a classic version of smoked-filled-room politics—would select its own chairman. While President E. B. Harris was the dominant public personality for the Merc, its front man for the world, the chairman tended to be an "inside" man.

Melamed recalls that he was elected to the board "on a wave of enthusiasm. I had the highest vote total of any of the 12 candidates. That was very unusual for an outsider." He had helped cattleman Robert J. O'Brien get elected chairman of the board that year. In response to his broad support and O'Brien's backing, Melamed was named secretary to the board, an unheard-of elevation for a freshman board member.

The slight, swarthy Melamed had a talent for conciliation, and with the exchange roiled by the turmoil resulting from success and change, his political talents were frequently called upon. He represented a younger, faster generation, and in 1969, when he decided to make a bid for exchange chairman himself, the old-timers saw that the younger crowd was behind him.

As Melamed tells it, he ran on a platform based on making the management of the exchange more representative of all the members. The membership at the time felt it had no say in governing the Merc. Committees existed only as a formality. A reform-halting quorum rule required 300 of 500 exchange members to be present before an official meeting could be called. "I knew the rank and file was very dissatisfied," says Melamed, who promised to promote the power of committees and lower the quorum requirements for meetings. He also proposed a referendum rule that allowed the membership to petition the board to act on a particular issue. Ironically, that rule would be used effectively against Melamed 20 years later when his entrenched power base riled a new generation of Merc traders.

Melamed's experience on the new commodities committee gave him some hope that the Merc product line could be expanded and strengthened. He was also angered by the way the Merc board had handled the onion debacle. "I thought it was an atrocity that it had gotten to that point—that the corner wasn't broken up before it became such an issue. It was more than I could comprehend, as an attorney or as a seat-of-the-pants economist," Melamed explains.

Melamed's legend has been polished over the years, his ascendancy to the chairmanship described often as a revolution of the "young turks" over the old guard. Melamed himself has perpetuated this carefully honed version in press interviews. But not everyone sees it that way: Many view the young turks story as overly romanticized. There was no power struggle; rather, Melamed and his group took custody of an ailing institution.

Glenn Andersen, who was on the board at the time, agrees that the young turks story is overblown. Melamed was a bright, aggressive, and charismatic young man whom some viewed as overly ambitious. But he headed no revolution. "We thought it would be good to have a lawyer in the job," Andersen says simply. "Those of us who liked Leo, who understood what he wanted to do, got behind him."

Melamed was elected chairman of the board in 1969, the youngest person ever to hold that position. For the next two decades, he would retain a tight hold on the political reins of the exchange, remaining chairman of the Merc, or its offshoot, the International Monetary Market, until 1976. He then turned the chairmanship over to a rotating band of three associates who alternated terms in office through the next 13 years. After 1976, Melamed accepted the title Special Counsel to the Board. When that nebulous title confused status-conscious Japanese regulators, Melamed quickly claimed the title Chairman of the Executive Committee. He had acted in that capacity since he came to power in 1969.

While Melamed's rise at the Merc was no revolution, it was most certainly a changing of the guard. He came to power and placed his friends in power, keeping the politics of the exchange concentrated within a narrow group of men, much as it had been for the previous five decades. Whatever his title, throughout his years in power, Melamed would leave no doubt in the minds of Merc members that he and he alone was the driving force behind the exchange and its explosive growth in the 1970s and 1980s.

□ □ □

IN HIS EARLY YEARS at the helm, Melamed had two objectives for the exchange: to improve its image, and to diversify its product line. The exchange's image was terrible. Wags at the Board of Trade referred to the Merc as "the whorehouse." Corners, squeezes, and other manipulations were standard. There were rules, but the structure and organization were fathoms below Board of Trade standards. "The rules were so loose they were more a joke than a reality," Melamed says.

The rule book at the time was in the keeping of Merc secretary Ken McKay, who would paste in rule revisions by hand as the Board approved them. Copies of the changes were rarely distributed to members. Frequently, the Merc's board members could not remember what their rulings had been. "It wasn't that we didn't have a rule book," Melamed said. "It's just that everyone had a different version. If it wasn't in McKay's book, it didn't count."

Melamed began writing his own rule book and quickly acquired an able ally—Jerrold Salzman, a new attorney with the Merc's law firm of Freeman and Freeman. Fresh out of Harvard law school, Salzman had caught Melamed's attention while representing the old guard in early skirmishes with the young turks. Once elected, Melamed asked Freeman and Freeman to put Salzman at his disposal. Given the Merc's inconsequential size at the time, the young lawyer was more than up to the task. Without office, title, or even a membership, Salzman would become one of the most powerful people at the Merc.

Melamed told Salzman he wanted to reorganize the Merc's rules and create a committee structure that worked. During 1969 and 1970, the exchange conducted a year-long "constitutional convention" with 20 exchange members, many of them the same men who had helped put Melamed in power, meeting three nights a month at the Bismarck Hotel, the legendary home of Chicago's Democratic Party. The traders went step-by-step through the rule book, seeing what was needed and what needed change. Jerry Salzman wrote it all down.

Finding the means to quell the market corners and the egos that attempted them was not easy. The new rules created a Business Conduct Committee empowered to stop corners. But Melamed, as chairman, still had to face down traders twice his age and persuade them to unload their positions. Frustrated in one attempt to clean up the egg pit, Melamed called Alex Cauldwell, then the CEA administrator in Washington. Cauldwell was a friend of Melamed's, and while the CEA had no real authority over corners—that rested with the exchange—Melamed decided to bring out Cauldwell and walk him around the egg pit to put some fear into the hearts of the most blatant offenders. Cauldwell took the tour but could not exact the fear Melamed had hoped for. Corners and squeezes remained fashionable.

□ □ □

WITH HIS VISION OF GROWTH FOR THE MERC, Melamed recognized that the exchange needed more generous trading space for traders and for the new contracts he planned to introduce. In 1970, Merc members, crowded into the obsolete 5,000-square-foot trading floor on Franklin Street, were more concerned about their own trading conditions than about the condition of the markets. The solution: a new $6.5 million trading complex that used the air rights of the Union Station Company at 444 West Jackson Boulevard, next to the Chicago River. The Merc moved into the squat, girder-and-glass building with its 14,000-square-foot trading floor over Thanksgiving weekend of 1972. The new building was meant to serve the exchange until 1990, but would suffice only until 1983.

Trading boomed, and five years later Harris and Melamed were sitting in Mayor Richard J. Daley's office, seeking approval to expand the Merc's trading floor out over the street. They needed a zoning variance to start construction, and despite the best efforts of several teams of attorneys, the mayor had withheld approval.

As Melamed and Harris sat politely, Daley regaled them with stories of coho salmon fishing on Lake Michigan, and praise for Senator Everett Dirksen. When Daley grew tired of the conversation, he asked what they had come for, and Harris explained that the overhanging addition would shelter the sidewalk from the rain and provide a handy spot for a bus stop. Melamed one-upped Harris, promising the expanded Merc would be the center of finance in the country west from New York to Chicago. The mayor liked the thought, and the building variance sailed through the city council that week.

With the new rules codified and a new trading floor on the way, Melamed explored ways to capitalize on the changing economic winds of the time. In addition to improving the Merc's image, Melamed's mission as chairman was to diversify the exchange's business. He had seen the Merc nearly extinguished because of its dependence on single product lines—first eggs, then onions. The meats were providing good income and trading when Melamed came to power, or "inherited the exchange," as he thinks of it. But meats were still only one product.

The Johnson and Nixon administrations brought on inflation financing the Vietnam conflict, and investors began to flock to real assets like gold and other hard commodities. As strains on the global system of fixed exchange rates increased in 1970 and 1971, Melamed began to dream of a futures market that could be used to hedge currency risk. The most significant of the international monetary agreements, the Bretton Woods accord, appeared headed for collapse. Drafted shortly after World War II, Bretton Woods had prescribed a narrow band for price fluctuation between most major European currencies and the U.S. dollar. If Bretton Woods broke down, as Melamed and others expected, the world's currencies would trade in volatile ranges and would be ripe for a hedging vehicle.

Melamed claims the idea for trading futures on foreign currencies dawned on him during a social conversation with economist Milton Friedman, then a professor at the University of Chicago, the shrine of free-market economics. Friedman, anticipating the collapse of Bretton Woods, wanted to speculate in the interbank market for foreign currencies but was told by the big banks that he was too small a player for them to service. Friedman wondered why a futures exchange couldn't fill the need.

At the behest of Harris and Melamed, Friedman wrote a paper on the concept. Melamed and his band of supporters shopped Friedman's white paper all around Washington and New York, meeting mostly ridicule or indifference. But Treasury Secretary George Shultz, another University of Chicago faculty alum, voiced no objections, nor did powerful Federal Reserve Board Chairman Arthur Burns. In the end, foreign currency futures were launched in 1972 because no one was strongly opposed to them and because Melamed's determination to have them was so strong.

Preparing Merc members for currency futures trading was another matter. Traders were willing to try it, but the concept of trading money was entirely foreign, not just to the old egg traders, but also to the newly arrived meat traders. "We supported it, but we didn't understand it," Thomas Dittmer, head of Refco, Inc., recalls.

Despite the cattle trading boom, existing Merc clearing firms did not have nearly enough capital to support billions of dollars worth of interbank foreign exchange trades. Merc members wanted to attract that capital but also stay out from under the thumbs of the big New York banking and trading communities. They also wanted to avoid sharing the rights to their existing pork barrel through a membership expansion that would be absolutely necessary to handle all the new trading.

Melamed devised a workable compromise, which he dubbed the International Monetary Market. The IMM was chartered in January 1972 as a separate but affiliated entity of the Merc. Each of the 500 existing Chicago Mercantile Exchange members was given one membership on the new exchange for a $100 subscription fee. Another 150 memberships were offered to the public for $10,000 each at a time when full Merc memberships were selling for around $100,000. A few blocks away, the Board of Trade was creating the Chicago Board Options Exchange and granting CBOE seats to Board of Trade members.

Melamed became chairman of the new 650-member IMM, which in May 1972 launched futures in seven foreign currencies. At first, trade in the currency contracts was dismal. Melamed loyalists, including his former law partner, his bridge buddies, and his in-laws, took turns leaving the booming pork belly, live cattle, and hog pits to stand in the near-dormant currency pits for a few hours each day. New York banks were slow to catch on to the concept of futures trading, since they already hedged risk using sophisticated forward spread arrangements in the interbank currency markets. The small-time investor that Milton Friedman envisioned never showed up.

Lacking many "commercials" to trade with, the floor traders swapped currency futures back and forth. They knew little about the underlying fundamentals of the foreign exchange market and were constrained, more or less, by rules against "wash" trading—buying and selling with no economic gain or loss for either party. That kind of trade, a violation of CEA rules, was tempting as a means of boosting volume in those early months. Despite the efforts of Melamed loyalists, IMM volume in the first full year was a dismal 417,310 contracts, although some pits, such as the deutsche mark, were busier than others.

Scrambling to build business, Harris and Melamed created a new class of clearing membership on the IMM. The new Class B clearing firms would be allowed to join the Merc to perform arbitrage, a trading strategy designed to capture minute differences between prices in the interbank foreign exchange markets and the IMM's currency futures. Class B members could not sponsor, or clear, trades in the Merc's agricultural markets. Financial institutions with the know-how and capital to make IMM currency futures work snapped up the new memberships.

By September 1975, an IMM seat traded at a then-high $40,000. Total IMM volume of 643,000 contracts contributed meaningfully to the Merc's 5.7 million contracts. In 1976, the Merc and the IMM merged, with Merc members given the right to trade all IMM contracts. Handled delicately to preserve the power of full Merc members, the merger concentrated voting rights three to one in the hands of the Merc badge holders. The tilt was necessary to convince wary Merc members to accept the merger, and it also kept the political power within the merged exchanges concentrated in the hands of Merc members loyal to the Melamed regime.

□ □ □

WITH THE MERGER of the IMM behind it, gold trading was the Merc's next big challenge. The United States legalized the private ownership of gold on December 31, 1974, and in the process created the biggest opportunity ever seen in the futures industry. Every futures exchange in the country prepared a gold futures contract, and the competition was so fierce that the Board of Trade did not wait for its regular business day to launch its contract. It inaugurated gold futures trading at 12:01 A.M. on December 31, 1974—the minute it was legal—with a midnight champagne reception.

The splashy start hardly helped the Board. After the first week, the battle for the gold market was primarily between the Merc and the New York Commodity Exchange, the Comex. The first day, the Merc gold pit saw turnover of 2,131 contracts, and by 1977 the Merc gold pit's volume was close to one million contracts a year, neck-and-neck with gold volume at the Comex. By late 1978, though, Comex volume pulled away, while the Merc's volume peaked. The Hunt silver debacle in 1980 helped quash the market, and by 1985 the Merc's gold futures were dead.

As the Merc's gold market declined, floor traders griped about "the guys who stole the golden egg." Certainly, in the flurry of new business, gold brokers had so much business that they could not service customers properly. But prevailing wisdom at the Merc was that the gold contract was killed by the domination of a few prominent individuals. Customers and floor traders alike complained bitterly that the gold pit routinely shaved points off customer trades, but no major exchange action was ever undertaken in the gold pit.

While it lasted, the gold market put a big-time gleam in the eyes of many of the Merc's pork belly traders. They drifted in, established their dominance, and traded like soldiers warring for the good of the exchange and their own financial empires. Merc veterans leased their new IMM seats—which carried gold trading rights—to young traders whom they backed financially in return for a share of their winnings. The young traders in turn became wealthy enough to buy their own seats.

□ □ □

THE MERC'S GROWTH was not limited to the trading floor itself. The young traders who had helped establish Melamed's power were moving off the floor to launch clearing firms and organize retail operations to serve public customers. The success of their firms relieved many of them from the financial need to be jostled in the pits.

Melamed had already joined forces with his old law partner Maury Kravitz to form Dellsher Investment Co. Brian Monieson, a computer whiz turned pork belly trader, started GNP Commodities. Jack Sandner, a young featherweight boxer encouraged by Kravitz, rose to become chairman of the livestock trading firm Rufenacht, Bromagen & Hertz. Thomas Dittmer had already built his father-in-law's old-line meat trading firm, Refco Inc., into one of the biggest firms in the country. Barry Lind, a Melamed contemporary and kindred spirit, started B. J. Lind Co. and then expanded it with the concept of discount brokerage to become Lind-Waldock & Co. Lind was vice-chairman of the committee that created the IMM gold futures contract, and he would play a behind-the-scenes role in nearly every Merc innovation in the 1970s and 1980s.

As the young turks left day-to-day trading and the old-timers proved too slow for the pace of the financial pits, a new breed of young traders gained dominance on the Merc floor. The membership expansion during creation of the IMM brought in a group of traders who were not schooled in the old-line etiquette of pit trading and who needed to form their own alliances in order to survive. Traders who had arrived in the belly pit just a few years earlier became deans of the floor and heroes of its popular culture. Harry "the Hat" Lowrance was among that group, a pit broker who would rise to become floor chairman and hold that appointed position under a half dozen different Merc chairmen without ever being elected to any capacity by the membership.

In the enormous context of global financial markets, the concerns about market corners and price manipulations became less relevant. Instead, tax dodges and the temptations of skimming off some of the wealth surging across the trading floor became more serious dangers to futures customers and to the integrity of the markets. Regulation, particularly self-regulation, was slow to respond to the shifting slant of commodities transgressions.

The trading boom of the 1970s created such riches for traders that for many, winning became as much a matter of outwitting the tax man as of reading the market correctly. In many cases, losing in the markets let traders win in the tax arena by allowing them to preserve and reinvest their bloated reserves of capital. Legal year-end tax dodges known as straddles became a mini-industry as traders took advantage of a federal law allowing them to roll over their futures market profits, tax-free, year after year.

The emphasis on tax-driven trading was bound to invite trouble, and did. In a famous case in 1974, old-line Merc member Joseph Siegel sought to curry favor with millionaire copper trader Harold Brady with a promise to shelter $2 million of Brady's wealth using futures straddles. Carrying out his promise, Siegel conducted one of the most ambitious schemes in the Merc's history.

Siegel was the principal of Siegel Trading Co. and the brother of Sam S. Siegel, the man who launched the fatal onion corner at the Merc. Eager to please Brady and gain a bigger chunk of his business, Siegel did not take any chances with the big trader's account when Brady wanted $500,000 in tax losses in 1974. Siegel suggested huge straddles in the IMM's Mexican peso futures contracts. Siegel instructed, with the help of Alvin Winograd, a floor broker who was on the Merc's board of governors at the time, to arrange the trades with other Merc members, putting Siegel accounts squarely on the other side of Brady's trades. Then, after arranging the sham trades, Winograd reported them to the clearinghouse as legitimate, even though pre-arranging trades and falsifying trading cards were major violations of Merc rules.

Ignorant of Siegel's trading methods, Brady was so pleased with the tax losses that he asked Siegel to shelter an even larger amount— up to 2.0 million—in 1975. Siegel, not wanting to tamper with success, had Winograd execute the peso spreads in even larger amounts: 1,000 contracts at a crack. On the days these spreads were put on, Merc records show that the Brady trades represented as much as 98 percent of the Mexican peso futures volume.

Even the Commodity Futures Trading Commission, in its first year of operation, noticed the large volume in such a slow pit with so little price variation. CFTC officials visited Brady's office and asked if he knew that Siegel Trading was taking the opposite side of his Mexican peso spreads. Angered by the news, Brady sued Siegel Trading and instructed Siegel to liquidate his accounts. Siegel, noting that "there is very little volume now being traded in these contracts, probably due in large part to the intimidating effect upon the market caused by the CFTC's investigation," asked Brady's permission to take the other side of his trades. "There is so much paranoia rampant," he complained in a letter to Brady.

After the case overwhelmed the young CFTC, the U.S. Attorney's office in 1978 indicted Siegel and Winograd for conspiracy, tax fraud, and violations of the Commodity Exchange Act. The complaint alleged that Brady had received $800,000 in fraudulent tax benefits and that Siegel Trading had received $90,000 in commission from the Brady trades.

Appearing as a witness for the government in the case was Melamed's former law partner, Maury Kravitz. Facing the possible suspension of his law license as well as his trading privileges because his trading account allegedly was used to park some Brady spread trades, Kravitz enlisted the services of the Jenner & Block law firm. A young lawyer named Anton Valukas, his primary counsel, arranged for Kravitz to become a prominent government witness at the trial, and successfully maneuvered to keep Kravitz out of a defendent's chair. The actual start of the trial had to be delayed, however, so that Kravitz could represent the Merc at a gold trading seminar in London.

Siegel and Winograd were convicted of conspiracy, tax fraud, and Commodity Exchange Act violations. They were fined and given brief trading suspensions. Today, both men remain registered Merc floor brokers.

□ □ □

THE LONG-RUNNING MEXICAN PESO CASE was not a distraction for the Merc's growth in the late 1970s. The gold pit was on the downslide, but currencies flourished. Meanwhile, the Merc introduced a series of short-term interest rate futures contracts on the IMM that were as promising as gold had been: three-month Treasury bills in 1976, domestic certificates of deposit in 1981, and three-month Eurodollar CD's in December 1981.

The interest rate products were viable because of another turn-around in government policy. When Federal Reserve Board Chairman Paul Volcker decided in 1979 to let interest rates "float," they jumped above 20 percent the next year and then declined, creating volatility that fueled a futures market. Expanding federal debt and Fed fine tuning of the economy nurtured both the supply and demand sides of the interest rate market through the 1980s.

The history of corners in the futures markets prompted the Federal Reserve Board to undertake a detailed study of the potential effects of futures markets on the cash T-bill market. The Fed held up approval, fearing that the deliverable T-bill supply could be cornered and the price of the huge government debt manipulated, as had happened with wheat and other commodities.

Even when the Fed's study produced favorable results, the CFTC felt it did not have the authority to approve a futures contract on Treasury bills. It passed the buck to Secretary of the Treasury William Simon. Fearing that the contract application would stall, the Merc had its old friend Milton Friedman phone Simon. The good word helped, and the contract was approved almost immediately.

With Merc volume reaching 22 million contracts in 1980, and a new marketing office in New York generating more business, the Merc needed new blood and bodies to keep up with the growth. Melamed and newly elected chairman Jack Sandner in March pushed through a 25 percent expansion of the Merc's membership, pushing the total to 2,500 members. The new members, and a new division called the Index and Options Market, were poised to trade an exciting new contract: futures on the Standard & Poor's 500 stock index.

With its high capitalization and tendency to move quickly, the S&P quickly became a favorite among local traders, who took the other side of the huge institutional orders that the S&P attracted. The climate in the pit quickly earned the new futures contract, launched in April of 1982, the nickname "pin-striped pork bellies." Plentiful and cheap, IOM seats were picked up by runners, clerks, and established Merc traders who planned to lease them on a speculative basis, hoping for a price appreciation. To appease Merc members, IOM traders were given even less voting power than the IMM members had been given: one-sixth of a full Merc member's vote.

Much of the income from the sale of new memberships was earmarked to finance a move into a new building, made necessary by the success of the IOM and the S&Ps. The Board of Trade in 1979 had rejected a city bid to house both the Merc and the Board in one facility, leaving the two exchanges to upgrade their facilities independently. In November 1983, 11 years to the day after moving into the 444 Jackson Boulevard building, the Chicago Mercantile Exchange moved into a new, leased headquarters at 30 South Wacker Drive. The building, designed with the idea that the wild expansion of the 1970s would continue through the 1990s, housed 70,000 square feet of trading space on two levels, suspended between two 40-story office towers.

But the go-go expansion of new products and trading volume was to go the way of tax straddles and inflation. Aside from a variety of new options contracts, S&P 500 futures were the last successful new futures contract the Merc would launch in the 1980s. Attempts at trading such varied contracts as crude oil, an over-the-counter stock index, and the European Currency Unit would all fall flat.

Lacking excitement at home, Melamed and other exchange leaders turned their attention to franchising the Merc's success in far-flung international locations. In 1983, they guided the creation of the Singapore International Monetary Exchange, which had contracts that matched the Merc's currency and Eurodollar futures. Modeled after the Merc, the SIMEX was Melamed's experiment with the Far East's appetite for futures trading while he planned a more high-tech mechanism for 24-hour global futures markets.

As the big guns were spinning their globalization dreams, everyday floor traders, now numbering in the thousands, pursued wealth and action in the Merc's active trading pits. With the advent of the IOM, the floor became the realm of very young men. Thirty-five-year-olds who had made their millions in the pits were relieved to "go upstairs" to trade, only half joking that they lacked the physical stamina to stay in the pits.

Regulators during this period struggled to catch up with the phenomenal growth of the markets. The CFTC disposed of its heavy agenda of new contract applications and became more sophisticated about market surveillance. The National Futures Association had been created to qualify and register people selling futures products to the public. However, the slowly expanding reach of the government regulators still did not extend to the exchange trading floors. The exchanges remained the kings of their realms, maintaining discipline and enforcing rules as they saw fit.

In the early days, when there were only 500 members at the Merc and volume was less than 500,000 contracts a year, the honor system among traders kept most traders in check. A half-century later, with membership quadrupled and volume as heavy in a day as it once was in a year, self-regulation by the exchange had serious shortcomings. "In the old days, if you got out of line, somebody would come over and talk to you," says an old-time trader who has had several brushes with the CFTC. "Now nobody knows anyone, and the CFTC is more interested in administrative crimes—traders exceeding position limits, what your advertising looks like—than addressing the problem of people stealing on the trading floor."

The Merc's clearing and computer surveillance operations rivaled any in the country. But the booming volume and the huge floor population reduced the chances that any particular misstep would be detected. With the odds of being wiped out by a single disastrous trade far outweighing the chances of getting caught breaking the rules, traders adopted a distinctive floor culture. Be cutthroat on a trade, this culture stated, but give other traders a break. They'll return the favor. The customer is supposed to get the edge; but, of course, the trading floor is a place to make money. If money falls in your lap, take it.

Justice by the exchange's disciplinary committees was arbitrary and spotty. Rank-and-file traders complained they would be charged for violations for which bigger, better-connected traders would get a pass. Traders who were disciplined two and three times for pre-arranged trading would see their fines and suspensions increased, but would almost always be allowed to return to the floor.

By 1985, the growth of institutional business had changed the definition of a customer on the Merc trading floor, particularly in the financial pits. The proverbial "little guy" had all but vanished. Customers for Eurodollars were huge multinational banks and brokerage firms hedging millions of dollars with a single trade. The customer entering an order in the S&P 500 futures pit was often an arbitrageur or a fund manager investing a billion dollars of someone else's pension fund.

Floor traders learned that with some exceptions, no institutional customer would quibble over a tick or two on a futures trade. In fact, some desk managers discovered that the longtime exchange tradition of giving the edge to the customer sometimes irritated Wall Street computer jockeys, who craved precision and did not understand the vagaries of futures. "These guys don't understand futures," one S&P broker complained. Brokers who worked hard to get their customer the best price would be dismayed to find that customers complained.

"They yell, because they want exactly 50 contracts at 345.00, not $344.90. A different price messes up their computer model," the broker explained. "They ask you to write up a different ticket. So what do you do with the two extra ticks?" Two ticks on 50 S&P 500 futures contracts is $2,500. In some cases, customer demand created the temptation to just stick the profit in a friendly account.

□ □ □

THE NATURE OF THE FLOOR TRADERS was changing, too. The newest traders often lacked the price of a membership, leasing their seats from established members who might offer to back a promising new local. By 1985, a few veterans of the 1960s pork belly heyday saw the opportunity to formalize these relationships. They established groups of employee brokers and partners who owned their seats. Groups often shared customer business, offering cheaper execution rates within each of the IMM pits and enabling members to share expenses.

Two or three large broker groups that solidified during these years captured business with the best cutthroat marketing methods: undercutting established commissions; awarding reduced rates to firms that gave them business in every pit on the floor; and, in some cases, offering kickbacks to floor managers who switched their business from an independent broker to the broker group.

These methods alienated the independent floor brokers. Many of the broker group employees were abrasive and inexperienced, and some established their positions in the pits more with fisticuffs than with trading prowess. Moreover, members of a broker group traded among themselves and with favored locals to the exclusion of others. Dual trading—which allowed brokers to handle customer orders while also trading for their own accounts—entrenched the groups' monopoly.

By early 1987, some prominent local traders and independent floor brokers, angry about conditions on the floor, drafted a petition seeking to limit the activities of broker groups and ban dual trading in the S&P 500 futures pit, where the petitioners thought trading abuses were particularly virulent. The petition quickly garnered the 350 signatures needed to bring the matter to the attention of the board of governors and resulted in limited floor reforms. It showcased the concern of many traders that Melamed and his followers had lost touch with the trading floor. It was a rare instance where dissenting members, defying Melamed, had garnered enough signatures to put a petition before the board of governors. When the press picked up on the controversy, it put an uncomfortable spotlight on a matter that ordinarily would have stayed within the insular confines of the exchange.

Coming to terms with the issue belatedly, but with substantial skill, Melamed and the board of governors imposed limited restrictions on dual trading in the S&P 500 futures pit. The reform also required broker groups to register their members with the exchange. An accompanying rule limited the number of trades brokers could make with other members of their associations.

The exchange stepped up disciplinary actions in the S&P 500 futures pits almost immediately. And by June, the Merc boosted the fines and sanctions for floor trading abuses. In 1987 and 1988, the exchange handed out more than $1 million in fines for trading abuses, more than double its previous record.

The effort to reform the S&P 500 futures pit came during the heyday of the stock market rally of early 1987, which brought the Dow Jones industrial average to historic new highs nearly every week. That ended abruptly when Black Monday hit the stock market. The Dow dropped 508 points that day, and S&P 500 futures skidded nearly 1,200 points in heart-stopping action that left futures traders white-lipped and clammy with fear, and left the S&P contract permanently disabled.

By that time the FBI had planted two of its men on the Merc floor. Agents using the aliases Peter Vogel and Randy Jackson had first set foot in the S&P 500 futures pits five months before the crash. And on Black Monday, they emerged from the melee as shaken as real traders, with real economic losses to boot. The agents would disappear for a time after the crash. Upon returning to the Merc, they avoided the S&P 500 pit, drifting instead to the foreign currency pits. "The pace is a little easier," Vogel explained to a reporter.

□ □ □

By any measure, the Merc's rebirth and growth is a story of stunning success. Beginning with the emergence of Melamed and the young turks, the exchange changed from a second-class regional market to a center for global finance. Its membership diversified from a few local produce companies to representatives of all the largest financial institutions in the world.

The success also provided a natural shield against criticism: Don't tamper with something that works. The philosophy had led the Merc's member banks and financial firms to overlook certain floor irregularities. It was convincingly deployed against regulators seeking tighter reins on trading. And it supported Merc leadership in nearly any new venture it fancied.

Melamed and his associates had been, after all, less reformers than practical businessmen. When cleaning up the Merc's image paid off with profits, a cleanup was worth the effort. But by the 1980s, it was better business to search the world for new Merc clients than to stay home and take another look at the rule book. So long as the customers were not complaining, the exchange felt it was doing its job.

CHAPTER SIX

——————— □□□ ———————

Leo & Co.:
The Merc Today

BY THE LATE 1980s, the Merc and the Board of Trade were impressive institutions where the world's stock, bond, currency, or grain markets could go to find a buffer between short-term panic and long-term catastrophe. This remarkable success was the heritage of decades of struggle as well as the harvest of recent bursts of imagination. Without their history of fighting corners, bucket shops, regulators, and reformers, the exchanges would never have climbed to their positions of prominence. And without the imaginative and driven people who steered the exchanges through the early 1980s, they never would have realized their potential.

At the time the undercover FBI agents were plying their way through the Chicago markets, certain princes of the pits ruled the Board and the Merc. Through trading smarts, political prowess, or a combination of the two, they had formed cliques that made policy and influenced trading more profoundly than any other people in the world. At the Merc, the leadership headed by Leo Melamed consisted of one-time reformers who had held on to power long enough to become the establishment. At the Board of Trade, top tandem Thomas Donovan and Karsten Mahlmann were merely the latest products of a hierarchical structure that produced competent, if uncharismatic, leaders.

Despite their differences in style, the two exchanges shared certain common purposes and practices, all carried out by the increasingly prominent people at the top. Year in and year out, the exchange leaders worked together to minimize the effects of regulation, to keep their markets competitive, and to promote their business overseas. They served together in the same industry lobby groups and self-regulatory agencies. They testified, usually with the same message, before the same congressional committees.

The exchange leadership extended beyond the people with the big titles. In some cases, as with one-time gold trader Maury Kravitz at the Merc, the most powerful and influential members were rarely bothered with committee work or goodwill tours. That hardly minimized their impact on trading. The power-brokers-without-portfolio often had the greatest impact on day-to-day trading activity because that was where their attention was focused and their influence felt.

Whatever their different approaches and purposes, the leaders as a group had a singular effect. The system they created worked alongside another, with its own set of rules. Certainly there were exchange rules, CFTC regulations, and even federal codes. But the rules on the books were no match for the rules on the trading floor. Floor rules were the ones that mattered most and the ones most closely followed. According to these informal rules, when brokers were stuck with a costly mistake or a missed order, local traders would help them out. Later on, the broker would return the favor, sometimes in spades. It was a sloppy, seat-of-the-pants system, but it worked.

That's all the customers really seemed to want. That's all Congress and the regulators really seemed to demand. And that's all that most floor traders felt it was necessary to give. As long as there were no major complaints, no blatantly greedy and abusive acts, as long as the markets seemed, on the surface at least, to continued to serve their purpose, few questions were asked.

The me-first attitude that defined the Chicago exchanges during this period was one that started at the top. And to understand why the exchanges functioned the way they did—why the government felt compelled to send undercover agents to work on a four-year investigation that cost more than $4 million—one must know more about the people who set the tone in the world's greatest futures trading city, Chicago.

It's fair to say that, in setting the tone they did and in failing to adequately police their markets, the exchange chieftains fashioned an environment in which indictments of lower-level traders would be inevitable.

□ □ □

LEO MELAMED IS THE LEADER nonpareil of the futures industry. Just ask him. Melamed mixes an astonishing string of remarkable accomplishments with an equally profound appreciation for his own accomplishments. No individual can claim as much personal responsibility for the stupendous growth of the Chicago markets over the last 20 years. Although he was not alone in conceiving the idea of financial futures, Melamed alone made them a success by aggressively marketing the concept to an establishment that was not so much skeptical as it was indifferent. The 1972 creation of futures on foreign currencies ushered in a period of growth that made the Chicago markets a center of world finance.

Only Melamed can lay claim to the title "the Father of Financial Futures," and only Melamed would. But on the Merc trading floor, the nickname cuts both ways. The father that comes to his critics' minds is not a sublime paternalistic presence, but an overlord surrounded by sycophantic subordinates, quietly dispensing favors and intimidating his enemies. At the height of his power during the late 1980s Melamed used the mystique his legend created to lay claim to all meaningful power at the Merc. It was Melamed who called all the shots, not whoever temporarily occupied the chairman's seat at the Merc. And although his name has never been connected with trading scandal, Melamed, because of his position, cannot completely deny responsibility for the wrongdoing that occurs around him because he is the architect of a system that has failed its self-regulatory mission.

The official Melamed biography is a source of inspiration to futures traders. The only child of Hebrew teachers, Melamed fled Poland eastward in 1939, as the clouds of World War II gathered over Europe. He was six years old then, and nearly nine by the time a freighter from Tokyo brought his family to America. Growing up in a middle-class community in Chicago, Melamed polished his oratorical skills in amateur Yiddish theater. After graduating from the University of Illinois, he attended John Marshall law school, a factory for part-time law students that for years has compensated for an unimpressive academic reputation by routinely turning out hungry young lawyers who have moved and shaken the city of Chicago.

Melamed was no exception. Driving a cab to put himself through Marshall, he stopped in at the Merc in 1953 while looking for a better way to finance his schooling. He sometimes claims to have thought that Merrill Lynch, Pierce, Fenner & Bean was the name of a law firm when he applied for a job there and was quickly handed a clerk's jacket. But other times he says he was answering an advertisement calling for a $25-a-week floor clerk.

Struck with trading, at age 20 Melamed borrowed $3,000 from his father to purchase a seat on the exchange. Because his father insisted he finish school, Melamed continued his classes in the afternoons while learning to trade in the mornings. In 1959, four years after graduating, he formed a law practice with Marshall classmate Maury Kravitz, who would become one of Melamed's closest friends and confidants. It was during this period that the young lawyer-trader abandoned his birth name, Melamdovich, for the Americanized Melamed. Once Melamed turned his full attention to trading in 1967, giving up annual law practice earnings of about $25,000, his rise to power at the Merc was as fast as it was inevitable. By 1957, he had formed Dellsher Investment Co., which would become a spawning ground for the Merc's future political leadership.

Dark, diminutive, with a receding hairline that emphasized his piercing brown eyes, Melamed was not an overpowering physical presence on the trading floor. But his voice, his facility with words, and his ability to sense the will of a crowd made Melamed an overnight political force at the Merc. Over the years, his clear tenor and carefully cadenced phrasing would become a siren song that would help transform the Merc from a fading butter-and-egg exchange to the second largest commodities exchange in the world. "I'm a leader. That's my makeup," he once told an interviewer. "I don't know how to do anything except lead."

In the early 1970s, Melamed recognized the meaning of global currency reform and had the determination to sell the Merc's members and the global financial community on the idea of financial futures, devising the name International Monetary Market primarily as a marketing tool. By 1976, his power base at the Merc was so entrenched that he stepped down from the chairmanship and assumed a new, unelected post, that of special counsel, from which he ruled the exchange throughout the 1980s and into the 1990s. In that role, he introduced successful new products like S&P 500 futures led the Merc on a building boom, pushed expansion overseas, and spearheaded negotiations with regulators. With the often-delayed introduction of Globex, the computerized after-hours trading system first announced in late 1987 but still not operational in 1991, Melamed hoped to bring the Merc's brand of financial innovation to the rest of the world.

Indeed, the Melamed myth is matched by only one thing: the Melamed ego. The Merc chieftain has never lacked for self-esteem, sometimes to startling effect. Melamed once waxed boastful about a plan to introduce futures trading to China. The idea "is bread cast upon the water," he explained to a reporter. "Another great man a long time ago said that before me."

Some critics complain (wrongly) that Melamed takes more credit for the Merc's accomplishments than he deserves. Others claim (rightly) that he embellishes his recollections to make them more dramatic. During a speech to an industry convention on the occasion of his second "retirement"—and given his current level of activity, it looks as if Melamed will some day have to announce a third—Melamed recounted the oft-told tale of his struggle to sell the concept of currency futures. Merrill Lynch Futures, in honor of his visit, had placed a quote board in its lobby listing global exchange rates. "I stood there, tears pouring down my face, and knew that this idea, this dream, would live," Melamed told the crowd.

John Conheeney, the head of Merrill Lynch Futures, doesn't quite remember it that way. "His eyes did look a little misty," Conheeney joked with a reporter a few minutes after Melamed's speech. "I thought he had to sneeze."

When he deals with the powers in Washington, the lawmakers who decide the industry's fate, Melamed can be surprisingly forceful. Lobbying against the tax straddle legislation in 1981, he commandeered the office of Senator Alan Cranston (D-California) for days at a time, inviting other legislators in for educational sessions. Again in 1988, when fighting a reform bill that would have given the Federal Reserve power to regulate stock index futures, Melamed and a group of Merc officials took over the office of Senator Donald Riegle (D-Michigan), sometimes even asking the senator to leave so they could conduct their business. On another occasion, years earlier, Senator John Glenn (D-Ohio) stopped at Melamed's office for a visit during trading hours. At high volume, Melamed made it clear to his secretary, and to the senator, that he would not be ready to receive visitors until the market quieted down.

Staying in tune with the market is a Melamed fetish. The invention of hand-held telephones and quote machines has enabled Melamed to watch the trading screen and order up trades while sitting on dais after dais from Chicago to Boca Raton, Florida, to Tokyo. Leaving his trading account in the hands of a friend while on a recent trip to the Moscow Commodities Exchange, Melamed planned ahead the hand signals for buy or sell he would use while being photographed with Soviet dignitaries—images he knew would be carried back to the Merc via satellite by news services. Melamed detests persistent rumors that he's not much of a trader, but he refuses to tell reporters how much he makes (or loses) in the markets and complains that his dedication to the welfare of the exchange has cost him millions.

Melamed has a stubborn streak. When the Globex system was first conceived, it needed a name befitting its grand ambitions, a lesson Melamed learned with the International Monetary Market. Globex was one of several ideas suggested at a Merc executive committee meeting and seemed to be favored by most of the members. Melamed wanted a different title, Post-Market Trading, or PMT for short. And PMT it was. But PMT had an unfortunate connotation in London, where the initials mean premenstrual tension to most people. Melamed stood firm for a time, until the Merc's partners at Reuters PLC, a British-based firm, eventually prevailed on him to change the name.

Melamed's proprietary attitude toward the Merc showed in the way he staffed the exchange. In 1988, he appointed personal assistant Alysann Posner, a 27-year-old DePaul University graduate, to the new post of vice president for special projects. Posner's only pre-Melamed exchange experience was in the promotions department at the Chicago Board Options Exchange. By contrast, another vice president hired to work in the surveillance department at the same time had a doctorate in statistics from Stanford University. The advancement of Melamed's confidante—who shared the dedication to his science fiction novel *The Tenth Planet* with Melamed's wife—caused disgruntled Merc staffers to complain about favoritism.

The special treatment for close friends and asssociates extended even to the Merc's board room, where the 12-person executive committee, the exchange's most powerful body, became home to Melamed's close friends, business associates, and even family. Howard B. Dubnow, an S&P 500 broker with no particular political or trading skills, has a near-permanent seat on the panel. He is Melamed's son-in-law and clears trades through Melamed's Dellsher Investment Co. Laurence M. Rosenberg, for years vice-chairman at Dellsher, holds a seat, as does M. Scott Gordon, another former Dellsher officer. Close Melamed friends like Brian Monieson and John F. "Jack" Sandner also had seemingly permanent executive committee spots throughout the 1980s.

The 30-person board of governors was peopled with a mixture of Melamed's personal associates and pragmatic political choices. Melamed nephew Scott Slutsky and Dellsher-backed broker Norma L. Newberger both became governors. When Susan B. Phillips resigned as chairman of the Commodity Futures Trading Commission, Melamed wasted little time in inviting her onto the Merc's board. Melamed wanted a politician on the board to strengthen the Merc's hand on Capitol Hill, so he asked the Merc's Washington lobbyist, C. Dayle Henington, for a recommendation. The response: former Senator Thomas Eagleton. It was an appointment Melamed would come to regret.

Over time the Melamed myth, the string of excesses, and the persistent complaints that he was not doing enough to ride herd on wrongdoing on the trading floor led to a decline in Melamed's popularity within the exchange and to some brief but unsuccessful challenges to his power. The fight over S&P 500 futures in February 1987 was the first sign that Melamed's base of support was beginning to erode. The source of the revolt was the practice of dual trading, in which brokers handle customer orders while also trading for their own accounts. Recognizing a source for potential abuse, traders clung fiercely to their dual trading rights. A gifted politician, Melamed recognized that the reformers meant business and co-opted their movement. With his plan to ban dual trading on the top step of the S&P pit and force broker groups to register with the exchange, Melamed preempted the reformers' call for an outright ban on the controversial and fraud-ridden trading practice. Thanks to the Melamed-led reform, dual trading continued in the S&P pit, but only for brokers willing to take one step down from the top tier, thereby rendering themselves ineffective.

Such was the fear of Melamed's wrath that none of the backers of the S&P referendum would go public with the group's complaints. "If you think we're afraid of what Leo would do, you're right," one reform-minded trader says. Years earlier, one of Melamed's closest friends, Barry Lind, had made a similar observation. "If you cross Leo, you'll never forget," he told a reporter. Melamed denies all assertions that he has ever used his power at the exchange to carry out a personal agenda.

Melamed managed to prevail over the S&P reform referendum, but after nearly 20 years at the top, he suddenly looked somewhat vulnerable. It wouldn't take long for the reformers to find another issue—the generous $500,000 salary awarded to Melamed by his friends on the Merc's board of governors in late 1988. Jack Sandner, the Melamed protégé who had just served his second three-year term as Merc chairman, was granted a $150,000 salary and the title special adviser to the board of governors. Even some of Melamed's most ardent critics grudgingly admitted that Leo probably was worth

$500,000 to the exchange. But the award to Sandner, a yeoman leader at the very best, riled the rabble. And the way the salaries were awarded, without seeking approval from the members, was the last straw.

Dissatisfaction over the salaries reached a head in the spring of 1990. After more than a year of behind-the-scenes campaigning, a group of Merc members thought it at last had rallied enough anti-Melamed votes to push through a referendum that would give members a vote approving salaries to unelected officers of the exchange. Melamed was the only officer who fit that description. Led by Douglas Bragan, a currency trader with a record of opposing Melamed, and Emmett Whealan, a cattle trader who previously had been a Melamed backer, the petition drive was the first bona fide political struggle at the Merc since Melamed's rise to power. While the petition ostensibly was about the salary issue, it also was an offshoot of suspicion among floor traders that Globex—the worldwide after-hours computerized trading system backed by Melamed—would threaten the open outcry system of trading that is the lifeblood of the trading floor.

The referendum prompted Melamed to simultaneously dig in and bail out. In a surprise announcement on March 5, Melamed said he would retire by year's end from his leadership positions at the exchange. He had already stepped down as chairman of the National Futures Association in December 1989, in an apparent attempt to resolve questions about conflict of interest in his roles as head of both the industry's self-regulatory agency and the Merc. But the March announcement still came as a shock.

Of course, Melamed had announced retirement plans at least once before, in 1984, and had never come close to reducing his power at the Merc. Many thought the 1989 announcement was a repeat of 1984. Some even saw the retirement, timed as it was to occur while the referendum was circulating on the Merc's floor, as an effort to raise a sympathetic anti-referendum vote from members. In characteristic fashion, Melamed sent facsimile messages about his retirement to 1,000 people worldwide, each of whom he thought would want to know immediately of the news. "All these people deserve my spending some time with them," he explained.

As support for the referendum continued to gain strength, the exchange mustered a battery of forces to defeat the proposal. Melamed even wandered down to the floor and confronted Gerald Ordman, one of the petition's backers. "How can I represent you if my authority is questioned by this referendum?" Ordman remembers Me-

lamed asking. In a scene somewhat akin to Nixon's visit to war protes-
tors at the Lincoln Memorial, floor traders gathered around, asking
Melamed why he was so concerned about losing face if he were about
to retire and challenging him to accept the fact that he would have
to be elected and held accountable to members.

As the June 19 vote approached, the exchange leadership played
hardball. In mailings to members, the board outspokenly opposed the
referendum, violating an exchange rule that limits discussion of issues
in exchange-funded mailings. The Melamed-controlled board ordered
William Brodsky, president of the Merc, to lobby each of the trading
firms that owned seats on the exchange to oppose the petition. Two
other Merc officials key to a firm's contact with the exchange—clearinghouse chief John Davidson and general counsel Gerald Beyer—also
were ordered to make calls. The campaigning by exchange staff enraged referendum proponents. "The staff works for and is paid by all
our members," said Bragan. "Having Brodsky interfere in our members' election process was an outrageous abuse of power." Abusive or
not, the lobbying apparently aroused enough off-the-floor opposition
to drive the referendum to defeat. But the petition garnered 41 percent of the vote, an unusual show of strength for the renegades.

The dissent still would not die, and the conflict turned ugly. Melamed's opponents sought to drag down the exchange's leader with a
campaign of rumor and innuendo. In anonymous mailings sent to
reporters, dissident members tried to discredit Melamed. No reporters took the bait, but during the trial of Swiss franc traders indicted
after the FBI probe, *The Wall Street Journal* published a story about
a trader who had pleaded guilty in exchange for reduced charges and
testified that Melamed's trading orders received special treatment on
the floor. The dissidents jumped on the chance to photocopy the *Journal* story and circulate it with an anonymous letter calling Leo Melamed "the Ivan Boesky of the Commodity Industry" and "the Ultimate 'Bagman.' " Though none of the mudslinging made its way into
the newspapers, the rumor-mongering outraged Melamed. "Everybody talks about investigating me," a frustrated Melamed told one
reporter. "Why don't you investigate the guy who's sending that garbage out?"

The darkest moment for Melamed was yet to come, in the form
of a novel defense employed in the trial of Japanese yen traders. Sam
Cali, one of the 14 yen traders to come to trial, defended himself by
claiming that everything he did was simply "standard operating procedure" on the trading floor and that his trading did not violate any

fiduciary responsibility to his customers because it was done in accordance with "custom and practice." To prove Cali's point, defense lawyer Thomas A. Durkin targeted the industry's biggest name, Leo Melamed, to help prove just how widespread certain seemingly fraudulent practices were on the trading floors. Quoting FBI investigative records, Durkin in a court filing contended that Melamed received special treatment from brokers who would regularly change prices on orders to please him. Moreover, the Durkin filing noted, one trader told FBI undercover agent Dietrich Volk that Melamed "doesn't tell you anything, he just threatens you" when seeking to have a price changed.

Melamed boiled over when word of Durkin's legal gambit hit the newsstands. The Merc's public relations man, Andrew Yemma, called the newspapers that had printed information from the court papers, told them they had been used, and complained about their irresponsible treatment of the matter. Melamed for his part refused to comment. "I'm not going to dignify that," he explained.

As the trials ground on, it appeared that the government had tried but failed to implicate Melamed in wrongdoing. To defense lawyers, the prosecution's decision to release investigative files without expunging the names of Melamed and others was a sign that the government had no case against the Merc chief. They suspected that the prosecution had chosen nonetheless to sully the names of Melamed and a few close associates by leaving them in full view of lawyers who would gladly drag the big names into court to help clear their clients.

The controversy in court hardly slowed down Melamed, who showed no signs of retiring at the end of 1990. In October, Melamed accepted a position as co-chairman of a joint Merc–Board of Trade committee considering merger of certain noncompetitive functions of the two exchanges. In November, he flew to Budapest and Moscow to promote futures trading in those former communist cities. Meanwhile, he worked toward the 1991 introduction of Globex. To critics and supporters alike, it looked as if Melamed was headed for an unusually active retirement.

□ □ □

THE BACON-LETTUCE-AND-TOMATO CYCLE brought Brian Monieson into the futures markets, and a stint in the frying pan may force him out.

Monieson, who started a computer-programming business in the early 1960s after graduating from Northwestern University, befriended Leo Melamed after joining the Merc in 1971. The pair started out together as champion bridge players and wound up as two of the most important figures in the history of the Merc.

Melamed has always kept his name clear of serious allegations of wrongdoing. Not Monieson. He became embroiled in a CFTC proceeding which found that he failed to supervise two traders, one of them his closest friend, as they blatantly ripped off customers of Monieson's trading firm, GNP Commodities.

Brian J. Monieson is not the type one normally associates with the free-for-all world of commodities trading. Bookish, wearing Coke-bottle eyeglasses, he would look more at home in a computer lab than in a trading pit. And it was the computer lab that got him started. Monieson founded Indecon, a computer consulting firm, in 1965, when the computing revolution was in its infancy. One of the company's first programs was an econometric model for picking winners at the harness track. Since childhood, Monieson and his friend Myron Rosenthal—an Indecon partner who later would cofound GNP Commodities—had loved playing the ponies.

By 1971, a pork processor had hired Indecon to develop an inventory model for pork bellies. When the program, which ironically was never used by the customer, proved uncannily accurate, Monieson and nine associates each contributed $5,000 to form a partnership to trade bellies. The bacon-lettuce-and-tomato cycle—which stipulates that pork belly inventories fall sharply in June, July, and August, as people eat BLT sandwiches—made the group nearly $500,000, or ten times the original investment.

With that, Monieson was on his way in the futures business. Trading in the hog pit at first, he soon was drawn to the currencies and other financial futures just starting up at the time. Monieson and Rosenthal formed GNP Commodities in 1973 to avoid paying brokerage commissions. Around this time, Monieson was also drawn into a friendship with Leo Melamed, as the two by chance were paired in bridge tournaments on the Merc's commercial team. When the pair won a national corporate tournament in 1975, their friendship was cemented. (Monieson to this day claims he is the better bridge player of the two.)

As Melamed's hand-picked candidate, Monieson in 1983 was elected chairman of the Merc. The greatest accomplishments of his three-year term were the Merc's move into its new building at 30

South Wacker and the launch of its first international partnership, with the Singapore International Monetary Exchange, or SIMEX. Although the Merc later unceremoniously dumped SIMEX in favor of the Globex computerized trading system, the link with the Singapore exchange for a time was considered the wave of the future.

Monieson's record as chairman would not go untarnished, however. Their fascination with pork bellies still strong, Monieson and Rosenthal traded actively in the commodity—too actively, it seems. In 1986, a Merc disciplinary committee found that the pair had violated exchange rules by taking excessively large speculative positions.

A Merc investigation of the case would find that three associates at GNP held positions nearly identical to those held by Monieson and Rosenthal and that the two men used a company they controlled to lend the other traders more than $6.5 million to fund their trading activity. Monieson, who later would call the fine "a parking ticket," paid $10,000, becoming the first exchange chairman ever found guilty of exchange violations while running the Merc. Rosenthal, who had a previous violation on his record, paid a $70,000 fine.

One of the traders apparently working with Monieson and Rosenthal was Norman Furlett. Monieson considered Furlett, with whom he shared vacations and family activities, his closest personal friend. But with friends like Furlett, Monieson needed no enemies. Furlett joined GNP in 1983 to head the firm's retail commodities department. In 1985, broker Ira Greenspon joined Furlett in the retail department from the Atlantic Corp., a firm with a long list of compliance problems. Although Monieson apparently did not know it at the time, while working at Atlantic, Greenspon had entered trading orders without assigning them to specific customer accounts and also fraudulently allocated losing trades to customers and winning trades to himself.

The same pattern would soon become familiar at GNP. Between January and May of 1986 alone, Greenspon and Furlett on at least 100 occasions fraudulently placed losing trades in 30 different customer accounts. The profitable trades they kept for their own personal accounts. All told, the two men pocketed $117,000 in winning trades and dumped $214,000 in losses into customer accounts. The scheme went so far that the two set up a separate telephone line that, in violation of GNP rules, did not tape-record conversations with customers. A CFTC administrative complaint against Monieson charged him with failing to supervise Furlett and Greenspon from 1984 to 1986.

The Furlett and Greenspon cases were not the only troubles GNP had during that time. Regulators also found that the firm had failed to oversee four high-pressure sales firms that brought it business. What's more, GNP had to reimburse customers of Chilmark Commodities Corp. of New York, a GNP-affiliated firm that shut down operations while facing CFTC fraud allegations.

Monieson's defense was simple. He claimed that, as chairman of the Merc during most of the period in question, he had had little time to concentrate on GNP's business. But testimony in the Furlett and Greenspon hearing established that Monieson had been warned, both in person and in writing, by at least five employees about fraudulent trading by the two. An internal GNP accounting of the fraudulent activity was even drawn up, listing the suspicious activity trade by trade, but Monieson claimed not to remember ever reviewing the document. Nevertheless, Monieson recalled hearing rumors about his friend's activities, even from people on the Merc's trading floor. On one occasion, Monieson warned Furlett, "Your integrity is the only thing that matters in this business. You're getting a bad name."

It was Furlett who tarnished his friend's name, and his business. In January 1987, Monieson had struck a deal with Banque Indosuez, the French financial giant, which had agreed to purchase GNP for up to $40 million. But when the Federal Reserve, which had veto power over the sale, learned of the CFTC investigation, it refused its okay. An irate Monieson phoned the CFTC and warned the agency's general counsel, Kenneth Raisler, that the collapse of the GNP sale would cause "an international incident." Indeed, Indosuez had written Fed Chairman Paul Volcker, voicing concern about possible damage to the bank's reputation in international markets. Shortly after the deal collapsed, Monieson broke ties with Furlett but agreed to set up his friend in business in California.

The Furlett and Greenspon incident also killed another chance to sell GNP, this time to Nomura Securities Co. of Japan. Not long after the Banque Indosuez sale collapsed, the Japanese trading behemoth Nomura had agreed to buy GNP, but only if Monieson would settle all outstanding charges against him and the firm. The CFTC offered Monieson a $100,000 settlement. But acting on advice from lawyers, Monieson refused. "I figured, if you think somebody is wrong, then fight it," explained Monieson, who has spent nearly $2 million in legal fees and now admits that contesting the case was probably a mistake. For the CFTC proceeding, Monieson hired Jerrold Salzman, the powerful outside counsel to the Merc, to serve as his personal attorney.

The Monieson case would become a symbol of the futures industry's failure to adequately regulate its own affairs. Former Senator Thomas Eagleton of Missouri, already aching to distance himself from the exchange in the wake of the commodities investigation, would use the case as a pretext for quitting the Merc's board just weeks before his term was set to expire. On November 7, 1989, Eagleton resigned his board seat after Leo Melamed and then-Agriculture Secretary Clayton Yeutter, who had served as Merc president while Monieson was chairman, agreed to testify on Monieson's behalf. Calling self-regulation "the Chicago mirage," Eagleton said he was particularly upset that the Merc had allowed Salzman, its outside counsel, to appear on behalf of Monieson while the former Merc chairman faced charges brought by the industry's regulator.

Even with such heavyweights as Yeutter and Melamed coming to his defense, Monieson could not win the case. On May 25, 1990, administrative law judge George L. Painter expelled Monieson and his firm from the futures business and fined them each $500,000. Furlett and Greenspon were each fined $75,000 and expelled from the industry. "The shame of this case is that GNP and Monieson were so callously indifferent to the wrongs done to their most vulnerable customers," Painter said.

The ruling so far has had little effect on Monieson. His firm was acquired by E. D. & F. Mann Commodities of New York, but Monieson still sits in the same corner office on the Merc's ninth floor. GNP logos still adorn the firm's reception area. And many of GNP's original employees remain with the firm. While Monieson plans his appeal, he continues to trade and manage most of GNP's daily activities. What's more, he is unbowed by the experience. "I elevated the stakes," he says ruefully. "I had Clayton [Yeutter] testify. I had every leader in the industry there."

"I never knew what a witch hunt was before this," Monieson says. "I've been crippled unmercifully . . . You can be innuendoized to death." Or at least to a lengthy appeal process, it seems.

□ □ □

TO SMALL INVESTORS SEEKING ADVICE on high-yielding retirement plans, the John F. Sandner story was irresistible. A scrappy kid from Chicago's South Side, Jack Sandner had fought his way out of his working-class neighborhood on the amateur boxing circuit and used the values of a successful boxer—discipline and preparation—to graduate from Notre Dame law school and become a millionaire commodities trader.

Impressed by the credentials of the go-getter Sandner, novice investors opened accounts at Rufenacht, Bromagen & Hertz, a Chicago-based commodities firm he headed. They received assurances that Sandner personally would make the managed-account trading decisions. To the uninitiated, it seemed a safe bet. Sandner, after all, was not just chairman of the firm; he was chairman of the Chicago Mercantile Exchange. He held an international reputation as a spokesman for the futures industry.

The routine pitch at RB&H, as described in customer complaints to the CFTC, was pursuasive: potential customers were given a quick tour of the exchange and Sandner's office, with its private bathroom, sauna, and mini-gym, and a rendition of the Sandner story. It was easy to decide to entrust their funds with RB&H and try for a piece of the same American dream.

If they lost most of their capital in the ensuing months, they could chalk it up to experience or bad luck. Some were pursuaded to add to their initial investments to recoup losses. Others complained to the CFTC.

Small investors often get burned in the futures markets. But RB&H customers were atypical because they weren't just investing in futures: They were buying the Jack Sandner mystique. RB&H salesmen were trained to feature Sandner in their sales pitches, scripted to sell his success as part of their product.

The Jack Sandner story has two sides. The public image sells well: the successful and dedicated futures executive who has been a central force in the rise of Chicago's futures markets. Sandner has been Merc Chairman no less than seven times—a record for the exchange and the industry. During rule-imposed retirements from the chairman's seat, Sandner has remained in advisory positions, most recently as senior policy advisor to the Merc, a $150,000-a-year position. He has been a member of the Merc's central executive committee, its most powerful panel, since 1978. Like Melamed and Monieson, Sandner can claim that his history during those years is the Merc's history. His guidance was instrumental in the development of the exchange into international prominence.

Sandner is attractive, compact, and athletic. His blue eyes and sandy blond hair complement a likable, boyish face. For years, to offset the puckish image, he wore a full beard and trimmed mustache. He stands 5'5", or a little taller in his cowboy boots. Unlike some traders, Sandner eschews gaudy belt buckles and tasteless ties. Though his dress once was somewhat scruffy, today he presents a diplomatic front in custom-tailored suits and carefully coiffured hair. Usually mild-mannered and levelheaded, Sandner has a temper, friends say, that sometimes boils over.

Building his image along with that of the Merc, Sandner became a well-respected futures executive and a spokesman for the industry. His office walls are lined with photos taken with presidents, senators, ambassadors, and influential congressmen. If the wall photographs are not enough, he has pressed dozens of others into three-ring binders open for visitor perusal in the anteroom of his office. Sandner's résumé lists service on dozens of exchange and industry committees, including several formed to limit abuses in the trade.

The other face of the Sandner story is less savory. It is the tale of a man who may have battled for self-regulation out of self-interest, the story of a man who climbed to prominence at the Merc with the aid of powerful insiders and who has rewarded them by always being predictably friendly to their interests. As chairman, Sandner has operated the Merc seemingly for the benefit of floor brokers. In his own business, he hired employees with known track records of customer abuse. Although publicly an advocate for strong self-regulation, Sandner failed to apply tough standards to his friends and collected some questionable business associates. When serving on industry regulatory committees, Sandner repeatedly exposed himself to situations where conflicts of interest were clear.

Christened John Francis Sandner by his Irish father and Italian mother, Jack Sandner was at 15 a high school dropout in the mean streets shadowed by the belching smokestacks of Chicago's Republic Steel works. Sandner strapped on boxing gloves at the urging of a friend and was soundly beaten in his first pick-up bout in a Catholic Youth Organization gym. It was there in the neighborhood gym that Sandner was discovered by the legendary 1940s middleweight world champion, Tony Zale. With Zale as coach, Sandner fought 60 matches as a Golden Gloves featherweight, winning his first with a 45-second knockout and losing only twice.

Gaining a charismatic self-confidence on the fight circuit, Sandner returned to high school, won a boxing scholarship to college, and then entered Notre Dame law school, after personally convincing the dean to admit him. Sandner distinguished himself at Notre Dame, winning first place in the moot court competition the year he graduated. He emerged from Notre Dame in 1968 with a polish that glossed over the tattoo on his left arm and the fight-promoter friends who had helped arrange summer jobs dealing blackjack in Las Vegas.

His excellent record at Notre Dame allowed Sandner his choice of jobs at prominent Chicago law firms. Instead of serving time as a rookie at a blue-blooded partnership, Sandner struck out on his own. He joined forces with some of the best trial lawyers in Chicago to gain courtroom experience. It was during this time he forged a friendship with Fred Lane, an expert at trial procedure and a well-known Chicago attorney. The spring he left law school, Sandner visited the Loop law office of a friend, Maury Kravitz. The two had met at a South Side Christmas party while Sandner was in law school, and they had kept in touch.

Sandner showed Kravitz the job offers he'd gotten, and then asked the older man a favor: He didn't have $20 to put gas in his car, much less the money to print up stationery, but he told Kravitz that he wanted to work for himself. Kravitz, who also owned a trading firm called Dellsher Investment Co. with another lawyer-turned-commodity-trader, Leo Melamed, made Sandner a deal. The younger man could have an office, the half-time use of a secretary, and his own stationery and could pay things back when he had the money.

Sandner practiced law for several years, often defending his friends from the old neighborhood. He followed Kravitz to the Merc in 1971, after defending the wife of Merc president Everette B. Harris in an auto accident case. Harris, a tireless promoter of everything connected to the Merc, liked Sandner and encouraged him to buy a seat. Kravitz seconded Harris's suggestion and encouraged Sandner to borrow the $82,500 price.

In less than two years, Sandner had parlayed part-time trading during his law firm lunch hours into a full-time occupation. "I learned I could make a lot more money trading commodities than being a lawyer," Sandner unabashedly told an interviewer. Even in his high-heeled cowboy boots, he was small for the rough and tumble cattle pit, but his athletic conditioning helped compensate. Sandner's early trading was not always successful, and he was bailed out of his first major loss by a loan from Kravitz, who encouraged him to keep trading.

Sandner hit the committee process at the Merc at almost the same time he began trading full-time. Committees are the central cog in the Merc's self-policing efforts. They are also a political ladder, and Sandner was heading for the top. Melamed, who long before had established his dominance in Merc politics, sensed a kindred spirit in Sandner and nominated him to the Merc's arbitration committee, which rules on disputes between members. For a relative newcomer, the appointment was a signal honor. Judicial committees are the most powerful on the exchange. Arbitration, business conduct, and floor practices committee members all sit as judges over their compatriots on the trading floor.

Sandner expanded his power base under the tutelage of Kravitz and Melamed. By 1976, he had been named to the Business Conduct Committee, one of the Merc's most powerful because it hears disciplinary cases brought against members by the exchange's compliance staff. Sandner also sat on a committee that trained new floor brokers and on another committee that would pass judgment on commodity firms accused of cheating customers.

That year he also joined RB&H as a vice president. Robert Rufenacht, Glenn Bromagen, and Fred Hertz had started the entrepreneurial livestock trading firm in 1969, and the business was expanding. Sandner would typically spend the morning on the trading floor and the afternoon tending to RB&H business or attending exchange committee meetings. He would then head home in the evening to his wife Carole and five children.

A year later, in 1977, Sandner reversed the original business arrangement between himself and Maury Kravitz. He hired Kravitz to head RB&H's monetary division, an arm of the firm that specialized in recruiting customers to trade futures on gold, interest rates, and foreign currencies. A departure from the firm's traditional business, financial futures quickly became RB&H's major commission base. Kravitz's reputation as a heavy-hitting gold trader was touted to RB&H customers, along with Jack Sandner's appealing life story.

Apparently Sandner didn't see any impropriety in hiring Kravitz, even though he was aware that his friend was then embroiled in one of the most serious disciplinary cases the U.S. government had ever brought against the Merc, the Mexican peso tax straddle case. Kravitz was suspected of allowing two fellow Merc brokers to park pre-arranged trades in his trading account. Sandner sat on the Merc's Business Conduct Committee during the time the Mexican peso trials were being held a few blocks away in U.S. district court. But the committee never issued a judgment on Kravitz's role in the case; Kravitz ultimately appeared as a witness for the government and emerged unscathed while a jury convicted traders Siegel and Winograd.

Kravitz's attention to RB&H's business enabled Sandner to continue his focus on exchange politics. Sandner rose rapidly to the

Merc's chairmanship. He was first elected to the Merc's governing board in 1977, and a year later was named vice-chairman and a member of the executive committee. Once on the board, Sandner chaired one group that reviewed exchange rules and another that dished out coveted assignments for booth space and telephone service on the trading floor. In 1978, Sandner also moved up to become president of RB&H. And by 1980, the diminutive but determined former high school dropout had been elected chairman of the Chicago Mercantile Exchange.

The chairmanship exposed Sandner to Washington politics. In 1981, accompanied by Melamed and other senior Merc officials, Sandner made 34 trips to Washington to lobby for favorable tax treatment for commodities. A novice at the Capitol, he quickly learned the ropes, aided by the exchange's lobbyists and backed up by political action committee dollars. The Reagan administration approved the tax law, allowing Sandner to announce the triumph in a speech to members.

Washington would become Sandner's special area of expertise. He successfully discouraged legislation designed to remove the making of margin rules from the hands of the exchange, blocked the CFTC's attempt to protect customers from abuse by tightening the order-tracking process, and deflected charges of manipulation in the cattle futures market with a barrage of defensive publicity. In Washington, he preached the merits of self-regulation and held out the Merc as an example of its success. At home, in reports to the membership, Sandner warned of the enemies to free enterprise lurking in Washington. "Free Markets for Free Men," the motto of the exchange, was embroidered on the breast pocket of every RB&H trader.

In 1983, Sandner stepped aside as chairman but remained on the executive committee; in 1986, he regained the chairman's post as another insider, Brian Monieson, stepped aside. Merc members were riding high on a record expansion of the industry, and the board of governors saw valuable continuity in Sandner's second term as chairman.

By 1986, Sandner was a mature politician. No longer a scrappy street kid or an aspiring outsider at the exchange, he knew exactly how the trading floor was run, where the strengths and weaknesses of the regulatory agencies were, and what his constituency wanted most—to be left alone to trade as they always had. Sandner's committee appointments in 1986 show he had no thought of shaking the trees. Floor governance and floor practices remained much as they always had. Sandner left Harry "the Hat" Lowrance in place as floor chairman, the boss of the trading floor.

Lowrance had held the appointive position for years and had the final word on what went on in the pits. To a floor broker, Lowrance's power—shared by his pit committees—to change or adjust official prices, negate (or "bust") trades, determine opening and closing ranges, and arbitrate small pit disputes could mean millions of dollars in gained or lost profits. The responsibility made the colorful Lowrance one of the most feared traders on the floor. Lowrance lived his reputation. A tall, burly man with shaggy, thinning hair, "the Hat" had a legendary appetite for wild parties. He arrived at the Merc each day in a black chauffeured limousine, and often kept the limo on call all day outside of the front door of the exchange.

Lowrance has never been accused of any wrongdoing at the Merc. Some consider him a tireless worker with a thankless job. However, rival brokers point out that Lowrance's membership in at least four interlocking broker groups made it nearly impossible for him to make a price adjustment decision without affecting one of his own close business associates. His critics say that his power, and his years of accumulating favors due from other traders, leave him beyond the reach of the exchange's judicial committees.

The judicial committees that Sandner picked in 1986 were dotted with traders who themselves had been shown to have abused customer orders and pre-arranged trades. The most flagrant example was the agricultural floor practices committee, charged with ruling on trading ethics and conducting investigations and hearings. In 1986 nearly one-quarter of the men on the committee, which oversaw the livestock pits where Sandner had made his millions, had histories of exchange sanctions for pre-arranging trades and abusing customer orders.

Sandner shrugs off the questionable committee appointments, saying he delegated the work of committee selection to other members of his board of governors. He notes, correctly, that he violated no rules in appointing members with disciplinary histories to the exchange self-governance committees.

The conflict between self-regulation and self-interest is highlighted by Sandner's ties to the Merc's powerful and widely criticized broker groups. As chairman, Sandner played down his connections to the Merc's largest group, ABS Partners. When mentor Maury Kravitz joined forces with James Kaulentis to form ABS Partners, Kravitz quietly left his official capacities at RB&H. But the departure was mostly window dressing. Kravitz still rents space in the RB&H office and shares RB&H staff. Through a restructuring of RB&H ownership, Sandner in 1988 obtained part ownership in ABS Partners. And RB&H

itself garners thousands of dollars a month processing ABS Partners trades as its clearing firm.

Sandner's ownership in the broker group did not become widely known to Merc members and the exchange's regulatory staff until after the FBI probe became public. Sandner began receiving income from the group in 1989, shortly after he agreed to sit on the blue ribbon panel the Merc formed to review trading practices after the investigation became known. Among other things, the panel considered recommendations to limit the influence of broker groups on the trading floor.

The contrast between Sandner's public dedication to strong self-regulation and customer protection and the way he conducted his private affairs also appears in his work for industry groups like the National Futures Association. Sandner was an early advocate of the NFA, an industry-sponsored self-regulatory group that emerged during his first term as Merc chairman and is designed to protect customers from unscrupulous futures salesmen. He was named chairman of the NFA's central region business conduct committee when the group was formed, and he remains at its helm. Through his executive role at the NFA, Sandner should have known that the agency was investigating serious abuses at a brokerage firm called First Commodity Corp. of Boston. The NFA and the Commodity Futures Trading Commission drove FCCB out of business in 1986 after proving the firm ran a boiler room operation that used high-pressure sales tactics.

The shady FCCB history did not stop Sandner in 1988 from hiring the firm's former Chicago branch manager, Bruce Piazza, as a $4,000-a-month consultant. Piazza's job: to set up a precious metals investment program at RB&H. After all, RB&H could not hire Piazza as a broker or a broker supervisor because the CFTC had charged Piazza with defrauding customers and would not approve the NFA registration Piazza needed for those jobs.

The CFTC's misgivings mattered little once Piazza walked through the door at RB&H. While Piazza was hired to set up an investment program that did not involve futures, former RB&H salesmen say Piazza acted as their sales manager and instructed them in making sales pitches to customers. Apparently RB&H liked the special talents of FCCB salesmen. In addition to Piazza, the firm hired at least 11 other former FCCB salesmen.

Piazza's tenure at RB&H ended in December 1989. Two months later, a federal grand jury indicted him for allegedly bilking FCCB customers out of more than $744,000 between 1980 and 1986. Five of the other former FCCB salesmen who had worked at RB&H were indicted in the same probe. At about the same time, just weeks before the FBI investigation of the Merc's trading floor became known, Sandner shut down RB&H's retail sales operation. "Thinking back on it, we might have done things differently," Sandner told a reporter when questioned about Piazza a few months later. Sandner says he had no knowledge of Piazza's history at FCCB at the time Piazza joined RB&H.

CFTC records show that the agency received 27 customer complaints against RB&H in the period between 1983 and 1990. That is not extraordinary for a big futures firm. RB&H, like many futures firms, settled complaints before they reached the CFTC's official record. Even so, the CFTC in 1987 found that RB&H and four of its Iowa-based salesmen used false advertising, traded customer funds without authorization, and illegally allocated trading profits and losses. Moreover, RB&H failed to register salesmen and handled orders in such a shoddy manner that customers were at risk. RB&H hastily settled the ten-count administrative complaint, agreeing to cease and desist. The firm paid a $10,000 fine and the Iowa salesmen were sanctioned.

The case is unremarkable in the history of futures trading abuses. However, it is extraordinary that Sandner, president of RB&H and chairman of the Merc, was chairman of the NFA's business conduct committee at the time of the CFTC sanctions and remained there after they were settled. Except that in the case of John F. Sandner, conflicting bonds of duty, business, and friendship are hopelessly intertwined.

□ □ □

MAURY KRAVITZ, MILLIONAIRE COMMODITY TRADER and the mastermind behind the biggest group of broker-traders at the Chicago Mercantile Exchange, is a student of Genghis Khan. Kravitz admires the Mongol barbarian's highly organized armies and his successes in conquest. He dismisses Khan's legendary cruelty as a fact of life at the time. Kravitz's 38-foot yacht is named "Temujin," which was Genghis Khan's birth name, and the same word graces the license plates on Kravitz's Mercedes Benz.

To Kravitz's way of thinking, Khan may have raped, pillaged, and devastated, but he also ran an efficient empire. The Mongol leader managed to conquer three-quarters of the known world by organizing his armies into units of ten men who chose their own leaders, who were in turn formed into groups of ten, and so on. The units were carefully supplied with food, transportation, and intelligence, giving them an advantage over their adversaries.

Kravitz's own trading-floor army, Associated Brokerage Services Company (known as ABS Partners) is similarly well organized. His broker-partners and employees occupy nearly every futures and options pit at the Merc. They coordinate their trading tasks and pool their administrative expenses, and by aggressively cutting brokerage fees—the amount paid to a broker to execute a futures order—Kravitz's broker army has captured an increasingly broad share of the market. The business is lucrative, amounting to tens of thousands of dollars a day.

While CFTC documents in 1989 showed 22 floor brokers enrolled in the ABS group, that understates the group's true reach. Interlocking memberships—traders who belong to both the ABS group and as many as four others—expanded the ABS reach geometrically and pushed its influence into the narrowest corners of the trading floor.

The extent of the group's influence, and the checkered histories of Kravitz and some of his major partners in the ABS venture, have made the group controversial on and off the trading floor. Its power attracted the attention of federal investigators, who targeted group members for special scrutiny during the nearly two years that FBI agents worked undercover on the Chicago Mercantile Exchange.

Kravitz's connections to the entrenched Merc leadership add to the group's aura of power. A businessman, not a politician, Kravitz has lined his office walls with the stuffed heads of African gazelles and other beasts, not photographs of prominent Washington friends. However, Kravitz has been an effective behind-the-scenes general for the Merc's more politically minded men. He formed Dellsher Investment Co. with Leo Melamed in 1957, after the two had shared their law practice. Kravitz is mentor and friend to Jack Sandner and is even godfather to Jack Sandner's son, Nicholas. (That arrangement was complicated by the fact that Kravitz is Jewish, and the Catholic baptismal service requires the godfather to acknowledge the deity of Jesus Christ. Sandner found a priest willing to bend the rules, Kravitz found a surrogate who would answer the difficult questions in the service, and the two men were able to cement their friendship and business relationships with a family tie.)

Brokers are central characters in a futures pit. They fill orders from customers and provide a steady stream of liquidity into the pit from the outside world. Since the number of orders entering a pit is finite, locals compete to complete trades. Although exchange rules require a broker to award orders to the trader offering the best price in open outcry, in the fast-paced, volatile pits, the temptation lurks to favor a friend or fail to see an unfamiliar trader with a competing bid.

If nothing else, filling customer orders puts brokers at financial risk. At the Merc, brokers must "eat" their errors. If a broker makes a mistake that costs the customer money, the broker writes a check to make up the difference. On the other hand, if the broker makes an error that creates a windfall profit, the customer is entitled to all of the windfall, and the broker keeps none. Outtrades—mistakes made in recording or reporting trades—also put brokers at risk. One outtrade, one bad price or missed order, can cost a broker an entire day's work, and more. The risks of being a broker are offset by the generous income. Clearing firms pay brokers $1 or $2 per contract. For a broker holding a moderate-sized deck of orders, that could translate into about $40,000 a month in income, which can be supplemented by the broker's own personal trading.

Kravitz, a savvy businessman, recognized that franchising the broker concept and drumming up enough business to keep a couple of dozen brokers busy could bring him far more income than he could generate filling orders on his own. He hired brokers, put them on salary and commission, skimmed off the bulk of their income, and backed them and their errors with the hefty capitalization of his foundling partnership. Others had employed the concept at the Merc—but none would do so as effectively as Kravitz.

Kravitz formed the precursor to ABS Partners in 1986. He had first come to the Merc in 1954, taking over a Merrill Lynch runner's job when Leo Melamed got promoted. Kravitz bought, and lost, a Merc seat a year later, washing out in the onion pit. Shortly afterward, he was drafted into the Korean War and, because he could speak Russian and German, was given a special forces assignment in Germany. He returned to Chicago 33 months later to practice law and trade commodities on the side. A short, solid, fireplug of a man with a full, grizzled beard, Kravitz made a name for himself in the Merc's gold futures pit in the late 1970s, earning a reputation on the trading floor for a particular ruthlessness. Off the floor, he was portrayed as a gold expert and managed customer money in a gold futures fund.

Kravitz had decided to go after the gold business the moment the Merc began to draft a gold futures contract, before gold trading was made legal. Kravitz visited all the major firms who would be potential customers if gold futures ever flew and captured the promise of their business. His solicitations were so successful that when gold was launched, he had the business of 140 brokerage houses. "It would be easier for me to tell you the names of the nine houses whose business I didn't get," he boasts.

But holding 98 percent of the paper in a pit made it difficult to service customers efficiently. The Merc eventually called in Kravitz and ordered him to split his deck with other brokers. "They told me I was ruining the business," Kravitz says. "I had so many orders—when the whole pit looks to one little corner, one person, it isn't good." Kravitz split his business with a young trader named John Oberman, who eventually split off from Kravitz to form his own broker association. Kravitz also acknowledges that many Merc members credit him with contributing to the gold pit's demise. "There are all sorts of stories about that," he says.

Kravitz served on the Merc board of governors from 1978 until 1980, and during that time had a run-in with his friend Leo Melamed over the future of the gold market. Melamed thought the Singapore International Monetary Exchange would revive Merc gold, but Kravitz disagreed, noting that Hong Kong was Asia's gold-trading center and Singapore would attract little business. Later, when Kravitz proposed a special gold trading membership at the Merc, the Melamed-controlled board of governors refused, raising Kravitz's ire.

After the Merc's gold pit died in late 1984, Kravitz looked for other challenges and organized ABS Partners with a former rival, James J. Kaulentis. Kaulentis and Kravitz had been fierce competitors, with Kaulentis brokering orders in the front month of the Merc's pork belly pit, and Kravitz in the next-most-active month. The rivalry cooled down when Kravitz moved to the gold pit, but flared again when brokers employed by each man began competing head-to-head for customers in the currency futures pits in 1983. The two combatants held a parley and decided that a price war would tear their businesses apart. If they worked together, they'd be unbeatable. A truce was called, and the two broker groups joined forces.

The 45-year-old Kaulentis is taller than Kravitz and just as portly and rumpled, but the similarities end there. Kaulentis grew up on the Northwest Side of Chicago, where he learned the lessons of the streets, including a fierce loyalty to boyhood friends. Kaulentis and his friends were active cardplayers and gamblers, and those interests drew them to futures trading. Kaulentis sponsored several of his old friends for Merc membership and employed some of them in the ABS group. Kaulentis' brother Dean became his chief lieutenant in the livestock futures pits, and his early partner in the floor brokerage business was brother-in-law Mike Minnini. Minnini and Kaulentis would split before ABS Partners was organized, and Minnini would form alliances with Kravitz's former associate, John Oberman. Harry "the Hat" Lowrance, longtime Merc floor chairman, was another Kaulentis friend from the old neighborhood. Kaulentis' former room-mate, Michael J. Christ, became a floor broker and part owner in the ABS group, and Sam Cali, Dean Kaulentis' high school buddy, became a group employee. Both Cali and Christ were indicted for fraud in the FBI probe.

□ □ □

THE COMBINED FORCES of Kravitz and Kaulentis hit the Merc trading floor in 1986 like a Mongol horde. Independent floor brokers lost business as the ABS Partners broker group cut commissions well below the then-standard rate of about $2 per contract. There were plenty of other broker groups on the floor, but none was able to do business for such small fees.

Part of the ABS advantage, floor traders said, was its "franchise" agreements with young brokers, a cost-saving arrangement that helped fray the very fabric of the trading floor. The young traders' salaries were low in comparison to their colleagues, and the temptations, with millions of dollars swirling by, were great. What's more, the salary arrangement meant ABS brokers became dependent on their bosses, and not their trading acumen, for success. "The potential for abuses is enhanced, because brokers are controlled by the people who brought them into the group," said John Troelstrup, a former Merc compliance officer who is now an attorney in private practice.

Kravitz was aware of the temptation and encouraged abuse, according to former Merc trader Aric March. March worked for Kravitz in 1987, when the Merc was trying to restart its ill-fated gold pit. March complained to Kravitz that he couldn't make a living on brokerage in the moribund pit. March claims that Kravitz, a veteran gold trader who knew all the tricks of the trade, offered a matter-of-fact reply: "What's wrong, can't you steal enough?"

Kravitz's reported comment to March contradicts the upright image of its managing partners that ABS draws in promotional literature.

Floor traders chortle over one marketing brochure which, among other things, says that ABS "employs over 80 people, all with the same commitment to ethics and philosophy of service as the company's original founders."

□ □ □

THERE IS NOTHING INHERENTLY EVIL about broker groups. Supporters say that the broker group strategy is brilliant, and that given the high risks and costs of brokering in the futures pits, it is logical to pool resources by forming broker associations. But critics, many of them floor managers for clearing firms say groups with the size and influence of ABS Partners stretch the capabilities of the exchange surveillance system. They say the large number of cooperating brokers makes it easier to use illegal tactics that require a "friend" in the pit. And by cutting brokerage fees so low, the big groups have driven independent brokers out of business, leaving clearing firms with limited choices for brokers.

In a world where money is power, the heavy capitalization of the groups, particularly ABS Partners, also draws attention. Kravitz will not specify the group's assets, but he says ABS has more money than most Merc clearing firms, and the capitalization plays to the group's advantage. "People know that," he says. "The leadership here knows that." Kravitz boasts that ABS has never had a losing month and has never failed to pay monthly dividends to partners.

There are other complaints about the ABS Partners group. Lewis Borsellino, known as "LBJ" on the trading floor, is a major investor and an ABS trader partner. He enjoys a reputation as a tough character in the pit and has collected a host of "decorum" penalties for using profanity and "undue force" while trading. Borsellino cut his teeth on the Merc floor as a clerk for Kravitz in the gold pit. His mother, Florence, had been Kravitz's legal secretary.

Borsellino is the largest independent trader, or local, in the S&P 500 futures pit. As such, he trades his own huge positions and often works opposite ABS brokers with big customer orders. Floor critics say that when those brokers are Borsellino's broker group employees, there is an inherent conflict of interest, a tendency to favor his own group members.

All across the Merc's trading floor, broker group interrelationships are interwoven like a spoked wheel, with ABS Partners at the hub.

Fourteen major groups exist at the Merc, all of which have one or more members who also belong to ABS Partners. What's more, all but three of the groups have members with partnership interests in at least two other groups. Broker group members claim they are a force for good, saving customers money and standing in the trading pits during tough times like the 1987 stock market crash, when many independent brokers fled the hair-raising markets. The latter claim is contradicted by a postcrash study by the government-appointed Brady Commission, which found that almost all of the Merc's traders—independent brokers, group members, and even local traders—deserted the S&P 500 pit after the stock market collapsed on October 19, 1987.

Breaking down broker group conflicts has proven no easy matter. Even the reform efforts attempted after the 1987 revolt in the S&P's have proven ineffective in forcing groups to act equitably on the trading floor. Indeed, since 1988, the Merc has cited more than 75 instances in which broker group members violated limits on the amount of trading group members may do with each other. In fewer than ten of the instances, however, did the penalty exceed a $1,000 fine. Most often the penalty was nothing more than a letter of warning.

Vigilance against group improprieties picked up in the wake of the FBI investigation, just as they had briefly in the wake of the 1987 reform movement. In the most celebrated post-investigation case, Merc governor Richard Lowrance (younger brother of Harry "the Hat") in mid-1989 stepped down from the board just before he was sanctioned for pre-arranging trades with other broker group members, in an apparent effort to avoid limits on intragroup trading in the Merc's Eurodollar trading pit. Besides losing a board seat, Lowrance also was ordered to pay a $200,000 fine and suspended from trading for one month. Lowrance's timing was rather unfortunate: He was nailed during the height of the postinvestigation panic. As the spotlight from the investigation dimmed, the Merc's crackdown on broker group violations would decline once again.

□ □ □

EXCHANGES BY THEIR NATURE are conflict-ridden enterprises. Nobody trades alone. And traders become successful, wealthy, and powerful only with the help of others in the trading pit. Close business ties, close personal friendships are inevitable. And as long as they do not interfere with the fair conduct of business, they are proper and, to the extent they help the markets work, desirable.

Indeed, there are many Merc traders who have become successful, and sometimes even influential, without any apparent improprieties or conflicts of interest. John Geldermann, chairman of the Merc at the time the FBI investigation became known, is the strongest example. The head of a successful trading firm co-owned with his brother, Geldermann rose to influence at the Merc by dint of his reputation for fair-mindedness and his hard work on improving the Merc's trading systems.

Unfortunately for the Merc, Geldermann has been the exception, not the rule. With Melamed's retirement pending—if in fact he ever does retire—the exchange may face an opportunity to be run as a truly democratic membership organization. But like many powerful leaders, Melamed has done little to make way for a successor. An early candidate for the chairmanship in 1991, Steven E. Wollack, did not have the clout or charisma to inherit Melamed's mantle. Jack Sandner, the most ambitious successor-in-waiting, had seen his ambitions tainted by revelations of his ties to ABS and the troubles at RB&H. Nevertheless, with Melamed's backing Sandner handily won election by the Merc's board of governors to again become the exchange's chairman. And the reformers on the Merc's floor, much as they would like to unseat the old guard, have found no one who could hope to become the next leader of a new group of young turks—young, idealistic traders with grand ambitions for the exchange. He may have had his faults in running the Merc, but Leo Melamed was one of a kind.

CHAPTER SEVEN

□□□

Process and Potentates:
Inside the Board of Trade

THE LEADERSHIP STRUCTURES AT THE MERC and the Board of Trade could not be more different. A cult of personality pervades the Chicago Mercantile Exchange, from Leo Melamed at the top down to the broker groups that operate the pits. The Merc, after all, would not be what it is today, and might no longer exist, if not for Melamed and his oligarchy. Fealty to Melamed is the natural consequence of that fact.

The Chicago Board of Trade, by contrast, owes its prominence to no single person. Those who have made names for themselves over the years—from Leiter to Rice to the Hunts—have been more scoundrels than seers. If personality runs the Merc, then process runs the Board. Little happens at the exchange that a committee has not begotten, or at least blessed. A few committees dominate: the executive committee, of course, but also the Business Conduct Committee and the floor practices committee. At the Merc, people first sign on with the ruling clique; only then do they gain influence in the governing process. At the Board, they gradually build a power base through committee work; only then do they become part of a ruling clique.

Make no mistake: A clique definitely does rule the Board. But it is a clique in which the characters change, and not just in a Merc-style musical chairs charade. Every few years, the composition of the Board's executive committee changes substantially. Former chairmen drop from sight. New stars appear. Even a candidate passed over by the nominating committee can win election, as Leslie Rosenthal did to become chairman in 1981, or Patrick Arbor to earn his third term as vice-chairman in 1989. The institution moves forward, or at times backward. But it is the institution, above all, that survives and thrives.

At the time of the FBI investigation, the Board was run by one of its longest-lasting and most dominating ruling cliques. Karsten "Cash" Mahlmann began his third term as chairman a few days before Operation Sourmash went public. His two predecessors had served only one-year terms. After the probe, one of the Board's most controversial former chairmen, Leslie Rosenthal, capitalized on criticism of Mahlmann's handling of the crisis to jump back into exchange politics. Meanwhile, Thomas R. Donovan was in his seventh year as president in 1989. He had left Chicago's city hall to join the exchange as secretary in 1979 and was president by the time Rosenthal's second term as chairman expired in 1983. These are the people one must know to understand the Board during its time of crisis.

□ □ □

THERE'S NO NICKNAME IN THE INDUSTRY quite like it: "Cash." For years, the sobriquet fit Karsten Mahlmann well, and did him no harm, as he climbed toward the chairmanship of the Board of Trade that he would attain in 1987. He complained good-naturedly to reporters for overusing the nickname, but in a business where cash is king, queen, and duke, few could resist. Besides, his real name had fallen into near-absolute disuse—even his wife called him Cash. But the moniker would take on an embarrassing undertone in the summer of 1990. That's when Mahlmann's firm, Stotler & Co., fell short of money and eventually was forced into liquidation. The lack of cash, and a questionable transfer of $5.5 million of customer funds to help prop up the failing Stotler Group parent company, would lead Mahlmann to resign both from Stotler and from the Board of Trade. The incident would cap a remarkable career with a singularly embarrassing denouement.

Mahlmann could never have foreseen the twists his life would take when in 1957, at age 20, he boarded a U.S.-bound grain freighter as part of a planned world tour. The son of a Hamburg grain merchant, Mahlmann had embarked on the journey to learn the grain business so he could take over from his father. After the freighter docked in Port Arthur, Texas, Mahlmann took a train directly to Chicago. He carried in his breast pocket a letter of introduction to a Chicago commodities trader, Daniel F. Rice, the same Daniel Rice who had feuded a few years earlier with the Board of Trade over its grain-storage policies.

In the late 1950s, Daniel F. Rice & Co. was one of the Board's most powerful and active firms. Besides futures trading, Rice also conducted a busy cash grain business, enabling the commercial grain firms that were its primary customers to buy and sell the actual commodities that were the basis of the futures contracts traded at the Board. With his background, Mahlmann was a natural for the cash room. And that's where Daniel Rice sent the young German-speaking gentleman with the close-cropped hair to work as a runner.

In no time, Mahlmann was a fixture in Rice's cash grain operation. Traders, too busy to bother pronouncing "Karsten," nicknamed him "Cash." The name stuck, and so did Mahlmann. The other legs of his planned world tour never followed the visit to Chicago. The young Rice & Co. runner walked to work from his boarding room at the Lawson YMCA 11 blocks north of the Board on Chicago Avenue, saving the carfare he could not afford. While working at Rice he met his future wife. Years later, Loretta Mahlmann would fondly remember ironing Mahlmann's cotton shirts—meticulously starching the collars so they met his exacting specifications—back when the couple was starting out.

Mahlmann left Rice in 1963, three years after the firm was purchased by Shearson Hayden. The brokerage firm he joined, Stotler & Co., had four principals, two employees, and no futures trading operation. Mahlmann's job was to start up a futures arm to mesh with Stotler's grain trading business. Stotler was hedging most of its cash grain positions in the futures markets, and the firm's partners figured their customers might want the same opportunity. Mahlmann was proud of the Stotler partners' close ties to the trading rooms. "Nobody had an ivory tower position," Mahlmann once told a reporter. "If a customer called in and had a problem, you got hold of the partner."

As he built Stotler's business, Mahlmann also climbed the ranks at the Board of Trade. The Board uses committees to help identify and groom the exchange's future leaders, and Mahlmann was a leader. Mahlmann served first on the margin and member services committees in the 1970s and worked his way to the board of directors in 1983. By 1986, he was vice-chairman of the exchange, the post normally used to groom the next chairman. As vice-chairman, he made his mark spearheading the exchange's response to a Commodity Futures Trading Commission proposal that would have significantly increased the amount of capital that trading firms were required to keep on hand to insure their solvency in the event of a market crisis. Board of Trade chairman John F. Gilmore volubly attacked the CFTC and raised a $1 million "defense fund" to back the exchange's lobbying effort. Meanwhile, Mahlmann worked behind the scenes to prevent an increase in the existing requirement that a trading firm's capital must equal at least four percent of its customers' funds. The tandem approach by Gilmore and Mahlmann worked, and the CFTC proposal was never adopted.

When Mahlmann became chairman in 1987, his first major act was to open an evening trading session to capitalize on overseas demand to trade the Board's Treasury-bond futures. At the Merc, which had not yet publicly floated the idea for its Globex electronic after-hours system, night trading was greeted skeptically. Jack Sandner, Merc chairman at the time, called it "a step backward" and predicted that night trading would not work.

Mahlmann pushed ahead. "It's like a factory. You've got a physical plant, and it's foolish to just turn off the lights at the end of the day shift," Mahlmann explained. Night trading proved a success, leveling out at about 7,000 contracts a session, and gave the Board of Trade an intermediate step en route to the inevitable conversion to a black box after-hours system.

Mahlmann's next major challenge was the stock market crash on October 19, 1987. Mahlmann and Board President Donovan shuttled between Washington and Chicago more than 20 times in six months to plead the case of the Chicago exchanges. Stock index futures, of course, were primarily the domain of the Merc, but the Board's stock index contract, the Major Market Index, had attracted significant criticism. *The Wall Street Journal*, falsely it turned out, had charged that the MMI was manipulated on October 20 while the Merc's S&P contract had been shut down during tumultuous trading. Mahlmann and Donovan knew they had turf to defend—the MMI in particular, the industry's self-regulatory independence in general. And defend it they did. For his efforts, Mahlmann became the first Board of Trade chairman ever to receive a salary: $240,000 a year beginning in March 1988.

As big a crisis as it was, the 1987 market crash paled compared to the fury that erupted when Operation Sourmash went public with the subpoenas of dozens of Board traders on the night of January 18, 1989. Just two days earlier, Mahlmann had begun his third year as Board chairman. His first instinct in defending the Board's position was to close ranks, stoically take the heat, and hope the problem would go away. But that was not possible. Mahlmann was drafted to serve as point man in the Board's repeated forays to Capitol Hill to defend the industry's integrity and, as usual, the self-regulatory system.

Mahlmann's repeated protestations in favor of self-regulation by the exchanges would come back to haunt him. Days before the investigation went public, U.S. Attorney Anton Valukas had indicted 18 former officers and salesmen of the fraud-ridden First Commodity Corp. of Boston. In the finger-pointing frenzy that followed disclosure of the investigation, reporters quickly discovered that one of the indictees was a Stotler employee. The untimely publicity that former FCCB broker Michael N. Kolb worked at Mahlmann's firm was an embarrassment to Mahlmann and the exchange. Stotler's CEO, Thomas Egan, explained that Mahlmann had no say in employment practices. But the defense sounded hollow to a suspicious public, particularly when Egan insisted that Kolb could continue working at Stotler, where he handled customer business, until a jury might find him guilty or innocent.

Egan's words rang truer than most people realized. Few knew it at the time, but Mahlmann by 1989 had virtually no say in the operation of Stotler. Three years at the helm of the Board of Trade had cost him his power at the firm, thanks largely to a coup engineered by Egan, who had become Stotler's chief executive in 1987, when Mahlmann began spending virtually all of his working time in the Board of Trade's mahogany-paneled executive suite.

At Stotler's helm, Egan engineered an ambitious, even reckless, growth plan that would strain and ultimately drain Stotler's capital. The largest factor: the breathlessly expanding number of outside brokers whose ability to meet financial obligations was guaranteed by Stotler. At the end of 1986, the firm guaranteed 146 introducing brokers; by 1990, the number would grow to 390, more than any other futures firm. Growth of the brokerage force was funded in part by $4.36 million raised in a 1988 public offering by Stotler Group. But some of those funds also went toward the mid-1989 purchase of securities broker R. G. Dickinson & Co., which also became a drain on Stotler's cash resources.

Stotler's public offering, the first ever by a commodities firm, traded heavily on Mahlmann's reputation in the industry. Mahlmann himself profited handsomely. His 9.9 percent personal stake in Stotler was worth $2.7 million at the time of the offering. Ironically though, the stock sale came just as Mahlmann's power within the firm was ebbing toward oblivion. Egan, a master of office politics, had allied himself with the ambitious young Robert Stotler to chip away steadily at Mahlmann's power base. When the Board began paying Mahlmann the $240,000 salary in March 1988, Egan saw that Stotler stopped cutting him a check. The last blow in Mahlmann's downfall, according to sources close to Stotler, was his divorce from Loretta and his open romance with a Stotler employee, Dory Stage. The indiscretion lost Mahlmann the backing of key allies at the conservative, family-oriented firm, particularly Howard Stotler, one of the firm's founders and its spiritual leader. By 1988, Mahlmann had no say in the firm's day-to-day operations. When Stotler moved its offices out of the Board of Trade building and into a nearby office tower, Mahlmann's new office was used as a storage room.

The 1988 public stock sale, which looked like a coup for Stotler at the time, in retrospect was the first sign that the Egan-led expansion was endangering the firm. By early 1990, the Board of Trade was monitoring the firm's capital because of concerns about a possible shortfall. The National Futures Association also was concerned, but because there was no formal communication between the two self-regulatory bodies, each thought it was the only one with concerns and neither saw any reason for alarm. The CFTC apparently had no concerns whatsoever about Stotler. The agency's crackdown on Stotler did not begin until after the Securities and Exchange Commission, the CFTC's arch-rival in the battle for regulatory oversight of the futures markets, uncovered signs of serious financial distress at the firm. A routine SEC audit in the spring of 1990 discovered a questionable transfer of $13.4 million of debt from the Stotler brokerage unit to its parent company. The CFTC, called in by the SEC, soon discovered that a unit of Stotler also had transferred $5.5 million of customer funds to help keep Stotler Group itself afloat.

Despite his loss of power at Stotler, Mahlmann still was chairman of the firm, and he was a scapegoat for its problems. The revelations about Stotler's alleged improprieties were an acute embarrassment to the Board, and to Mahlmann. His role as an advocate for the industry was completely subverted—under the circumstances, he couldn't possibly go to Capitol Hill and repeat his refrain about the beauty of self-regulation. Mahlmann's standing among his peers was ruined, as was his personal fortune. His Stotler stock, suddenly worth only $552,925, had lost 80 percent of its value and would soon become worthless when Stotler filed for bankruptcy. Legal bills from the Stotler collapse were just starting to mount.

In an emotional board meeting on August 1, 1990, just hours after he had vowed to stay and fight, Mahlmann resigned from the Board of Trade. He was the first Board chairman to resign since 1855. Within days, the firm he had helped build closed its doors and left the futures business for good.

□ □ □

MANY LEADERS OF THE CHICAGO MARKETS have remarkable political gifts, but the only pedigreed pol in the group business is Thomas R. Donovan, president of the Chicago Board of Trade. After the feisty Jane Byrne defeated his boss Michael Bilandic in the 1979 Chicago mayoral race, Donovan fled to the Board, which he joined as vice president and secretary. Within two years, he was president. And since then, he has come to guide the exchange's political agenda both in Chicago and in Washington, working closely with the Merc's Leo Melamed when cooperation serves the industry's interests. Politics and politicians, particularly Chicago politicians, are Donovan's calling card in the markets.

The Chicago of Tom Donovan's early days was a city run by the clannish politics of Chicago's South Side. The red-haired, blue-eyed young Donovan had but one thing going for him: He was Irish, and Irish politics ran Chicago. He came from modest means, the son of a window glazier for the Chicago Board of Education. But Donovan was growing up in the predominantly Irish neighborhood of Bridge-port, where politics was as much a sport as street-corner baseball is in most other neighborhoods. And Donovan started in politics at an early age, canvassing for the local Democratic organization, making a name for himself in the local political machine. Before long, Don-ovan had made contacts with a prominent political family named Daley, and his prospects were good, indeed.

In the year 1969, young Donovan joined Chicago's city govern-ment. A graduate of DeLaSalle High School and the Illinois Institute of Technology, Donovan was working as a glazier for the Hamilton Glass Co. when he interviewed for an administrative job in Chicago's Department of Streets and Sanitation, perhaps the biggest patronage bureau in the Chicago Machine. The man who interviewed him was the legendary mayor, Richard J. Daley. Before the year was out, Don-ovan was on the mayor's personal staff, where he quickly became patronage chief, a job of major-league proportions in the Daley ad-ministration. By 1974, Donovan had moved his desk to an anteroom outside Daley's office. From there, he controlled access to the mayor as a steady stream of the wealthy and powerful passed by to see the most dominating big-city mayor in the nation.

Donovan was with Daley when he died of a heart attack in 1981. Along with Edward "Fast Eddie" Vrdolyak, he helped the little-known alderman Michael Bilandic, a Daley protégé, succeed Boss Daley. However, because the back-room dealing momentarily cut the powerful Daley clan out of the political picture, Donovan lost his ties to the city's strongest political family. When Byrne, a former Daley commissioner, won an outsider's campaign to unseat Bilandic in the 1979 mayor's race, Donovan was out the door.

The Board of Trade was a natural move. Donovan knew nothing about the markets, but he knew politics. And, just as important to the Board, he knew politicians. He had first met Congressman Dan Rostenkowski in 1969, when he joined the mayor's staff. By the time Donovan moved to the Board, he could be counted among Rosty's closest political pals. The Board's president at the time, Robert K. Wilmouth, had the business connections. Wilmouth had come to the Board in 1977 from the Crocker Bank of San Francisco, but was best known in Chicago as loser to the controversial A. Robert Abboud in a bitter horse race to become chairman of the First National Bank of Chicago in 1974. With Donovan's political ties and Wilmouth's business connections, the Board had a strong duo.

Donovan made his first mark in politics on the Board's behalf with the hard-fought battle to prevent implementation of a tax on commodity straddles. Although Wilmouth was the titular leader in the charge on Washington, Donovan played his Chicago connections well. The industry-sponsored bill that passed out of the House in 1981, which preserved a tax break for certain year-end finesses in the commodities pits, was introduced by Representative Marty Russo, a Rostenkowski protégé and industry supporter.

As the exchanges lobbied, throwing yacht parties for congressional staffers, commandeering Senator Alan Cranston's office for powwows with other senators, and inviting committee members to speak in Chicago, House Ways and Means Chairman Rostenkowski officially remained inactive in lobbying for the bill. Still, everyone on the Hill knew Russo would never sponsor such a controversial bill without Rostenkowski's blessing. Even so, the House version was defeated by a Senate bill, backed by Treasury Secretary Donald Regan, which severely reduced straddle tax breaks by forcing traders to figure gains and losses as if their positions had been closed on December 31. Despite the eventual defeat, Donovan had impressed the Board's leaders with his close ties to Rostenkowski and other powerful pols with Chicago connections.

Donovan's good reputation benefited him in short order. Wilmouth's days as Board president were numbered. The Board in 1981 had begun construction of a 24-story, $51 million annex to its original building, which would house an agricultural trading floor the size of three basketball courts. By April 1982, it had become clear that the Helmut Jahn–designed structure, with a 12-story atrium, was coming in more than $18 million over its original budget. When restive members, already angry about the loss on the tax straddle issue, forced Wilmouth's ouster, Donovan moved into the president's office.

Donovan's first year as president was marked by some remarkable successes. Jane Byrne, the nemesis who had ousted Bilandic as mayor, proposed a city transaction tax that would have cost the industry millions of dollars each year. Donovan engineered a program that combined heavy lobbying at the state capitol in Springfield with loud threats to move the Chicago exchange out of state, and he ultimately led state lawmakers to pass a law prohibiting any such city tax. During the 1982 reauthorization hearings for the CFTC, Donovan's political leadership helped the Board win sweeping victories on a variety of issues. A proposed user fee program that would have raised $23 million for the government also was defeated. Meanwhile, the exchange helped convince the CFTC to lift a ban on options on agricultural commodities. And in a move that eviscerated the CFTC's authority to intervene in market emergencies, the commission's emergency actions on the exchanges became subject to judicial review.

In his eight years at the helm, Donovan has solidified his power base both within the exchange and outside. He maintains strong ties with the former chairmen under whom he served—current board members Thomas Cunningham and Goldman, Sachs & Co. executive John F. Gilmore, in particular. He has helped engineer the exchange's campaigns against restrictive capital rules proposed (and eventually dropped) by the CFTC, and in favor of continued CFTC regulation of the markets.

As head of the exchange's political fund-raising effort, Donovan has consistently reminded members to contribute to the Board's Auction Markets Political Action Committee. By the time Sourmash went public, Donovan's frequent presence on Capitol Hill was an asset to the exchange perhaps as valuable as the millions collected over the years for the PAC. By then, all of the combined political skills and financial resources of Donovan, Melamed, and the rest of the players in the industry would be necessary to prevent a bloodbath for the pits.

□ □ □

CONSIDERING ITS COLORFUL, BUCCANEERING PAST, the Board of Trade in the 1980s was a rather gray eminence. The committee system was in charge, and the once-innovative institution had become tradition-bound to the point of immobility. The Chicago Mercantile Exchange had assumed a role as the innovative heart and soul of the futures markets. But that all changed when Leslie Rosenthal broke into the Board's hierarchy. No leader in the recent history of the Board has aroused such allegiance, antipathy, and controversy as the silver-haired, smooth-talking Rosenthal.

An independent trader who formed his own clearing firm, Rosenthal accumulated more baggage in his career than an airport sky-cap even before emerging as a force in exchange politics. In 1977, the CFTC charged Rosenthal & Co., Rosenthal himself, and a group of 15 employees with fraud in their marketing of tax-dodging commodity options contracts traded in London. The commission settled the charges in 1986 by ordering Rosenthal to pay $30,000 and allow an independent consultant to monitor his firm's activities. The charges had included a variety of abusive sales techniques. Salesmen and promotional literature allegedly understated the risk to customers, quoted deceptively low commission figures, understated the break-even point on options investments, and even created a fictitious "foreign service fee" that really was a fraudulent add-on to Rosenthal's regular commission structure.

The London options case still was an open file at the CFTC when Rosenthal was nominated in 1980 to serve as chairman of the Board of Trade. But it wasn't the only questionable activity in Rosenthal's past. Rosenthal was one of the four traders suspected by members of the business conduct committee in March 1979 of trying to corner the Board's wheat contract. He was the exchange's vice-chairman at the time. Despite his substantial personal trading position, Rosenthal participated in meetings held by the exchange's board of directors to discuss the wheat matter. Rosenthal did not actually vote when the directors decided to take no action to halt trading in the wheat contract, but his presence at the meetings influenced deliberations, according to members who were present. "Nobody was about to suggest any action with Les sitting there in the room," said one director who participated in the debates. "It was outrageous that he didn't excuse himself."

Election to the chairmanship did not change Rosenthal's style. He took control of the exchange's committee structure, ousting members who had opposed his election and putting close associates in their place. In the negotiations over the tax straddle, he refused to budge from the Board's position that was reflected in the bill Representative Russo introduced in the House. His intransigence helped bring about a defeat for the Board, for which Wilmouth ultimately took the fall. Rosenthal also conducted secret negotiations with the New York Futures Exchange, a struggling offshoot of the New York Stock Exchange that some traders feared as a potential competitor.

Surprise and outrage over the NYFE move was such that, when Rosenthal sought renomination for a second term as Board of Trade chairman in November 1981, the nominating committee instead chose his vice-chairman, Ralph Goldenberg. The normal, gentlemanly election process at the Board of Trade gave way to a rhubarb. Appealing to the growing contingent of Jewish members at the Board, Rosenthal took to calling his opponent "a showcase Jew," intimating that Goldenberg was a lackey for the Irish clique that normally ruled exchange politics. Goldenberg's forces, in turn, accused a Rosenthal ally, Henry Shatkin, of Chicago-style vote-fixing. Rosenthal had supplied Shatkin with 100 extra ballots when Shatkin explained that some of the many traders affiliated with his firm had lost theirs or were out of town. The Goldenberg allies claimed Shatkin was strong-arming members who cleared trades through his firm to vote for Rosenthal. In another instance of campaign high jinks, a trader posing as a reporter sought to obtain damaging information about Goldenberg from C. C. Odom, a Goldenberg ally running for vice-chairman.

When the smoke cleared, Rosenthal had won election to a second term as chairman. He purged the remaining committee members who weren't his allies and proceeded with the Board's aggressive and successful lobbying for the 1982 reauthorization of the CFTC. And he completed construction of the 24-story annex. That was only the start. Rosenthal also introduced a new series of partial memberships at the exchange. The new seats—designed both to increase access to the increasingly expensive closed club of Board membership and to fill new trading pits with traders hungry to succeed—have continued to arouse controversy even to the present time. Yellow-badged full members who resent the membership-interest holders campaign from time to time to eliminate the partial memberships.

Rosenthal stepped down after his second term, but he was not finished with exchange politics. In late 1989, he again ran for the chairmanship, seeking to prevent Mahlmann from serving a fourth term. In a raucous and glitzy campaign, Rosenthal attacked Mahlmann for his inept response to the FBI investigation and proposed selling the Board's building—an idea he claimed would fetch each member a $300,000 lump sum payment. He also proposed introducing a new series of contracts based on risk in the insurance business. All of this was spelled out in pamphlets mailed to members, a breakthrough in exchange politics.

But Rosenthal's past would haunt him. At a members' forum before the January 1990 election, a member rose to ask Rosenthal about his reputation. "I'm not sure I understand the question," Rosenthal snapped back at the trader. "But I certainly understand the intent." Members made their intentions clear in the election. Apparently buying Mahlmann's claim that Uncle Sam would be the biggest beneficiary of the sale of the building, and nervous about the prospect of Rosenthal appearing on Capitol Hill to defend the industry's integrity in the wake of the trading scandals, members elected Mahlmann to a fourth term by a narrow margin.

Despite the bitter election battle, Rosenthal apparently held no grudge. After Stotler collapsed and Mahlmann resigned the Board's chairmanship, Rosenthal hired the deposed former adversary to run the Rosenthal Collins Group's London office. One of many unwritten codes in the pits states that people who are up help out those who are down, so Rosenthal's gesture was hardly surprising.

□ □ □

WHATEVER THE POWER OF PEOPLE LIKE MAHLMANN, Donovan, and Rosenthal, the Board remained primarily a leviathan driven by corporate needs and challenges. The institution mattered more than the few leaders who occupied its top posts. The Merc was run by a personality-driven power elite. There were obvious differences between the two exchanges, but in the late 1980s the markets and their leaders had common, overarching interests: freedom from regulation, low taxes, a strong position against international competitors, an ability to introduce new products.

To obtain these goals, the exchanges would need more than market savvy. They would need cooperation with each other, and friends in Washington. And it was to Washington they would turn, again and again, to preserve the businesses that they had built.

CHAPTER EIGHT

□□□

Friends in High Places

WHEN ANTHONY CASTELLANO BURSTS OUT of the back side of the S&P 500 stock index futures pit, surfacing after a sweaty morning of trading, he looks the part of the hardscrabble floor creature that he is.

Castellano stands barely 5′6″ and weighs in at close to 225 pounds. His slate-blue trading jacket with the Dellsher badge on the breast pocket strains at the shoulders and can't contain his enormous stomach. His expensive, high-topped gym shoes are untied, his shirt is rumpled, and his whole demeanor appears slightly out of control. His one bow to fashion—a pair of eyeglasses with bright blue plastic frames—sits incongruously on a face both dull and pugnacious, trimmed with a middling black mustache and a shock of black hair.

To some, Castellano represents all that is flawed about the self-regulatory system that runs the futures markets. He has been disciplined by the Merc four times in less than ten years for pre-arranging trades, sometimes skimming profits from customer orders. His record makes futures executives shudder and reinforces the negative public image that futures brokerage houses must continually battle—the image that futures trading is rigged, that floor brokers have an unfair edge over their customers, and that futures trading is a game that the average investor will lose.

Castellano's career is worth studying because it is a laboratory of both the strengths and the weaknesses of self-regulation. Exchange self-policing in his case was apparently efficient: His abuses were detected, the cases were fairly adjudicated, and fines and suspensions were issued. He is even forbidden from brokering customer orders.

However, the fact that Castellano remains in the business and on the trading floor, wearing the trading colors of the firm run by the most powerful executive at the exchange, Leo Melamed, demonstrates the soft underbelly of the self-regulatory system.

Floor traders and brokers, the free-spirited and heavily bankrolled entrepreneurs of the futures markets, hold a special spot in the minds of federal regulators. They are exempt from many of the rules that govern other commodity industry professionals. They certainly are subject to exchange rules, but those rules are written and enforced by the traders themselves. Enforcement proceedings are secret, and details rarely travel beyond the walls of the hearing room, much less the exchange.

Proponents of self-regulation believe self-policing is necessary in the arcane, confusing, and fast-moving world of futures. Too much regulation, or regulation at the hands of those who do not know the markets, can kill the trade, or so the thinking goes. Many disagree. Critics say that the financial and political clout that has preserved floor traders' independence has created a system fraught with conflicts of interest, more devoted to self-interest than to customer interests.

Castellano may not be a typical case. Few traders have his record of repeated abuses. But in his tale lies the best and the worst of regulation in the futures industry: Each self-regulatory agency performed its assigned function, and yet together they still failed to protect the public.

□ □ □

ALTHOUGH A YOUNG 35, CASTELLANO is a veteran and a survivor. He came to the Merc in 1978 from the sales offices of a commodity brokerage house called Murlas Trading. The CFTC in 1989 would put Murlas out of business for a long history of churning customer accounts—trading accounts excessively in order to generate commissions. Castellano was not personally charged with any wrongdoing in the Murlas case, although as a sales manager at the firm he was probably aware of the company's sales practices.

When he arrived on the floor of the Merc in the late 1970s, Castellano was initiated into the habits and customs of a floor broker at the edge of the hectic gold pit. In those days, many brokers routinely matched customer buy and sell orders in the opening and closing ranges, and resolved trading errors by giving profitable "ticks" to the opposing broker or local rather than writing checks to cover the errors, as rules require. These practices were against the rules and against the law, but traders engaged in them as a matter of convenience. Few believed they harmed customers. And if customers were harmed, traders rationalized, they were paying only a small price to keep the pit in business. The floor's culture set its own limits of tolerance. Rule violations that blatantly harmed customers, particularly pre-arranging trades against customer orders, invited retribution and, in extreme cases, reports to the exchange's disciplinary committees.

Castellano first attracted disciplinary attention in 1983, when the Merc's floor practices committee found that Castellano and his business partner, a young floor broker named Jimmy Sonnenberg, had been running a scam. The two traders had misused customer orders to generate profits for an account held in the name of Castellano's father, Michael. For that episode, which the Merc committee considered a major rule violation, Castellano received a $15,000 fine and a 30-day suspension from trading.

In 1985, Castellano was in trouble with the Merc again, charged this time with selling a customer order at a price below the market, then quickly selling at a higher price for the benefit of Sonnenberg's account. Castellano settled the Merc charges and was given a 15-day suspension and another $15,000 fine. Castellano engaged in other pre-arranged trades that year. Merc records show he took part in a trade transfer scheme, this time with the aid of Sonnenberg and two long-time brokers for GNP Commodities, the firm owned by Brian Monieson, the Merc's chairman at the time. GNP brokers Gerald Woods and Walter Posner, with the cooperation of Castellano and Sonnenberg, put the winning legs of certain S&P 500 futures trades into one account, and the losers into another. The trades occurred in 1985, but the case was not decided until 1987. For his participation in the scheme, Castellano was fined another $5,000 and suspended for five days.

Castellano might have continued as a broker in the S&P pit if he had not decided in May 1987, to apply for membership in the MidAmerica Commodity Exchange, now part of the Board of Trade. The MidAm looked at Castellano's disciplinary history and told him he was not suited to be a member. That decision brought Castellano to the attention of the Commodity Futures Trading Commission, the top futures industry regulator. The CFTC reviewed Castellano's disciplinary history and, five years after his first Merc fine, revoked Castellano's registration to fill customer orders. If not for his rejection by the plucky MidAm, Castellano might never have been noticed by the CFTC.

The CFTC revocation, however, hardly meant that Castellano was out of the futures business. To the contrary, he still reports to the trading floor every day, where he is free to trade for his own account and where Melamed's firm continues to clear his trades. The CFTC found that Castellano did not deal fairly with public orders but allowed him to stay in the business. Likewise, the Merc kept Castellano on its membership roles.

Castellano's case demonstrates the perverse distinction regulators make between floor brokers and local traders. Brokers have to be registered with the CFTC because they fill customer orders. Locals are not registered because they trade exclusively for themselves. The rule overlooks the fact that local traders are in contact with the public every day, on almost every trade, taking the other side of customer orders. The trading practices of independent locals most certainly affect the welfare of the general public.

Consider Castellano once again: In November 1989, the Merc found that Castellano had again pre-arranged an S&P 500 futures trade, this time to cover an error. Already banned from handling customer orders, Castellano nonetheless helped take $3,000 out of the pockets of two customers. He was fined $10,000 and ordered to pay the customers back.

Fines and brief suspensions are commonplace at the exchanges, but expulsions are rare and seem to be beyond the will of the exchange disciplinary process. Merc leadership tolerates repeat offenders, and some member firms continue to employ brokers with long records of fraud. It is a system that protects insiders. As regulatory scrutiny increased in 1987 and 1988, the Merc and the Board of Trade did beef up their disciplinary actions. Even so, of 118 traders sanctioned at the two exchanges during those years, only five were permanently barred from trading.

Floor brokers are registered with the CFTC, but supervising them is left to the exchanges. And because of another regulatory quirk, outsiders face a formidable task in trying to discover a floor broker's disciplinary history. There is no central clearinghouse for the information. Brokers fined or suspended at one exchange can continue to trade at other exchanges where they hold memberships. The Merc and the Board of Trade don't share their disciplinary records, despite their overlapping memberships. Neither exchange shares records with the National Futures Association, an agency that registers futures traders and is designed to protect futures customers. The CFTC maintains public files on its own actions but releases only the most cursory information about the disciplinary files of the exchanges it supervises.

□ □ □

THE ELITE REGULATORY STATUS of floor traders and brokers is no accident. Futures exchanges and their members have fought aggressively to maintain their rights of self-governance. Because of inherent public suspicion of futures—Federal Reserve Board chairman Paul Volcker in 1986 referred to futures exchanges as "casinos"—those battles have been intense. But the futures industry has a powerful weapon in these battles: cash. Its wealthy members provide cash to grease the political processes in Washington, cash to provide jobs and other benefits to Chicago and the national economy, and cash to mount formidable public relations assaults on critics.

The Political Action Committees of the Chicago Board of Trade (known as AMPAC, for Auction Markets PAC) and the Chicago Mercantile Exchange (CFPF, for Commodity Futures Political Fund) have liberally distributed cash around Washington for 15 years. The payouts were first conceived, according to CFPF chairman Leo Melamed, to counter an appalling ignorance of futures on Capitol Hill. Over the years, the exchanges have done everything possible to get the most they can from their "education" dollars.

Content for the most part to ignore the futures markets during the sleepy days of the 1960s and early 1970s, lawmakers began to notice Chicago when volume exploded and new, exotic financial contracts surfaced. Highly sensitive to the changing winds and the closer scrutiny of Congress, both the Board and the Merc opened Washington offices in 1978. After choosing quarters just down the street from the White House on Pennsylvania Avenue, the exchanges hired well-connected law firms to lobby their cause. Adding to the exchanges' lobbying muscle was the industry's Washington-based trade group, the Futures Industry Association. And of course, member firms of the exchanges, like Archer Daniels Midland and Cargill Inc., also maintained Washington offices to look out for their own interests, which often ran parallel with the exchanges.

The industry also maximized its insider connections. Futures Industry Association president John Damgard learned the Washington ropes while an aide to vice president Spiro Agnew. Clayton Yeutter, who served as president of the Merc during the late 1970s and early 1980s, left Chicago for Washington to become Ronald Reagan's U.S. Trade Representative, then Secretary of Agriculture for George Bush, and in 1991, the chairman of the Republican National Party. Throughout, Yeutter maintained his ties with Chicago futures exchange policymakers. C. Dayle Henington, the Merc's principal lobbyist in Washington, was on the House Agriculture Committee staff for many years. David P. Prosperi joined the Board of Trade as communications chief in May 1990. He had been deputy press secretary to President-elect George Bush and was press secretary for vice presidential candidate Dan Quayle during the 1988 election campaign.

The well-cultivated Washington alliances have paid off repeatedly. The first big battle won by the futures lobby was a row over futures audit trails. In 1979, the CFTC called for a one-minute time-stamping rule aimed at detecting fraud on the trading floors. This market surveillance measure would have allowed the agency to better reconstruct the sequence of trades and ensure that the customer got the best available price. The CFTC commissioners approved the rule, naively thinking it would have to be implemented.

That audit-trail approval hurled the wrath of a powerful and antagonistic industry lobby at the CFTC. Chicago futures executives and their lawyers visited each of the CFTC commissioners and explained their opposition. They wrote blistering letters to the agency, saying the regulation would be burdensome to brokers and would bring trading to a grinding halt. Legislators who sat on the congressional committees that governed the CFTC were visited and "educated" by exchange representatives, who later sent them generous campaign contributions.

The lobbying effort produced stunning results. The CFTC commissioners reversed their affirmative vote and tabled the time-stamping rule for further study. Computerized audit trails and one-minute trade tracking would not be proposed again until 1986. The futures lobby had Congress wrapped up, and with it the industry's chief regulator.

"The fact is, a regulatory agency views itself as a creature of Congress and searches out the congressional will on issues," a defeated CFTC chairman James Stone said after the commission reversal. CFTC staffers agree that any perception that a federal agency is independent of Congress is a myth. "We always operated as if Congress was our boss, and we were always interested in what they wanted from us," said Marshall Hanbury, executive assistant to former CFTC commissioner Susan Phillips and now a lawyer in private practice.

Until the news of the FBI investigation surfaced in 1989, the CFTC still lacked support in Congress to further tighten trade-tracking procedures, or to ban dual trading. A 1989 Government Accounting Office study found that trade auditing was the biggest weakness in exchange self-regulation.

The lax oversight seemed to matter little to lawmakers influenced by the futures exchanges' big-bucks lobbying tactics. Besides, the free-market philosophy of the wealthy Chicago businessmen appealed to Congress and to Reaganite officials almost as much as their cash. Legislators who had no time to study futures felt they understood what made for good business and what did not. Meanwhile, the exchanges promoted a patronizing position that futures are too complicated for anyone but industry insiders to understand. "Very few of us have any idea what futures are. If we take the view that these guys are honest businessmen, and they don't want us to restrict their business, we can do that," one Washington staffer said.

Exchange lobbying efforts matured in the 1987–1988 election cycle, in part because 1988 was a presidential election year and the all-important year after the October 19, 1987 stock market crash. The New York securities industry went after the futures business with a vengeance after the crash, and the futures exchanges fought back. In that election cycle, the Merc and Board PACs ranked among the ten largest corporate PACs in terms of total receipts and available cash on hand, according to Federal Election Commission data. They collected a record $2.3 million from their memberships. The amount is remarkable because the exchanges' combined membership is less than 6,000 and because Merc officials contend that fewer than half their members make PAC contributions. Politically astute and well-capitalized traders often kicked in more than $1,000 each.

The size of the Chicago PACs dwarfs the political efforts of their Wall Street counterpart, the New York Stock Exchange. The NYSE during the same period collected only $41,000 from members, distributed $35,983 to candidates, and had a slim $32,617 on hand at the end of the reporting period. Although the securities industry does have active lobbying arms beyond the NYSE, it was unprepared for the futures industry onslaught in Congress after the stock market crash.

Predictably, the biggest Chicago handouts go to the members of Congress with the longest tenure in office and to those who hold the top spots on committees that deal with issues vital to the futures industry. Congressional favorites who sit on the House and Senate agriculture and banking committees regularly receive the maximum allowable contributions from exchange PACs—$5,000 for each primary and $5,000 for each general election. Many legislators accept the money even when they are highly capitalized and have not faced a seriously contested election in years.

The combination of big PAC money and an influential constituency back home is irresistible to the Illinois congressional delegation, the futures industry's most powerful asset on Capitol Hill. The 22-member delegation is led by heavyweight House Ways and Means Committee chairman Dan Rostenkowski. Rosty can be counted on to appear at the Chicago Board of Trade's bidding at almost any industry event. Behind the scenes, he is a strong advocate for tax preferences and regulatory independence for the futures industry.

The Merc is closely aligned with Senator Alan Dixon, who sits on the Senate banking committee. When the heat of the CFTC–SEC jurisdiction battle became almost unbearable for Chicago during the summer of 1990, Dixon made a personal appearance in the Merc's S&P 500 futures pit to reassure the troops with a vacuous stump speech. He swore to vanquish Chicago's enemies, which in this case meant he would try to keep the CFTC independent and in charge of regulating stock index futures. To the irritation of many traders, but to the delight of Dixon, the videotape of his three-minute performance was replayed on the trading floor in a continuous loop all of the following day.

Outside of the Illinois delegation, Senate Republican leader Robert Dole is most sought by the exchanges—they funneled $18,000 to the Kansas senator and his Republican leadership PAC (Campaign America) over the eighteen months ended June 30, 1988, and for good reason. He is one of the top-ranking Republicans on the Senate agriculture committee, which controls the CFTC. A fourth-term legislator who was not up for reelection and who had a large campaign surplus, Dole was an important ally in the 1989 reauthorization battles for the CFTC.

On the other side of the aisle, Senate Majority Leader Robert Byrd, a five-term West Virginia Democrat, took $20,000 in Board and Merc campaign contributions during the same period. Byrd was the top-ranking Democrat on the Senate appropriations committee, which drafts tax legislation that at times has been highly favorable to commodity traders, and which also rules on funding for the CFTC.

Senate banking committee members receive generous treatment from the exchange PACs, in part because they oversee the Securities and Exchange Commission, which has campaigned vigorously to take jurisdiction over the futures industry from the CFTC. New York Republican Alfonse D'Amato, an aggressive fund-raiser and banking committee member, received the maximum allowable $10,000 from the exchanges in 1988 for his "D'Amato in '92" campaign. D'Amato had virtually no record on futures-related legislation, but the exchanges decided not to overlook him, nonetheless.

Senators Richard Lugar (R-Indiana) and Pete Wilson (R-California), Senate agriculture committee chairman Patrick J. Leahy (D-Vermont), and Senator Jesse Helms (R-North Carolina) are the other Chicago favorites. House agriculture committee chairman E. "Kika" de la Garza (D-Texas), and members Glenn English (D-Oklahoma) and Dan Glickman (D-Kansas) have also been darlings of the Chicago PACs because they serve on committees with power over taxes or futures industry regulation.

□ □ □

AWASH WITH CASH, and obsessed with buying access, the exchanges do not limit themselves to direct contributions to federal candidates. The two PACs gave $111,000 to national Democratic party campaign funds for redistribution to candidates, and $58,000 to Republican fund-raising committees during the 1988 election cycle.

The PAC-to-PAC transfers to the national committees allow the exchanges to contribute beyond the $5,000-per-election limit. Uncounted thousands more go to "soft money" committees that do not report on a federal level, but provide support for national candidates. And of course, the flood of exchange "honoraria" is difficult to track but is broadly recognized in Congress.

Washington lobbyists credit the Chicago exchanges with elevating the system of honoraria from simple compensation for an appearance to a powerful lobbying tool. The Merc and the Board, under the guise of education, trooped nearly the whole of Congress across their trading floors between 1986 and 1988. The drill never changes. Anyone from Congress ripe for a junket can be invited. The visit usually includes a breakfast or lunch with a few exchange directors, a tour of the trading floors, and some backslapping photos with exchange officials.

The lawmakers depart Chicago $4,000 richer ($2,000 in honoraria from each exchange), with all their expenses paid.

The honoraria gravy train also brings members of Congress to the posh resorts where industry meetings are held, and if the lawmakers can't travel, the exchanges arrange "appearances" in Washington. In 1988, at the height of the battle to defend stock index futures, an impressive array of 16 congressmen and five senators visited the annual Futures Industry Association convention in Boca Raton, Florida, for cocktail parties and a few rounds of golf, and were paid for their trouble. Even that contingent was dwarfed by the 18 senators and 108 congressmen who attended a Merc reception in Washington a few months later.

The flood of influential visitors slowed after the first FBI subpoenas were issued in January 1989, when lawmakers began to worry about the appearance of accepting tainted money. News of the Justice Department's aggressive pursuit of Chicago commodities fraud sent ethical shivers through the clubrooms of Washington. The Board's Donovan and the Merc's Melamed were momentarily at a loss for a strategy. However, needing friends more than ever, the PACs redirected their capital stream and began giving more circumspect contributions to individual candidates while sending big sums to party committees for discreet redistribution to congressmen who might not want to publicly acknowledge a gift from the futures exchanges.

Giving to national dinner committees and sponsoring fund-raisers amplifies the exchanges' financial clout. In 1989, the Merc's PAC paid $15,000 each to the Democratic Senatorial Campaign Committee "Leadership Circle," the Democratic National Committee "Business Council," and the Democratic Congressional Campaign Committee's "Speakers Club." Similarly, the Board's Auction Markets PAC made big aggregate donations in 1989, directing $15,000 to the Democratic National Campaign Committee, $12,000 to the "Presidential Dinner" fund, and $15,000 to the Democratic Congressional Dinner Committee.

The Merc also remembered local pols, giving $30,000 to the primary campaign of Neil Hartigan, the Democratic candidate for Illinois governor. The PAC also gave $15,000 to the successful 1989 Chicago mayoral campaign of Richard M. Daley, son of the late mayor. The local contributions were important for more than appearances sake. As recently as 1982, handouts to local politicians had discouraged attempts to impose city taxes on futures trades.

□ □ □

WITH RONALD REAGAN READY TO LEAVE the White House, Chicago futures pols took an active interest in the 1988 presidential race. The deregulatory environment of the Reagan years had been wonderful for the industry, and exchange executives reasoned that a Bush win would help maintain that bloom by preserving the status quo, burying the stock index futures jurisdiction issue, and capping the battle that followed the stock market crash. If handled correctly, it could also keep congressional friends on their committees on the eve of CFTC reauthorization.

Melamed and Donovan told their memberships that exchange efforts in Washington in the year since the stock market crash had been successful. Not one bill affecting the markets had been passed, and the intense lobbying efforts had boosted the futures industry profile in Washington. Donovan termed incumbent congressmen "investments." The year's massive PAC spending was a method of protecting those investments by keeping the incumbents in office. Political donations "are a cost of doing business," Donovan explained.

In the summer of 1988, George Bush was struggling against a wimpish image in his presidential race against Democratic challenger Michael Dukakis and needed all the friends he could get. Board of Trade president Tom Donovan and Merc chief Leo Melamed were friends. Both were well connected in Washington and in the cash-rich heartland. They and their lieutenants, Board chairman Karsten Mahlmann and Merc chairman Jack Sandner, had visited Washington every week during the prior year, seeking and receiving relief from the hail of criticism that had landed on Chicago after the 1987 stock market crash. Bush knew that he could count on the Chicago futures exchanges for at least a million-dollar transfusion to his campaign.

A month before the 1988 election, both Melamed and lifelong Democrat Donovan had begun to worry about Bush's chances of winning. Bush was pulling away in public opinion polls, but Dukakis was still within striking distance, and the PAC chieftains were pushing for a Bush victory. They were hardly enamored of Bush's likely Treasury Secretary, Nicholas Brady, author of the postcrash study that largely blamed the futures markets for the 1987 crash and criticized the regulatory structure. But Brady was considered far better than Dukakis' probable choice, futures critic Felix Rohatyn.

Many of the Brady report's recommendations were hard for the exchanges to swallow. But the exchanges felt Brady was showing con-

ciliatory signs as the election loomed, and that he would lose interest
in his suggested reforms when the Treasury post provided other distractions. What's more, Donovan's political savvy told him that a chairman of the House Ways and Means Committee was worth more than
a Treasury Secretary. As long as Dan Rostenkowski was a friend,
Brady would get nowhere in a fight to change the regulatory jurisdiction of the futures industry. Besides, Donovan reasoned, "We know
Brady, we understand him."

As for the CFTC, Bush was certain to reappoint Wendy Gramm,
a Texan, to the chairmanship. Gramm, who knew little about the
futures markets when appointed by Reagan in 1986, had been a willing student of the exchanges. She had sided with the exchanges after
the crash and had proved an effective ally in the SEC–CFTC battle
over stock index futures. Her chairmanship had focused on reducing
the regulatory barriers to product innovation within the industry, and
on bolstering the CFTC's image in the eyes of Congress. Gramm was
also the wife of Texas Senator Phil Gramm. If Bush won, it would be
largely because of Gramm's efforts in Texas, and Bush was not likely
to put his friend's wife out of a job.

Dukakis, on the other hand, would be a total unknown. If he won,
it would do more than ruffle the industry's well-organized friendships
in Congress. The reformist and highly disliked Carter administration
CFTC chairman, James Stone, had come directly from under Dukakis' wing, serving as Massachusetts insurance commissioner during
Dukakis' first term as governor. The exchanges feared that a Dukakis
presidency would bring another crusading chairman to the CFTC.

Donovan and Melamed rallied their well-heeled troops and urged
total and unwavering support for Bush. PACs are prohibited by Federal
Election Commission rules from contributing to presidential candidates who accept public campaign funds. However, the exchanges
understood the vagaries of the campaign laws. Their tactic: organize
a massive fund-raiser.

The event, which featured a visit by President Ronald Reagan to
the Merc trading floor and a $5,000-a-plate dinner for selected busi-
ness and political leaders in the Merc dining club, raised $1.3 million
for the Bush Illinois Victory '88 campaign. Merc president William
Brodsky and the Board's Tom Donovan served as vice-chairmen of
the gala, and they mustered their machines vigorously. PAC lieutenants fanned out to sell $250 tickets to the cocktail party that preceded
the dinner, and the exchange staff manned ticket tables on the trading
floors. The week of the event, nearly all of the Merc's government

affairs, marketing, and special events staff was deployed full-time to attend to details. Merc employees returned the night of the party to serve as hosts and hostesses to the crowd.

To top off the fund-raiser's success, the Merc's CFPF donated $10,000 to the Illinois Victory '88 campaign the week of the party. Neither that donation nor the dinner proceeds had to be reported to the Federal Election Commission. The Chicago pols did not begin to suspect that they were pouring funds into the coffers of a Republican administration whose Justice Department was already deep into an investigation of their business practices.

□ □ □

THE BUSH CAMPAIGN WAS A SUCCESS, but the hard-won presidential victory would be savored only briefly by the Chicago exchanges. News of the FBI investigation broke just one day before Bush's inauguration, and the carefully constructed net of Washington friends would suffer considerable damage. In the light of the FBI investigation, Donovan and Melamed would discover that they had miscalculated the intentions of Nicholas Brady who, supported by renewed criticism of the futures industry, led the Bush administration on a campaign to shift CFTC responsibilities to the SEC.

The Chicago futures exchanges were not particularly fond of the CFTC, but through their congressional connections they had the agency carefully within their grip. Ever since the commission had backed down on the time-stamping rule in 1978, it had carried the image of a "puppydog" regulator. Years of disdain from Congress and its own regulatory constituents had left the agency right where it had started—underfunded and inept.

The Commodity Futures Trading Commission was born in 1974 from the ashes of the old Commodity Exchange Authority and left a starveling, understaffed and underpowered. It rarely stepped beyond its paper-pushing functions to take a close look at the trading floors or the exchanges' executive suites. Its commissioners often arrived through the revolving door of the industry, holding loyalties closer to the exchanges and their Washington allies than to the public trust.

Putting a new name and a new face on the old CEA did not automatically transform the agency into a fresh and efficient police force for the futures industry. The dusty, sluggish reputation of the Agriculture Department satellite remained, along with most of the old staff and much the same budget. Public money, billions of dollars of it, passes through the hands of a few thousand futures traders every working day. Trade surveillance is left to the exchanges, who must answer to the CFTC. However, the few CFTC staffers who do visit trading floors make it painfully obvious that they are bewildered by what they see.

The early ignorance of the CFTC staff was notorious. When Board of Trade president Warren Lebeck submitted his proposal for a Ginnie Mae–backed futures contract to the new agency in 1975, CFTC staff pored over the documents for weeks, then returned a reply. "Has the Board of Trade considered if there is adequate storage space for delivery of the new commodity?" the staff letter inquired. Lebeck, astounded, wrote back that yes, there was delivery space. He had an empty file cabinet in his office.

The CFTC's sluggishness amounted to benign neglect during the exchanges' growth years. The Board and Merc expanded their trading volumes by nearly 300 percent between 1980 and 1990. But a look at the CFTC's budget during that decade shows how regulation failed to keep up with progress. Congress in fiscal year 1981 funded the CFTC to the tune of $18.78 million for the oversight of 11 active futures exchanges. The agency had a staff of 479. A decade later, in fiscal 1990, the CFTC's budget had grown to $31.186 million, with staff creeping up to only 529, despite the futures volume explosion. By comparison, the Securities and Exchange Commission's budget was $166.6 million, and it had 2,209 staff.

Willing to leave floor supervision to the exchanges, the CFTC's enforcement and surveillance arms were focused on the old concerns of market manipulation and speculative excesses. The CFTC, critics said, scrutinized paperwork and not practices and spent most of its meager enforcement energies on making certain commodity firms' reporting requirements were met. The CFTC also took an inordinately long time to prosecute disciplinary cases. The London options scandals of the 1970s dragged on for a decade without resolution. The notorious boiler room operations bubbled on during endless administrative hearings and document reviews, with the offending firms sucking in new customers while the regulatory processes dragged on.

□ □ □

RECOGNIZING THAT A BAD PUBLIC IMAGE is bad for business, the futures industry trade group, the Futures Industry Association, in 1976 began framing plans for another regulator. The National Futures Association was to be the futures industry version of Ralph Nader—an agency chartered to look out for public customers and to ferret out negligent firms. Still, its structure was patterned after that of the futures exchanges. It would have members supervising members, making judgments on trade abuses in private tribunals.

As a stepchild of the exchanges, the NFA gave its parents the opportunity to extend their reach over non-exchange futures merchants—the mass of small firms and salesmen that peddled futures products to the public. In a rather subtle trade-off, the NFA's architects, led by Merc chief Leo Melamed and including luminaries of the industry from both Chicago and New York, agreed to tighter regulation for non-exchange firms while trimming the already-minimal federal oversight over floor brokers. The plan also carefully preserved the exchanges' self-regulatory oversight of the big firms that were exchange clearing members.

The NFA was a grand plan, worth a bundle in public relations value. The futures industry portrayed itself as demanding a new regulator to protect the public from unscrupulous futures salesmen. Its beauty was that the public—through a levy on every trade—would foot the bill.

By the time the agency was operational in 1983, the seven founders of the NFA—Melamed and Howard Stotler, former head of the now-failed futures firm that bore his name; Leslie Rosenthal, former chairman of the Chicago Board of Trade; Warren Lebeck, former Board president; John Conheeney, president of the futures division at Merrill Lynch; and George Lamborn and David Johnston, both executives at Balfour, Maclaine Futures, a now-defunct New York firm—had packed its executive committee. They also constructed a 42-member board of directors with such an unwieldy voting structure that few initiatives would come from anywhere but the executive suite.

The NFA's committee personnel is a roster of futures industry insiders: Leo Melamed was chairman of the board from the inception until he resigned his spot in 1989. The NFA made Melamed permanent special advisor to the NFA executive committee after he stepped down as chairman. Merc chairman Jack Sandner appears to have a lifetime lock on the NFA's central business conduct committee, where he has held the chair's slot since the committee's formation. Brian Monieson, another former Merc chairman, was one of the ten

committee members the NFA used to advise futures firms on proper
business conduct. Monieson's advice did not save his own firm, GNP
Commodities, from being ordered out of business by the CFTC for
fraudulent business conduct. Monieson served on the NFA committee
at the time the CFTC considered the GNP sanctions.

Merrill Lynch's John Conheeney took over as chairman of the
NFA board after Melamed's exit, insuring continuity. Although the
board has three "public" directors who are supposed to represent
non-industry interests, it remains an insider's club. One of the current
"non-industry" directors, for example, is Warren Lebeck, an NFA
founding father and former Board of Trade president.

Part of the insiders' deal to create the NFA was to make certain
that the NFA would have no jurisdiction over floor brokers or traders.
"Those guys [floor traders] are very contentious and arrogant, and
they didn't want anybody touching them," recalls Wilmouth, who has
served as NFA chief executive officer since the agency's launch.

Despite the exemption from NFA oversight, floor brokers can
solicit customer orders on or off the trading floor and can supervise
other futures salesmen. Once registered, a floor broker stays that way
unless he or she comes under revocation proceedings. In the spirit of
"paperwork reduction," the NFA in 1986 discarded the annual registration renewal required of floor brokers.

The registration process is further flawed because it relies on
voluntary disclosures on the part of applicants. The NFA and the
CFTC rarely verify the information. In the case of floor brokers, the
NFA by law is not allowed to receive details of exchange disciplinary
proceedings against floor brokers, and so cannot cross-check statements volunteered by the brokers who bother to update their registrations.

The case of Robert L. Schillaci, a 22-year veteran of the Merc,
is an example of the registration process gone awry. Schillaci was a
registered floor broker who also ran an office soliciting customer business. In his spare time, he was treasurer of the Merc's Political Action
Committee. In a 1983 registration application and in subsequent up-
dates, he failed to report that he had a history of rule violations at
the Merc, where he had been suspended twice and paid substantive
fines between 1980 and 1985. The NFA and the CFTC failed to detect
the omissions, even though the CFTC receives copies of all Merc
disciplinary actions.

Schillaci's omissions came to light only after the NFA received
multiple customer complaints about his firm, Masters Trading Or-

ganization Ltd. The NFA's complaint said Schillaci and the firm had used deceptive sales materials, engaged in high-pressure sales tactics, and conducted unauthorized trading in customer accounts. Schillaci settled the NFA complaints by paying a $38,225 fine. The Merc separately fined him $25,000 for pre-arranging trades connected to the scam and suspended him from the trading floor for two years. By then, Masters Trading was out of business, but Schillaci had set up yet another firm.

□ □ □

IN CONTRAST TO THE CFTC's constrained budget, the NFA's treasury ballooned along with futures exchange volume. The initial charge of 0.33 cents per contract for each customer trade drew such riches that the NFA voted to lower the rate repeatedly until it reached 0.20 cents in 1990. In the 1991 fiscal year, the NFA had a $28 million budget, with more than $14 million in cash reserves. Its staff of 316 included some 180 people devoted to compliance duties.

By 1987, when the FBI moles were first setting foot on Chicago's trading floors, the NFA had matured enough to bring regular enforcement cases against its ocean of small operators. When it turned up Florida boiler room sales operations preying on wealthy retirees, or stopped the distribution of misleading sales promotion material, the NFA excelled. Two of its best enforcement actions, according to NFA president Wilmouth, were against Presidential Futures, Inc., of Fort Lauderdale, and Great American Commodities, Inc., of Miami. Both firms were forced to liquidate after the NFA filed complaints alleging sales abuses. Both were relatively small companies with low profiles in the industry.

Those successes are admirable. Still, the NFA rarely takes the lead in cracking down on the members of its core constituency—the giant brokerage houses that are major owners of the nation's futures exchanges. Ruffling the feathers of the powers of the industry seems to be the last thing on the NFA's agenda. Critics charge that when the NFA does discover problems with a big futures trading firm, the agency bows out.

Wilmouth concedes that in cases like the 1990 funding incident that led to the demise of Stotler Inc., one of the country's largest futures firms, the NFA may have dragged its feet. While the Chicago

Board of Trade was Stotler's primary regulator, responsible for monitoring the firm's financial health, the NFA was responsible for safeguarding the funds of thousands of customers who invested with subsidiaries of the Stotler Group. Stotler's army of "introducing brokers," a larger number than in any other firm in the country, was under NFA jurisdiction. Additionally, the NFA was required to scrutinize the investments of Stotler's futures "pool" funds, which invested public money.

In mid-May of 1989, three months before Stotler's collapse, the NFA discovered that a Stotler futures fund had invested in debt securities issued by its parent firm, in violation of NFA and other rules. Rather than act, NFA administrators tabled the case. A few weeks later, the firm's funding problems came to light during an audit by a surprising outsider—the Securities and Exchange Commission. The incident was embarrassing to the NFA, and to all advocates of the futures self-regulatory process.

Wilmouth said the NFA would have moved faster on the Stotler case if it had known that the Board of Trade had Stotler on its "early warning list." Stotler, he said, had been under special financial scrutiny by the Board for more than a year. The transfer of public funds to the parent company would have taken on a different cast if NFA investigators had known of the Board's concerns, Wilmouth added.

The conflict-of-interest problems in the case are evident: Both Karsten Mahlmann, chairman of Stotler, and Howard Stotler, a principal in the firm, were on the NFA's ten-member executive committee at the time of the NFA investigation and during the months leading up to Stotler's collapse. Mahlmann was also chairman of the Board of Trade at the time. There remains the question of whether Mahlmann, in one of those roles, may have had a responsibility to disclose Stotler's financial difficulties to the NFA.

Sometimes the NFA bungles cases because it does not communicate with the CFTC. After receiving numerous customer complaints against Chicago-based Murlas Trading, the NFA began an in-depth investigation of the firm, assigning as many as ten staffers to the case. Despite this effort, the NFA had to table the case after the CFTC filed its own charges against the firm. The CFTC would not be able to force the firm out of business until six years after the initial customer complaints were filed.

When the NFA issues an enforcement action, few people hear about it. Like the futures exchanges, the NFA has held an insider's view of publicizing its disciplinary actions. Until recently, even when a major fine or suspension was rendered by the agency, the names of the parties involved were shielded and news of the action was distributed only to NFA members, and then only on a quarterly basis. Wilmouth explains that broader publicity of the actions would be bad for the industry—an odd worry for a regulatory agency.

This keep-quiet practice backfired in 1989, when shortly after the news of the FBI investigation surfaced, NFA members elected the object of one of the association's own investigations to the NFA board of directors. Larry R. Williams, a California-based money manager with a controversial background, gained a seat on the NFA board by campaigning against overregulation. His campaign letters did not mention his own troubles with the NFA, and the NFA did not bother to mention them either. Williams, according to the NFA, had overstated his investment record and engaged in misleading advertising. Williams was allowed to sit as a director for nearly a full year, an embarrassment to many in the agency, until he lost his appeal and was forced to step down.

□ □ □

THE RECORD OF AGGRESSIVE political contributions, a weak CFTC, and an inept NFA have combined to give the futures industry an unsettling legacy. People and institutions in the futures business who recognized abuses, observed patterns of favoritism, or simply sought a higher level of professionalism, had few places to turn. The exchanges themselves had promulgated rules making it a major violation for a member to publicly criticize the exchange.

With nowhere else to turn, it makes sense that a few insiders, mistrustful of the system, frustrated by the sluggishness of the CFTC, and longing for reform, ultimately turned to an unusual quarter for aid: the FBI.

PART III

CHAPTER NINE

□□□

From Abscam to Hedgeclipper

WITH HIS THINNING BLOND HAIR and blue eyes, his fetching all-American smile, FBI agent Richard Ostrom hardly looks like the direct descendant of an Arab sheikh. But the lineage is one of duty, not of blood. The FBI created a fictitious sheikh in the late 1970s and early 1980s to snare money-grubbing politicians in Operation Abscam. Nearly a decade later, Ostrom and three confederates hit the pits in Chicago's commodity markets to root out fraud on the floor. During the intervening period, the government turned Chicago into the nation's capital of white-collar stings.

Until Abscam, covert enforcement work by the FBI was limited to short-term jobs designed to set up known criminals for arrest. J. Edgar Hoover, the man who built the FBI, disliked undercover work because of its huge expense and the risk that agents acting like crooks would be overcome by the temptation to switch sides. As a result, undercover jobs pre-Abscam lasted only as long as needed to nab the mob chieftain, drug pusher, or fence that was the target of the sting.

Abscam changed both the size and scope of FBI undercover work. The probe, designed to nail corrupt public officials, started in 1978, when the government costumed an FBI agent in traditional Islamic garb and posed him as the head of Abdul Enterprises, a fictitious multinational company. Other agents and operatives then spread the word that the sheikh needed help with immigration troubles. The key operative in Abscam was Melvin Weinberg, a swindler performing as a crooked go-between looking for legislators who could be "helpful" in cutting through red tape. "We put out the word that money was available," Weinberg explained during one of the trials. "We had a honey pot and the flies came."

The bureau filmed reels upon reels of entertaining videotape, one of which featured Representative Richard Kelly of Florida gleefully stuffing money into his pockets in a Washington, D.C., hotel room. The payoff: convictions of six U.S. representatives and Senator Harrison A. Williams, Jr., of New Jersey and, not incidentally, loads of favorable publicity for the gumshoes.

The headlines did not go unnoticed by lawmen, in Chicago or elsewhere. In 1973, the FBI conducted 53 undercover investigations; by 1980, the year Operation Greylord got underway in Chicago, the number had climbed to 300. The various probes led to the convictions of New Orleans mob boss Carlos Marcello for union health insurance fraud; nearly 100 Oklahoma county officials who took kickbacks from a lumber contract; more than 50 Massachusetts fences; and Teamsters Union president Roy L. Williams together with mob hitman Joseph "Joey the Clown" Lombardo for attempting to bribe Nevada Senator Howard S. Cannon in a Las Vegas land deal.

There were a few dismal failures, too. Most notable was Cleveland's Operation Corkscrew, in which the FBI learned too late that the "judge" accepting bribes from hustler Marvin Bray was not a judge at all. The robed man was Bray's friend, only too happy to help him steal more than $100,000 from the feds in an ingenious turnabout scam. But the sting operations still netted enough big fish to whet the FBI's appetite for more.

All the stings shared common elements, including undercover operatives, wide use of electronic wiretapping, and videotaping. But there was more to the FBI's romance with undercover work than a fascination with concealed cameras and pint-sized tape recorders. The apparatus enabled the government to bolster what frequently was the weakest part of its case: the mob informant or street hustler who had agreed to serve the cause of justice. That often meant tying the government's fate to somebody who already was part of the crime problem. When such cases reached trial, the government lawyers knew they would have to defend the character and motives of their star witnesses, who often were getting a pass on their legal troubles by cooperating in the sting. That made the prosecutor's job tough. But in most cases there was no other way.

In Operation Greylord, the government was doubly blessed. Besides the latest recording technology, the probe of corruption in the Cook County courts also featured two undercover operatives with untarnished credentials. Terry Hake was a lawyer in the State's Attorney's office trying felony cases at the Criminal Courts Building at 26th Street and California, next door to the Cook County Jail in a rough South Side neighborhood. Twice he had applied to become an FBI agent, making the waiting list the second time. Still harboring ambitions to join the bureau, Hake was pleased when State's Attorney Bernard Carey and U.S. Attorney Thomas Sullivan asked him to play the role of a disillusioned young lawyer ready to become part of the fabric of bribes and corruption that ruled the county courts. In May of 1980, Hake agreed to participate if the FBI guaranteed him a job afterward. Greylord was underway.

The second Greylord operative was Brockton Lockwood, a thirty-four-year-old judge from Marion, Illinois, a rural town 350 miles downstate from Chicago. Lockwood had filled in during summer vacation for a Chicago judge and was shocked to learn that a prosecutor and a defense lawyer had fixed a case on which he had ruled. Furious, but suddenly suspicious of anyone in law enforcement in Chicago, Lockwood flew to Washington to bring his complaint directly to the Justice Department. Justice at first suspected that Lockwood himself was setting them up—that he was a double agent sent by the Cook County boys who, God knows how, had heard about Hake's secret mission. Eventually, Lockwood won the confidence of the Justice Department, and before long was playing the part of an unscrupulous, hard-drinking, womanizing, free-spending downstate judge who used his stints in the Chicago courts to raise some hell, and some cash. Nobody knew that inside his cowboy boots Lockwood wore a tape recorder wired up his back, over his shoulder, and down the front of his robes.

Hake and Lockwood would provide the entree into a court system rife with corruption. Because circuit court judges had to be slated by political parties to run for office, the bench in Cook County had become as rife with influence peddling and intrigue as any other part of the Chicago political machine. At the top of the slime heap, Hake and Lockwood found Judge Richard F. LeFevour. The chief of traffic court assigned potentially profitable cases like drunken driving and hit-and-runs—cases where defendants gladly would pay a $100 fee to escape conviction—to crooked jurists who would kick back part of the take to him. Honest judges got the less graft-prone cases like speeding or driving with expired plates.

Hake and Lockwood also found Judge "Dollars" Dan Devine, the only judge to accept money directly from Hake rather than through a bagman. They engendered the nation's first legal bugging of a judge's chamber, that of Judge "Warbling" Wayne Olsen. Each of them found that a close friend was corrupt, in Hake's case his best friend Arthur R. Cirignani, and in Lockwood's case a friendly police officer, Ira J. Blackwood.

At the time U.S. Attorney Dan K. Webb announced the first indictments on December 14, 1983, Greylord's undercover phase had nabbed only three judges, three lawyers, and three bagmen. But judging by the hype, one would have thought Webb was bringing the whole system down. The indictments were announced at a packed 2:00 P.M. federal building press conference. The boy-faced Webb was flanked by the top law enforcement officials in the state—Illinois Attorney General Neil Hartigan, Cook County State's Attorney Richard M. Daley, top Chicago FBI man Edward Hagerty, and Chicago Police Chief Richard Brzeczek—but Webb did all the talking. He made certain no reporter would underplay the indictment of nine people, only three of them judges. "In my judgment, when the project is over and all the cases are tried, I believe this will be viewed as one of the most comprehensive, intricate, and difficult undercover projects ever undertaken by a law enforcement agency," Webb promised.

Over time, Greylord delivered. Hake and Lockwood had collected incriminating information on a number of other judges, LeFevour and Devine included, though not enough evidence to bring charges unless early indictees testified for the government in subsequent cases. Greylord could not be a success unless the government won the early rounds in court. And that it did. Except for a setback in the case of Associate Judge John Lurie, in which Hake's testimony seemed contradictory, the Greylord trials rolled up a string of early wins. The U.S. Attorney's office became a processing house for would-be "flippers" ready to turn in their brethren in order to reduce their own jail sentences or fines. In all, nine judges, 37 lawyers, and 19 cops and clerks have been convicted in the Operation Greylord sting, which a decade after it started is only now being discussed in the past tense.

Still, for all its success, Greylord did not lead to sweeping reforms such as selecting judges by merit rather than by politics. Once elected, an almost automatic process after slating by the Democratic party in Cook County, judges can stay on the bench for life as long as 60 percent of the voters approve their retention. Webb, who continues to promote the merit selection concept, still brags that Greylord's conviction record made it the most successful undercover operation ever. But he once told a reporter he is frustrated that the investigation has not promoted sweeping reform. "In terms of institutional impact, Greylord has been a miserable failure," Webb admitted.

□ □ □

GREYLORD WAS A TOUGH ACT TO FOLLOW. It had shaken an entire court system and rolled up a nearly unbroken string of victories at trial. But the next major Chicago investigation was just as juicy. It was called Operation Incubator, and while it fell short of its most ambitious goal—probing for corruption in the mayor's office of the city of Chicago—Incubator did jail 14 people on corruption charges.

The biggest name brought down by Incubator was Morgan Finley, clerk of the Cook County courts. Aldermen Wallace Davis, Perry Hutchinson, Marian Humes, and Clifford Kelley were also brought down by the probe, as was Clarence McClain, Mayor Harold Washington's closest confidant before he got snared in the investigation. What's more, Incubator led to a companion operation in New York that developed into a major scandal in that city's Parking Violations Bureau and led to indictments against several close associates of then-mayor Ed Koch.

Incubator's record is impressive, amazingly so given the background of the government mole. Michael Raymond was sleazy even by comparison to the two-bit hustlers who often serve the government in such a role. In Cook County, his code name was "Muck," a fitting sobriquet. He kept returning to crime the way some people go back to the bottle. Raymond's first known brush with the law came in 1955, when a Manhattan prosecutor summoned him for questioning regarding the disappearance of $40,000 worth of his customer's stock certificates. In 1964, he was arrested by the FBI for allegedly using bad checks to buy securities worth $84,000. Two years later, he was charged with stealing $1 million in securities from a Wall Street messenger. By 1971, he was a hooded witness in a Senate hearing, testifying how he had bribed three New England judges. On December 16, 1983, he was released from federal prison in Texarkana, Texas, after serving 16 months of an eight-year prison term for trying to sell $1.5 million in stolen securities to European investors.

A few weeks later, Raymond landed a job at Systematic Recovery Services, a company competing for Chicago's lucrative parking-fine collection contract. By July, after yet another arrest while carrying a loaded machine gun en route to a planned break-in on an insurance executive's home in Nashville, Tennessee, Raymond suddenly found himself holding two jobs. Besides SRS, he also was working for the U.S. government as an undercover mole. Why a man of Raymond's questionable character would be considered as a possible government agent has never been made clear. But apparently, Raymond was good at his job. In less than a month, he was making his first payoff, $6,500 to a deputy city revenue director.

Ensconced in posh quarters on the 15th floor of the landmark Lake Point Tower apartment building near Chicago's Navy Pier, Raymond went to work. FBI agents in a unit next door filmed and recorded as Raymond—using the alias Michael Burnett—wined, dined, and lined the pockets of several aldermen, courts clerk Finley, and mayoral confidant McClain. The FBI kept such close tabs on Raymond that they even telephoned him during parties to feed him specific questions for his quarry or ask him to have his guests repeat key phrases the tape recorder had missed.

Meanwhile, Raymond's boss at SRS, Bernard Sandow, foolishly bragged to Raymond about his bribing of New York parking officials. Sandow was pressed into work as a government mole in New York after agents played back Raymond's tapes to him. Despite repeated efforts to meet Mayor Washington, Raymond never got any closer than McClain, who received a $10,000 gratuity in return for helping SRS win the city contract but never did make the introduction sought by the mole.

The FBI and the U.S. Attorney's office in Chicago were not the only ones keeping tabs on Raymond's clandestine activities. Beginning in January 1985, a Florida magazine writer named Gaeton Fonzi was also on his tail. Fonzi was working on a story about the swindler Michael Raymond for *Miami/South Florida* magazine when he tripped across a lead that Raymond was working as a government agent in a Chicago sting. The reporter contacted the Justice Department in Washington and told what he knew. He was willing to hold his story, but only if the feds played ball and gave him a briefing on Raymond's activities. If the government did not go along, Fonzi threatened to sell his information to the *Chicago Tribune*, thereby blowing Raymond's cover just as he was making the first inroads among Chicago aldermen and power brokers.

The Attorney General's office, with the cooperation of U.S. Attorney Webb of Chicago, decided to deal with Fonzi. Twice under Webb's reign, FBI agents from Chicago flew to Florida to brief Fonzi on their progress in the investigation. Then, when Anton Valukas succeeded Webb in May 1985, one more meeting took place. Finally, late in December 1985, with Fonzi again threatening to go to press if the feds could not convince him that he would sabotage a vital operation, Valukas and the Justice Department said no. On Christmas Day, both Chicago newspapers carried stories about an undercover probe aimed at Chicago aldermen close to Mayor Washington. Fonzi's patience had paid off: He received $10,000 from the *Tribune* for the background information he provided to the newspaper about Michael Raymond.

Valukas today regrets the arrangement with the mercenary Fonzi. Although he claims the agents "revealed only generically what was going on," Valukas knows the deal tainted his office's image. "I was really embarrassed by the stories, because everybody naturally presumed we were leaking the information," he says. Valukas took steps to make certain his assistants did not get the wrong message and start freely doling out leaks to favored reporters. He called his two top assistants, Ira Raphaelson and Daniel Gillogly, into the office and laid down the law on Operation Incubator: "If anybody leaks anything on this investigation, or puts out any more information, they're history," he barked.

Valukas followed up his verbal outburst with a memo distributed to every lawyer, clerk, and secretary in his office. The new U.S. Attorney was making his point: No leaks, no questions asked. But the incident would taint Valukas's office for the rest of his term. "What it made us look like, to put it bluntly, was an office of whores," Valukas recalls. Three years later, when the *Tribune* broke the news about Operation Hedgeclipper and Operation Sourmash with a detail-packed first-day story and several impressively precise follow-ups, the Fonzi incident would be remembered. Certainly there had been a tip, if not an outright leak. Reporters and defense lawyers throughout the city wondered, with varying degrees of doubt, if somebody in Valukas's office had played ball again.

□ □ □

THOSE WHO KNOW HOW VALUKAS ran his office know that game playing was not his style. He earned the nickname "Tough Tony" for his uncompromising approach to pretrial negotiations and hard-nosed decisions on charging accused criminals. The tough-guy approach produced mixed returns. Valukas likes to point to his many successes—indictments of 50 El Rukn street gang members and the resultant demolition of The Fortress, their aptly named headquarters; convictions in a series of precedent-setting bank fraud cases; indictment of the principals in a nationwide money-laundering scheme—but most of these cases must still come to trial. Two other cases once counted among Valukas's big winners recently became high-profile losses. Three former managers of the Sundstrand Corp., which agreed to a $115 million settlement with the government for overcharging on defense contracts, in October 1989 were acquitted of wrongdoing. And two seedy sports agents, Norby Walters and Lloyd Bloom, in September of 1989 had a guilty verdict set aside on appeal.

Whatever the other results, it is by the commodity cases that Valukas's term as U.S. Attorney will be judged. When the commodity sting idea was placed on his desk in his first days on the job, Valukas was the person for the job. The son of Cook County Circuit Court Judge Anton J. Valukas was born in the all-white Marquette Park neighborhood in Chicago, where Martin Luther King, Jr., would later face a cursing crowd of bigots in one of his most famous civil rights rallies. But by that time, the Valukas family had moved to Palatine, a middle-class community northwest of the city.

After undergraduate work at Lawrence University in Appleton, Wisconsin, Valukas attended law school at Northwestern University, graduating in 1968. He first worked for the Ford Foundation, then in 1970 landed a job on the staff of U.S. Attorney James R. Thompson, as part of the "Kiddie Corps" of young lawyers whose work would help the crusading Thompson build his bridge to the governor's mansion.

After leaving the U.S. Attorney's office in 1977 to join the politically connected law firm of Jenner & Block, Valukas had his first exposure to commodities litigation. Most of his commodities work came in exchange-level disciplinary proceedings, where he successfully defended such high-profile traders as Maury Kravitz. At the Board of Trade, Valukas unsuccessfully defended clients accused of nefarious activities including stealing points from customers and misallocation of winning trades.

In his biggest commodity case while in private practice, Valukas defended Richard C. Groover, a 50-year-old soybean trader at the Chicago Board of Trade. Groover, together with four other traders, a salesman, and a customer, was charged with fraud by U.S. Attorney

Sam Skinner in June 1977, after a 15-month investigation. Groover was accused of working with fellow floor traders Edward A. Arnold and Robert N. Meyer, Jr., who was legally blind and had a dog in the trading pit with him, to rip off customers by skimming profits at the opening and close of trading. Meyer's blindness was a help to the prosecution—his clerk kept detailed written records of all of Meyer's legal and illegal trades. The group traded only with each other, allotting customer profits to their own accounts and making their customers eat the losses, picking prices from within the opening range and closing range of trading to help hide their tracks. It was a tactic that would become familiar to FBI undercover agents a few years later. In the Groover case, Valukas negotiated a guilty plea to 3 of 62 counts against his client, but also agreed to a $100,000 fine: a mixed result for Groover.

On another case during this period, Valukas pulled out all the stops. He claimed that the grand jury process had been abused, charging that information collected in the criminal investigation was improperly shared with the CFTC. Valukas's claim was discredited when Assistant U.S. Attorney Stephen J. Senderowitz proved that Valukas's key witness to the supposed grand jury indiscretions, was romantically involved with one of the defense lawyers and thus had a motive to help thwart the prosecution.

Years later, after Operations Sourmash and Hedgeclipper first went public on January 18, 1989, the newspaper accounts played up Valukas's private practice experiences as a key to the investigation. "Commodities Interest Gives Valukas Edge," sang the *Tribune*. Valukas laughs at the hype. "My prior involvement in commodities had little to do with what happened here," he says now. Still, associates explain that Valukas often fretted that the exchanges, owned by members, were run solely for the benefit of members. He complained that the opening and closing ranges were fraught with abuse of customer orders. Trades were regularly "busted" so that one or another trader could dodge a loss, leaving a customer's profit opportunity as worthless as the torn-up order tickets strewn on the floor.

□ □ □

VALUKAS IS RIGHT ABOUT HIS COMMODITIES experience being overblown. Certainly, it meant that the man who oversaw most of the sting operation did not need basic schooling about the markets. But that was a bonus. What was most important was that the FBI and the U.S. Attorney's office should understand commodities. And that they did. For nearly a decade, beginning in late 1979, the two agencies had worked together on a series of successful and far-reaching crackdowns on commodities fraud. Most of the work concentrated on bucket-shop activity off the exchange floors, but the early experience served as a primer for some of the key players in the eventual undercover investigation.

The first of the scam shops that caught the attention of lawmen was Archaray Enterprises, a New York City firm that marketed commodity options investments to unsophisticated investors. Commodity options at the time were illegal, but that made little difference to Raymond Day, Archaray's owner. At its height, Archaray employed 45 salesmen who did cold call telephone selling, urging their marks to buy options on gold, silver, platinum, and heating oil at rock bottom, before prices rose. "These guys were prophets because silver just went up and up," recalls Paul Jenkins, the FBI agent who headed the investigation. There was just one hitch: The customer money was never invested. When Archaray was raided in September 1979, only about $20,000 in assets was found. The $2 million customers had invested at the time would have been worth $19 million thanks to the soaring price of silver and gold. Raymond Day would later be a star witness at congressional hearings about commodity fraud, bragging about his skill at ripping off customers. The customers would never get their money back.

Archaray was only the first of many boiler rooms that Jenkins, together with Assistant U.S. Attorneys Senderowitz and Scott Lassar, would find during several years of commodity rip-off investigations. Senderowitz, whose nickname "TV Stevie" was an apt recognition of his love of hype, would bring the scams to the public's attention with frequent comments in the press. Along the way, Jenkins recruited Jeffrey Frank, a young CPA new to the FBI's Chicago office, to help him with paperwork. It was Frank's first exposure to commodities, a good primer for his future job of running day-to-day business for Operation Sourmash.

After uncovering the blatant fraud at Archaray, Jenkins asked Senderowitz why such an outfit was not more closely regulated. "I thought, well, there's got to be somebody who regulates these guys," Jenkins recalls. Senderowitz suggested that the CFTC would have authority, but when Jenkins called on the agency's Chicago office, he could not believe the lack of savvy. "I said, 'Well, what do you do?' "

he recalls. "They handed over a white book of regulations. When they went to crack down on a shop, they weren't getting responses to their requests for records. I thought, what's wrong with this picture?"

Amazed at the CFTC's timidity and naivete, Jenkins invited the CFTC's top Chicago enforcement officer to the next raid, at the Clearwater, Florida, offices of Jefferson National Investment Corp. that November. For John Troelstrup, who liked to call himself the commission's "Top Cop" in Chicago, the invitation was the start of a working relationship that would serve all three organizations—the CFTC, the FBI, and the U.S. Attorney's office—when the undercover operations were launched a few years later. The enforcement trio was together again in March 1980 on a bust of E.K. Capital Corp. of New York City, also a boiler room peddling illegal precious metal options. Eventually, they would be the first to use federal racketeering laws to bust on a boiler room operation.

After a while, the different scam shop busts seemed to run together, because all the boiler rooms used the same strategy: Get the money from the customer with a high-pressure sales pitch; don't invest it anywhere; hope that the price goes down, so the customers will believe the money was lost in the market. There was one hitch. If the price went up and the customers wanted their money, there was trouble.

The real paydirt came when the Commod Squad crossed paths for the first time with Jack Rose. It was a case that fell in their laps when two employees of Rose's firm showed up at the FBI offices in Miami and said they wanted to turn in their bosses at First Guaranty Precious Metals. Only later would the feds learn that the pair of apparent do-gooders were themselves under suspicion by the firm for embezzlement. But that was a relatively minor matter.

Rose was an operator unlike any other. Jenkins considered his setup "the 7-11 of boiler rooms." He had started as the protégé of another accomplished scam artist, David Bentley of Fort Lauderdale, Florida, but it was not long before the pupil surpassed his mentor. Before Rose eventually was put out of business, he had opened Atlantic Gold Coins boiler rooms across Florida and in Meditri, Louisiana, and a New York City shop called Empire Precious Metals. Some of the salesmen Rose trained would spread out to the West Coast to set up shop.

After First Guaranty was forced out of business, Rose and two associates established Whitehall Investments International. It was a dream come true for the seasoned scam artist: a real, live trading firm that actually sent customer orders away to be executed on the exchanges. Rose had an almost poetic notion about what Whitehall could mean to his fortunes. Describing it later to government agents, he called Whitehall "a license to steal."

The object of Rose's new game was to make money by generating huge commissions from excessive trading. As long as the accounts were churning, nobody even cared if the market went up or down. So it was that Whitehall's sales manager, Billy Wolf, would stand in the firm's sales room and utter three simple but elegant words: "Sell, sell, sell."

All that business was lucrative—Rose took in $75 million from one of his businesses alone from 1982 to 1983. But in his current home in a Florida prison, where he bides his time along with David Bentley, Jack Rose does not have much of a chance to spend any of it. In any event, the government long ago seized the funds.

□ □ □

AS THE RECORD OF BUSTS BEGAN TO BUILD, Senderowitz, Jenkins, Frank, and Troelstrup would hear a familiar refrain. "They would tell us, 'You guys are looking at the wrong place,' " Jenkins recalled. "The commodity exchanges are where you ought to be." The advice made sense. The boiler-room salesmen commonly were veterans of legitimate trading firms who had left the business to make money the easy way. Senderowitz, before he left the U.S. Attorney's office, had catalogued enough fraud to make a prosecutor's stomach churn. With the publicity the crackdown was getting, boiler shop activity actually seemed to be slowing down, so the trading floor seemed a logical place to turn.

The time was right. All the government needed was an opportunity. They would not have long to wait.

The market in action on the floor of the Chicago Board of Trade. The "open outcry" trading system puts a premium on strength, size, and vocal power as traders jockey for position in the pits.

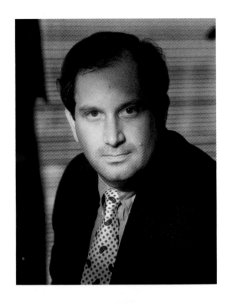

Right: Assistant U.S. Attorney Ira Raphaelson, whose late-night visits to traders' homes unnerved traders and outraged their lawyers. Promoted to Acting U.S. Attorney, he led the successful prosecution of soybean traders. (Kevin Horan)

Below: FBI Agent Randall Jannett (badge JXN 327) at work undercover in the Chicago Mercantile Exchange currency pit. Trading under the assumed name of Randy Jackson, he was a passable local trader but bungled his way through a day as a Swiss franc broker. (© Chicago *Tribune* Company. All rights reserved, used with permission.)

Left: Dwayne Andreas, politically powerful chairman of grain-trading giant Archer Daniels Midland. A longtime critic of the Board of Trade, he offered to train FBI agents even as his own firm made questionable trades in the Board's pits. (Noel Neuberger)

Below: William Brodsky, president of the Chicago Mercantile Exchange, and Merc executive committee chief Leo Melamed address reporters after disclosure of the investigation. The Merc's image-makers nimbly put the best spin possible on events. (© Chicago *Tribune* Company. All rights reserved, used with permission.)

Leo Melamed

Right: John F. "Jack" Sandner, seven-time chairman of the Chicago Mercantile Exchange. Revelations about his ties to powerful broker groups and hiring of former salespeople from a scandal-plagued trading firm came to light in the midst of the public outcry over the FBI investigation. ()

Bottom: Karsten "Cash" Mahlmann, who advocated a closed-mouth approach to the scandal as chairman of the Board of Trade. Improper transfers of customers' funds at his firm Stotler & Company forced him to resign from the Board. (Michael L. Abramson)

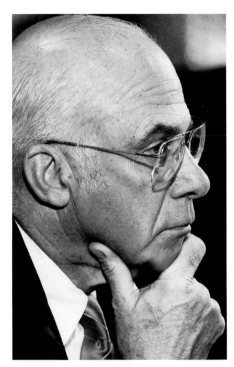

Left: John Geldermann, elected chairman of the Merc just days after the investigation went public. He strongly favored computerization in the pits to help eliminate trading improprieties. (Reprinted with permission from the Chicago *Sun-Times*)

Below: Clayton Yeutter, former Secretary of Agriculture and now National Chairman of the Republican Party. His past ties to the Chicago Mercantile Exchange came under scrutiny as part of the FBI probe. (Chicago Mercantile Exchange)

The first meeting of the Merc's "blue ribbon committee," formed to review trading practices after disclosure of the FBI sting. Several heated arguments punctuated the proceedings. (Wide World Photos)

"Cash" Mahlmann and Board of Trade President Thomas R. Donovan, testifying in defense of futures industry self-regulation before the Senate Committee on Agriculture, Nutrition, and Forestry. (Chicago Board of Trade)

Left: Wendy L. Gramm, chairman of the beleaguered Commodity Futures Trading Commission, defending the commission's enforcement record before a Senate Agriculture Committee in 1989. She was kept in the dark about the undercover sting until days before it went public. (Wide World Photos)

Below: Former U.S. Senator Thomas Eagleton, embarrassed by his link to the Chicago exchanges, resigned from the Merc board after claiming that self-regulation was the "Chicago mirage." (Wide World Photos)

Left: "If we have to instill the fear of God into any member of this exchange, we will do that."—Merc executive committee chairman Melamed on August 3, 1989, the day after the government announced the indictments. (Reprinted with permission from the Chicago *Sun-Times*)

Below: U.S. Attorney Anton Valukas announces the indictment of 45 futures traders and one clerk, culminating the two-year undercover investigation. From left to right: FBI Director William Sessions; Valukas; U.S. Attorney General Richard Thornburgh; CFTC chairman Wendy Gramm. (Reprinted with permission from the Chicago *Sun-Times*)

CHAPTER TEN

□□□

The Origins of the Sting

IN THE OFFICE OF DWAYNE O. ANDREAS, atop the headquarters building of grain-trading giant Archer Daniels Midland, hangs a reproduction of *Dinner for Threshers*, one of painter Grant Wood's masterpieces. In Wood's straightforward, naturalistic rendering, a group of spruced-up field hands eats an abundant meal at a long boardinghouse table. The view is obtained because one wall of the building has been cut away in the manner of a Hollywood studio set. The overalls-clad threshers, hungry and tired from a day in the fields, go about eating their hearty meal without once glancing over their shoulders to see that they are being watched.

The vantage Wood offered of rural life in 1934—the opportunity for observation without being observed—was the same one that, 50 years later, the iconoclastic Andreas offered to the FBI. But the focus of the bureau agents was very different from the threshers' sublime dinner: life in the hurly-burly of Chicago's commodity pits. For years, the Chicago office of the FBI could only dream about the chance to monitor the actions of the mysterious, tightly knit world of commodities trading in its raw, unadulterated form. Now Andreas would help make the dream come true.

Andreas' commodity trading firm, ADM Investor Services, would train an agent or two, help them fit into the fabric of the trading floor, and let them go to work enforcing the nation's laws. If the FBI was good at its job, it could capitalize on this rare opportunity. This would be the agency's best chance to impose law and order in a place where, the FBI suspected, the rule of market men overwhelmed the rule of law.

The southern Illinois river town of Decatur would seem an unlikely birthplace for an undertaking aimed at the brawny, hustling commodities markets of Chicago. Surrounded by boundless acres of black-dirt Illinois soybean farms, Decatur is a crusty company town of 94,000 inhabitants. The only corporation that matters to Decatur is ADM, the nation's largest food processor and by far the city's biggest employer. Steam from the firm's grain milling smokestacks fills the air, and trucks loaded with ADM's corn and soybeans fill the streets. When the farm belt blossoms, Decatur booms, but when grain prices fall, the city falters.

Nowhere is the ebb and flow of the farm economy felt more keenly than in the spacious office of Decatur's first citizen, Dwayne O. Andreas. He rules every facet of the nation's largest grain-processing firm, a company with $7.9 billion in revenues, and Illinois's second-largest exporter (behind equipment maker Caterpillar Inc.). With the agricultural sector improving from the depression of the mid-1980s, with strategic positions in Europe and the Soviet Union, with an unmatched record of successful lobbying for farm interest legislation thanks to the one million dollars in campaign donations Andreas has made since 1979, ADM is the nation's most successful food processing company.

All of that makes Andreas, a craggy-faced, diminutive man of 72, one of the agricultural economy's most important citizens. He's come a long way from the Minnesota-born farm boy who grew up in Lisbon, Iowa, where his father ran a grain elevator. Andreas dropped out of Bible-thumping Wheaton College when a lack of spiritual yearning convinced him the ministry was not his calling. Instead, he went to work running his family's Honeymead Products Co., which he promptly sold to Minneapolis grain giant Cargill just as he was drafted to fight in World War II. But the war ended before Andreas entered the military, so he went to work for Cargill. Then, in 1965, he joined the struggling ADM, along with his brother Lowell, as a turn-around team.

The two Andreas boys certainly did the job, although Lowell, who was perhaps more responsible than Dwayne for ADM's early success, would not live to enjoy the fruits of his work. Today, ADM has processing plants throughout the United States and Europe. Besides being the largest grain processor in the nation, ADM is also a major producer of gasoline substitute ethanol, a major producer of corn sweeteners, and a leading developer of biodegradable plastics impregnated with cornstarch. Years of courting Soviet leaders appear poised for a payoff, and new processing plants in the United States and Europe will meet the growing need for growth-promoting animal feed. Andreas's personal holdings of ADM stock is worth around $83 million, and he earns a salary topping $1 million per year. Four of the company's 15 board members are Andreas relatives.

The company owes a large measure of its success to Andreas's shrewdness as a lobbyist for farm interests, ADM's in particular. An inspired back-room dealer, he has been credited with preserving tax abatements for ethanol, promoting the government's Export Enhancement Program that subsidizes soybean oil and wheat exports to the Soviet Union, and maintaining an import tax that protects domestic sugar from foreign competition. On Capitol Hill, Andreas gets a key assist from fellow ADM board member and master lobbyist Robert S. Strauss.

Still, Andreas's disarming aw-shucks manner, knowledge of the issues, and ample political war chest make him a potent lobbying force in his own right. A political gameplayer, golfing buddy to everyone who matters in Washington, D.C., and closest American pal of Soviet President Mikhail Gorbachev, Andreas is a man who gets his way. When he doesn't get his way, he gets even—a lesson Chicago's commodities exchanges learned all too well.

□ □ □

NO MAJOR COMMERCIAL TRADING FIRM has ever had completely amicable relationships with the Board of Trade. From Cargill in the 1930s to Ferruzzi Financiaria S.p.A., which allegedly tried to corner soybeans in 1989, commercial firms have always complained about market conditions, grain quality standards, and warehousing procedures—seemingly trivial and technical matters, but gripes that amount to big money when millions of bushels of grain are involved. ADM is no exception. A Board of Trade member since 1927, Archer Daniels Midland has had any number of reasons to dislike the Board.

Andreas's main beef is about the Board's rules that designate only Chicago and Toledo as acceptable delivery sites for grain and soybeans, two of ADM's primary raw materials. He has long complained that the Board's opening and closing price ranges invite manipulation of customer orders, and that the practice of establishing closing settlement prices is also fraught with fraud. "It's really gotten to the point where it's nothing but a gambling den up there," Andreas complains. "The prices on the Chicago Board of Trade bear no resemblance to reality, to the true prices anywhere outside Chicago."

Andreas's continuing frustration with the Board of Trade, his persistent perception that the exchange's trading floor was a rigged market where not even honest members of the exchange could get a fair price, prompted him to complain to the government about conditions in the markets. In late 1984, Andreas sent ADM's director of security, Michael Cheviron, to Chicago to knock at the government's door, complaining about market manipulation and the rough-and-tumble world down on the trading floors.

Cheviron first approached the Chicago office of the Commodity Futures Trading Commission. The CFTC referred the informant to the FBI—a proper move, but one that would cost the beleaguered agency a chance for a much-needed publicity boost when the investigation eventually went public. Rather than becoming an image-building coup for the CFTC, the investigation became a nightmare in which the commission was portrayed as uninformed and inactive, a regulator asleep at the switch. Even so, with the Chicago FBI office's broad experience in commodity matters, the bureau was the best agency to handle this type of investigation.

And besides, the CFTC's Chicago supervisor, Dennis Robb, knew quite well that Ernest G. Locker, Jr., the FBI's methodical and tenacious head of the Chicago white-collar crime unit, had been searching for an opening to the Chicago commodities markets for more than a year. In numerous preliminary meetings with FBI agent Paul Jenkins in Chicago-area hotels, then with Locker and other FBI agents from the bureau's Squad Seven, ADM security chief Cheviron put his complaint simply. "We're a major player down there, and things are just not right," participants in those early meetings recall Cheviron saying.

The ADM complaints might have raised little more than a sympathetic shrug if it were not for the legacy of commodity rip-off cases brought by the U.S. Attorney's office in Chicago during the early 1980s—from Archaray Enterprises, to David Bentley and Jack Rose, to Board of Trade broker Mark Caruso, a floor trader nailed by the FBI for fraudulent trading after complaints by his customers. For the FBI agents who had worked those cases, ADM's sudden appearance on the scene was a windfall. "We were being told that if you were an honest man in the pits, you couldn't make it because nobody would do business with you," recalls one former investigator who was present during the initial meetings. "Nobody believed me, until this guy showed up."

Satisfied that the ADM complaints were legitimate, and assured that the firm would do whatever it could to discreetly assist an undercover operation, Locker set up a meeting with the U.S. Attorney's office in Chicago, as the first step toward securing Justice Department approval for a full-blown undercover investigation. The U.S. Attorney who agreed to meet with Cheviron late in 1984 was Daniel K. Webb, who was in the final months of his term of office. By the time the new U.S. Attorney, Anton Valukas, would bring charges against traders on August 2, 1989, Webb was in a flourishing private practice at major Chicago law firm Winston & Strawn. His client list included a number of traders charged or under scrutiny in the very investigation that he initiated. One of his clients, Howard J. Goberstein, would be the first trader to plead guilty to racketeering—a major victory for the investigation Webb helped initiate. Moreover, when the Board of Trade needed a criminal law expert to advise the exchange and its members on defending against charges under the Racketeer Influenced Corrupt Organizations Act, it turned to none other than former prosecuting attorney Webb.

□ □ □

THE FIRST MEETING IN WEBB'S federal building office was crowded with prosecutors, FBI agents, and ADM officials. Webb, at least one Assistant U.S. Attorney, Locker, and another FBI agent represented the government. And ADM security chief Cheviron ushered in a five-person delegation that included Andreas himself, participants recall. The meeting was brief and to the point, and the result was expected. Andreas and Cheviron outlined ADM's complaints, then the FBI outlined its proposal: a plan to infiltrate the exchange. With ADM's help the undercover agent—only one covert operative was contemplated at first—would work his way up the system at the Board, from ADM's back offices to runner to clerk to floor trader. His rise would be swift, but he would cover all the bases, so as not to arouse suspicion. The agent would project the image of someone on the make, looking for all the angles, happy to break the rules to make a quick buck. Word would get around. It always did on the floor. Once inside the pits, the agent would look for bad guys, try to win their trust, and hope the kinky business would come his way.

Andreas agreed to the plan. For the government agents, that meant it was time to start work. The operation would not come cheap, or easy, and it was not a guaranteed winner. This would be harder than simply outfitting an agent to look like a crooked city worker or a lawyer with cash in his briefcase. There was the matter of buying a $300,000 exchange seat, setting up house in the tony Presidential Towers apartment complex, requisitioning a Mercedes sedan from the bureau's undercover car pool, buying a Rolex watch, and landing a membership at the swank East Bank Club where many traders exercise.

There were also expensive and vital housekeeping details. For each undercover agent, probably five or six people would need to work behind the scenes at the federal building. Once the agent got going, there would be tapes to transcribe, catalog, and cross-reference. Trading records would have to be checked with the help of the Commodity Futures Trading Commission—aside from some coaching of agents, that agency's lone contribution during the undercover phase of the investigation. A mind-numbing surfeit of government forms would have to be kept. The trail of evidence would have to be impeccable. Traders were not street thieves who would roll over and die when the government said "boo." They would hire the best legal talent in town, and a minor evidentiary mistake could cost the government its case.

Before any of the operation could proceed, there was the matter of winning approval both from the bureau and from Justice. This would be classified as a Group One undercover project, the highest risk, highest priority designation. It would need approval from U.S. Attorney Edwin Meese and FBI Director William Webster. One of the FBI agents involved in Sourmash from the beginning describes the hurdles that had to be crossed. "The project had to go through intense review similar to a Title Three [wiretap] form," the agent explained. "You can't just go bug somebody's house because you think you might find something." He ticked off the obstacles one by one: "You've got to have probable cause, you've got to have a reasonable chance of success. You've got to have a very specific proposal outlining what kind of manpower you're going to need, how long it's going to take, what you're going to find. It has to pass the undercover committee. Then the director has to sign off on it."

The project also needed a code name for use by the two agencies. After some noodling, someone devised the name "Sourmash," a fitting tribute to ADM because it was a term used in processing grain, and an ironic-sounding turn of phrase.

The proposal first went to the FBI's local undercover review board in the Dirksen building. After receiving the okay, Special Agent in

Charge Edward Haggerty signed an approval form. From there, the proposal went to Washington for review by the bureau's top undercover review panel. And for a moment, it hit a snag. "It was a very hard sell to the bureau at headquarters," remembers Paul Jenkins, the former FBI special agent whose boiler room work in the early 1980s led to his involvement at the beginning of Sourmash. "We told the bureau that this was not going to be a quick-hit type of thing. We suspected that it was going to take quite some time after the undercover agent went down there, particularly somebody new, to be accepted." After questions about cost, probable cause, and chances for success were ironed out, the committee approved the proposal. Webster signed off, and several months after the initial meeting in Webb's office, Operation Sourmash was a go.

□ □ □

WITH SOURMASH APPROVED AND UNDERWAY, it was an odd time for what ADM allegedly did next: turn a quick trick in the soybean oil market. In March 1985, according to charges considered by the Board of Trade's Business Conduct Committee, ADM's soybean-oil traders devised a scheme to make a quick, automatic profit with a gambit that for one day would manipulate the price of soybean oil.

This was no cornering attempt that would take months to see through. Rather, it would have the opposite effect from a corner—it would drive prices down briefly so ADM's traders could make money on the rebound. According to Board of Trade charges and interviews with exchange staff and former directors, ADM's traders quietly sold short a significant number of soybean-oil contracts late one afternoon as the March expiration approached. This put the firm in a position to profit if prices went down, just as ADM's traders would expect if the alleged scheme worked correctly.

The next morning, ADM registered a large number of soybean-oil storage receipts with the Board of Trade's registrar's office. Traders register delivery receipts to announce they have a supply of a commodity available for delivery. The predictable result is that prices fall, because registration is a sign of increased supply of the commodity. Sure enough, soybean-oil prices fell after the ADM registrations. When the market hit bottom, ADM bought back the contracts it had sold the day before, pocketing a handsome profit. Then, after the close of trading, the firm removed the receipts from the registrar's office, again reducing the known supply of soybean oil in the marketplace. Angry traders, caught off guard by the soybean-oil shell game, cried foul. The Board's Business Conduct Committee investigated and brought manipulation charges against ADM.

That's when the case took an unusual turn. Andreas refused to allow anyone from ADM to appear before the committee, only the second time in the exchange's history that a member firm had done so. Instead, he sent lawyers from the Jenner & Block law firm. Arriving in the Board's wood-paneled fifth-floor boardroom, Andreas lawyers explained that ADM felt the charges were baseless. No ADM representative would appear to answer them.

A shocked Business Conduct Committee quickly dismissed Andreas' representation, and just as quickly ordered a $50,000 fine for the affront. "We've never seen anything like it, before or since. That's just not the way the game is played," said a Board official. ADM's unorthodox response particularly shocked board members who had hoped that the firm's attitude toward the exchange would soften after Michael Andreas' term as a director of the exchange. Still, the hardball ADM tactic worked impeccably. The manipulation charges were dropped for lack of evidence. Even worse for the Board, the company later successfully appealed the fine for failing to testify and had it reduced to $25,000.

For Dwayne Andreas, the incident undoubtedly confirmed his feeling that the Board lacked the ability to keep its own house in order. His firm, a major player at the Board, had been publicly upbraided for what he considered an incidental indiscretion in one of the exchange's minor trading pits, yet all across the floor real crime was taking place—pre-arranged trading, matching customer orders in a noncompetitive fashion, shaving points from customers during the opening and closing ranges. It was high time for the exchange to learn what its priorities should be, and Andreas was happy to be helping in the education.

Cagey as ever, Andreas still will not talk directly about his role in Operation Sourmash. Asked about it, he at first denies any participation. Reminded that the government discussed minor details of ADM's role, Andreas has an odd response. "We didn't have anything to do with it," he says. "And if we did, I'd lie to you about it anyway."

□ □ □

AT THE FBI'S CHICAGO OFFICE, Locker and his colleagues were occupied with weightier matters. In fact, one agent claimed the FBI was not even aware of the soybean-oil episode until press reports after the investigation went public. The first order of business for Operation Sourmash, and probably the single most important decision of the entire project, was choosing the right agent. Jeffrey Frank, the special agent Locker designated to run the day-to-day aspects of the operation, recalls that finding the right person was no easy task. Locker preferred someone with an accounting background, both for the financial skills and for the frame of mind. An accountant himself, Locker thinks accountants make the best undercover agents because they are trained to be objective, analytical, and clerically skilled: three important attributes for someone charged with gathering and compiling complex, detailed information. Moreover, the kind of mind-numbing drudgery necessary to learn the skills of accountancy would have its parallel in the long, sometimes redundant hours of transcribing, filing, and cross-referencing records that would be needed to create a paper trail thorough enough to win convictions in the investigation.

The technical skills were a necessity. But there was another, equally important necessity: social skills. The undercover agent would have to assimilate to life in the pits quickly enough to fit in, become known as rule breaker, and observe illegal activity without raising suspicion. Of the three, breaking into the social fabric of the Board would be the biggest challenge. "The whole idea is that this is a closed society," said an agent involved in the investigation. "The interrelationships are amazing. One person knows somebody because they used to belong to the same synagogue, they're a fourth-generation Irishman, or they've played golf together for years. You can't just show up out of the blue and become part of that."

Frank and Locker also were concerned about keeping the agent's head straight in the fast-lane life of commodities traders. The bureau needed to guard against a corollary to the "Stockholm syndrome," common in kidnappings and hostage-takings, in which hostages become sympathetic to their captors. "You had to choose somebody who was levelheaded enough to drive a Mercedes and not get drunk on that," the agent said, "FBI agents aren't getting rich on the job. They have to be frugal. For some people, it could be too much."

The FBI's central computer has in its files the names of 8,000 agents volunteering for undercover assignments. The files include complete background information on each person's life experiences, education, interests, hobbies, job history—anything that might yield a good match of agent and assignment. It was to this talent pool that Locker and Frank turned to find the right person for the Sourmash undercover work. "If you plug into the computer and say 'We want someone who's traded commodities for four years and has a Harvard MBA,' we don't get a lot of those," quipped Frank.

For security sake, the names were cross-checked against any number of potential coincidences that might blow the cover off the operation. "Nothing could be worse than having a guy undercover down there and have him bump into someone he went to high school with who knew he was with the FBI," explained a bureau source. High school and college yearbooks were checked against the Board's membership list. Prospective applicants were asked whether they knew anybody at the exchanges or the clearing firms. If even their wives knew anyone, it was cause for disqualification. The agent definitely had to come from somewhere outside Chicago and had to pass a psychological examination.

For Frank, the computer work was really just a back-up. He had an agent in mind even before crunching any data: Richard Ostrom. A former teammate on the Eau Claire, Wisconsin, high school football team, and still a close friend, Ostrom was aptly suited to the job. A balding, blond-haired, stocky man of 31, Ostrom had taken an accounting degree from the University of Wisconsin–Eau Claire. After working two years at the Milwaukee office of accounting firm Touche Ross & Co., he had joined the FBI. Bureau work took him to Peoria, Illinois, and then to New York City, where he worked on white-collar crime and antiterrorism, but now he was anxious to move back to the Midwest.

Frank knew Ostrom had more than a background profile that would please Locker. He had the social makeup, too. Ostrom had a gregarious but low-key personality that suited him to the job at hand. Frank gave him a ringing endorsement, and Locker seconded the choice. When the computer printed out Ostrom's name among several dozen qualifiers, the choice was made.

□ □ □

SOURMASH WAS UNDERWAY at the Board, but that meant the initial phase of the undercover probe was only half started. The bureau had nothing going at the Chicago Mercantile Exchange, and a Merc operation was vital. First, having stings at both exchanges would protect the operation from charges of favoritism toward either exchange. And besides, Locker and others at the bureau suspected that the Merc was at least as bad as, and probably worse than, the Board of Trade. The Merc's membership list is full of surnames that are familiar to the bureau's mob enforcement unit. In addition, the existence of a cliquish ruling group with Leo Melamed at the top fed persistent rumors about favoritism in the rule-enforcement process. There were occasional rumors about a high-ranking government official with ties to the exchange leaking information to Merc officials before official release times. And the history of the scandal-tainted collapse of gold trading was still another reason a Merc operation was a necessity.

Months passed. Before the bureau could make any inroad at the Merc, Ostrom was working his way into the soybean pit as a would-be trader named Rick Carlson. A second agent, Michael Bassett, was placed on the Board as a clerk named Michael McLoughlin, with an assignment to eventually become a trader in the Treasury-bond pit, the Board's most active. Then, at long last, the bureau found a way into the Merc, through a ten-year veteran trader, William Todd.

Diminutive by traders' standards at 5'7" and 155 pounds, Todd had worked for eight years as a floor broker for Heinold Commodities, but had left the firm when it was acquired by Geldermann Inc. At age 44, with thinning white hair and a pasty complexion, Todd was practically a graybeard at the Merc. He had cut his teeth in the gold pit, probably the most notorious locale in the history of the Chicago markets, before it collapsed under the weight of its own bad reputation. On his own for the first time in his career, with his seat leased to another trader so he could not even trade on the floor, Todd still was on the trading floor daily, making rounds in the gold-colored trading jacket of a Mercantile Exchange clerk. Always one with a taste for gossip, he particularly liked swapping stories about the latest ups and downs in the Merc's executive suite.

On those rounds, Todd apparently saw much he did not like. And viewed from a distance, rather than from within the chaos of the trading pit, the transgressions of traders looked especially tawdry. Tired of watching the big brokers constantly slough off prime business to their favored local traders—the customer be damned—Todd was more than willing to help the government by introducing two young men into life at the Merc.

By May 1987, Todd was walking the floor and halls of the Merc with two new faces in tow. One was a silver-haired, athletically built man going by the name Peter Vogel; the other, a dark-haired, bearded, and pudgy Randy Jackson. Todd explained that he knew the young men from his Peace Corps days in Peru during the mid-1960s. One of them had a rich uncle who wanted to stake the two go-getters to commodities careers. "I'm going to teach these men the futures business," Todd told acquaintances. And FBI agents Dietrich Volk and Randall Jannett had their feet on the floor.

Nobody at the Merc knew that the rich relative was really Uncle Sam. Operation Hedgeclipper and Operation Sourmash were under way. It was time for the real sting work to begin.

□ □ □

CHAPTER ELEVEN

Life as a Mole

NOBODY SAID LIFE AS A MOLE would be glamorous, or easy. But at least it was supposed to be exciting.

Apparently no one had passed the word along to Archer Daniels Midland. The grain giant was intent on showing FBI special agent Richard Ostrom, undercover as Rick Carlson, the commodities business from the fields to the grain bins to the trading pits. But after more than three months on the job, the plodding education process seemed to be going nowhere. Except for a two-week hitch early in the ADM orientation program, he had not even visited the Board of Trade. More than 150 miles south of Chicago in Decatur, Illinois, Carlson was worlds away from the action.

Even so, on January 22, 1986, Carlson got his first whiff of wrongdoing in the grain markets. At a meeting with a dozen grain elevator workers, ADM manager Tim Breem reported industry rumors that an ADM competitor was tampering with grain quality standards. The competitor's warehouse employees were supposedly bribing grain inspectors with liquor and loading barges with two feet of sour grain, then piling good grain on top of the bad.

Carlson dutifully reported the rumor in the first of hundreds of FBI Form 302 reports he would complete over the next four years. But the sour grain incident was hardly the kind of commodity scandal Carlson was looking for, even if it did give a new twist to the code name Operation Sourmash.

The incident intensified Carlson's frustration. "We've got to get this thing moving," he complained to FBI case agent Paul Jenkins one day over the telephone. Jenkins and his bosses shared the sentiment and started pressuring ADM to let their agent go.

At last ADM did. By April 1, Carlson was in Chicago, working as a runner at the Chicago Board of Trade. Even at that lowly station, he began to experience the petty corruption that pervaded the Board. Local traders who wanted to curry favor with ADM constantly offered sizable gratuities for Carlson's most routine efforts. Christmastime was like winning a jackpot. And when he donned ADM's royal-blue jacket to begin brokering the firm's orders, Carlson was buffeted with stealthy requests for information about ADM's order flow.

To fellow traders, Carlson explained his fast rise on the floor by intimating that he had "a godfather" at ADM who wanted to see his career advance quickly. Certainly, Carlson had a godfather: ADM's chairman, Dwayne Andreas. And at least four other executives at the firm knew he was an undercover FBI agent. Only later would Carlson learn that one of the executives, in an effort to make certain that no ADM employees were implicated in the investigation, had told the firm's floor manager about Carlson's secret identity.

Traders dealing with the new ADM broker wanted all the angles—tips on ADM's business, breaks on trades, the usual chicanery of the pits. But as part of the deal with ADM, Carlson was not yet tape-recording their antics. That part of the undercover operation would start only when he was trading on his own. And by May 1987, he was.

Carlson's first task as an independent trader was to find a firm to clear his trades. He approached Daniel Henning, a barrel-chested bull of a wheat trader who was a partner in a prominent clearing firms for floor traders. As Henning laid out the package he would offer—charging 85¢ per contract to stand behind his trades—Carlson probed.

"I want more," he said, again and again. The conversation struck Henning as strange. At first, he wrote it off to the brashness of Carlson, who had shot out of the hordes of clerks on the floor to trade on his own in near-record time. Either he had lots of money, or he was representing someone else who did. Only two years later would Henning finally surmise that Carlson was fishing for a payola deal of some kind. He did not find it with Henning.

At last, Carlson came to terms with USA Trading, a relative newcomer to the clearing business that was still building a stable of smaller local traders whose risk it could bear. For USA, Carlson was a typical new client, a young trader on the rise, trying to earn enough through trading to buy his own seat. Even so, floor trader/FBI agent

Rick Carlson with the proud red-white-and-blue USA shield on his chest was irony undercover. Uncle Sam himself would have liked the uniform.

□ □ □

EVERY PERSON BUILDS A LONG PAPER TRAIL over a lifetime—from a birth certificate to school registrations to credit cards to a marriage license to a death certificate. For two FBI agents in early 1987, the first major concern of Operation Hedgeclipper was to create a lifetime's worth of history in a few weeks of work. Special Agents Randall Jannett and Dietrich Volk had done it before. But this one would be particularly challenging. With the Merc and the National Futures Association both expected to check the backgrounds of all applicants, the identity trail would have to be able to withstand a thorough background check.

For starters, the agents adopted aliases: Peter Vogel for Volk and Randy Jackson for Jannett. Vogel's application listed his actual college and graduation year—the University of Kansas at Lawrence, class of 1976—but his prior place of employment was fictitious, Peach State Capital of Georgia. For Jackson, even the school was falsified. He never attended St. Mary's College of California in Morgana, but he did phone the school several times during the early days of his undercover work to gather information about the curriculum and the atmosphere on campus, to help him keep up a convincing front.

After arriving in Chicago in mid-April of 1987, the two agents' first task was to build up these rudimentary identities. Supplied with drivers' licenses and social security numbers, the rest was up to them: applying for credit cards, opening bank accounts, renting apartments. There were also perks to help them fit in. Vogel, an avid weightlifter, particularly prized his membership at the tony East Bank Club.

Creating a false identity was just the start. With no background in commodities trading, or even in financial markets, the two had a challenge on their hands: learning the jargon of the pits and how to trade. Their cover story was simple enough. The two supposedly were cousins, in town to trade on the floor for Vogel's rich uncle from Uruguay, Friedrich Krupp. Floor traders and managers of trading firms at the exchange were completely taken in. The head of Shatkin Trading Co., a Jewish-controlled brokerage firm, even phoned the

Simon Wiesenthal Center to make certain that Krupp was not listed in their records as a Nazi war criminal.

By early May, the two newcomers were touring the Merc's trading floor in clerks' jackets, following Bill Todd, a struggling former broker for Heinold Commodities who seemed to see the newcomers as an entree to new capital and a possible return to the pits. The choice of Todd as a business partner raised some traders' suspicions that the two strangers had an anti-Jewish bias. The pasty-faced Todd railed against the exchange's Jewish power brokers, Leo Melamed in particular.

The agents had attended a six-week undercover training course at the FBI's training ground in Quantico, Virginia. But nothing at Quantico could give them the knowledge they needed to operate in the pits. For that, they turned to the most rudimentary of sources, the *Commodity Trading Manual* published by the Chicago Board of Trade and *Futures* magazine, a monthly covering the commodities markets. Their formal instruction in the futures business amounted to three afternoons of classroom instruction in mid-May. Taught by floor traders, this Merc orientation program amounted to little more than a stream-of-consciousness litany of war stories from the pits, followed by a mock trading session.

After registering with the National Futures Association brokers' test and paying $1700 a month to rent space for their newly formed Dolphin Trading Co. on the Merc building's 12th floor, Vogel and Jackson entered the Standard & Poor's 500 stock index futures pit on June 15, 1987, wearing cotton blend trading jackets with cardboard-thin tape recorders in their left front pockets. They noted suspicious activity on their trading cards and charts. Jackson even pretended to work cross-word puzzles so traders would not wonder why he was writing so much.

Customer complaints earlier that year had forced a reluctant Merc hierarchy to reform some trading practices in the S&P pit, but rumors persisted about continuing corruption there. What's more, the stock market was nearing the apex of a bull run that had begun in August 1982. All of the Merc's heavy hitters had a hand in the S&P's, and the FBI wanted to be there, too.

October 19, 1987, changed all that. The stock market crash brought the S&P market thundering down, too. It also nearly bankrupted Operation Hedgeclipper. Vogel was rumored to have lost more than $200,000 on Black Monday, though the actual figure was just about $30,000. By Christmas, with the S&P pit all but dormant, Vogel and Jackson were part of a crowd fleeing the pit for safer and more active markets elsewhere on the Merc floor. By January 1988, Jackson was in the Swiss franc pit, and Vogel was in the Japanese yen pit. With the unsettling lessons of the S&P's behind them, they were ready to deal.

□ □ □

WORKING IN THE HEART of the soybean pit, Rick Carlson quickly became an expert in the art of commodities trading. Not the kind of trading one reads about in the textbooks, but the kind practiced under the rules of the trading floor, the "floor rules" that always gave the edge to traders in the pits. Everywhere he turned—from the big soybean broker Martin J. Dempsey, with his reams of customer orders, to local traders Charles Bergstrom or James D. Nowak—everyone appeared happy to help instruct Carlson in the ways to beat the official rules.

On September 9, 1987, Carlson was working in the soybean pit's illegal after-hours curb market, waiting to see where he might be needed, when broker Thomas P. Kenney discovered he had made a mistake and needed to sell 95 contracts even though the market was officially closed. If Kenney could not get the contracts sold, the loss would come out of his pocket because the customer order should have been filled. Turning to Bergstrom, Kenney asked, "How am I going to get it back without looking terrible?"

Bergstrom, who had learned his craft while working for the Board's Office of Investigations and Audits during the 1970s, quickly arranged the deal. He would buy 95 contracts from Kenney, then quickly sell them to Carlson, who would sell back to Kenney. The order would get filled, but it would be a "wash trade" in which none of the floor traders had to hold the position overnight. What's more, they would set the prices so each participant made a little money.

Nervous about what OIA might think, Kenney was not immediately comfortable with the plan. "That's going to look terrible, isn't it?" he asked Bergstrom.

"It's going to look beautiful," Bergstrom claimed.

□ □ □

OF ALL THE UNDERCOVER OPERATIVES, FBI special agent Michael Bassett had the toughest job. His assignment was the Board of Trade's Treasury-bond market, the world's most active commodities pit and the most dangerous for an individual trader. Newcomers usually have little luck in the T-bond pit, where major international banks and insurance companies, and even the treasuries of nations, guard against rising or falling interest rates.

With his alias as Michael McLoughlin fixed, Bassett went undercover as an ADM clerk in March of 1987. Thanks to Carlson's work, he had been spared the lengthy tour of ADM's off-site operations. By September, he was trading on his own.

Even so, by the time the investigation would wrap up, Bassett had only three suspects safely on the hook. One of them, Melanie Kosar, was the only woman nabbed by the two undercover operations. The cases were clean—all three defendants would plead guilty—but they seemed to lead nowhere, at least for now.

The big boys in the Board's T-bond pit remained safe from trouble with the FBI.

□ □ □

FOR JAKE MOROWITZ, USA Trading was more than just a clearing firm from which he made money. Of course, as owner of USA he did make money. But Morowitz also took young traders and helped them learn the business the right way.

Too many promising young people busted out of the markets for lack of discipline, skill, and the proper temperament. Morowitz tried to reduce the odds of such brief and unprofitable careers for the 80 or so traders he cleared for during the late 1980s.

Rick Carlson was a natural student for Morowitz. Carlson kept an office in the Insurance Building west of the Board of Trade, but he was a regular visitor to USA's suite on the 16th floor of the Board's annex building. One day, he told Morowitz that he was having a hard time learning how to trade.

Morowitz jumped from behind his desk, gesticulating vigorously. A former philosophy student at the Chicago campus of the University of Illinois, Morowitz remembered all too well how tough it had been at first—the bashfulness about screaming out trades, the brief hesitations that can kill a trader.

"Get your hands up faster," Morowitz said. "Make your voice louder. *Sold!*" he yelled.

"Sold!" Carlson mimicked.

□ □ □

FRIENDS IN THE SOYBEAN PIT quickly taught Carlson a vital lesson: Keep an eye out for OIA. The Board's Office of Investigations and Audits was mostly a do-nothing outfit, but that did not stop traders from worrying almost endlessly about trouble with the OIA.

"Wait a second, the sheriff is in the pit," broker John Ryan warned Carlson one day when they were trading on the curb. On January 28, 1988, another curb session, Ryan was a little more blunt when three OIA investigators were in the pit after the close: "They come over here, we'll beat the shit out of them," he suggested.

Charlie Bergstrom drew on his OIA experience to outline detection-proof strategies for Carlson's benefit. He ridiculed the OIA's inadequate computer capabilities and advised Carlson to say simply, "I put it on the wrong card," if OIA asked about an errant trade. The fatherly Bergstrom's advice was summed up in a simple phrase. "Just deny, deny, deny," he told Carlson. Bergstrom credited his lawyer with creating the strategy.

□ □ □

RANDY JACKSON HAD SPENT just over a month in the Swiss franc pit, and nothing of interest had turned up yet. Trading 30, sometimes 50 contracts a day, he had started to get a feeling for the pit. He traded at first near the price reporter's stand, but he was now standing near the group run by brokers Gary Kost and Michael Joyce. Another broker with the group, Robert Mosky, also traded a lot of customer paper.

Jackson was trying to become an outlet for the Kost group's trades, and on February 13, he finally had his chance. He had sold three contracts to Mosky. But Mosky immediately needed to buy four back at a lower price, a price below where the market was trading.

Jackson took the trade, and a $12.50 loss. That took Mosky out of his jam. "What's the bid now?" Mosky asked in a quiet tone while fingering a customer's sell order.

Jackson hesitated. "One bid?" he asked, naming a still-lower price and not even specifying how many contracts he would buy.

"Sold you nine at one," Mosky blurted, handing Jackson an instant $100 profit on the deal. For Jackson, it was a breakthrough. For taking a $12.50 loss and helping Mosky out of a jam, he had been handed a risk-free $100 profit on a different customer's order.

An hour later, Mosky bumped into Jackson at the edge of the trading pit. "Good things happen to those who help out," Mosky explained in a big brotherly tone.

"That was the best deal I had all day," Jackson replied. For the FBI agent with 11 months undercover in the pits, it was the best deal yet.

□ □ □

SOMETIMES RICK CARLSON STUMBLED over shenanigans without even being on the scene. In the months after December 1986, when the government had forked over $350,000 to buy his seat, Carlson had become intricately woven into the spider web of associations that ran the trading pits.

He left the soybean pit for 40 minutes on March 4, 1988, and when he returned, Charlie Bergstrom and James Nowak informed him that he had been used as a scratch trader. While he was out of the pit, he had bought from Nowak and sold to Bergstrom in a $2,000 money pass. It was his job to make certain his trading cards fit the scenario.

Returning to his office later, an unhappy Carlson found that the tape recorder had malfunctioned, and the audio record of the event was lost. Not long afterward, the recorder concealed inside a pocket calculator was replaced by a slimmer model hidden in the lower-left pocket of his buff-colored USA Trading smock—a more reliable machine.

□ □ □

THE MOVE FROM THE S&P 500's to the currency pits had meant starting over for Randy Jackson and Peter Vogel. Each had begun working his way into the trading pits, but they had made no progress penetrating the inner circle of men who ran the exchange—Leo Melamed, Jack Sandner, Maury Kravitz, and the others from whom all power emanated. They needed an introduction, if not to the Merc's top brass, at least to one of the biggest broker groups.

The pair turned to Alan Fleishman, a floor veteran known throughout the exchange as a down-on-his luck trader who had repeatedly sought financial help from his relatives and friends.

Fleishman had also been partners with a broker named Bill Sturch, and he could offer information about a 1986 incident in which one of Sturch's clerks went to breakfast on a busy trading day with a fistful of orders in his pocket. The market moved 200 points while the clerk was away, leaving Sturch hung on hundreds of thousands of dollars in customer orders. The agents had heard that Merc floor chairman Harry Lowrance salvaged the situation by busting nearly every trade for the prior hour, changing prices, and logging them into the Merc's surveillance system as revisions, until the mess became manageable. If the agents could get the story from Fleishman, they would have a better look at the inner workings of the Merc floor.

Fleishman, with his rumored financial problems, seemed like an easy target when the agents invited him up to the Dolphin Trading offices. But Fleishman was suspicious from the start. Perhaps he had heard rumors from the S&P pit, where a trader once asked Vogel if he was an FBI agent.

Fleishman would not talk until he had frisked the two men, checking for tape recorders, unaware that the audiovisual equipment in the room made wearing wires unnecessary. Probing questions from Vogel and Jackson further aroused Fleishman's concerns, and the conversation went nowhere.

As he left, Fleishman issued a warning. "If you guys are with the government, you're going to have bullets in your brain," he said. After some checking, the two agents found reason to take Fleishman's warning seriously. He had been arrested at least once in Chicago for a firearms violation.

□ □ □

RANDY JACKSON HAD NEVER FILLED orders before. He had always traded as a local, handling just his own personal trading account and a few orders from Dolphin's customers. But on April 14, broker Robert Mosky of the Joyce-Kost group needed help. It was a trade figure day, when the government's release of data on the size of the trade deficit had the potential to send the market rocketing or plummeting. The volume of orders would be huge. And Mosky asked Jackson to help fill them.

"Don't fuckin' try to squeeze them," Bob Mosky warned Jackson before the opening. "Don't be a hero. Just get 'em done. Otherwise, it's going to cost you money."

As Jackson organized the deck of orders, the pit was filled with jostling and last-minute negotiating before the opening bell. Brokers Mark Fuhrman and Michael Fishbain negotiated a deal. "You gotta buy one, I gotta sell one," Fishbain said.

Furhman proposed a pre-arranged trade with Fishbain. "We'll split the opening range," he suggested.

"Take the high of the opening range, man, what's your story?" Fishbain complained, apparently unhappy that Furhman would not make his customer pay more so Fishbain could sell at a higher price.

The market opened with the Swiss franc trading at 7391 and paused there momentarily. At 7:30 A.M., the bottom dropped out. In a second, the Swiss franc contract dropped 17 ticks, a change of $202.50 per contract. A minute later, the bid had dropped another 23 ticks, meaning the contract had lost another $287.50. Buyers bid at 50 at the same time sellers offered at 73—the market reeling and jumping in confusion.

The chaos overwhelmed Randy Jackson. His voice rising in panic, he bid furiously to fill the dozens of customer orders Mosky had handed him. He paid 7350 to buy eight contracts, but quickly discovered he was supposed to be selling and busted the trade. "I'm sorry, it was a sell," Jackson explained. "Sorry, I fucked up."

"Eight at a half. Eight at a half," Jackson shouted.

"What half?" trader Danny Scheck wondered, confused by the incomplete information in Jackson's frantic bidding.

Jackson thrust his arms skyward, bidding again and again. "Hey, you're dropping the fucking paper," a voice from behind him shouted.

"Ah, for Christ's sake," the flustered agent said, stooping to pick up customer orders strewn at his feet amid the clutter on the floor.

"C'mon, get it up, man," the other trader said.

The market jerked higher, to 7325 before Jackson could fill more than a dozen orders in his deck. He would owe the customers money if he couldn't get them filled. "Buy these fuckers," Jackson said.

"Did they just come in?" asked Fuhrman, who tried to nurse Jackson through the panicked opening while filling Joyce-Kost group orders of his own. "You didn't buy them?" he asked increduously.

"Mark, these gotta be filled, don't they?" Jackson asked, showing Fuhrman a handful of customer orders that had been left behind by the fast-moving market. "I gotta buy 15 at a half. Who's a good guy for that?" Jackson asked, hoping Fuhrman would recommend a partner for a pre-arranged trade.

"Huh?" Fuhrman wondered.

"Who can I get those from?" Jackson explained.

"Put that one away," Furhman said, advising him to pocket the order until the market slowed down enough to clean up the mess.

The pattern became almost comical. The market kept moving, and Jackson could not keep up. "I missed this one. I missed this one," he said.

"Son of a . . . damn, you gotta get 'em filled," blurted Fuhrman, exasperated by Jackson's ineptitude.

Busy as he was with his deck of orders, Mosky could not ignore the calamity going on next to him. "Are you still stuck on those?" he yelled, shocked that Jackson had failed to fill more orders as the market dropped 10, then 20 ticks.

When Jackson said yes, Mosky reached into his deck and pulled out a few sell orders. "Here, use these to match them up and clear it out later," he said. "Match them up and stick it in your pocket."

When the "A" bracket ended at 8:00 A.M., Fuhrman stopped trading a minute to look at Jackson's trading cards. The two brokers tried to assess the wreckage of the crazy morning and plan an explanation for Mosky. "We're going to tell Bobby that we lost some points to somebody and we'll take care of it," Fuhrman said.

The morning was not a complete disaster for Fuhrman. He had been able to give one trader extra points from a customer order to help reduce a $2,500 debt. "I got stuck for a little bit," Fuhrman explained. "You better believe it's not coming out of my pocket."

Mosky, checking on Jackson, found that the broker did not even know how to correctly endorse completed trades. "You don't know how to fill an order yet?" he asked, startled. A few minutes later, Mosky checked on Jackson again. "What the fuck?" he wondered, looking at a stack of half-hour-old orders Fuhrman had handed to Jackson.

"Fuhrman's an asshole," Mosky muttered. Jackson offered to take care of the orders, but Mosky wanted none of it. "Wait a second. Fuckin' dick Fuhrman. Just hold on to these, I'll make him eat them."

With the market quieting, Jackson apologized to Mosky for the mess he had created. "I, you know, I'm not too good at this stuff," he explained.

"I know," Mosky said sympathetically. "Don't worry about it. Don't worry about it."

For Jackson, the day would not be a complete loss. Back in his Presidential Towers apartment, playing and replaying the tapes in an effort to sort out the confusion and chaos that had overwhelmed him during the day, Jackson found seven transactions that looked promising for the investigation. One of them had even resulted from Fuhrman's trying to clean up the mess on an error Jackson had made. Jackson had blown a 15-contract trade, which Fuhrman took and executed with Scheck. Ultimately, Jackson's sloppy trading led to criminal charges against the two men.

□ □ □

THE APRIL 14 TRADE-FIGURE OPENING had been crazy in the yen pit, too. Peter Vogel needed a break. Stepping away, he ran into Ray Pace, a dark-haired, olive-skinned yen broker.

"Listen to me now, I'm going to write something down on a card," Pace said as they walked toward the men's washroom. "All you gotta do is copy it the exact way I write it, okay?"

Pace stepped into the john while Vogel waited outside. He emerged with the card in his hand. "Pete, alright, 50 by 50. You bought 50 cars at 80 from SCL," he said, pointing to the trader's acronym on the card. "Copy it exactly the way it is."

Five days later, the pair met at the River Front Cafe across Monroe Street from the Merc to settle up business. Vogel carried with him a white envelope that held a dozen $100 bills. When they left the restaurant, the envelope was in Ray Pace's breast pocket.

□ □ □

WEDNESDAY IS USUALLY DOCTORS' DAY on the golf course. But for commodity traders, any day is a day for the links. And Wednesday, May 18, was a beautiful day for a golf game, particularly for Randy Jackson.

Mark Fuhrman was not noted for his discretion, even in the Merc's crowded Swiss franc pit. Let loose on the golf course with Jackson, Furhman's mouth ran like a cat on the loose.

After surviving together through the wild April 14 trade-figure day when Jackson had dropped his trading deck, the two had developed a rapport. One of the lesser lights in the Joyce-Kost broker group, Fuhrman laid out his strategies for ducking mistakes, stealing extra profits from customer orders, and doling out just enough profit to local traders like David Zatz to keep them willing to take losses down the line.

"I don't worry about errors," Fuhrman boasted. "That's why I have idiots like DIZ around." It was a reference to acronym Zatz's.

"I keep DIZ 200 points ahead," he added. "That's why he helps me."

Furhman knew he ran risks trading the way he did—on the curb, in side deals, basically any way he chose. He did not take the same kind of risks he once had, like the time in 1978 when, as a desk clerk for Madruff & Co., he'd been nabbed diverting a customer trade that made $1,500 in the market into a personal account.

In case he ever got caught, Fuhrman had a plan. "If, God forbid, anything ever happened to me someday, I would take down some big guys," he confided. "I'd turn state's evidence."

Something about golf builds camaraderie among men. "Hey, Jackson, stand near me, I'll give you stuff," Furhman said. "I'll help you out."

Jackson could not have been happier. "Mark, I'll take your losers," he said.

□ □ □

ON MAY 23, SOYBEANS opened up and stayed high on big volume. It was an opportunity just waiting for someone to grab it. Broker John Eggum asked Rick Carlson and Charlie Bergstrom if they still had their cards from the opening.

Carlson had handed his into the clearinghouse, but Bergstrom still had his. On busy days, Bergstrom liked to hold onto his cards, knowing they might come in handy. In fact, Bergstrom often left blank lines between entries on his cards, just in case some profitable revisionist history was necessary.

Lucky Charlie. Picking a price out of the opening range, Eggum quickly arranged a trade with him, using a customer order that Eggum had neglected to fill. Sheldon Schneider, another local, also helped out. Profit tally: Bergstrom $450, Schneider $1,570.

□ □ □

IN EARLY SUMMER OF 1988, USA Trading's Jake Morowitz was doing what he did every day: checking the accounts of the traders he cleared. Without close monitoring, a big loss by any trader could put USA out of business in a day, maybe less.

One notation jumped out at Morowitz. Rick Carlson, the rookie, had a big outtrade—$20,000 in his favor. For a guy who normally traded five, maybe 15 lots at a time, a $20,000 mistake was serious business. Never mind that this one happened to favor him.

When trading closed, Carlson answered Morowitz's summons to his office. "What's going on with this outtrade?" Morowitz wondered.

"It was just an outtrade," Carlson explained, in a deferential manner. "I guess I just got lucky."

"Watch out," Morowitz warned. "If it happens the right way, it can happen the wrong way."

Two weeks later, Morowitz again picked up a string of small outtrades in Carlson's account. This time they were losers. "You're lucky you were a winner the first time," Morowitz said.

"Yeah, I know," Carlson replied. "But don't worry. I'm paying them back."

□ □ □

CARLSON'S WORK WAS PAYING OFF. He had become bagman to Marty Dempsey, one of the biggest brokers in the soybean pit. As bagman, he worked like a kind of bank for Dempsey, a place where the bald-pated, bulldog-faced broker could put money for safekeeping. Or from which he could take money when the markets moved against him and Dempsey wanted to pay off debts.

The relationship between Carlson and Dempsey was widely known. Such things were hardly kept secret in the pit. At one point, broker John Eggum even compared Carlson to his own personal bagman. "Sheldon Schneider does the same thing for me that you do for Marty Dempsey," Eggum told Carlson.

And Carlson did quite a lot for Dempsey. On one occasion, Dempsey had put a $26,000 losing trade into Carlson's account after the close of trading on a Friday. But a weekend rain caused the drought-driven soybean market to turn around. At the opening on Monday, Dempsey reclaimed his trade, suddenly a $36,000 winner.

Sometimes a bagman's job got complicated. To keep his accounts manageable, Carlson arranged a deal with an accommodating trader happy to swap debts as long as no one lost money. Carlson owed $2,000 to Thomas Kenney, and Kenney owed the same amount to Dempsey. But paying Kenney with the customary pre-arranged trade would risk detection by OIA, so Carlson simply took on Kenney's debt to Dempsey. The debt Carlson owed Kenney was cancelled. "It's smarter that way," Kenney agreed. The swap had no effect on Dempsey's debt to Carlson at the time: $19,700.

Dempsey's debit sheet was running high on another occasion. Haplessly, he looked at his deck of orders and explained his repayment plan to Carlson: "If I can see anything here in these decks or something where I can pump money into you, I will do that."

Bagging had its privileges, Carlson found. Trading on the curb after the market closed one day, Dempsey suddenly shushed Carlson. "Be careful of writing, be careful, be careful," he said.

Carlson wondered why.

"OIA is around here," Dempsey said.

In an effort to throw OIA off their tracks, Dempsey once created an outtrade with Carlson on which Carlson lost $1,500. Dempsey promised to repay him later with a profitable trade. The next day, using a customer order, Dempsey made good on the promise.

"I'm going to get you some money," Dempsey said on a separate occasion. "I'm always trying to pick you."

Carlson certainly appreciated his efforts.

□ □ □

EVERY PIT NEEDS ITS STREETCORNER philosopher-comic, and in the bean pit, John Vercillo fit the bill. A former Chicago cop, the black-haired, fast-talking Vercillo was a joking, gregarious trader who knew his way around the pits.

During one particularly active curb session after the bean pit's 1:15 P.M. close, Vercillo bemusedly looked at his watch. "What's the point of coming in early?" he wondered to his fellow curb traders. "I might as well just come in at 1:15."

On another occasion James Nowak could not decide what price to place on a customer order, and Vercillo revealed his philosophy on handling customer business. "Make it the highest possible price if it's a buy," Vercillo advised. "And the lowest price possible if it's a sell."

Vercillo listened in once as Nowak described to Carlson how he was pre-arranging a trade with Craig LaCrosse in order to settle a debt. "You need to know how to do these things," Vercillo sagely advised the neophyte Carlson.

The Vercilloism to top them all came during the midst of the drought of 1988. Carlson's "banking" business—bagging profits and losses for brokers—was booming. The market often closed limit up within minutes of opening, so the few trades that could be made had great value. With the market volatile and illiquid, the brokers kept Carlson busy, buying and selling to him, adjusting their accounts as necessary. Dempsey, Nowak, Eggum, and Kenney practically lined up at banker Carlson's window.

July 17 was just such a day. With the market up limit and no customer orders getting filled, Carlson heard a voice behind him remark, "Boy, I bet all those customers who aren't getting filled are going to complain."

Vercillo's observation was brief, and to the point: "Fuck the customer."

Carlson winced, knowing he had not activated his tape recorder. But this was too good to pass up. He reached into his pocket and pressed the switch. "What did you say about the customer?" Carlson asked.

"Fuck the customer," Vercillo repeated. This time Carlson caught the comment on tape.

□ □ □

IT WAS THE FIRST PERSONNEL CRISIS among the undercover agents, and it was not going to go away easily.

Until now, everything in Operation Sourmash and Hedgeclipper had seemingly gone well. The agents were showing the typical signs of fatigue. They wanted to get back to the office, carry their badges and guns again, not have to live double lives.

Even one of the FBI's biggest early fears—that the riches of the commodities markets would lure the agents away from the bureau, or possibly corrupt them—had apparently been groundless. Besides, the bureau had contracted with each agent to remain with the FBI for five years after the undercover phase was closed. None of them seemed likely to try to walk out on that.

No one had foreseen this particular problem, though. Jackson wanted to get married. Randy Jackson, Swiss franc trader, had met the woman of his dreams, and the nuptials could not wait until Operation Hedgeclipper was history. Jackson wanted permission to blow his cover to his fiancée to avoid marrying her under false pretenses.

Jeffrey Frank, Ernie Locker, and the other FBI managers at first tried to persuade Jackson to maintain his cover. "It's too big a risk," Locker explained.

But Jackson dug in his heels. "I am not going to marry this woman unless she knows who I really am," he said.

The standoff was absolute. Jackson had not explicitly threatened to leave the project, but that was a possibility. With nowhere for the bureau to turn, permission was granted.

☐ ☐ ☐

THE SUMMER OF 1988 HAD BEEN HOT, and in hot weather, crazy rumors run through the grain markets. This early September rumor was not a market-mover. Rather, it was a bomb threat: Rick Carlson might be FBI.

Marty Dempsey, Charlie Bergstrom, and James Nowak huddled in the Board's third-floor members' lounge speaking in low tones. Dempsey had heard the rumor from William Barcal. The sandy-haired Barcal had met a woman at a party over the weekend, a runner for the Refco Inc. brokerage firm, who had told him she knew an undercover FBI agent in the soybean pit named Rick Carlson.

"I find that hard to believe," Bergstrom announced. Carlson had worked in the pit for nearly two years. If he were FBI, he would have wandered away by now, looking for more crime somewhere else. The bean pit did not have a patent on suspicious trading, after all.

Bergstrom decided to use his contacts as a former Office of In-vestigations and Audits investigator to check out the rumor. "I still have some friends in OIA. I'll make a couple of calls," he said.

Back in the pit a few days later, Bergstrom came in empty-handed. "I couldn't find anything out," he told Nowak. Even so, he still did not buy the rumor.

Dempsey did not know whether to believe them or not, but he was taking no chances. He owed Carlson $10,700 and needed some way to clear the debt without causing more problems for himself or helping Carlson, if he was an FBI agent, to build a better paper trail.

Nowak had an idea: a debt exchange in which no money actually changed hands. Carlson was in hock to him, and Nowak could cancel part of Carlson's debt. Nowak would pretend he owed the money to Dempsey. That way, Carlson would understand why Nowak suddenly was forgiving a big debt. "I'll tell him to take the $10,700 off what he owes me," Nowak volunteered. "And, Marty, you can take care of getting the money back to me."

On September 16, Nowak outlined his plan to Carlson. Describing his supposed debt to Dempsey, Nowak explained, "I owe him a chunk." Carlson and Nowak had arranged a 50/50 split of profits from the illegal trade that had generated Carlson's debt, but Nowak suddenly acted quite generously about that debt.

"Whatever Marty owes you, why don't you just take it off double?" he magnanimously said. Then, to close the loop on the cover story: "I'll take care of Marty."

Of the three, only Dempsey stopped his dealings with Carlson. Just three days later, Nowak and Bergstrom were back in business— working out a deal to park $5,000 by falsifying a 50-lot trade.

"They just got my card," Nowak complained about the clearing firm, explaining why he couldn't do the deal with Bergstrom himself. Then, seeing empty lines on Carlson's trading card: "You can squeeze it in."

Carlson was more than happy to help out.

□ □ □

RICK CARLSON WALKED INTO USA'S SUITES after another day of trading, and Elsie McElligott, the secretary, happened to look up and notice him.

"Rick Carlson," she said. "I remember that name. He's the guy from 'I Led Three Lives.' " The original Richard Carlson was an actor in the 1950s television show, in which he played Herbert Philbrick—private citizen, undercover agent, and FBI counterspy.

Carlson turned white, tried to smile, and walked past McElligott. He offered no reply.

□ □ □

PETER VOGEL WATCHED AT HIGH NOON as Tommy Braniff, one of the yen pit's more active brokers, walked up to Robert Bailin, a small-time local. "Fifteen I bought at three," he said, sticking Bailin with a losing trade.

"Tommy, you got to get that back to me," said Bailin, who was in the midst of a miserable September. "I'm not doing well this month."

"What?" Braniff asked.

"I'm not doing well. You need to get this back to me. I'm not doing well right now," Bailin complained.

"What?" Braniff asked, though he obviously had heard.

Bailin repeated for the fourth time the embarrassing admission. "I said I'm not doing well," he said. A few moments later, he bought 15 yen contracts to get out of the trade, netting a $947.50 loss. "This is terrible, you know, it's every day," he groused.

Braniff's pal, Michael Christ, a broker with the powerful ABS Partners group, had observed the action. "You stuck him with it?" Christ asked Braniff, feigning naivete. "Is that what they do over here, stick the locals with it?"

Vogel intervened in the touchy situation. "Tommy, if you ever get stuck, you know I'll help you out," he said. "Listen, for you, I would take a thousand points."

□ □ □

ON SEPTEMBER 30, 1988, President Reagan visited the floor of the Merc, where he would appear later that night for a George Bush fund-raiser. But business as usual prevailed in the yen pit. Peter Vogel was subbing for Tommy Braniff, handling the Refco Inc. deck for the close of trading, and even though orders are supposed to remain secret until announced to the pit, the local traders gathered to find out what Refco had going on the close.

For the moment, Vogel refused to let Aric March, the tubby local, get a glimpse. "You're turning into a Nazi on me, Vogel," March complained.

"Lumpy, what's going on, man?" asked Mike Greenfield.

"Just trying to steal a few dollars before the weekend," March explained.

"He's an honest thief," piped up Ray Pace.

Vogel's discretion wavered. As Reagan peered over the floor from a catwalk, Vogel told local Robert Bailin to sell five on the close, and told Pace to sell two—pre-arranging the trades. "Reagan's looking pissed over there," Refco broker Mark Jansen told Vogel, momentarily confusing him. "He sees what you're doing, he sees you're crossing trades," Jansen joked.

When the after-hours curb market finally halted, Jansen checked Vogel's trade record. "Pete, you're going to command respect in this pit," he said.

Chuckling, Vogel said, "They can make money off me. Let's call a spade a spade."

"They know you can be bought, Pete," Jansen said.

"Just trying to get along with the world, Mark."

"Right," Jansen answered. "Comes with the territory down here."

□ □ □

HALLOWEEN OF 1988 was just a few days away, and it was trick and treat time for Rick Carlson and broker Bradley Ashman.

Ashman sold 65 contracts, mistakenly thinking he was filling a customer order. He quickly discovered the error, which left Carlson short 65 contracts with the market moving against him. Ever the accommodating local, Carlson accepted the trade and the $3,000 loss on the deal.

The repayment negotiation began. The two decided to split the cost, with Ashman owing Carlson $2,000. But first they subtracted a $150 debt Carlson had accrued in a trade on July 12. On that deal,

Ashman had asked simply, "Can I give you a little money?" before parking some customer funds with Carlson. At the time, the $150 had seemed so inconsequential that Ashman did not even mark it on the card he kept in the breast pocket of his trading jacket to tally debits and credits with other crooked traders.

The $2,000 sum settled, Ashman explained that he already had a standing $1,900 debt to another trader, Brian Novak. Carlson would have to wait until a market opportunity enabled Ashman to repay Novak. The legal method—repaying an outtrade debt by check on the day it was accrued—was not even considered.

Carlson agreed to wait. Ashman pulled out his pocket balance sheet, which often was littered with traders' acronyms and sums they owed, and marked his debt to Carlson. "These are the people I owe," he said, swiping a finger toward the list. "These are the bad ones."

Ashman eventually paid back the money by selling six contracts to Carlson at a below-market price. "I sold it to you at six," Ashman said, selling a customer order at a penny-and-a-half below the market price. "Get out of it."

"Get out of it" was the phrase traders used to advise each other that they had been handed the chance to make some money, but only if they acted quickly before the market moved against them.

□ □ □

FOR HIS TRADER COMRADES, breakfast was a time to blow off steam. For Peter Vogel, it was time to work. November was a particularly busy month, and a time for traders to complain about how their jobs were affected by corruption at the Merc.

On November 10, Vogel and three other traders sat down to eat at Mrs. Levy's Delicatessen in the first floor of Sears Tower. In a rambling conversation that also included brothers Brian and James Sledz, trader Joseph O'Malley, a broker who had recently abandoned his deck of orders to trade only for himself, held forth. "A broker who has a good volume of business cannot fill honestly and legally without losing money," O'Malley complained.

In 1986 and 1987, O'Malley had written personal checks totalling $101,000 to compensate customers for mistakes he had made. "Because I wasn't good at getting, stealing a hundred grand a year," he explained.

Six days later, the breakfast club met again at the Merc Club on the third floor of the Chicago Mercantile Exchange building. Brian Sledz complained about how broker John Baker had taken advantage of a $1,250 trading debt to launder up to $60,000 through Sledz's account over a three-month period. "He gives me 15 grand one day and says keep 50 points of it and give the rest to this, and this, and this, and this," Sledz griped. "It gets in my fucking way. I don't need the aggravation."

□ □ □

THERE WAS MORE TO THE MERC CLUB than breakfast. The drinks that were served there proved a useful tool for Vogel in his pursuit of John Baker, one of the yen pit's biggest brokers, who considered himself a "mechanic" of trading improprieties.

Seldom successful in engaging big-time brokers in the pit, Vogel first befriended Baker in a lengthy October 4 Merc Club conversation. Baker reminisced then about bygone days of customer rip-offs. "Before now, I mean it was so gravy train," he said. "That's what the bagman thing came out of."

"There are certain things that you can't admit to," Baker added. "There is a system. You don't tell the world about it." Vogel listened all morning, plying Baker.

It was the start of a drinking partnership that would lead to some of the most gossip-filled discussions of the investigation. Meanwhile, back in the yen pit, Vogel joined in when traders poked fun at Baker, mocking his eccentric dress and relative old age. "Old Blue Hair" and "Mutant Peacock" were two of Vogel's favorite nicknames for Baker.

Paydirt came during a beer-drenched 10:00 A.M. conversation on November 11, when Randy Jackson joined Baker and Vogel at the Merc's bar. Working together, the two pumped Baker for dirt on the Merc's power elite.

Baker explained that Leo Melamed pressured his brokers. "You don't want Leo's stuff," he claimed. "You're stuck." He intimated that Melamed tried to coerce brokers. "Do it at this price," Baker said. "He doesn't say anything, he just threatens you," Baker added of Melamed.

"It's beyond that, isn't it?" Vogel asked, hoping to draw Baker into a more specific and incriminating discussion of Melamed. "I mean, you have to do better than trade."

But Baker ignored the lead and took the conversation elsewhere. A few minutes later, Vogel raised another big name: Clayton Yeutter, the former Merc president who was President Reagan's U.S. Trade Representative. Vogel's FBI bosses suspected that Yeutter was a source of government news leaks to the Merc.

"You think Clayton ever, like, like, would tip Leo off on the trade figures and stuff?" Vogel asked.

"No, I think Leo has inside information," Baker replied. "I don't think he needs Clayton Yeutter for something like that."

The conversation rambled on, gossiping about some of the bigger traders in the yen pit. But Vogel did not let the time idly slip by. With Jackson pitching in, he laid the groundwork for one of the investigation's big-time production numbers: a tax-dodge scheme that would include a videotape of Baker in the Dolphin Trading office.

□ □ □

AN UNEXPECTED TELEPHONE CALL would dramatically affect Richard Carlson's work during the remainder of Operation Sourmash: The voice on the telephone informed him his wife had fallen down a flight of stairs. The retinas in both eyes were detached.

For the next two weeks, with his wife's eyesight in serious jeopardy, Carlson had more than the usual concerns about working on the project. When he could, he stole away to visit her at the hospital. Relatives and friends were helpful, but as a spouse and father he needed to be with her.

Over time, the crisis would pass. But for Carlson, the difficulty of visiting and caring for his wife while remaining undercover was another inconvenience of the project.

□ □ □

THE CROWDS IN THE TRADING PITS always thin out a day or so before big holidays. Traders leave town or simply stay home with their families. But on this Wednesday before Thanksgiving, a pair of increasingly nervous soybean traders worried about a face missing from the crowd.

"Where's Rick? In Washington?" Marty Dempsey asked Jim Nowak, referring to the mysterious Carlson and his equally mystical identity. Dempsey could not believe Nowak was still trading with a guy who might be FBI.

"Hey Marty, that's not funny," Nowak replied, shuddering at the thought of the blond-haired trader visiting FBI headquarters in Washington. Nowak turned his back and returned to trading.

□ □ □

FRIDAYS WERE ALWAYS INTERESTING for the agents. Nobody wanted to go home with empty pockets, so traders' temptations were great. But on this particular Friday, the day after Thanksgiving, action in the Swiss franc pit was slow for Jackson. Slow, that is, until Aric March started talking. "I want to give you a lot of money," March proclaimed out of the blue.

This obviously was not charity. March wanted to pass a big winner to Jackson so he could take the money out later. "I'd like to make about $85,000, $80,000 right here," March stated. "I'd like that Bentley Turbo. I want that Bentley Turbo for my birthday in February."

By February, of course, March would have other things on his mind. Subpoenas and a possible jail term would replace a coveted English sports car as his main concern.

□ □ □

CARLSON HAD BEEN WARNED that the job would not be easy. But he could never have anticipated how much of a grind the work would become. Trade all day, transcribe tapes most of the night, try to socialize enough to pick up tidbits at the East Bank Club or one of the local bars.

Month after month, it had never let up. In early 1987, he had worked double-time passing along his experiences to Michael Bassett, the FBI agent going under cover in the Board's Treasury bond pit.

Several times a week, particularly in the early going, he contacted Charlotte Ohlmiller at the CFTC's Chicago office to consult about certain suspicious activity.

The false identity, the trading, the transcribing, the recordkeeping, the meetings: It was all getting to be a grind. Early one evening in December, Carlson was transcribing a set of tapes, dictating his Form 302 reports from the day's activities. His wife found him fast asleep, his infant child sucking a bottle under one arm, the dictaphone dangling from the other.

□ □ □

SHOWTIME.

The hidden camera was ready to go for the proposed John Baker tax dodge. Vogel and Baker had worked out the details in late November. To cut his tax bill, Baker wanted to lose about $10,000 a week in the market and be repaid in cash.

On the morning of December 16, Vogel and Baker put the first phase of the operation into effect, working out a trade in which Vogel made a 380-tick profit, enough to set up some $4,750 in tax losses for Baker. Refund time came later that day. Baker went to the Dolphin Trading offices and sat in an easy chair across a desk from Vogel. With little small talk, the two got down to business.

Vogel handed the cash across to Baker, saying simply, "That should square us." Without counting the money, Baker stuffed it into his front pants pocket. Randy Jackson would have Mark Fuhrman count out the money for the benefit of the camera in a similar deal, but Vogel opted to eschew the formality with Baker.

The deed done, the two talked for some 20 minutes, discussing New York City's high crime and slow traffic, fast cars, and their commutes to work. Baker mused about the $2 bill he kept folded in his wallet, a souvenir of his first day of trading on April 13, 1976.

After the show was over, Vogel realized a serious error had been made: He had shorted the government till by $2,375. The trading profit, it turned out, had been only 190 points, not the 380 the two thought they had arranged. On December 19, Vogel tracked down Baker in the Merc Club bar. He explained the mistake, and Baker agreed to adjust the problem in the market the next day. "The thing, the irony of it is that we are both sitting there figuring it out and screwing it up," Vogel said.

□ □ □

THE TIME WAS COMING TO WRAP UP the undercover phase of the operation. Jackson and Vogel had gotten the Baker and Fuhrman deals on tape. Carlson had his suspects cold, and McLoughlin was not likely to make more progress.

The bureau feared that the cover might blow. And for good reason. On the floor of the Merc, broker Bob Mosky pulled aside trader Bill Walsh and nodded toward Randy Jackson. "There's a rumor he's with the government," Mosky said. "Don't trade with him."

Talk about Carlson was spreading at the Board. And there were signs that word of the investigation was starting to leak out of the U.S. Attorney's office to the press.

The Christmas season would be the last hurrah. The agents continued their undercover ruse. Vogel wore his wire while attending a Christmas party thrown by Baker and his partner, Thomas A. Crouch, in Countryside, Illinois. Carlson attended at least one Christmas function at a trader's home.

Just after the New Year, all four traders had left the floors of the Chicago Board of Trade and the Chicago Mercantile Exchange. Their disappearances went all but unnoticed. In the markets, people come and go all the time.

Their reemergence a few weeks later—wearing badges and guns, carrying tapes of incriminating conversations, asking questions, and identifying themselves as Richard Ostrom, Michael Bassett, Randall Jannett, and Dietrich Volk—would make headlines.

CHAPTER TWELVE

□□□

Running for Cover

IN RETROSPECT, JAKE MOROWITZ of USA Trading figured he should have seen it coming after he sent Rick Carlson a Christmas gift. Even though Carlson had stopped clearing trades through USA, the young trader had been a friend, the kind of guy who would appreciate the Fruit-of-the-Month-Club package.

A few days later, in early January, the gift was returned. The Post Office had stamped a simple statement next to the mailing label: "Moved Left No Address."

The returned package made Carlson's sudden disappearance all the more mysterious. But Morowitz would not have to ponder the mystery for long. Carlson was not a trader. Neither were three of his associates in other Chicago pits. They were FBI agents who were about to make the good old days at the Merc and the Board of Trade shatter like a piece of fine crystal.

Beginning with the late-night visits to the homes of traders on January 18, 1989, Operation Sourmash and Operation Hedgeclipper crashed down on the heads of Chicago's exchanges in a two-week burst of intense public scrutiny. Fueled by a headline-chasing frenzy in the newspapers, the undercover probes became the top story in financial centers from New York to Chicago to Los Angeles, and throughout the farm belt.

To some, the press seemed to work hand in glove with the prosecution, identifying and practically indicting traders and the futures industry as the story developed day by day. The government's tip to the *Chicago Tribune* gave the early stories a heavy prosecutorial slant:

Defying reason and reality, the newspapers quickly compared the Chicago affair to the indictments of Ivan Boesky and Michael Milken, whose insider-trading frauds netted them hundreds of millions of dollars. In fact, as gradually became clear, the comparison was embarrassingly overblown.

The other groups involved in the case hardly stood still. Within days, the defense lawyers mobilized their own publicity campaign, and headlines decrying Assistant U.S. Attorney Raphaelson's commando tactics and the heavy-handed use of RICO began sharing newsprint. *The Wall Street Journal*'s editorial page, its anti-regulatory bias ever intact, called for Valukas's resignation.

The exchanges practiced variations on a theme: "It's just a few bad apples." The regulators moved to prove they had been vigilant. Traders tried to lie low. Eventually, even reporters wound up defending themselves against charges that their frenzied coverage had made them tools of the prosecution. It was time to run for cover.

□ □ □

JONATHAN R. LAING, a reporter for *Barron's* magazine, walked into *The Wall Street Journal*'s Chicago office on Wednesday afternoon, January 18. He had heard rumors on the Board's trading floor about a sting operation, talk of G-men visiting traders' homes Tuesday night. If true, the story would be out by the time the weekly *Barron's* hit the streets, but Laing knew the *Journal*, *Barron's* sister paper, would be interested.

The *Journal*'s office jerked into action. Sue Shellenbarger, the bureau chief, told all four available reporters to drop their other work and ferret out the story. The U.S. Attorney's office, the exchanges, the CFTC, the brokerage firms, lawyers: Call them all. Then she jumped on the phone to New York, to pass along Laing's tip. New York loved the story, but only if the Chicago crew could nail it down.

It was 3:00 P.M. in Chicago, two-and-a-half hours before deadline. There still might be time.

Reporters Bob Rose, Jeff Bailey, and Robert Johnson left to interview traders, hoping to snare one who had been indicted. Scott Kilman, the farm futures reporter, stayed to work the phones and take reporting from the field. Meanwhile, Shellenbarger phoned Scott McMurray, the *Journal*'s lead commodities reporter, who was at home ill.

An hour before deadline, Shellenbarger called Washington to ask for reporting from the Justice Department. But the Washington bureau came up empty.

A half hour to go, and the *Journal*'s reporting machine had turned out enough nuggets to flesh out a story. There definitely was an investigation: They had a few names of traders who had received subpoenas, and even a Chicago Mercantile Exchange response to the rumors. But still there was no confirmation of the probe from the government, and the reporters had not located anyone who actually had been visited by the government.

The New York editors were antsy. If this was true, it was a big story. But if it was just another rumor-induced panic from the pits, the "Bible of Business" would look stupid.

Finally, New York made the decision. The details were too sketchy, the confirmation too thin. This was too big a story to hang on rumors. The 13-paragraph version could not go in the *Journal*. It was a tough call. But the editors thought it was the right one to make.

The *Journal* ran only four paragraphs, buried inside the back section of the paper. The headline was an anemic "Subpoena Rumors Sweep Chicago Board of Trade." The story was no stronger.

Shellenbarger tried to rally her spent troops. But she could rouse no enthusiasm, not even her own. They had come so close, only to fall short.

□ □ □

AT THE *CHICAGO SUN-TIMES*, the number two Chicago newspaper, the beige telephone on the assistant business editor's desk rang at 4:00 P.M. The financial section's 6:00 P.M. deadline was closing in.

As usual, assistant business editor Gavin Maliska was sitting at the end of the business copy desk, "the slot." He was editing stories, prodding pokey reporters, processing copy for the January 19 *Sun-Times*. The tabloid's business section had developed a reputation for missing deadlines, a rap Maliska was trying to beat. Besides, he had a train to catch.

When he picked up the phone, Maliska did not recognize the voice. "There's been some indictments on the commodities exchanges," the caller said. Maliska pushed for details, but none came. The caller refused to identity himself, and hung up.

Greg Burns, who had started covering commodities in the fall of 1987, had left early that day. Burns's predecessor on the beat, who had been promoted to write a Chicago business column, was not in sight. Maliska decided to make the next call himself.

He phoned the U.S. Attorney's office and asked for Anton Valukas. Instead, he got Daniel Gillogly, an assistant U.S. Attorney who handled most of Valukas's press calls. Gillogly would not confirm or deny anything. Maliska made a note to pass along the tip to Burns in the morning and returned to editing copy. It was a deadly error for a competitive newspaper: Good stories do not keep overnight.

In the cityside newsroom, reporter Deborah Nelson's telephone rang and rang. Her desk was ten paces from the main newsroom's switchboard, but no one seemed to hear the phone. Nelson wasn't in anyway; whoever it was could call back.

Waiting on the end of the line, listening to one, two, three rings and more, was one of Nelson's government sources. A longtime investigative reporter, Nelson had contacts in the Justice Department and the IRS, and one of them was trying to reach her. The source had a tip about a sting on the commodities exchanges. And he knew the story was about to blow wide open.

The telephone rang and rang. And then it stopped.

□ □ □

LATE ON THE NIGHT OF JANUARY 18, 1989, the Freedom Center presses whirred. By midnight, the first of more than 750,000 *Tribunes* were spilling off and getting bundled, loaded, and shipped. For much of Chicago—the 6,000 traders, the 30,000 people employed directly or indirectly by the markets, the lawyers and regulators, the businessmen, even the taxi drivers and cops—the headline would jump off the front page: "Government Probes Futures Exchanges," it read. "FBI Tapes Key to Fraud Investigation."

From top to bottom, it was an amazing story. An unspecified number of FBI agents, wearing concealed microphones, for two years had worked the pits of the Chicago commodity exchanges. Up to 100 traders and executives might be implicated. U.S. Attorney Anton Valukas had been to Washington the week before to get Attorney General Richard Thornburgh's okay to subpoena traders. FBI agents and prosecutors had fanned out across the city, making late-night raids on traders' homes. The government's Racketeer Influenced Corrupt Organizations law, dubbed RICO, might be used against the traders. For the guilty, it could mean a loss of homes, cars, even exchange memberships.

The story was complete, with a wealth of detail. Few significant questions went unanswered. To many readers, it looked like a direct leak from the feds to the *Tribune*, a blockbuster handed to them sealed in plastic, ready for the day's press run.

Few of the *Trib*'s competitors held such suspicions. Most reporters figured the *Trib* had a few days' head start and had made the most of it. The tip obviously came from Washington, or else Washington correspondent Christopher Drew would never have had the lead byline. The source clearly was quite knowledgeable.

But a leak, with all the i's dotted and the t's crossed? If only life were that easy.

□ □ □

For Greg Burns, January 19 started like any other morning. He walked the dog, dressed for work, and bade farewell to his wife, Ann. The walk to the train was cool, but not frigidly cold.

When he got to the station, Burns caught a chill that cut to his bones. Glancing at the *Tribune*'s coin-operated honor box just before climbing the platform, he saw a headline that stole his breath. Burns had been scooped, and scooped big.

Burns considered fleeing to the house, grabbing the car, and driving downtown. Thinking twice, he waited for the train, hoping the Evanston Express would be quicker than backtracking.

After an interminable ride, Burns rushed to the fourth floor of the *Sun-Times'* squat seven-story gray building on the north bank of the Chicago River. Some colleagues averted their eyes from the lean, boyish reporter, as if someone had died. Burns felt like it had been him.

He swiped a notepad and the press badges that would get him access onto the trading floors and hopped a cab south to the exchanges. Once there, the work of collaring traders and asking for their thoughts took his mind off the larger problems. The *Trib* was obviously a mile ahead on this story; they would assign legions to cover it. The *Journal* would jump on board. And Burns, in contrast, would be all but alone.

Rushing back to the *Sun-Times* building before lunchtime, Burns rode the elevator to the fourth floor. He stepped off the lift just as Kenny Towers, the newspaper's editor, was about to step on.

"Greg, we got scooped," Towers said.

"Yeah, I know," Burns replied, hoping for understanding, if not support or advice, from the avuncular editor.

"Greg, we got scooped," Towers repeated.

Burns mumbled. There was little to say in reply to Towers, a payroller pushed to the top of the *Sun-Times* masthead by four ownership changes in the prior six years.

As the mauve-painted elevator doors slid shut, Towers made one last utterance, his final comment to the *Sun-Times'* commodities reporter throughout the remaining coverage of the story: "Greg," he said again, "Greg, we got scooped."

□ □ □

THE AD HOC GROUP THAT MET in *Tribune* business editor Bill Neikirk's office on January 19 was not the usual *Tribune* committee, discussing irrelevancies in meticulous detail. This committee had a job to do: plan coverage of the commodities scandal. Ideas were fired out, taken up, or dropped dead in rapid succession. It was free-form, assignment by association.

With the ten-by-twelve-foot financial editor's office packed with a half-dozen business staffers and a handful of investigative reporters from the metropolitan desk, Neikirk was not running this meeting so much as monitoring it: Who were the moles? How many of them? Who did they get? How long were they there? How did they get on the floor? Did they buy seats? Lease them? We need to contact the firms. We've got to call defense lawyers. Let's check the exchanges' disciplinary records.

Officially, Neikirk was heading the *Trib*'s coverage of the scandal. It was, after all, a business story. But right away, the *Tribune*'s commanding voice of the coverage was Dean Baquet, the *Trib*'s new investigations editor and a recent Pulitzer Prize winner. Baquet was part of a *Trib* team that explored conflicts of interest on Chicago's city council. The topic was like shooting fish in a barrel, but the slickly packaged series was made to order for the Pulitzer committee. Knowing the commodities story might be the *Trib*'s next Pulitzer bid, the reporters all wanted on board.

Neikirk and Baquet handed out assignments. Drew would write the second-day story. Bill Crawford, who had covered the federal building for a decade before moving to the commodities beat, would work the courts and the pits. Anybody who had ever covered commodities received assignments: Laurie Cohen, once the bane of the industry for her hard-hitting reporting, would dig through regulatory files; Carol Jouzaitis and Sallie Gaines would chip in writing background stories.

Baquet set loose four investigative reporters on the story, too. He was three months into a project with two other reporters, but their study of homicide coverups by the sheriff's office would have to wait. "We knew at that point we had a hell of an interesting story," recalled reporter Thomas Burton of the two-foot-thick stack of sheriff's office files on his desk. "The last thing either of us had in mind was to drop what we were doing." But drop they did. Over time, more than 20 *Tribune* reporters would work on the commodities story.

For years, newspapers have used their business sections as dumping grounds for the inexperienced or the inept. And watching Baquet smoothly insinuate himself into this story revived lingering insecurities. "They smelled Prize, and they came after this thing like crazy," recalled one business staffer. "Baquet was masterful, the way he handled it."

The rules of interoffice engagement were clear from the start. Neikirk told the group that Jack Fuller, the heir-apparent to editor James Squires, would call the big shots, and Fuller was playing by strict rules. Anonymous sources would be approved, but two confirmations would be necessary before anything went to print. Reporters would have to be prepared to tell editors the identities, or at least the titles, of their sources.

The toughest rule: The *Tribune* would not print the name of any person subpoenaed by the government without obtaining confirmation from the trader or his lawyer. It was quite a tough restriction. And it would cost the *Trib* a scoop the next day, because the *Journal* had no such rule. But with the headline madness that was certain to set in, somebody had to set the rules.

□ □ □

FOR ERIC BERG, it was a costly visit to the dentist on January 19. The *New York Times'* Chicago business correspondent was new to the city and barely knew his way around Chicago when the commodities story hit. Berg did not even have a press pass for the trading floors.

This particular morning, Berg had not bothered to check the Chicago newspapers before spending the morning in the dentist's chair. The first call from New York came to Berg's office at 9:00 A.M. Chicago time. No Berg. The second call came an hour later. No Berg. As the day wore on, Chris Bockelman, the assistant business editor running the New York desk that day, accelerated the pace of her calls. The receptionist in Chicago wasn't any help. Berg had left no word of his whereabouts.

By the time Berg stepped into the office at 2:00 P.M., a pile of pink message slips littered his desk. His reporting assistant had put a copy of the *Tribune* on his desk. Together, the two messages spoke volumes. The moment he saw them, Berg suspected he was in trouble. And he was right.

The *Times* carried a story the next day, but Berg may as well have photocopied the *Tribune*. On the biggest Chicago business story of the decade, the nation's newspaper of record would never really catch up.

□ □ □

CELESTA JURKOVICH had been through some strange days running the Chicago Board of Trade's Washington, D.C., lobbying office. But the Thursday before George Bush's inauguration would set a new benchmark. It was the day the Board and the Chicago Mercantile Exchange would jointly host a pre-inaugural dinner for the House Ways and Means Committee. It was also the day the sting story broke.

One minute, the telephone rang with a call about orange muffins for the party. The phone rang again, and it was ABC News, asking her to describe the practice of bucketing trades. Every news organ within a telephone's reach of Washington called. Most of them seemed never to have heard of commodity futures, let alone understand how somebody might steal while trading them.

For Jurkovich, the ordeal was wearing. The Board's two choosy chiefs, Chairman Karsten Mahlmann and President Thomas Donovan, had not even arrived yet, and already the day had been long. She stuffed handfuls of telephone messages in her jacket pocket and never returned most of the calls.

Of course, Mahlmann and Donovan did not stop by the office. That would not make sense. There was too much lobbying to do, and inauguration weekend was the perfect time for it. The usual distractions of Washington life—junkets to foreign countries, visits to home districts, fund-raising parties in Hollywood—would not apply. This was the lone night every four years that would make Washington the social center of the nation. Bush's inaugural bash might not measure up to Ronald Reagan's, but this still was one event not to be missed.

Mahlmann and Donovan's first stop was at the CFTC's headquarters on K Street, a bureaucratic outpost set well away from the mainstream of the federal triangle. There, the two exchange leaders met the CFTC's newest commissioner, William Albrecht. Next came the meetings with staff of the legislative panels that held the regulatory future of the industry in their hands, the Senate and House agriculture and banking committees.

Already, Mahlmann and Donovan had the rap down well. All they knew of the investigation, they had read in the papers. The U.S. Attorney's office hadn't even extended the courtesy of a warning telephone call. The CFTC officially was keeping mum but was believed to have been involved in the probe. Whatever the newspapers might say—and it was obvious they'd have plenty to say because their anonymous sources would babble on at will—the scandal still did not change one fact: "We've got more than 3,000 members at the Board of Trade," Donovan reasoned. "When you have that many people, whether it's banking, insurance, even politics, you're going to have a few bad apples." He figured that the exchanges had done their best to root out corruption. If they and the CFTC had missed a handful of traders, it was not for lack of effort. After all, the Chicago exchanges had recently responded to CFTC prodding and spent more than $1 million developing their Computerized Trade Reconstruction system, dubbed CTR.

Donovan thought the pitch went over rather well. But it was hard to tell with staffers, who don't always have the same political instincts, the survival skills, of the representatives themselves. Where a politician's outrage might be tempered by thoughts of the exchanges' hefty PAC power, staffers tended to see only the specter of customer rip-offs and lawless floor trading.

"It was a very unhappy time, right at the inaugural," Donovan would remember. "But fortunately, it gave us a chance to talk to a number of members of Congress and their staffs and tell them our side of the story."

Whatever the importance of the meetings with the staffs, the Board of Trade delegates knew where the most crucial three hours of their trip would be spent: at the Grand Hotel. In the wake of the scandalous revelations, the Ways and Means dinner would be a vital first move toward seizing the issue by the throat and gradually, but oh, so forcefully, strangling it to death.

The Board would not struggle alone. This was one time when it would be good to have the Merc team along. The nearly constant stream of CFTC reauthorization proceedings had taught the two Chicago exchanges to accommodate one another when their fates were dangling together in Washington, and this was just such a time. The great stock market crash of 1987, in particular, had taught them to come out swinging together from the same corner in order to preserve their markets, their regulators, and most important of all, the right to set the rate for margin payments required of traders—the very lifeblood of their business.

The Merc's Leo Melamed was never so fully in his element as when he was in Washington. Leo had made his mark in the markets, but he could well have been a politician. His rhetorical flourishes, his keen instincts, his expansive ego would have served him well. As head of the Merc and as a legend in his industry, Leo had achieved a certain political stature in his own right, a regular and respected face on Capitol Hill.

Donning his tuxedo for the pre-inaugural party that night, Melamed half-listened to the Cable News Network on television in his Washington hotel room. Suddenly, something anchorman Lou Dobbs said jerked Melamed to attention. "Government agents served subpoenas on Chicago's commodities markets today," Melamed thought he heard Dobbs say. "Among those receiving subpoenas was Leo Melamed, chairman of the Chicago Mercantile Exchange."

Melamed snatched the telephone receiver. His first instinct was to call Dobbs and perforate his eardrum. Either Dobbs was wrong, or Melamed's people had failed to inform him. Instead, he dialed Merc public relations man Andy Yemma. Melamed ranted and raged and then asked Yemma to kindly pass his thoughts along to Mr. Dobbs, or words to that effect. Of course, CNN had gotten it wrong. Like many firms, Melamed's Dellsher Investment Co. had received a subpoena, but Melamed personally had not been served any papers.

By the time the party started, Melamed had cooled down some. None of the lawmakers said anything about the CNN report. That meant they either hadn't heard it, or did not have the nerve to bring it up—Melamed couldn't tell which. Certainly, if they wanted to, they had plenty of chances. The investigation was the talk of the night.

Across the room, Donovan was getting a read on Congress's reaction. "People in politics are less apt to rush to judge someone else based on what they read in the newspapers," Donovan would later explain. "They've all been the targets of an unfair attack. They learn to be somewhat suspicious of headlines."

Still, he couldn't deny the pall hanging over the proceedings. The crowd of 90 people—members of Congress, their spouses, the Board's officers and key members, and their wives or dates—should have been alive with anticipation of the inauguration. Instead, they grouped in whispering huddles.

Donovan could not help feeling depressed. The exchanges had fought for two years to rehabilitate their image after the stock market crash. Their contributions had built a solid political foundation with Bush. Just when all seemed clear, the headlines hit. "It was one of those situations where you know you're going to have to struggle for a year just to get back to where you were yesterday," Donovan said.

Leave it to Dan Rostenkowski, the old Chicago street pol, to save the night. The powerful chairman of Ways and Means put a beefy arm around Donovan's shoulder and turned to his old friend. "Hold your head up," he said. "You believe in yourself. That's all that matters."

□ □ □

FOR A BIG CITY, Chicago can be a very small town, for people in the commodities markets in particular. They move within a six-block area, bounded roughly by the Merc and the Board of Trade. Many even live just blocks away. Walking in the Loop business district, their pastel trading jackets stand out like lettermen's sweaters did in high school, setting them apart from the suitcoat and briefcase set. Most traders know each other by face and by badge acronym, if not by name.

For Bill Walsh then, running into Robert Mosky, a fellow broker from the Swiss franc pit, downtown on the evening of January 19 was hardly unusual. But the place of their meeting was extraordinary: They were both in the waiting room of Elliot Samuels, one of the defense lawyers whose name had circulated at the Merc on the morning of the FBI visits.

It had been one hell of a morning. At 6:00 A.M., Walsh had met with the two big Swiss franc brokers, Gary Kost and Michael Joyce, to map strategy. When Walsh had come home the night before, he had two messages on his answering machine—one from Kost, one from Joyce, both of whom had been visited by the FBI. A few minutes later, there was a knock at his door. One of the three visitors was Randy Jackson, the trader, whom he soon knew as FBI agent Randall Jannett.

The morning meeting near the Swiss pit was to the point. Walsh, Kost, and Joyce swapped stories and compared what they had told the agents, which wasn't much. They all agreed not to "flip" and cooperate with the government. Walsh was tight for money and Joyce, who headed the broker group that the three belonged to would promise to help pay Walsh's legal bills by taking only half of the commission he normally received from Walsh's trading.

The balance of the day had gone quickly, though it was hard to concentrate on the market with the constant talk of the investigation. Walsh felt better knowing so many others had been visited by the feds. So when he walked into Samuels's office and Mosky, his wife, Leslie, and their daughter were sitting in the foyer, Walsh was barely surprised. As they waited, Richie Endless, another trader from the pit, walked out of Samuels's office, just another scared face in the crowd. Before seeing Samuels, Walsh and Mosky decided to meet after their appointments.

Their visits with the lawyer were brief—the traders described the FBI visits, the types of questions the prosecutors had asked, and what kind of liability they thought they had. They discussed Samuels' fees, but no decisions were made. Samuels clearly was interviewing them as much as they were screening him. Lawyers wanted clients who were willing to fight.

Leaving Samuels's office, Walsh and Mosky went to Lloyd's Chicago, a mid-priced restaurant on nearby Madison Street. Mosky had strong opinions about the case, just like he had strong opinions about everything. "The tapes aren't going to be any good, anyway," Mosky told Walsh.

But Walsh was worried. A small-timer always trying to fit in, he tended to brag a lot, stretching the truth. And Walsh had bragged to Jackson/Jannett about capers in the pit. He had even paid off a $9 blackjack bet to Jannett with a pre-arranged trade of a customer order. "Now we're even," Walsh had told Jannett. "You pay the taxes." The line was good for a laugh at the time.

Mosky seemed indifferent to Walsh's story. He was convinced that the government was trying to strong-arm everybody, to use the press to get people scared. Mosky knew he hadn't talked to Jannett except in the trading pit, and there was nothing incriminating that he could remember.

The biggest risk was scared people talking to the feds. "Stick together, and everything will be fine," Mosky told Walsh. "If nobody says a word, they won't have a case."

□ □ □

IF REPORTERS AT EITHER OF THE CHICAGO PAPERS had doubted how big a story this was, the *Journal* cleared up all confusion with a bang-up story on Friday. Occupying the prominent right-hand column of the front page, the lengthy, in-depth story more than made up for the *Journal*'s embarrassment of the day before. The *Journal* had names of government moles and traders under suspicion, information nobody else had printed.

But it was the lame *New York Times* story that grabbed the most attention in competitors' newsrooms. For Bill Neikirk at the *Trib*, the *Times'* flop was a thrill. There, on the newspaper of record's January 20 front page, was a story that cited the *Tribune*, not once, not twice, but six times.

As he tacked the *Times'* front page to his bulletin board, Neikirk chortled with glee. During his years in Washington, he had been *Times*ed again and again—had his scoops stolen and reprinted in the gray lady from New York with never a credit. "For me, this is the ultimate thrill," he told a colleague. "This is a highlight of my career."

The *Trib* staff took time to gloat.

□ □ □

FRIDAY, JANUARY 20, WAS ANOTHER unhappy morning at the *Sun-Times*. Jim Schembari, the paper's business editor, called Greg Burns, Assistant Business Editor Gavin Maliska, and one of the paper's business columnists into his office to try to count the injuries.

First, the *Trib* beat them on Thursday. Then, the *Journal*'s Friday powerhouse blew them out again. It was time to assess blame.

The columnist beefed about Maliska's Wednesday evening fumble. "What are you doing calling the government?" he demanded, still outraged at the editor's attempt at reporting. "I wouldn't have taken a 'no comment' from them."

"Well, I'm sorry," Maliska said, sarcasm sharpening his voice. "I didn't know you're the only one around here who can call a source."

Burns griped that he needed more help. "Look at this list," he said, pointing to the italic byline at the bottom of the *Trib*'s story. "They've got everybody on it. We can't do it alone. Jim, you've got to get us some help."

Schembari fretted that the drubbing from the *Trib* was making him look bad. "You guys didn't advance the story," he said. "If it weren't for Art Petacque, we would have looked like shit."

Petacque, the *Sun-Times'* Pulitzer Prize–winning crime reporter, indeed had moved the story ahead. Dictating a story from a Las Vegas hotel room, he had conjured an item seemingly straight out of Dickens' *Oliver Twist*. The FBI had discovered a band of crooked old-timers that, Fagin-like, had taught young traders how to cheat.

Petacque's piece was great copy. Except, of course for one minor detail: It wasn't true.

□ □ □

THE COMMODITY FUTURES TRADING COMMISSION had faced a simple quandary: to leak, or not to leak. And already, it was looking like the decision not to leak had been the wrong one.

In every newspaper story, every television clip, all anybody talked about was the FBI agents and the U.S. Attorney's office. In all the publicity, the CFTC was barely mentioned. To make matters worse, it was a reauthorization year, and if the word didn't get out soon, nobody in Congress or in the pits would ever believe the CFTC had a hand in the project.

The irony was that the CFTC did play a role. Director of Enforcement Dennis Klejna had worked with the U.S. Attorney's office and the FBI from the beginning. Charlotte Ohlmiller, an enforcement staffer in Chicago, had tutored the agents and helped with their recordkeeping on an almost daily basis. For the last two years, as the project gained steam, it had taken up virtually all her time. There even were some good fights about how much of Ohlmiller's time Klejna was commandeering. "Hey, I've got an investigation I've got to close here," one of the department heads remembered asking Klejna during the thick of the project. "When can I get Charlotte?"

And what was the CFTC getting for all that? Not a peep. Somebody at Justice was singing to the press, and the folks on K Street were keeping mum.

In the debate about leaking, Klejna himself had favored the silent act. The discussion began almost as soon as he made his rounds the week before subpoenas were served in Chicago. One by one, Klejna had knocked on the commissioners' doors and laid out for them the broad brushstrokes of the investigation: undercover FBI agents in four different pits, from late 1984 to the present; the cooperation from insiders; the scope of the expected first round of subpoenas; the involvement of the CFTC, and the need for secrecy throughout, even within the agency.

Of course, the first commissioner he visited was the chairman, Wendy Lee Gramm. None of the three people who had served as chairman of the CFTC while the investigation was conducted, Susan Phillips, interim chairman Kalo Hineman, and Gramm, had been told. Klejna's silence during the undercover phase made him either insubordinate or a hero—the former if the investigation didn't pan out or got leaked too soon; the latter if everything went okay and the chairman could still be informed in time to take the appropriate bows. In retrospect, the decision to keep the project secret from the chairman's office appeared sound. There was no way Klejna could have foreseen that Phillips would join the Merc's board promptly after leaving the commission. But had she known, and still joined the Merc, it would have been a security disaster.

All the commissioners wished they could have known. But all professed they understood Klejna's reasons for keeping the operation secret. As head of the enforcement division, that was his prerogative. Until he told his peers in the other departments—Andrea Corcoran, head of the division of trading and markets was most directly affected—Klejna was the only department head who knew about the super-secret investigation of the Chicago exchanges.

With the investigation now on the front pages of the nation's newspapers, though, Klejna and company were in a fix. Each new Justice-praising headline spelled just one thing for the CFTC: a public relations disaster. Klejna knew he would have to turn the problem around. It had been his project. Now that it was time to make sure the CFTC got credit, it would be his job to do that, too.

Klejna first called Valukas about the publicity problem Friday afternoon, January 20. In the *Chicago Tribune* and *The Wall Street Journal*, stories featuring the escapades of the FBI and the boys at the U.S. Attorney's office had ignored the CFTC. "I'd like to know where all this stuff is coming from," Klejna told Valukas.

"It's not me, and as far as I know, it's nobody on my staff," Valukas said. Neither of them doubted the source—the Justice Department in Washington. Attorney General Thornburgh was no stranger to the well-placed press leak. "What do you want me to do?" Valukas asked, as if something could be done.

The Friday conversation was hardly the last. At times, it seemed it would have made sense to just leave an open line between Washington and Chicago, as well as one among the commissioners, Klejna, and Corcoran. Valukas sympathized with Klejna's position. But then, flattering instant profiles in the *Tribune*, *New York Times*, and *Wall Street Journal*—all while the initials CFTC were nowhere to be seen— probably helped ease his mind.

Finally, on Sunday morning, came the last straw. It was Attorney General Thornburgh on "Meet the Press." "Obviously, I can't discuss in detail what's a pending investigation," Thornburgh said. "I don't want to, obviously, make any predictions. But the investigation is far- reaching, it is significant."

At home, the CFTC's Andrea Corcoran practically jumped out of her chair. "There he is telling the whole country it's his investigation," she complained. "He's practically going on the Carson show and we're still not saying anything." Corcoran had lobbied from the beginning for discreet cooperation when reporters called. She was publicity- savvy enough to know how bad the agency would look if it did not appear to be involved in the sting. But in the end, Gramm had sided with Klejna and against any leaks.

The Thornburg appearance on "Meet the Press" was the end of the line for the CFTC. In yet another phone call, Klejna finally de- manded some help from Valukas. "Tony, we're getting killed on this," he said.

Valukas agreed. He had wanted to make no public comment about the investigation until the grand jury returned indictments. The Op- eration Incubator fiasco—the embarrassment over the leaks to the Florida magazine writer—had taught him that much. But there was no choice on this one. Thornburgh blabbing on television had sealed it.

"I'll come out with a statement tomorrow," Valukas promised.

The U.S. Attorney's statement, a three-sentence letter thanking Gramm for the CFTC's help in the investigation, was his first public acknowledgment of the probe. The CFTC released the letter publicly, but the damage had already been done. To outsiders, the missive looked like an obvious whitewash, professional courtesy from Valukas, covering for the CFTC as it headed into reauthorization hearings. The press openly scoffed. The CFTC wasn't up to a job like this. It was too ineffectual, perhaps even unreliable. The commission had been left completely out of the loop.

For four days, with reporters turning over every rock they could find, the CFTC had been nowhere to be seen. Not one source mentioned its cooperation, and none of the stories credited the agency for playing a part. Everything was FBI and U.S. Attorney. The press was not about to change its story now.

□ □ □

THE OFFICE OF THE *Tribune*'s business section, normally a mausoleum on weekends, was abustle. Four teams of reporters were combing the city and suburbs, visiting the homes of traders whom the *Trib* considered suspects in the probe. Two business reporters were working the phones, methodically calling the homes of traders on a photocopied list.

In the home of David Alpert, a veteran yen trader from the Chicago Mercantile Exchange, the phone rang like Ticketmaster's before a hot concert. When Linda Alpert picked up the phone for the umpteenth time, a *Trib* reporter was on the other end. "Rumor has it that your husband was subpoenaed," she said. "I'd like to talk to him right away."

Linda Alpert said nothing and knew less. Under the circumstances, with the papers full of scandal, the call scared her silly. Her husband, David, was on a business trip to the West Coast. When he finally returned on Sunday, the phone rang again. "I have a list of people who have been subpoenaed and your name is on it," a *Tribune* reporter said. Tired of the telephone terrorism, Alpert asked where the list came from, but the reporter would not say.

Only later would Alpert deduce that the list was probably nothing more than names in the Merc directory. The *Tribune* was obviously fishing for so-called targets. But still, that didn't stop his stomach from churning, or his anger from boiling.

□ □ □

LEO MELAMED STEPPED THROUGH the glass doors leading to the trading floor of the Chicago Mercantile Exchange. In itself, Leo on the floor was not unusual. He was there from time to time, when not jetting to some distant continent promoting the Merc. But this was Leo's first trip to the floor since the scandal broke, and everyone who noticed him was watching.

Melamed walked purposefully down the center aisle, between the meat pits on the left and the S&P 500 pit on the right. He veered southwest, toward the currency quadrant of the trading floor. Once there, he waded into the yen pit, heading directly toward broker David Horberg.

The Wall Street Journal that morning had identified Horberg as a target of the investigation. It had noted prominently that Horberg, one of the biggest traders in the yen pit and in the past year a co-chairman of the exchange committee responsible for discipline in the yen pit, cleared through Melamed's firm, Dellsher. The story had not mentioned that Horberg handled Melamed's personal trades. Even so, Melamed was not going to stand for this kind of publicity.

Melamed confronted Horberg and told him he was finished. Dellsher was done clearing his trades. The two argued for a few minutes, but Horberg clearly was getting nowhere. Melamed turned and walked out of the pit. A few minutes later, Horberg did, too. After the public dressing-down by the Merc's most powerful leader, it took Horberg months to find another firm to clear his trades.

Before Horberg's name had surfaced, Melamed had argued that runaway press reports were denying traders the presumption of innocence. He complained that innocent people were being unfairly tarred by leaks from the government. He defended the Merc's decision to allow subpoenaed traders to continue handling customer orders. "This is still a democracy," Melamed said. "People still have rights."

But now Horberg—only subpoenaed but not indicted—was being kicked off the floor. "I did it on advice of counsel," Melamed would rationalize, pegging Merc lawyer Jerrold Salzman with making the decision. "This is bigger than me. This is bigger than Dellsher. The exchange has a lot at risk here, and my counsel advised me of it."

Suddenly, all that talk about ideals and innocence was sounding rather hollow.

□ □ □

BILL CRAWFORD HAD NEVER HAD IT SO EASY. There, on the Board of Trade's 12th-floor, walked two goons with thick, brown accordian folders. A story on the Knight-Ridder Financial News Service had brought him down to the Board.

As soon as he saw the two squares, Crawford knew the tip was a good one. As the G-men made their way from office to office, serving papers at every clearing firm in the joint, Crawford tagged along. He buttonholed whomever he could in the firms, just to make sure the papers were, in fact, subpoenas.

Crawford felt comfortable calling the government wallpaper job "a sweeping escalation" of the probe in his January 25 *Trib* story. But that was too tame for the *Sun-Times*. With nuclear-powered calculators, the tabloid figured that the feds were seeking "ten billion trading documents" in a move that signaled a focus on "trading firms rather than individual traders and brokers."

The competition was getting deep.

□ □ □

DEFENSE LAWYER THOMAS A. DURKIN sat across the desk from prosecutor Daniel Gillogly, but not for long. After a few seconds had passed, both men were on their feet.

Durkin knew precisely how to make Gillogly's temper rise. Although the two generally kept on good terms, baiting Gillogly had become one of Durkin's favorite pastimes over the years, especially when he thought it might help a client.

This time, it was more than a game. Durkin was appearing for the first time on behalf of Sam A. Cali. A longtime yen broker, Cali had made some regrettable statements to agents the evening of January 18, not the least of which was a promise to cooperate with the government. Now it was Durkin's job to let Gillogly know that Cali would not be flipping after all.

"I can't believe you're doing this," Gillogly complained, the tone of his voice edging toward a whine. "Your guy said he was flipping." Gillogly hinted that some big-time trader had probably pressured Cali to change his mind.

Now it was Durkin's turn to get hot. "That's bullshit, Dan, and you know it," he said. Durkin explained how cynical he considered the entire investigation. The feds were nailing small-timers like Cali because they hadn't been able to get any of the big guys. "You think I'm standing in for somebody?" Durkin said, suspicious the government was hammering Cali in an effort to get to bigger, and presumably more culpable traders. His voice rising as he jumped to his feet, Durkin leaned across Gillogly's desk. "If you do, let's hear about it." he said. "Let me know who you think it is. Let's make a deal."

For the time being at least, Gillogly was not playing ball. Valukas, living up to his "Tough Tony" nickname, had ruled that nobody could get a deal without pleading guilty to racketeering charges.

"Nobody's getting any deals," Gillogly vowed. "Not without RICO."

□ □ □

A WEEK HAD PASSED SINCE DREW had written the first story, and he was casting about for the next day's lead.

Tom Burton was chasing down a tip that the FBI still had two undercover agents on the trading floors, trying to catch incriminating conversations among traders. The lead was iffy but would probably still make page one if Burton could nail it down. Still, Drew wanted something brand-new.

Suddenly, it came. Sallie Gaines called from the Merc's public relations office. "Melamed's giving interviews," she told Drew. "I'm in Yemma's office. Leo's summoning us up one by one."

"Wait there," Drew replied. "I'll come right over and join you."

"Go straight to Leo's office," Gaines told him.

Drew raced to a cab and reached the Merc building in less than five minutes. Melamed was the first exchange chief to break silence, and Drew couldn't wait to grill him.

He jumped an elevator to the Dellsher offices on the 19th floor. Gaines wasn't around. Drew identified himself to the receptionist, who used the phone to declare his presence.

Out walked a short-haired, petite woman who obviously was not Leo Melamed. "Mr. Yemma has left explicit instructions that under no circumstances are you allowed in to join the interview," she stated flatly.

Drew was miffed. The Merc had griped about the *Trib*'s zealous coverage since day one. Here was their chance to complain to the source, and they were blowing it. "I was over there willing to be educated by Mr. Melamed, willing to listen to anything he had to say," Drew would recall. "And he wouldn't let me in the door."

□ □ □

THE *SUN-TIMES* MEETINGS were held in a cramped, dingy conference room, steps away from the smoking dungeon with its nicotine-coated walls. At the *Trib* and the *Journal*, reporters were fighting to stay on the story. At the *Sun-Times*, they were angling to get off. The paper would score some minor hits—discovering the codenames Operation Sourmash and Operation Hedgeclipper, revealing ADM's suspected 1985 manipulation of the soybean oil contract, the first reporting on the content of the FBI's tapes—but by and large, the *Sun-Times* effort was a disaster. And everyone working on the story knew it.

Mark Eissmann, the 30-year-old assistant to the editor, was in charge of the *Sun-Times'* motley and demoralized crew. It was a tough job. Chuck Neubauer and Deborah Nelson, the only two *Sun-Times* reporters devoted to investigative reporting, were dragged in early on but within days had started avoiding the meetings, hoping to drop out of the picture. Art Petacque, who had added a spurious report about money laundering at the exchanges to his earlier "scoop," now known as the "School for Scandal" story, was never in the office. Greg Burns busily worked his sources, but other business staffers were back to their assignments, ducking the commodities beat. Charles Nicodemus, an investigative veteran, dutifully catalogued most of the reporters' activities. As each person dropped out, the list of daily tasks grew: calling defense lawyers, contacting traders, running down tips, checking for court filings.

Some days after the story first broke, only Nicodemus and Burns showed up for the daily meeting. It was the last time they even bothered.

□ □ □

IT WAS 9:00 A.M. THURSDAY MORNING, JANUARY 26. Chris Drew, hair still wet from his shower in the Marriott Hotel across Michigan Avenue, doughnut in hand from the *Trib*'s first-floor galley, occupied the seat across from Neikirk's desk. Bill Crawford and another reporter sat on the two-seat couch. Investigations editor Dean Baquet sat beside Drew.

With the *Trib*'s competitive furor still running high, the drill boiled down to this: Whoever had the best tip of the day would get the lead byline. Whoever contributed the most reporting to the story would be number two. Everybody else would go in the cast of thousands at the tail of the story.

Certainly, the main competition was the *Journal*, or maybe the *Sun-Times*. But there was competition right inside the office, and everybody knew it. Neikirk canvassed the room. John O'Brien, a metro reporter, spoke best, saying that sources told him 30 traders were cooperating.

"That's our lead," Neikirk said.

As the discussion strung along, Tom Burton left the room. A few moments later, he was back. He had confirmed that a trader named Bill Todd had introduced the moles into the Merc.

The number was wildly optimistic, and wrong. But heck, it made great copy. For traders and lawyers, it heightened the paranoia running rampant through the exchanges. But among reporters inside Tribune Tower, there was only one thing that really mattered: O'Brien and Burton had earned the top byline for the day.

□ □ □

TRIBUNE PHOTO EDITOR JACK CORN had given up. He must have searched through a thousand old photos, shot whenever the market moved up or down. Pretty quickly, they all looked the same: traders in the pits, arms jutting skyward. And they all lacked the same thing: a trader with the badge JXN.

As Corn walked away, photographer Ernie Cox came running after him. "I got it, I got it," he said.

Serendipity: The photo showed a bearded, balding, bespectacled man with a concerned look on his face. His badge clearly showed the letters JXN, a phononym for Jackson, Randy Jackson. It was the first look any reporter had of a mole.

The next day, January 29, the *Trib*'s more than one million Sunday readers got a look, too. To some traders reading over their coffee tables at home, it would look like the *Trib* must have obtained the photo from government files. At the *Tribune*, the photo scoop won Bill Crawford's story of life in the pits a spot on page one.

□ □ □

FINALLY, THE WALL CAME CRUMBLING DOWN. Cash Mahlmann and Tom Donovan had maintained a stony silence ever since the news first hit the papers, but the Board's members had prevailed. Mahlmann and Donovan couldn't even go on the trading floor, knowing they would be mobbed by traders desperate for information.

Here it was, January 31, and more than 400 Board of Trade members were gathered on the agricultural trading floor to hear what their leadership had planned. And they expected a lot.

The Merc had announced formation of a blue ribbon panel, and the Board was silent. The newspapers reported that dozens of traders had flipped and were cooperating with the government, and the Board was silent. Valukas was taking bows in Washington, an appointee to a new six-city task force on white-collar crime, and the Board was silent. Even the CFTC was claiming it was involved in the investigation, and the Board was silent.

But the silence had to stop. It had the members frustrated and angry. Too many of them thought the public construed their silence as an admission of guilt. The Merc, as usual, was outflanking them on public relations. They wanted action, a defense of their livelihoods, not this damned stoic, self-defeating silence.

Mahlmann made the opening remarks. Blowing into the microphone, he said, "This may not be the only one in the room," a dry joke that loosened up the members. Mahlmann told the traders they were an honest group of people, unfairly vilified by the press and ambushed by the U.S. Attorney's office. The Board was planning to sink $1 million into improvements of its trading surveillance systems. But he claimed the systems hardly needed work.

"We uncovered evidence of suspicious trading by a member known as Richard Carlson several weeks before leaks to the press," Mahlmann said, his methodic voice rising. By now, every trader knew Carlson was one of the moles. Mahlmann explained that the investigation was not complete enough to bring to the exchange's disciplinary committee before the headlines flew.

It seemed there were no secrets on the floor any more. All the traders had heard of another mole, who went by the name Ron Hansen. He never got beyond clerking for traders in the T-bond pit. But Hansen had shown up on the trading floor one day handing out subpoenas. Such indignities riled the traders.

Mahlmann swore the Board would defend its way of doing business. He said the exchange would fight to retain self-regulation and protect "dual trading," the practice that allows brokers to trade for themselves while also handling customer orders. The vow drew cheers from the crowd. Then came the big surprise: The Board of Trade had hired Dan K. Webb, Valukas's predecessor as U.S. Attorney, to give legal advice to the exchange and its members about ramifications of the racketeering laws.

Perhaps Webb, now a lawyer at the law firm of Winston & Strawn, was a better choice than even Mahlmann knew. He could certainly bring firsthand insight into the government's thinking on the matter: Webb was still U.S. Attorney when Operation Sourmash got started. When asked months later about Webb's dual role, Board officials said they were not aware of the direct conflict of interest Webb had as both originator of and defender against the investigation. "I asked him if he had any conflicts, and he said no," explained Scott Early, the Board's general counsel. "They have a conflicts committee at Winston, and they apparently saw no problem."

When Mahlmann threw the meeting open to the floor, the talk ran wild. One trader complained that he did not like being embarrassed about his job. Another described the visit he received from FBI agents, who pushed again and again for him to cooperate and fink on other traders.

Before long, the talk turned to what was, for many traders, the top concern of the day: Mahlmann's mishandling of the events. Paul F. McGuire, a member since 1948, rose. "I think this institution is being dragged through the mud, and I don't think you're doing enough to stop it," McGuire said.

For Mahlmann, the meeting went downhill from there. McGuire was just the tip of the iceberg. At that moment, a campaign to take Mahlmann's job in the next election, to blame him for the mishandling of the investigation, was born. Leslie Rosenthal, the controversial onetime chairman of the exchange, suddenly saw that the once-invincible Mahlmann suddenly was beatable.

□ □ □

THE STORY WAS TWO WEEKS OLD, and by now it was almost a grind. Still, the scandal had been on page one for 13 days running. And hell, it had even knocked the presidential inauguration below the fold on the *Tribune*'s front page. Finally, on February 2, Operation Sourmash and Operation Hedgeclipper were going inside the paper for the first time.

Drew, Baquet, and Neikirk worked until the paper went to bed at 11:00 P.M., the final deadline for their story. Then they took dinner together, planning the next day's assignments, swapping war stories from the day just done.

As usual, the restaurant was a nearby Chinese place. Two factors recommended the joint: It was near the Tower, and the food wasn't bad. Sitting in the red-carpeted, red-chaired, windowless Chinese restaurant, the three barely looked at the menu. They already knew it by heart.

After they finished eating, the trio could not miss noting what happened next. A large black rat scampered across the dining room and into the kitchen. Drew called the waiter, who protested. What the reporters just saw could not have happened, the waiter insisted.

It was a fitting metaphor for the last two weeks: rats running for cover, and officials denying what they knew to be the truth.

CHAPTER THIRTEEN

□ □ □

Damage Control

IN 1989, JANUARY WAS THE CRUELEST MONTH, by far. The last two weeks in January, really. But for futures traders, who expect the world to change moment by moment when a new price flashes across the exchange's quote board, two weeks in the spotlight had seemed like a year.

By month's end, the pace slowed. The headlines grew smaller and then moved off the front pages. The newspaper stories seemed to reflect a deeper understanding of the markets. And one or two even criticized the government—for its heavy-handed tactics, the threat to use RICO, in particular.

The time had come for damage control. To somehow turn the tide. To try to make the investigation yesterday's news. To get out the story of Chicago's free markets, and the benefits of self-regulation. At the Board of Trade, there was an encouraging sign: a stack of letters from customers more than two inches thick, coming to the defense of dual trading. The letters were carefully filed away, image ammunition for future use.

The worst part was the waiting. From the outset, the government sources leaking to the *Tribune* had said that they expected indictments in six weeks. Defense lawyers had scoffed, and predicted six months. Most people expected somewhere in between.

For the exchanges, business had to move on. The damage had to be repaired with customers, with Congress, with regulators, maybe even with the press. The task wouldn't be easy. But there wasn't any choice.

□ □ □

THE MERC HAD CALLED IT a blue ribbon committee, formed January 26 to study surveillance and regulatory systems and rule on the fate of broker groups and dual trading. But for a few seconds, it was a blue language panel, too. "You're a sneaky, lying son of a bitch, and I don't believe a word you say," blurted Thomas F. Eagleton, the former Missouri senator.

Eagleton's wrath, the first sign of trouble ahead for the committee, was directed at Jerrold Salzman, the Merc's outside counsel. Salzman had been explaining why the Merc, as soon as the government investigation went public, had backtracked its auditing system and reconstructed the trading activity of the two FBI moles who had worked on the Merc floor.

Eagleton's attack on Salzman was hardly an auspicious start for the February 1 kickoff meeting of the panel Leo Melamed had formed to help clear the Merc's name. In doing so, he was taking a page from the manual of late Chicago mayor Richard J. Daley. To Daley it was an axiom: Nothing kills controversy like a committee.

Nobody was surprised then, when the Chicago Mercantile Exchange annointed a blue ribbon committee just a week after the investigation went public, to buffer the exchange from the publicity glare. Melamed announced that nine people "beyond reproach" would investigate the Merc's surveillance, compliance, auditing, and trading systems. He would constantly refer to the panel as objective "outsiders," but that was a stretch. Only one person, Chicago Corp. brokerage firm chairman John A. Wing, was not already a Merc board member. At least no one could have blamed Leo for expecting the tame, deferential tones so common at Merc board meetings.

Eagleton's sudden outburst made clear that Leo's deck was not very neatly stacked. Eagleton thought he smelled obstruction of justice. Edgy already about the exposure his reputation was suffering in the trading scandal, Eagleton wanted no part of an obstruction controversy.

Already, U.S. Attorney Anton Valukas had summoned the Merc brass to his office and demanded an explanation of what they were doing. Valukas gave them a provisional okay to proceed with routine rule enforcement. But before they left the meeting, Valukas pointedly warned Leo Melamed and John Geldermann not to interfere with the government's work.

Eagleton felt that Valukas' warning was going unheeded, and he wanted no part of it. What's more, he was throwing his weight Salzman's way, letting the lawyer know he was a former U.S. Senator who knew how to go on the offensive when he had to.

When Salzman asked the retired lawmaker to step into an anteroom, more than one person on the nine-member panel wondered whether the two might come to blows. Instead, Salzman produced a letter from the CFTC acknowledging that the Merc had not only the right, but the responsibility to continue guarding against trading abuses. The letter seemed to appease Eagleton. "I apologize for what I said," he told Salzman.

The two had reached a truce, for the time being, at least.

□ □ □

NOW THIS WOULD BE AN ORDEAL. The last person in the world *Tribune* reporter Chris Drew wanted to spend time with was John Troelstrup, the former CFTC official, former Merc enforcement lawyer, and current private attorney. But the two had appeared on John Callaway's February 2 "Chicago Tonight" public television show, and Troelstrup had asked for a ride back downtown. It would be more than rude to leave him stranded at the WTTW studios on the city's far Northwest Side.

Besides, Drew could drill Troelstrup for some information. After all, with his background Troelstrup might have something worthwhile to say. Before the show, Troelstrup had even told Drew that he once proposed installing hidden cameras on the Merc's floor, but was turned down by the exchange brass. Then, when Drew raised that topic during the show, Troelstrup parried the question. Slippery, Drew thought.

As Drew drove the white *Tribune*-owned Chevrolet downtown, he carefully worked on Troelstrup. The lawyer claimed the Merc's disciplinary committee never prosecuted 50 percent of the disciplinary cases he investigated. Drew didn't have to hear another word from the blow-dried, silver-blond haired lawyer. With that tip about the Merc, Troelstrup had earned his ride home.

Gradually, Troelstrup took control of the conversation. It took him a while, but he finally got to the point. "Why do you think that Valukas didn't just hold a press conference and announce this thing instead of letting it come out in bits and pieces?" Troelstrup asked.

"I don't know why they did what they did," Drew replied. He drew a contrast with a previous investigation he had covered, a scandal at the Pentagon, which the government revealed via a major news conference. "I don't know why they did one thing in that case and something else in this one," Drew concluded.

Troelstrup thought he had it. To him, Drew had just confirmed he was the recipient of a major government leak. Drew obviously had taken the prosecution's line on the investigation without skepticism. And Troelstrup detected in the young reporter a strong but well-concealed ego, an ego tied up in making sure the investigation turned out big. As soon as he could, Troelstrup would spread the word that the *Tribune* story had come directly from a government leak, a claim that rang true to traders and defense lawyers.

Drew felt he had ducked the question. The last person he would tell about his sources was Troelstrup, who had come off as a creepy character to him. Drew hadn't even told Dean Baquet where he got the tip, and the *Trib's* investigations editor had been groomsman in his wedding. All Drew cared was that he had wrenched a good tip from Troelstrup about the Merc's disciplinary process.

The next day, *Tribune* reporter Carol Jouzaitis went to Troelstrup's office to check out the tip about the Merc's less-than-vigilant enforcement efforts. When Jouzaitis asked about the number of discipline cases the Merc's enforcement committees had rejected, Troelstrup repeated the same gambit he had pulled on Drew during the Callaway show the night before: He ducked and dodged.

□ □ □

THEY SAW THE FUTURE, and they weren't very impressed. To floor traders at the Board of Trade, the idea of computerized after-hours trading had never been popular. That was even before the government had prompted congressional leaders and newspaper pundits to discuss eliminating pit-style trading.

Now, on February 6, the Board was calling another members' meeting, to show its version of trading in a box. To many members, the contraption looked like it belonged in a pine box, about six feet underground. Dubbed Aurora, it featured Nintendo-style graphics that simulated pit activity.

Questions from the floor were hardly supportive. Several traders wanted to know Aurora's cost, but got no firm response. They asked why they had not been asked for more input. They asked if there was any guarantee the system wouldn't put them out of business.

If the meeting was designed to distract the press from the investigation, it did not work on that count, either. Afterward, a frustrated Tom Donovan and Cash Mahlmann talked with reporters for the first time since the investigation was made public. Donovan, visibly angry but not quite banging his shoe on the table, complained that news stories were "based on leaks and possibly plants."

Already, the Board suspected that one of its enemies in Washington, former Treasury Secretary Donald Regan, had convinced then-Attorney General Edwin Meese to sick the FBI on the Chicago exchanges in 1984. Some Board officials, Donovan included, thought Regan had a score to settle from one of the tax-straddle fights. If that were really the case, the Board's directors figured, then it could be expected that someone in Washington would leak the story to the *Tribune* to get the most bang out of the investigation. Although such scenarios were widely discussed within the Board of Trade, exchange officials decided to keep such thinking to themselves.

On the heels of Donovan's statement, Mahlmann chimed in. "We have the best exchange in the damned world on cost, on price, and on integrity," he said.

Then the two vowed that their decision to spend $1 million to upgrade the Board's Computerized Trade Reconstruction System was not a reaction to the investigation. They didn't even wink when they said it.

□ □ □

AT FIRST, DROPPING BY TRADERS' HOMES had been exciting for the *Tribune's* Tom Burton, but now it was routine, and almost demoralizing because so little came from the commando house calls. Other than a few new epithets, he had learned little.

The talk with yen trader Thomas A. Crouch on February 4 changed all that. Burton had met Crouch maybe once on the trading floor, but it was during a visit to Crouch's home that the big-time broker turned into a big-time talker.

Crouch described Peter Vogel, the yen mole, and his courtship of crooked traders. He talked about a "breakfast club" at the popular Lou Mitchell's restaurant, he even mentioned the tax scams that Vogel proposed and that Crouch pitched to other traders while himself declining to participate. "Tom, I lost my ass on the S&P's last year," Crouch remembered Vogel saying. "I have this big loss carryover, and I'm willing to sell it to guys who've made a lot of money."

As the bespectacled Crouch, frumpy, red-headed, laconic, spun out his yarns, Burton could not believe what he was hearing, and on the record at that. He knew it would be a great story—the first glimpse anybody had of a big trader who had been snared by the FBI probe. But Crouch claimed he wasn't alone. If he was guilty of breaking the law, so were some of the biggest names at the Merc. "If I have to go to court," Crouch vowed, "I'm going to take the big boys with me."

□ □ □

JOHN KOTEN HAD AN IDEA, and he liked it.

Ever since Koten took over as *The Wall Street Journal's* Chicago bureau chief the day after the scandal hit, the *Journal* had had a pretty good run of stories. The *Chicago Tribune* had started with a big lead on the story, but the *Journal* had more than closed ground. Its reporters had turned up some major news: the first identification of targeted traders by name, a provocative profile of the wild culture of the Japanese yen pit, breaking the story that the giant ABS Partners group had banned dual trading, two stories on exchange executives hiring former salesmen of the scandalous First Commodity Corp. of Boston. Some of the stories would not age quite as well, such as an overly expansive prediction that the Merc part of the investigation focused on 125 traders. Less than two dozen Merc traders would wind up with indictments.

But by mid-February, there was no denying that the story was running out of steam, and it was Koten's job to stoke it up again. The idea hit him: Why not a poll? Koten knew he was no George Gallup, but he figured a survey of traders would give readers a sense of who traders were and what they thought. It might also tip the *Journal* to some leads.

Koten asked each of the five reporters working the story to kick in ideas. By the end of the day, they had a page full of questions, and with a little work the survey was ready for a February 24 mailing. To a question asking how often traders suspected that curb trading, front-running, bucketing, and pre-arranged trading occurred, the survey offered only "Not very often" and "Too often" as possible answers. Other questions focused on the power of broker groups, dual trading, and the appropriateness of the FBI's investigation. It was obviously a survey straight out of the newsroom, anything but a scientific poll— not that any readers would know the difference.

Almost as soon as the first survey reached the first trader on February 25, Koten knew it was a success. The Merc's Andy Yemma called to complain, griping that the survey was biased against the exchanges. The Merc issued a memo to traders calling the survey "an unwar- ranted and unprecedented intrusion." The Board of Trade was sim- ilarly miffed, asking its members, as the Merc did, to ignore the survey. "This is totally inappropriate," Board of Trade public relations man Ray Carmichael told Koten. The *Chicago Sun-Times* even carried a story about the flap.

But before long, the *Journal's* fax machine whirred as the first response came across. About a quarter of the traders responded, in some cases expressing a surprising amount of criticism about the activities of their brethren on the trading floors. Koten knew it was a good idea.

□ □ □

WHATEVER GOOD MIGHT HAVE BEEN ACCOMPLISHED, in the eyes of Congress, Operation Sourmash and Operation Hedgeclipper were most directly responsible for one thing: the elimination of the all-expenses-paid, political-baggage-free trip to the Futures Industry As- sociation's annual convention in Boca Raton, Florida.

Virtually all of the members of the House and Senate committees that oversee the industry had been guests of the industry at the Boca convention at least once. Many repeated the pilgrimage time and again, making the early March migration to the Boca Raton Hotel and Club a rite of spring. A free rite of spring, at that.

For regular attendees, the program was comfortingly predictable. Upon arriving at the peppermint pink resort on Friday afternoon, the lawmakers would be treated to a festive dinner as guests of the ex- changes. On Saturday morning, Representative Dan Rostenkowski (D-Illinois) of Chicago would deliver his traditional go-back-to-sleep breakfast speech, a shopworn review of congressional action that made the muddiest cup of coffee look fresh. The dozen or so legislators then would be split into two panels. There, they each would earn their trip to one of capitalism's most decadent destinations with a 15-minute discussion of an issue vital to, well, vital to someone, no doubt. For their troubles, they would receive a $2,000 speaking fee. That done, the legislators would find much-needed rest on the Boca golf course, a fine place to tee off their enjoyable weekend away from the strains of conducting the nation's business.

For junket-happy legislators, the commodities scandal was bad news indeed. It meant a one-year hiatus from one of the easiest freebies they knew. Suddenly, some of Boca's most enthusiastic veterans lost the wanderlust. House of Agriculture Committee chairman E. Kika de la Garza (D-Texas) was a no-show. Sudden, no-doubt unavoidable conflicts also arose for Senator Patrick Leahy (D-Vermont), chairman of the Senate agriculture committee; Representative Edward Madigan (R-Illinois); and Representative Thomas Coleman (R-Missouri)—industry oversight committee members all.

A few legislators could not resist the Boca summons, but suddenly didn't want the Boca bucks. Representative Glenn English (D-Oklahoma), a prominent agriculture committee member, decided to travel at committee expense and decline his usual Boca speaking fee. Representative Dan Glickman (D-Kansas) accepted travel from the Commodity Exchange of New York but turned down the fee that in the past had always fattened his pocket for the trip home.

The industry's true friends, of course, were those willing to accept the speaker's fee largesse even when the chips were down. In that group belonged Rostenkowski, who gladly accepted an honorarium for his "effort" speaking at the convention. Senator Alan Dixon (D-Illinois), whose "Al the Pal" nickname is apt, and Senator Thomas Daschle (D-South Dakota), also appeared with open palms.

Then there was gray-templed Representative Marty Russo (D-Illinois), the poor-man's Rostenkowski. Through an aide, Russo explained to reporters that "there's no attempt to walk away or be embarrassed" by the industry. "They're a bunch of quality people down there," the aide explained.

Those quality people would have to spend their quality time at Boca Raton without at least one friendly congressman. Representative Russo was a no show.

□ □ □

SINCE THE DAYS OF SENATOR JOSEPH MCCARTHY, holding a list in one's hand has been a simple way for a U.S. congressman to gain attention. So it was that on March 9, at the end of a three-hour hearing on the subject of reauthorizing the Commodity Futures Trading Commission, Senator Patrick Leahy held a list in his hand and asked the chairman of the CFTC to prepare responses, pro and con, to his list of 11 questions.

Leahy's list, though, was anything but tough. His questions—from asking if exchanges should devote more resources to compliance, to querying whether more outsiders should serve on exchange boards, to wondering if perhaps members with lengthy disciplinary records should be barred from exchange disciplinary committees—were a study in powder-puff politics.

Welcome to hardball regulation, futures markets style. To the exchanges, it was time for their "investments" in Congress to pay off, and pay off they did. When it came to cracking down after revelations of the scandal, legislators overseeing the exchanges talked loudly, carried a lot of shtick, and did little.

In her first post-scandal appearance before the Senate agriculture committee, CFTC chairman Wendy Lee Gramm was given the list. She also was allowed to duck a question about the origin of the investigation, and to decline to identify the nature of the CFTC's involvement. When Senator Robert Kerrey wondered aloud whether the CFTC might want authority to conduct undercover operations, Gramm demurred. "It is my view that we have a good cooperative effort" with the FBI, she said. Later on, when the CFTC would respond to less than half of Leahy's list of questions in time to meet his 30-day deadline, the Democratic senator from Vermont simply thanked the commission for its input, and moved on.

With the CFTC still suffering from the perception that it did almost to nothing to help the investigation, many observers had expected finger pointing and fireworks at Gramm's interrogation. Those expectations were never met, although Senator Leahy did take the opportunity to do some extra grandstanding. Leahy had jumped on the investigation early as a headline-making opportunity, and his list of questions was only a start. The senator also announced plans to meet privately with Attorney General Dick Thornburgh for a briefing on the investigation. Another committee member, Senator Robert Kerrey (D-Nebraska), disclosed plans to invite testimony from U.S. District Court Judge Marvin Aspen, who had vilified the Board from the bench, calling it a "cesspool of corruption" just weeks before the investigation made news.

Neither happened. Aspen never was invited. And Thornburgh spoke to the committee in a private session along with U.S. Attorney Anton Valukas, but only after indictments had been announced and the CFTC reauthorization program was well underway. The Thornburgh briefing offered little that hadn't already been disclosed in the newspapers. "They basically just repeated what they had said at the press conference, and elaborated a little more about where the investigation was going," one agriculture committee staffer said. "They didn't name names or anything like that."

Representative Glenn English, chairman of the House agriculture subcommittee that oversees futures markets, in June would propose a dual-trading ban that was virtually a photocopy of the watered-down reform initiated by the Merc's blue ribbon committee. Just as had happened at the Merc, English's proposal was softened during committee wrangling in the ensuing months.

Few people would deny that self-regulation was responsible for many of the problems that led to the undercover investigation. But thanks to the accommodating actions of Leahy, English, and their colleagues, the Chicago exchanges eventually would bluff their way into maintaining the bad old ways of self-regulation.

□ □ □

THE EAGLETON MATTER WAS NOW a full-blown crisis. As was his habit during crises, Leo Melamed gathered his closest advisers around him: In this case, Jack Sandner, Brian Monieson, and Jerrold Salzman were available.

Thomas Eagleton, the former Missouri senator, was threatening to quit the Merc's blue ribbon committee. Since the blow-up with Salzman, his attitude had gotten worse, not better. He was the only blue ribbon committee member to have a lawyer accompany him to meetings. And Eagleton's repeated objections, often preceded by the phrase "Let the record reflect," had nearly prompted some committee members to throttle him.

But this Eagleton gambit was serious. Maury Kravitz had testified on behalf of ABS Partners, presenting his views on broker groups in a slickly prepared presentation, complete with glossy binder. Then, as soon as Eagleton started asking questions, Melamed had cut him off. Eagleton protested, but Melamed complained that the meeting was behind schedule.

Eagleton's threat to quit the committee and, by inference, the Merc's board, was no bluff, and Melamed knew it. If he quit, he'd go out with a bang and subvert the carefully managed "reform" process. As the Merc power brokers conferred, Monieson complained about Eagleton. The two had argued at the first governors' meeting after the investigation went public. "That's what you get with politicians," he said. "A politician smells trouble, he can't handle the pressure."

The group tossed around a few suggestions. To a man, they wanted to let Eagleton go, but they all knew the Merc could not afford the public relations fallout right now. Finally, Salzman proposed the compromise: Let Eagleton write a dissenting letter to the blue ribbon report. That would keep him on board, at least through release of the reform package.

Of course it was the only solution. "I'll call him," Melamed said. The call to Eagleton would be added to the list of sacrifices Melamed had made on behalf of the Merc.

□ □ □

FOR JAMES FOX, A VETERAN DEFENSE LAWYER representing bond trader Melanie Kosar, Jeff Bailey of The Wall Street Journal was like an itch that would not go away.

Fox had refused once, twice, any number of times to let Bailey interview his client. The reporter left notes at her father's home, tried calling her at work. Finally, Bailey had cornered Kosar on the trading floor. When Kosar called Fox to complain, the lawyer suggested maybe they should cooperate. He felt Bailey might be sincere about doing a story that would describe the pressures of trading in a male-dominated world. Perhaps he would write about more than just the investigation.

Finally, the three sat down in Fox's office, tape recorders for both sides whirring. Bailey went through the motions of asking about her background, her thoughts on trading as a woman, even the horrendous story of Kosar's four-hour interrogation while wearing only a bathrobe late on the night of January 18.

At last, Bailey got to the point. He asked if Kosar knew people on the exchange thought she was cooperating with the government.

"That's a rumor," Kosar shot back. And she knew the rumor was a threat to her life in the pits. Nobody would trade with a snitch.

Bailey backed off, but was back to the subject moments later. "I think some defense lawyers are fairly certain that you're cooperating, and told their clients: 'She's cooperating. Stay away from her.' "

"They can believe what they want to," Kosar mumbled. Bailey dropped the subject again and carried the conversation long enough that Kosar felt, after he left, that the session had gone pretty well. Fox agreed.

When they saw the April 13 *Wall Street Journal*, they both knew they were wrong. The headline—"While Chicago Traders Are Eyeing the Market, One Trader Eyes Them"—was just an opening salvo. In the first graf, the story stated flatly (and correctly) that Kosar was a government informant. Her "no comment," down in the body of the story, rang hollow.

As Kosar walked into the pit, traders turned their backs to her. After 20 minutes of futile effort, she could not make a single trade. Kosar left in tears. On two subsequent sorties, she was hooted out of the T-bond pit before she could even step in.

Kosar gave up her leased seat, and today works in the dry cleaning store owned by her father.

□ □ □

THE MERC'S BLUE RIBBON COMMITTEE on April 19 made its report to the public. After hearing from more than 250 witnesses from every facet of the industry—from broker groups to locals to customers to brokerage firm officials—the panel had issued its report. The scene was a gala Merc press conference, with Leo Melamed and Merc president Bill Brodsky at the head of the Merc's huge oblong board of directors' table. It was quite a contrast with lawyer Jerrold Salzman's harried appearance the day the investigation made news.

The presentation was slick. On cue, Merc counsel Gerald Beyer adjusted oversized storyboards depicting the Merc's proposed reforms. Each of the mob of reporters received a binder describing their scope: limiting, but not eliminating dual trading; doubling the Merc's 10-person floor surveillance staff; picking up trading cards every half hour; and inviting one outside representative onto each major exchange disciplinary panel.

Broker groups emerged virtually unscathed. Limits on the amount of trade within a group were imposed floor-wide, but that was it.

Reporters probed, seeking to determine if the reforms, presented as housecleaning, were really just window dressing. The questions focused on the loopholes in the purported ban on dual trading, and the lack of attention to broker groups. No reporters or blue ribbon committee members knew at the time that committee member Jack Sandner had begun taking a salary from the ABS Partners group. And none seemed curious about former Senator Eagleton's dissenting opinion: They figured that was typical for a man many reporters considered a blowhard.

The press questions barely grazed Melamed. "We trust and hope that you will agree with us that these are very careful, thoughtful, tough, but sensible recommendations," he told the throng. Such sanitized phrasing, a stark contrast to the invective that had prevailed during some of the committee's meetings, typified the session.

Only later would industry observers recognize a Trojan horse that was included within the reform package. The panel quietly inserted a recommendation to study "block trading," a style of trading common in equity markets in which institutions can match their buys and sells before sending them to the market. To people outside the Merc, the block recommendation was a shocker because the controversial trading style was anathema to the open outcry system. "Block trading is pre-arranged trading, which is illegal," Board of Trade lawyer Scott Early groused.

Block trading, leaving broker groups virtually unaffected, setting loophole-filled limitations on dual trading: reform, Merc style.

□ □ □

THE MERC WASN'T READY FOR REFORM. Among many people outside the Merc, the blue ribbon committee's proposals were considered measured, if unambitious. The committee report seemed likely to serve as a blueprint for the industry, and for congressional efforts. But on the trading floor, there was one group of reform measures that had caused an uproar: the dual-trading proposals. Any change in dual trading, any effort to prohibit brokers from also trading for their own accounts, was too much.

For almost a week after the blue ribbon committee report was issued, the floor was quiet but restive. At last, the revolt to save the sacred cow of dual trading started in the cattle pit. Tim Brennan,

Emmett Whealan, and Glenn Laken, veterans from the Merc's meat pits, led an exodus from the floor after cattle stopped trading at 1:00 P.M. More than 300 traders marched with them to the Merc's second-floor conference room.

"We can't let them do this," Brennan exhorted the crowd. "We're not going to give up our livelihood. We're not going to give up dual trading." In the meat pits, the trading volume was lower than anywhere on the floor, and traders felt they could not survive without the combined earnings from brokerage and trading.

To skeptics from other pits, the Brennan revolt looked too neatly staged. There seemed to be a silent hand controlling events. Brennan, after all, cleared his trades through RB&H, Jack Sandner's firm. Perhaps Sandner had put him up to this, some thought. A floor revolt would give the exchange leadership the opportunity to backtrack on dual trading, while at the same time telling Congress they had tried but failed to convince their membership.

Before Brennan could stop talking, the Merc's chairman, John Geldermann, walked into the room, quieting it immediately. It was the first time that Geldermann, as chairman of the exchange, felt like an alien among his own members.

The lumbering, soft-spoken Geldermann quickly soothed the crowd. "Nothing is set in stone," he said, promising that the exchange's board still would decide whether to adopt any of the committee's recommendations, particularly dual trading. Members would get a referendum vote, too.

The revision of reform was underway.

□ □ □

DAVID SKRODZKI had never wanted to play Junior G-Man, and indeed, he had not volunteered for the job assigned to him for May 11, 1989: trying to go undercover in the soybean pit to nail bean broker Edward Cox. The government had asked him to do it after they busted him for fraud in the soybean pit. If Skrodzki wanted to avoid a racketeering rap, he had no choice. Wearing a wire into the soybean pit was the price of pleading guilty and agreeing to cooperate with the government, the only way to avoid having his assets seized.

It had been a far, fast fall for Skrodzki. Less than two years earlier, he had it made, brokering trades for one of the biggest trading firms at the Board, Shatkin Trading Co. But that did not last.

Skrodzki's first career mistake was a trade he handled for Patrick Arbor, the vice-chairman of the Board of Trade and an officer at Shatkin Trading Co. One day in late 1987, while holding an Arbor order to buy ten contracts of beans, Skrodzki first purchased 50 contracts for his own account. But before he could buy the ten bean contracts for Arbor, the market rose, and Arbor's order could not be filled. It was illegal for Skrodzki to trade for himself ahead of a customer's order. But normally, nobody would have known. On this particular trade, though, Skrodzki had some bad luck: Arbor was standing at the edge of the pit, watching him trade.

Arbor could have pushed to have Skrodzki thrown off the trading floor. He could have reported Skrodzki to the CFTC. Indeed, as a Board member and exchange officer, he was obligated to report the infraction at least to the Board's Office of Investigations and Audits. But Arbor decided to keep the matter quiet. He simply took away Skrodzki's deck of orders and commanded the trader never to handle customer business again.

At the time, Skrodzki figured Arbor had done him a good turn by not turning him in. But in retrospect, in the wake of a surprise visit by government agents in late January of 1989, Arbor's lenience looked more like an ironic stroke of bad luck. It was during the year of trading as a local that Skrodzki had gotten himself into trouble dealing with Rick Carlson, the undercover FBI agent.

Now Skrodzki himself was undercover, though his cooperation was not a very well kept secret. A few days before he agreed to wear the wire into the bean pit, he had received two threatening telephone calls from other bean traders. The anonymous calls shook him up. But despite the threats, going undercover did not scare him as much as the thought of having his assets seized.

Skrodzki was wired for sound and wading into the soybean pit to nab his friend Eddie Cox. The two had plenty of history together: Cox's name was entered or erased frequently on the trading card Skrodzki used to tally other traders' debts and credits, a card used so much that the edges were frayed. Skrodzki was a bagman to the broker Cox, just as Carlson had been to bean broker Marty Dempsey. They matched trades together frequently, often using the opening or closing price ranges to help Cox rip off money from customers. When Cox wanted to steal some money and needed somewhere to put it, Skrodzki was his favorite bank. And when he wanted to withdraw, it was simple: In one instance, Cox's only personal trade during an entire day was a $3,000 money pass into his personal account from Skrodzki.

On the morning of May 11, 1989, though, their relationship was one of suspicion. The soybean pit, indeed, the entire trading floor of the Board, was overcome by paranoia. Nobody trusted anyone, and Skrodzki was among the top "flipper" suspects. Still, Skrodzki pushed ahead, following the script outlined by Carlson and Assistant U.S. Attorney Ira Raphaelson. He tried to coax Cox into talking about trades the two had made with two traders who were in a broker group with Cox. And he needed to get Cox's confirmation that the broker had intended to pass money through a local trader on a 100-lot sell-then-buy trade that Skrodzki and Cox had arranged.

But Cox was having none of such talk. During a 20-minute conversation, in which Skrodzki prodded and probed, Cox studiously avoided making any incriminating statements. Fear of feds was running rampant. And Cox had heard the rumors about Skrodzki. He was not about to allow a confederate of the FBI trick him.

"Everything we've done down here is 100 percent legitimate, and you know that, Dave," was Cox's final, definitive statement to Skrodzki. With that even Skrodzki realized that his undercover identity had blown. He left Cox in the pit and did not come back.

□ □ □

THE DEFENSE LAWYERS DECIDED Eddie Genson would make the call to the prosecutor's office. As the senior defender and counsel on one of the most challenging cases, local trader Robert Bailin, Genson was the logical choice.

The lawyers could not believe events had taken them this far. Negotiating individually, none of the half-dozen lawyers cooperating with each other on the yen case had been able to get the prosecutors to budge. Unless their clients would plea to RICO charges, the government would make no deal. The attorneys were unwilling to accept the harsh seizure sanctions, so it was no deal at all.

It was time to see if the standoff might be broken. Indictments were coming soon. The lawyers had to make their moves. Tom Durkin came up with the scheme: Offer the G a group package, six defendants, maybe more. All willing to plea, in return for reduced charges. Of course, no RICO.

Eddie Genson placed the call. He outlined the group's proposal to Daniel Gillogly, the chief prosecutor in the yen case. "We all take a step down," Genson said. "You get prosecutions."

Gillogly's response came back as if from a script: No RICO, no deal.

It was a last-ditch effort. Finally the lawyers knew they would wind up at trial. It was frustrating, trying to negotiate with Gillogly. It was obvious his hands were tied. The government was not going to move—not at least until ten weeks later. Just days before the bean trial, Assistant U.S. Attorney Ira Raphaelson dropped RICO charges against a defendant. In return for a plea, the trader agreed to testify at trial. The yen lawyers screamed.

□ □ □

NOW THE *TRIBUNE* KNEW how it felt to be stung.

First had come the March issue of *Chicago Lawyer*, which had hit like a brick through the window when it landed on *Tribune* business editor Bill Neikirk's desk. "Commodities Investigation—The Story Behind the Story" the headline read, blandly enough. But beneath the headline was a story by David Protess, professor at Northwestern University's Medill School of Journalism, slamming the *Tribune* and its approach to the commodities story. Protess held that the *Trib* had been used, knowingly and willingly, to drum up paranoia that favored the prosecution. He even implied the story had been fed by the government to the newspaper.

By May, Protess was in *Chicago Lawyer* again, criticizing the *Journal*'s coverage of the Melanie Kosar story. "Melanie Kosar made two unfortunate acquaintances," the subheadline read. "The first was an FBI agent, the second a reporter. Together they did her in."

Together, the stories painted an ugly picture of gung-ho journalism. Reporters running roughshod over traders' privacy, misleading them about a fictitious list of the investigation's targets, trampling into their Easter garden parties, abusing them over the telephone, directly lying about the focus of their stories: It was dirty work, sometimes done with questionable ethics. But the worst sin, Protess felt, was the way the newspapers had let themselves be used by the government. "There can be little doubt that the leaks that led to the *Tribune*'s initial story came from government sources," Protess declared.

The journalists reacted like prima donnas scorned. Neikirk, furious about the first *Lawyer* story, dialed Medill's dean, Edward Bassett. "Do you know what's going on?" Neikirk demanded of Bassett during a highly charged conversation.

Fishing for a red herring, to help distract Bassett from the validity of Protess' story, Neikirk complained that Protess had a conflict of interest because his wife worked as a lawyer for the National Futures Association. When Protess, in effect, defended the futures industry, he also was defending the self-regulatory system of which his wife was a part. Almost as soon as he hung up, Neikirk regretted letting his anger get the best of him. "If I had it to do over again, I wouldn't make that call," Neikirk says now. "I was angry. Sometimes when we're angry, we do things we regret."

Tribune reporters went to work. Unable to overcome Protess' criticism that the press had helped the government drive the markets into hysteria, the *Trib* defenders instead tagged the letters *NFA* on everything Protess did, as if he were a modern-day Hester Prynne. When Protess sold a reworked version of the *Lawyer* stories to the widely read *Columbia Journalism Review*, *Trib* investigations editor Dean Baquet phoned *CJR*'s managing editor to sound alarms about Joan Protess's job at the NFA. He also claimed Protess's story was factually inaccurate. Neikirk called, too. Uncowed, *CJR* still ran the story.

Then the calls went to the NFA, inquiring about Joan Protess's responsibilities at the agency. Protess felt *Trib* reporters Thomas Burton and Bill Crawford were harassing his family when they made the NFA calls, and that the conflict-of-interest charges were a red herring.

Burton also phoned Protess and, in a testy conversation, challenged his methods as a journalist. Indeed, in his press post mortem, Protess had strung out some strange yarns. He reported that *Sun-Times* editor Mark Eissman claimed he did not bite when the government had tipped him to the story on January 13, nearly a week before the *Trib* story. *Sun-Times* reporters guffawed—if Eissman had any advance warning, he told nobody, not even the newspaper's two commodities reporters. And in attempting to portray Kosar sympathetically, Protess had ignored the possibility that she might be guilty of trading crimes—which she was.

Protess's advocacy journalism also backed him into some tight rhetorical corners. "If the *Tribune* had not written a word about the probe when Drew received his leaks in January, the public still would have been fully informed about its nature and scope when the government announced its indictments a few months later," he claimed in a business journalism newsletter. It seemed an odd point to make, particularly for a professor of journalism who normally professed to a high regard for the public's right to know. Besides being utterly unrealistic—with subpoenas flooding the pits the very day the *Trib*'s story was printed, the investigation could never go uncovered—Protess's suggestion was also dangerous. In such a world, the press would report only what official sources said, only when they wanted to say it.

□ □ □

ON A HOT FRIDAY AFTERNOON, July 28, one of the biggest and most expensive pools of legal talent ever assembled in the city of Chicago—attorneys for all the traders implicated in Operation Sourmash and Operation Hedgeclipper—met in the federal building. Their host: Paul Coffey, the U.S. Justice Department's expert on racketeering law.

The lawyers had made repeated complaints from the defense bar about their difficulty in assessing how the government would approach the nuances of RICO; Valukas had deigned to fly in Coffey. The trip's purpose was twofold: to inform the attorneys about RICO, and to convince their clients that this really was their last chance to cooperate before charges flew.

They met on the Dirksen building's 16th floor, in the same room that the soybean case's 23-person grand jury had met to deliberate the fate of the lawyers' clients. Defense lawyers do not attend grand jury proceedings, so many in the group had never before been inside. "It was the only time you'll ever see a lawyer voluntarily enter a grand jury room," quipped Royal B. Martin, Jr., one of the lawyers who attended.

Coffey surprised nobody. Negotiations, to the extent they took place, had proceeded steadily since February. The lawyers could see that the local boys were getting their RICO marching orders from Washington, probably from Coffey himself.

Coffey's talk was unsettling, nonetheless. There would be RICO charges against most, but not all, of the traders. The exchanges would be named as a "racketeering enterprise" and most of the traders charged with conspiracy. The government would attempt to seize all assets gained as part of the racketeering scheme, including exchange memberships, homes, cars, trading profits, even the fabled jewels that had become legend on newspaper editorial pages.

Then came the warning every lawyer expected. "This is the last call," Coffey said. If any lawyers wanted their clients to avoid RICO charges, they would not have another chance. Once the charges were filed, RICO was not going to be plea-bargained away.

The defense lawyers protested, but weakly. They knew the RICO decision was made. And besides, they knew better than to argue with Coffey. They would save their air for the judges and juries. The process was too far along to change course now. Indictments were just days away. Five days, to be exact.

CHAPTER FOURTEEN

□□□

The Reckoning

WHEN BIG NEWS IS BREAKING from the federal prosecutor's office in Chicago, nobody walking by the Everett M. Dirksen federal building has to guess. They can count the television vans parked outside. A couple of trucks means a story of mild general interest. Four TV vans means every station in town is covering. Four vans, each with its receiving dish extended on a pole 20 feet into the air to broadcast live, and it's a blockbuster.

In the afternoon of Tuesday, August 2, 1989 four vans was just the start. More than six TV vans parked bumper-to-bumper on Adams Street. Trying to get an edge, the van from the CBS affiliate, WBBM-Channel 2, pulled up on the sidewalk next to the building. To anyone who had paid attention to the news in Chicago, it was obvious what was going on inside: The commodity indictments had come down.

The press conference would not be held until 2:00 P.M. that afternoon—the same time and same day of the week that the Greylord indictments had come down. Over the years, the U.S. Attorney's office had learned the art of staging press conferences. At two o'clock in the afternoon, TV reporters had enough time to get the tapes back to the studio and work out their stories, but not enough time to contact defense lawyers for second opinions. The evening news shows, starting as early as 4:00 P.M. in Chicago, would carry only the prosecution's version of the story. It was a gimme of a first victory in the war to win public opinion.

Though there still were hours before the press conference, U.S. Attorney Anton Valukas would have no trouble keeping busy. Valukas had to work out the wording for his formal statement. An overstatement, a misstatement, an omission: Any one could be cause for a defense motion to dismiss the indictment. Such a motion would be defeated of course, but Valukas did not want to give the defense a chance to create a little harassment.

The statement would have to wait. One of the prosecutors came in with a problem. The assistants were expecting at least 200 press, but the big IRS conference room on the second floor was reserved. "We'll have to use the one on 25," Valukas said, shuddering at the thought of crowding such a mob into a room half the size that was needed.

The next assistant into the office was a puzzled-looking Dan Gillogly, who had headed the Merc investigations. "We've got a problem," Gillogly said. "Some of the grand jurors want to come to the press conference."

Valukas was floored. In his years as a prosecutor, he never had heard of a grand jury attending a press conference announcing its indictments. It was a sign of how much publicity the case had received. The jurors were still considering several possible indictees, and Valukas knew it would expose the prosecution to charges of abusing the grand jury process. But Valukas could think of no way to order the jurors not to attend without alienating them, and he still needed their goodwill.

"I guess they can come," Valukas said. "But I want you to do everything you can to dissuade them. If they do come, I want seats for them, and I want somebody with them the whole time," Valukas added. "I don't want any reporters to get near them."

Gillogly left, promising to do his best.

Valukas rose for the next visitor to his office. It was Attorney General Richard Thornburgh, his boss, in town for the big show. The publicity-conscious Thornburgh had known from the beginning that this case would generate good press, and he was not about to miss the grand finale. He had flown in from Washington, showered in the FBI's suite of offices, then come straight to Valukas's office.

Thornburgh, six feet tall and balding, congratulated Valukas on bringing the investigation to the indictment stage. "We're not done yet," Valukas told him. Then the big boss went to meet with the assistants who had run the case, Ira Raphaelson on the Board of Trade side and Gillogly on the Merc. He wandered through the offices, shaking hands with everybody who had worked on Sourmash and Hedgeclipper, visiting briefly with a few of the others. He even stopped to have his picture taken with a few. Everybody, of course, wanted to press the flesh with Thornburgh.

With Valukas in tow, Thornburgh then rode the elevator down to the FBI offices on the eighth floor. Along with FBI Director William Sessions, Thornburgh went through the same drill with the FBI agents, meeting personally with Ernie Locker and Jeff Frank, talking briefly with the undercover agents—Ostrom, Volk, Jannett, and Bassett.

If ever an event had set itself up to be anticlimactic, the press conference for the commodities indictments should have been it. The hype that had reached a crescendo in late January had died down some, but the papers were still covering every nuance of the investigation and its aftermath as if it were the latest dispatch from the Western Front. To match the buildup, this would have to be some show.

Certainly, none of the press would miss it. In the hallway outside the conference room, reporters clambered to show their credentials to the security guard standing behind a lengthy folding table that served as a barrier between him and the throng. Scott McMurray, *The Wall Street Journal*'s commodities reporter, a head taller than the rest of the crowd, was waving his wallet at the guard, as was the reporter from *Crain's Chicago Business*. But in this instance, merely announcing "I'm a reporter" was not enough to gain entry: Everyone packed in the corridor was press. And none would be allowed to pass the threshold until proceedings were well underway and wire service reporters had started running for the phones.

At the pay phones in the hallway, there was a battle to hold lines open. Jennifer Allen, chief commodities reporter for Knight-Ridder Financial News, controlled the telephone just steps away from the conference room. Once the press conference started, Knight-Ridder reporters from inside the conference room would start a relay, carrying news to Allen, who would dictate a story to an editor in Knight-Ridder's newsroom in the Merc building. From there, the news would travel to traders huddled around the K-R screens on the trading floor, and around the world.

On the phone next to Allen was a television news producer, performing much the same task. Both were surprised when a woman approached them from a nearby stairwell. "Please," she said. "A man has had a heart attack and I need to call for help."

The plea was addressed to the TV producer, but he wasn't budging. "I can't give up the line," he told the woman. "I have my office in New York here and too many people are depending on it."

Allen offered her phone, allowed the woman her call, and was back on the line before the press conference started. "It may have been hot news," she would say later. "But no one's life was depending on it."

Back in the conference room, the throng quieted when Thornburgh led in a mob of officials. Valukas was behind him, flanked by the FBI's Sessions and Commodity Futures Trading Commission chairman Wendy Gramm. Each of the honchos wanted to cast their imprimatur upon events. For Gramm, especially, in the midst of a battle to save her agency from an overhaul by Congress, a convincing performance might boost the CFTC's standing. Every Valukas assistant who had ever heard of the investigation was there, as were ample FBI agents.

The group further crowded a sweaty, hot conference room into which reporters were packed like dirty clothes in a suitcase after a long vacation. A semicircle of 30 chairs three rows deep was filled with reporters; they were sitting shoulder to shoulder on the floor, and some were even stuck behind view-blocking television cameras in the rear.

Taking up seats in the overstuffed arena were two dozen people who obviously were not reporters. They weren't hustling for position, and they had no notebooks. Only a few reporters would figure that they were members of the grand jury itself. Who else would be escorted by a phalanx of three government lawyers? Gillogly had done his job.

Valukas was right to anticipate the jurors' attendance would cause problems with the defense lawyers. The jury was taking a quick coffee break and hearing what crooks the traders were. Afterward, they would return to the grand jury room and consider charges against a number of traders. Defense lawyers later filed several outraged but unsuccessful pretrial motions. "They went and heard this massive praise, high government officials lauding the performance of all of the parties on the government side. Then they were supposed to go back to work and be impartial," complained defense lawyer Harvey Silets. "That was totally prejudicial. It was a foolhardy thing to allow them to do. It was totally foolhardy."

Thornburgh and crew did their best to hype the product. "This probe is part of an expanding Department of Justice crackdown on white-collar crime from Wall Street to LaSalle Street to Main Street, with all stops in between," Thornburgh boasted. Valukas attempted to head off an expected defense parry by claiming the charges were more than just "technical violations." Gramm played up the CFTC's role and promised a new set of trading rules was not far off. Sessions said that since the probe went public in January, the FBI had issued 500 subpoenas, conducted well over 500 interviews and reviewed more than a million documents. "The FBI used extraordinary means to detect extraordinary fraud," Sessions said.

As Valukas outlined the specific charges, assistant prosecutors not otherwise serving as bookends at the podium passed out four doorstop-weight copies of the indictments, one for each pit in which an undercover agent had worked. The cases went by the name of the key defendant in each, *U.S. v. Dempsey* in the soybeans, *U.S. v. Goberstein* in the Treasury Bonds, *U.S. v. Mosky* in the Swiss franc, and *U.S. v. Bailin* in the Japanese yen. In all: 1,275 pages, 608 counts against 46 defendants.

A few blocks away, at the National Futures Association headquarters, a horde of reporters waited for the first copies of the indictments to arrive. They had arranged in advance to obtain personnel records from the NFA, so they could draw thumbnail sketches of the indicted traders. When the names came, some of the more seasoned reporters were surprised. There were a few notable names, but none of the exchanges' big names. For now, at least, it looked like the power brokers and major bagmen had dodged a bullet.

For those who were charged, this was serious business. The indictments included accusations of trading ahead of customer orders, pre-arranged trading, off-market trading, and destroying records. There were commodities fraud, mail fraud, wire fraud, and, of course, RICO charges. But there was no mention of how much money had been stolen in aggregate. Alleged rip-offs of as little as $12.50 were mixed haphazardly with those reading into the tens of thousands of dollars.

The omission was significant. The commodities cases always had been likened to Wall Street's insider trading scandal, but a look at the charges showed it wasn't even close. Compared to the $100 million settlement of arbitrage investor Ivan Boesky and the $200 million settlement of the case against junk bond king Michael Milken, the numbers in the commodities cases were nickel-and-dime. After all the hoopla, the government could not even bring itself to place a dollar amount on the crimes that allegedly were perpetrated—creating speculation that the figure was embrassingly small.

Defense lawyers jumped on the point. It helped them reinforce the public image of an overly zealous prosecution. Therein was born a defense tactic that claimed the government was bringing the full weight of its prosecution against crimes that allegedly had no victims. "It's an incredible case of overkill," griped lawyer Thomas A. Durkin.

Spin control from the exchanges began immediately. The Board of Trade, which had rolled up inside a shell after the investigation first became publicly known, held a press conference immediately. "We believe in the integrity of our markets and our membership," said Karsten Mahlmann, the exchange's chairman.

Thomas Donovan, president of the Board of Trade, unveiled publicly a line he had enjoyed using in private since the scandal began. "Where there's smoke, there's not always fire," he reasoned. "But where there's smoke, there's always smoke damage." All the smoke in the world could not hide the fact that the exchanges, 45 traders, and a clerk all were in for a real tough time. The damage, whether by the smoke of accusation or the fire of guilty verdicts, would be substantial. And it wouldn't clear for months, or years, to come.

The Merc would wait until the next day to gather reporters in its boardroom for a press conference. An animated and angry Leo Melamed recited a litany of the Merc's proposed trading reforms, though not enacted in the wake of the sting. Then, bouncing in his chair, pounding the mahogany table, Melamed nearly shouted to the assembled reporters: "We will put the fear of God into anyone who breaks the rules of this exchange." Melamed would be a hard act to follow, and his promise a tough one to keep.

□ □ □

AS THE FIRST NEWS BULLETIN about the indictments came across the Knight-Ridder and Dow Jones news terminals, traders in Chicago packed around the wire machines, looking for familiar names on the list of indictees. Others watched the press conference on television in the privacy of their offices, waiting for the late edition of the *Sun-Times*, the only Chicago paper to print an afternoon edition, to get the detailed list of names.

By the following morning, traders had a clear picture of what had happened: Those unlucky enough to have traded within spitting distance of an FBI mole stood a good chance of facing indictment. The randomness of the targets shocked the same traders who in January had called for the bad apples to be culled from the business. It seemed to some that the moles had found crime almost everywhere they went. To many others, the charges seemed an unfair crackdown on practices that were commonplace on the trading floor. And the names on the list were hardly impressive. A few of the indicted brokers belonged to the highly disliked ABS Partners broker group, but several brokers most notorious for corruption had apparently gone unnoticed. Even brokers and traders whom the Merc and Board disciplinary committees had nabbed for repeated big-dollar offenses had not been indicted.

Some traders who had been visited by the government but escaped indictment were not bashful about gloating. On the Merc trading floor Thursday morning, a few yen traders slapped high fives with their unindicted brethren. Others greeted friends jubilantly and moved toward their usual spots in the pork belly and S&P 500 futures pits. David Horberg, the yen broker prominently named as a target by *The Wall Street Journal* and then summarily stripped of his Dellsher clearing privileges by Leo Melamed, received congratulations all around the floor.

The traders had good cause for celebration. Despite the raw number of traders indicted, Operation Hedgeclipper and Operation Sourmash had fallen far short of their goals. At its inception, the investigation had set out to indict a system in which, the government agents believed, corruption started at the top and creeped its way to the bottom. "Everyone down there is crooked," said one of the government officials who headed the investigation in an interview not long after the indictments. "To be successful, you have to be part of the system. The system is crooked, so even if you're upstairs, even if you haven't been on the trading floor in years, you still know how the system works down there. To get where you are today, you worked the system yourself."

Meeting a reporter in a quiet restaurant, away from the excitement of press conferences and trading floors, the official tapped index finger to index finger and ticked off names from a list that sounded like a *Who's Who* of the Chicago futures markets. There were the men the FBI had eyed as it began the probe. "You've got the Melameds, the Sandners, the Moniesons, the Mahlmanns, the Rosenthals, the Kravitzes, the Kaulentises. You've got other names down there that are well-known to anybody on an organized crime unit," the official continued. "They all came up from the floor. They all know how the system works. They're the ones who run the system, and until we change the system, this thing won't be finished." Time would show that this docket of big names was little more than an investigator's wish list. None of the names of those who "run the system" were sullied by the investigation.

The initial products of the investigation showed how few of the government's goals had been met in the long and expensive undercover sting. In nearly every pit, the agents discovered a pattern of activity, often long-standing practices, that flouted the rules of the exchanges and the law of the land. Sometimes formalized relationships of greed became apparent, confirming the government's suspicions that the system was corrupt. However, the investigation failed to reach other ingrown problems of the markets. Despite their skill at aping the jargon and attitudes of the pits, the agents failed to penetrate the off-the-floor cliques that were the heart and soul of the exchanges. The people who called the shots had drifted so far from the trading floor that by the time the FBI had arrived, their only presence in the pits was in the trades they sent to brokers on the floors.

□ □ □

THE COMPETENCE OF EACH AGENT affected the size of his catch. The soybean and Japanese yen probes racked up far more indictees with more serious charges than the Swiss franc and T-bond probes had done. At the Board of Trade, agent Richard Ostrom had discovered an old-boy network of soybean futures brokers and traders who ran "bank balances" of ill-gotten gains with each other. They pre-arranged trades to soften the blow of brokers' mistakes or simply to rip off money. When locals took losing trades, brokers repaid them later by giving the locals profitable trades, profits skimmed from their customers' orders. They created false trades by fabricating records on their trading cards, then passed along the proceeds either in cash or through pre-arranged trades. Many tallied debits and credits from illegal trading on cards they slid into their breast pockets.

Ostrom's work led to the indictment of 18 soybean traders and one clerk, whose salary barely topped the minimum wage. Four indictees were major brokers in the pit, and ten of the 19 were charged with RICO conspiracy. Ostrom's indictments went deep into the bean pit. "It looked like [Ostrom] had set a bomb off in the pit," said one brokerage firm executive who traded soybean futures. The agent's performance as a mole had been so convincing that even after the subpoenas were first handed out, some Board traders had trouble believing he was an FBI agent.

Perhaps hardest hit by agent Ostrom's investigation was Martin J. Dempsey, the 52-year-old soybean broker who was a 20-year veteran of the pits. He had made the mistake of choosing a gumshoe as his bagman. Dempsey's specialty was trading ahead of customer orders, tipping his friends in the pit by saying, "You just bought five, now get out of it," and leaving his compatriots to cash in on their own. The son of a Chicago police sergeant, Dempsey was tall, beefy, and balding. His lavish life-style had attracted the attention of federal prosecutors. When they visited him in January 1989 to elicit cooperation in the investigation, prosecutors threatened to repossess his $600,000 suburban home, his green Jaguar, and his orange BMW under the RICO statute. During the conversation, Dempsey explained that he disliked the term "bagman" and preferred instead the more dignified sounding "accommodating local." True to the government threats, Dempsey was charged with RICO and 121 other counts. He pleaded innocent and went to trial.

Trader Charles Bergstrom was another big catch for Ostrom. The 42-year-old former employee of the Board's Office of Investigations and Audits used his knowledge to thwart the exchange's surveillance systems. He sometimes served as a "foreign ambassador" to broker James Nowak, travelling across the pit to repay Nowak's outtrades through pre-arranged money passes. Substituting for Nowak one day as a broker, he pre-arranged trades to Ostrom, then got the money kicked back the next day. Bergstrom also advised Ostrom to always trade with a director of the exchange, in order to avoid trouble with the disciplinary committees. He left blank spaces between lines on his trading cards so he could insert fictitious trades when the opportunity arose. Charged with RICO and 112 other counts, he stood trial.

Broker James D. Nowak spent 14 years as a commercial banker at Continental Illinois Bank and Trust Co. of Chicago before moving to the markets. He worked for the Board's clearinghouse before starting as a local trader who served as cobagman, with Bergstrom, on broker David Skrodzki's trades. When he became a broker, Nowak used Bergstrom and FBI agent Ostrom—undercover as Rick Carlson— as his own tandem of bagmen. Nowak used his knowledge of clearinghouse operations to counsel fellow traders on how to cheat in the pit and not get caught. But after he was snagged in Operation Sourmash and charged with RICO and 239 other counts, Nowak admitted to ripping off more than $150,000 from customers with Ostrom's help.

His plea of guilty to racketeering conspiracy and one count of filing a false tax return, just days before the soybean trial, shook the other major defendants, who recognized that Nowak would become a star witness for the government.

David J. Skrodzki, at 32, was the Shatkin Trading Co. broker who was caught trading ahead of exchange director Patrick Arbor's order. Forbidden to handle customer business, Skrodzki began trading as a local on the other side of the soybean pit, where he became a bagman to broker Eddie Cox. Skrodzki had grown up comfortably in suburban Northbrook and had worked at the Board since 1978, when he started as a runner. Skrodzki, with his floor history, was an easy mark for Ostrom. When he was visited by the FBI at his home in January, he almost immediately agreed to cooperate with the government. He aided the investigation by wearing a tape recorder in the bean pit in a failed effort to trick Cox into incriminating himself. The charges against Skrodzki were relatively minor because of his early and enthusiastic cooperation: one count of mail fraud and one count of pre-arranged trading.

Thomas P. Kenney, a 35-year-old broker, often used agent Ostrom and local traders like John Eggum to help with pre-arranged trades. He also matched trades with other members of his broker group, organizing some of the most complex money passes in the soybean pit. He pleaded not guilty to RICO conspiracy and 27 other counts. Together with Bergstrom, Kenney would also face separate CFTC charges for helping trader George Segal park soybean trades in excess of limits on a speculative trader's activity.

Craig LaCrosse, 40, was another local who traded heavily with Nowak. He pleaded guilty to two trading violations and cooperated. LaCrosse admitted to accepting a winning trade from Nowak that did not belong to him and repaying part of the profits in a cash kickback. In front of Ostrom, Nowak laughed at LaCrosse for his ineptitude at stealing. LaCrosse also admitted to illegal trades directly with agent Ostrom.

Scott Anixter, 40, was a wealthy local trader with a comfortable suburban life-style. Described by the government as a bagman, he first pleaded not guilty, then flipped before the trial and admitted to four counts of trading violations.

Bradley Ashman, a 28-year-old University of Illinois graduate and Chicago yuppie, was charged with RICO conspiracy and 14 other counts. He did not even start trading until February 1988, well after Ostrom had arrived in the soybean pit. But Ashman quickly learned the ropes, stealing as a broker and meticulously marking other traders' debits and credits with him on a trading card that served as a tally sheet. Ashman once complained that Ostrom had not been available when Ashman had wanted to send some pre-arranged trades his way. He would be the first defendant to take the stand in the bean trial, where his equivocating responses to prosecutor Raphaelson's questions did him more harm than good.

William A. Barcal III, 35, was a broker who belonged to a group that included John Eggum, Sheldon Schneider, Kenney, Ashman, and Dempsey. The group members often matched customer trades amongst themselves. Barcal several times made legitimate trades with Agent Ostrom, but while verifying the trades he and Ostrom changed prices. He suffered a serious automobile accident in March 1988 and missed three months of work. He stood trial on charges of RICO, mail fraud, and Commodity Exchange Act violations.

John J. Eggum, 47, an affable broker who also traded frequently for his own account, moved over to soybeans from the wheat pit about a year before the indictment. He quickly fit in, serving as a scratch trader in a three-way money pass with Ostrom and Kenney. He also matched customer trades with Ashman and other members of his broker group. Eggum pleaded guilty to two counts of mail fraud and agreed to testify against his fellow traders.

Edward Cox III was a 28-year-old broker with a degree in economics. He handled the sell side of a deck for a broker group and used Skrodzki as his bagman. He was never taped or involved in an illegal trade with Ostrom. Instead, the government would rely largely on the testimony of Skrodzki to try him on charges of RICO conspiracy and 37 other counts.

Joel J. Fetchenhier, at 49, was a 14-year veteran of the bean pit, where he always traded his own account. Fetchenhier took a $4,000 loss from one day and was partly repaid the next day in the illegal after-hours curb market. A month later, Nowak told Agent Ostrom to repay $500 to Fetchenhier. Fetchenhier stood far away from Agent Ostrom, across the pit, and never traded directly with the agent. He stood trial on RICO conspiracy charges and 11 other counts.

Kenneth Gillen, 29, was a minor local trader. Charged with one count of pre-arranged trading, he pleaded guilty, agreed to cooperate, and was not even called to testify at trial.

Bruce W. Mittelstadt, 49, a prominent broker from a family of grain traders, stood close to Agent Ostrom in the bean pit. He also stayed close to John Ryan, a local trader who would take Mittelstadt's mistakes, expecting to be repaid after the close of trading. Mittelstadt was charged with RICO conspiracy and 56 other counts. After first pleading innocent, he later changed his mind when the government agreed to drop the RICO charges on the eve of the trial. He pleaded guilty to one count of mail fraud and one count on a trading violation.

Harry O. Patten III, 39, a former insurance claims adjuster, was a broker and a local. He was charged with two counts of violating the Commodity Exchange Act after he pleaded guilty and agreed to cooperate. During a conversation with Ostrom and Bergstrom in the Board of Trade's lobby, Patten explained how the pit's dishonor system worked. "We all have skeletons down here and that's what keeps us afloat," he said. "If one guy tells something about that guy, the other guy will tell something else."

John Ryan, 49, another veteran, took outtrades from broker Nowak. Ryan traded mostly as a local, accepting brokers' errors and receiving paybacks though pre-arranged trades. Even though he was indicted on four counts of mail and wire fraud and ten violations of the Commodity Exchange Act, the total value of Ryan's alleged thefts was a mere $125. He pleaded not guilty and stood trial.

Sheldon H. Schneider, 46, a local trader, was a latecomer to the bean pit. He began soybean trading in May 1988, long after Ostrom had arrived. He was the favorite bagman of broker John Eggum. He stood trial charged with RICO conspiracy and nine other counts.

John A. Vercillo, 44, the son of a garbage man and an office clerk, was a Chicago police officer before he became a trader. The affable, gregarious Vercillo called himself a "mechanic," and he excelled at fixing trades. His humorous and salty language, entertaining as it was to traders in the pit, would prove damaging in court. When Agent Ostrom complained about the market, Vercillo had simple advice. "You got a big bag at home. Take a few shekels out of it," Vercillo said. "You were here until four o'clock with me yesterday," trading after the market closed. Vercillo was charged with RICO conspiracy and 20 other counts. He stood trial, where his lawyer told the jury that foul language is not a federal offense.

Michael Weiser was a 21-year-old clerk who had first worked for Skrodzki and then for Dempsey and Nowak. Weiser would walk across the pit carrying cards on which Nowak had dictated trades, expecting Ostrom and other locals to copy onto their own cards the false trades he had created. With a reported income of $7,784 in 1987, he could hardly afford his defense at a lengthy trial. He pleaded guilty to three counts of trading violations and one count of failing to file a federal income tax return, and cooperated with the government.

□ □ □

IN THE TEEMING BROTH OF BODIES that makes up the Board of Trade's Treasury-bond futures pit, FBI Agent Michael Bassett could not match Ostrom's success in the bean pit. The T-bond pit has the biggest volume of any futures contract in the world, and its climate is much more aggressive than in the staid agricultural pits across the hall. It is the place where most of the United States Treasury's huge debt is hedged, and because of the pit's size, success there is dependent on a trader's geography—his location in the pit.

Spanning the diameter of the huge, loud pit with a shout and a trade is a feat that requires operatic vocal projection and skilled hand signaling. Newcomers inevitably must either make large trades and demonstrate the ability to ride major risks, or be relegated to the farthest fringes of the action. As an inexperienced newcomer, Bassett never made it to the top tier of the bond pit. His investigation netted only three traders. One was a middle-range broker; the others, small locals.

Broker Howard J. Goberstein was a 33-year-old accountant turned commodities trader who traded during the day while earning his MBA degree from DePaul University in the evening. He was charged with RICO and 127 other counts. A client of Dan K. Webb, the former U.S. Attorney who helped launch the undercover sting, Goberstein became the first trader to plead guilty to a RICO charge. His plea of guilty to one count of RICO conspiracy was a boost for the very investigation that Webb helped initiate. It cemented the government's resolve to stand by the RICO charges against other traders seeking to arrange plea agreements.

Local trader Melanie Kosar worked her way up from a runner to a trader in the eight years she spent at the Board after finishing high school in suburban Chicago. At 25, she was relatively new to the bond pit, trading small numbers. Kosar pleaded guilty to one count of mail fraud and one count of pre-arranged trading. The charges stemmed largely from admissions she made during the FBI's visit to her apartment late on January 18, 1989.

John Myskowski, 36, joined the crowd in the T-bond pit not long after Agent Bassett did. Myskowski started as a clerk in 1986, after studying criminal law for a time at the University of Illinois at Chicago. He pleaded guilty to one count of mail fraud and one count of pre-arranged trading.

□ □ □

AT THE MERC, agents Dietrich Volk and Randall Jannett leased an office together and entered the S&P 500 futures pit in tandem, hoping to familiarize themselves with the language and culture of the most hectic pit on the floor. Unlike their colleagues roving the Board, the two Merc agents aimed to uncover wrongdoing by a specific group of traders, including members of some of the Merc's powerful broker groups. They also suspected mob involvement among some Merc traders. The charges would have been hard to prove, even if the agents had not been novices in the pit. Because of their inexperience, they fell short of their most ambitious goals.

Poor timing compounded their problems. A few months after the agents arrived, the Merc imposed dual-trading restrictions on S&P 500 futures brokers, cutting down on opportunities for fraud. Then, in October, the stock market intervened. The disastrous Black Monday crash of October 19, 1987, left Jannett and Volk stunned and crippled. Volk later told friends he had lost $30,000 in the crash. The two split up in early 1988 and headed into separate foreign currency pits.

In the Swiss franc pit, Jannett discovered a small group of brokers and traders who worked closely to defuse the risk of trading errors and big losses. But Jannett proved a less than competent trader who never became part of the fabric of his pit. He had only superficial contact with several traders charged in the case.

Robert Mosky, 33, was a broker in the Swiss franc pit who used local traders to "help out" when he made a trading error or missed filling a customer order. Mosky was a competent broker in the group with Gary Kost and Michael Joyce, but when he traded for his own account while also brokering, he made mistakes that got him in trouble. Charged with RICO conspiracy and 63 other counts, he stood trial.

William A. Walsh, 23, was a Swiss franc broker who had been a business partner of Mosky's. A consummate hustler, he had worked as a salesman for Wealth Unlimited, a scandal-tainted investment "educational" firm in Chicago's suburbs. Nailed for a pre-arranged trade arranged by Jannett, he pleaded guilty to one count of wire fraud and one count of pre-arranged trading and would testify against Mosky at the trial.

Mark Fuhrman, 39, a local in the Swiss pit, sometimes also acted as a broker. Agent Jannett befriended Fuhrman more effectively than he did any other Swiss franc trader. Fuhrman had made illegal trades directly with Agent Jannett and was captured on videotape arranging to pass him cash. Fuhrman pleaded guilty to one count of wire fraud and one count of pre-arranged trading, and would testify.

Danny Scheck, a young and successful local in the Swiss franc futures pit, was a favorite of Mosky and others in the Joyce-Kost group. He never traded directly with Agent Jannett and had no substantive conversations with him. On one trade for which he was charged, Scheck's only recorded comment was this: "I have to go to the bathroom." His indictment would not be announced until well after the August 2, 1989, press conference, leading his lawyer to complain that the grand jury was prejudiced by its visit to the indictment extravaganza. He was charged with non-RICO counts.

David Zatz, known as DIZ on the trading floor, was a small local in the Swiss pit who also was not part of the original indictment. He was indicted after the others, on grand jury testimony by cooperating witnesses Fuhrman and Walsh. Zatz complained when brokers tried to force their errors on him. "Get it back to me," he once told Fuhrman. "I don't want to be a loser." At trial, his lawyer would argue that Zatz was not smart enough to pull off trading scams—a tactic that came to be called "the village idiot defense."

□ □ □

AGENT DIETRICH VOLK found a rich harvest of wrongdoing in the Japanese yen pit. He made cases against 21 traders, four of them members or former members of the powerful ABS Partners group. Among the others were two independent brokers who held large decks of customer orders and a few local traders, some of whom were reputed bagmen who helped brokers steal from customer trades.

There was no telling how Volk's indictments would stand up at trial. Having spent only a year in the yen pit, he had delivered two more indictees than Rick Ostrom had produced after three years in the soybean pit. And Volk had not received the formal training that had made Ostrom such an effective pit trader. With only three indictments returned by his Merc partner Randall Jannett, Volk looked like the more productive agent when indictments were returned on August 2, 1989. That original impression would not hold up by the time the yen verdicts were returned some 18 months later.

John M. Baker was the 50-year-old broker with the wacky trading jackets and a taste for drink who allowed the FBI to interview him in his home for three hours in January 1989. He allegedly took up Volk on a tax-loss trade the agent proposed, netting some of the 47 counts against him, including RICO. After videotaping Baker accepting cash from Volk in the agent's Dolphin Trading Co. offices, the feds wrapped up the Merc investigation. Among Baker's alleged misdeeds: bragging to Volk that he knew four people willing to take $100,000 outtrades from him and handing Brian Sledz a 100-contract trade that earned $120,000 then accepting a $60,000 repayment check. Baker's adopted nickname, "The Master Mechanic," would sound sinister before the jury. "We are in a business here, and there are certain things you don't admit to," Baker told Volk. "There is a system, but you don't tell the world about it."

Thomas A. Crouch, known on the trading floor by his badge, "ATOM," was a business partner of Baker and also a yen broker. Crouch had been a broker in the livestock futures pits until shortly before Volk arrived on the trading floor. In his most damaging trade, Crouch allegedly handed Brian Sledz a card with buys and sells written on it and directed Sledz to copy the notations onto his trading card. The profit, an $18,000 check from Sledz, went toward the purchase of a new Mercedes. Crouch was charged with RICO and 40 other counts. He pleaded not guilty and stood trial.

Sam A. Cali, 38, a yen broker for ABS, was a high-school friend of Dean Kaulentis, the brother of one ABS co-owner, James Kaulentis. Cali resigned from the group when it became clear he would be indicted, and Dean Kaulentis called Cali the morning after he was subpoenaed on January 18, 1989, and cautioned him not to talk to the government. By that time, it was too late. Cali had been drawn into the net by friends Brian and James Sledz. Incorrectly described in the press as a major broker, Cali had a reputation as a bumbler who benefited from his friendship with Kaulentis. He was charged with RICO and 96 other counts.

Michael J. Christ, known as "Chi Chi" on the trading floor, was a 43-year-old broker and local who also was part-owner of ABS. Christ was born in Greece and in high school became friends with the Kaulentis brothers. He was a 16-year veteran of the Merc and had served on Merc pit and floor practice committees. He watched bemusedly as Thomas Braniff forced Robert Bailin to take a losing trade that Bailin could ill afford. Christ was charged with four counts of mail and wire fraud and six Commodity Exchange Act violations.

Ray Pace, a 33-year-old former Golden Gloves boxer, was another ABS broker. Pace allegedly stole money from customers to make up for losses in his personal trading. "If it's [in] the deck and you want to use it, fine," he explained. In the indictment, he was accused of RICO conspiracy and 118 other counts.

Michael D. Smith, 34, worked as a broker for ABS but had no ownership interest. After allegedly handing Brian Sledz a 100-contract trade that earned $125,000, Smith took a $28,000 check from the trader. The traders, allegedly cooperating with broker Cali, had agreed to subtract one-third of the profit to pay Sledz's taxes. Smith was accused of RICO conspiracy and 31 other counts.

Aric March, 33, worked with ABS Partners for a time in 1987. A veteran local trader, he had gained a reputation for unscrupulous trades. He traded with nearly all of the local traders charged in the case. March agreed to cooperate with the government early and submitted to 22 interviews with the FBI to feed information about other traders on the Merc floor. With rumors of March's not-very-secret cooperation rampant, broker Gary Wright challenged him at a Merc Club breakfast. "If you've rolled over on me, you're through," the diminutive Wright told the beer-barrel built March. March admitted to two felony counts, for an illegal trade in the S&P 500 futures pit in 1987, which protected him from sentencing guidelines instituted after 1987.

Joseph P. O'Malley, 38, had been Baker's business partner for a time, but he was on his own as a local by the time Operation Hedge-clipper went public. Rip-offs, O'Malley confided to Agent Volk, "can be done without the customers feeling the pain. It's like they expect you to do it." He stood trial on four counts of mail and wire fraud and six Commodity Exchange Act violations.

Robert H. Bailin, 36, was a yen local who protested to FBI agents that he was "just a small fish" who made $100,000 per year. He suggested they look at big brokers, including James Kaulentis. In allegedly pre-arranging a trade with Volk, Bailin suggested changing prices. "Otherwise, it looks like shit," he said. A complainer, Bailin griped that brokers Thomas Braniff, James Marren, and Cali owed him points from losing trades they had forced on him. He faced 29 non-RICO counts.

Thomas M. Braniff, 33, a broker and a local, was Refco Inc.'s man in the yen pit. With Agent Volk watching over his shoulder, Braniff arranged a trade with Christ. "All right, take out a card," he said. "I bought four." Braniff also traded with Volk after the market closed, advising the agent to assign part of the trade to a trader who was not present. Braniff pleaded guilty to two counts of mail and wire fraud and cooperated with the government.

Donald E. Callahan, 45, was who filled customer orders on the Merc trading floor. Callahan reportedly is a devoted family man who regularly attended 5:00 A.M. mass in the Loop's St. Peter's Church before trading. He pleaded guilty to one count of mail fraud and was not called to testify.

James M. Marren, a 39-year-old broker, was charged with RICO conspiracy and 25 other counts. When agents visited him, Marren acknowledged that he had never written a check to a customer to cover his trading mistakes, implying he was either perfect or had stolen. He stood trial.

Michael I. Greenfield, a 28-year-old local, was hit with 12 non-RICO counts. Greenfield chose an unfortunate time to enter the commodities business. At the Merc's orientation class, he sat beside a would-be trader whose true identify was FBI agent Dietrich Volk.

Kenneth M. Maslak, 37, was a local trader in the yen pit. Like many traders, he tallied debts and credits from allegedly illegal dealings on a trading card slipped into his breast pocket. Only a single trade was cited in his 9-count indictment. He pleaded not guilty.

Matthew A. Newberger, the 29-year-old son of Norma Newberger, who sits on the Merc's board of governors, pulled out a pocket calculator, figured the profit from an allegedly pre-arranged trade, subtracted one-third for taxes, then allegedly paid Braniff $3,000 in cash, all as Volk watched. Facing a seven-count indictment, Newberger would endure the prolonged trial.

Daniel Parz, a 34-year-old broker, pleaded guilty to one count of wire fraud and one Commodity Exchange Act violation. He was a member of a broker group headed by John Baker and Thomas Crouch.

Martin J. Riley, 31, was charged with one count of mail fraud and two Commodity Exchange Act violations. Riley originally pleaded not guilty, but by the time the trial started, he was nearly destitute. His lawyer asked for, and received, a plea of no contest. Riley was spared the ordeal of a lengthy trial.

Michael L. Sidel, a 42-year-old local trader, was charged with ten non-RICO counts. He stood trial.

Brian E. Sledz, the 29-year-old local who received one of the first subpoenas from the government, agreed to cooperate and implicated his friend Cali. An active trader and voracious real estate buyer, Sledz would implicate numerous traders but do the most damage to broker Baker. Sledz sold his Merc seat for $350,000 shortly after the FBI investigation was disclosed. He pleaded guilty to one count of wire fraud and one count of violating the Commodity Exchange Act.

James G. Sledz, Brian's younger brother, was also a local in the yen pit. He cooperated with the government and testified against the other indictees at the yen trial. After accepting a $25,000 loser from Crouch, James Sledz went to discuss the problem with Crouch's partner, Baker. The veteran broker pulled out a card listing half a dozen traders in the pit who owed him money. On another deal, Sledz paid $3,500 in cash to Baker in the Merc's washroom. For his cooperation, he pleaded guilty to reduced charges—one count of mail fraud and one Commodity Exchange Act violation.

Gary A. Wright, a 28-year-old local and alleged trade fixer, explained to Agent Volk that pre-arranging trades "is part of the game. That's why you paid for your seat." Trying to set up an alleged money pass with broker Pace, Wright needed a trader in the middle to help out. "Do you want to get in the middle of a ten lot?" he asked Volk. Wright pleaded not guilty to 11 non-RICO counts. For his alleged Merc Club threat against March's cooperation with the government, Wright garnered an obstruction of justice charge.

□ □ □

THE GOVERNMENT had taken its opening shot. But the war had only begun. In the next few days, the traders targeted by the investigation had to run gauntlets of reporters and television cameras simply to file their pleas of guilt or innocence. Over the next several months, defense lawyers and prosecution lawyers would feint and parry with court filings and delaying tactics until, at last, in May of 1990, the trial of three Swiss franc traders opened under the gavel of Judge Ann C. Williams, a respected law-and-order jurist.

The government plan was to win early convictions, and move slowly but inexorably up the ladder of the hierarchies at the exchanges. It was a tactic that had worked in Greylord and other investigations. From the government's point of view, there seemed little reason the same technique would not work in the pits.

The FBI and the prosecuting attorneys figured they had the goods to win convictions; it was only a matter of making the jury understand. "We've got to make certain the jury gets it," Valukas repeatedly advised his underlings. But making the juries "get it" would be no mean feat. In fact, as testimony in the trials would show, at times even the FBI agents and the prosecuting lawyers seemed confused by what went on in the pits. What's more, the government knew that the much-ballyhooed audiotapes, which had sounded so intimidating in press accounts, would rarely live up to their billing. Too often, they were ambiguous, and at times indecipherable. And the agents' discretion in switching the tape recorders on and off to fit their needs was certain to become a point of contention.

The key to the results of the investigation would rest with one element: juries. As the prosecutors would soon find, juries don't always follow the government's script. By the time the first round of trials would come to an end, the juries would write their own script—an interesting one, indeed.

CHAPTER FIFTEEN

□□□

The Aftermath

BY EARLY JANUARY OF 1991, two years after prosecutor Ira Raphaelson had led the first midnight raids in Chicago's winter chill, the city's futures exchanges had largely succeeded in distancing themselves from the investigation and the ensuing trials. The three-month trial of three Swiss franc traders, ended in August, had resulted in a mixed verdict from which both defense and prosecution could claim victory. The jury hung on 85 counts of the 115-count indictment. A single juror explained during deliberations that he was not convinced that the apparent violations qualified as felony crimes. The jury's decision to return no verdict on the racketeering charge against broker Robert Mosky gave at least temporary encouragement to defense lawyers who believed the government had overstated its case.*

After some initial hoopla at the opening of the two major show trials of 12 Japanese yen traders and 10 soybean traders, the commodities cases had all but disappeared from the public consciousness. The exchanges were back to business as usual, running their markets and concentrating on expanding abroad and retaining the regulatory status quo at home. The U.S. Attorney's office turned much of its attention to other areas of law enforcement, particularly a crackdown on political corruption called Operation Gambat. The individuals caught up in the web of Operation Sourmash and Operation Hedge-clipper had long since given up hope of returning to normal life.

*For a complete list of current trial results, see "The Verdicts to Date" at the end of this chapter, beginning on page 300.

The apparent order broke down on January 9, 1991. After a four-month trial and three weeks of deliberation, the federal jury in the soybean trial returned a sweeping victory for the government, guilty verdicts on 250 of 303 counts, including racketeering convictions on eight of the nine traders charged with RICO. Broker Marty Dempsey fell hardest, receiving guilty verdicts for 52 felonies, including racketeering and racketeering conspiracy. Broker Edward Cox was convicted even though he had never traded with agent Richard Ostrom; the testimony of former trader David Skrodzki helped do him in. Local trader Charles Bergstrom also took a major hit. William Barcal, the only bean trader to beat a RICO rap, still was found guilty of 23 felony counts.

Valukas's successor, new U.S. Attorney Fred Foreman, for the first time threw all his weight behind the commodities probe, an effort he had eyed warily when he first took office. "When I came in, I knew I had just adopted this investigation, but I didn't know if I would be a good father," Foreman said days after the soybean verdict. "Now my kid just graduated from Harvard."

But Foreman's "Harvard graduate" would fail its next major test. On March 13, the jury that had sat through the six-month yen trial returned after more than 20 days of contentious deliberation. The result: not a single guilty verdict among the 240 counts at trial. Two defendants were acquitted of all charges against them, the first defendants to walk completely free. The jury remained hung on 101 of the counts, including racketeering charges against brokers John M. Baker, Jr., Thomas A. Crouch, James M. Marren, and Michael D. Smith.

In the yen courtroom, broker Matthew Newberger broke down and wept when the verdict was read. Broker Smith was defiant. "The government made us look like monsters," he charged. "I felt we were the victim of a monster. The biggest crime was what they put us through." A few blocks away, a cheer rolled across the Merc floor when the Dow Jones news screen hanging over the trading floor bulletined the news. Later, broker John Baker bought drinks for the house at a jubilant, impromptu party of traders and their lawyers at the Merc Club.

The verdict's timing was perfect for the leaders of the futures industry, gathering that very day for their annual conclave at the Boca Raton Hotel & Club. Merc officials crashed a cocktail party held for reporters. They verbally high-fived, gleefully entertaining questions from the press and declaring the investigation "now largely behind us." Merc President William Brodsky attacked the government. "At what cost to the taxpayers were these investigations conducted?" he wondered. Brodsky stated that "difficult and hard questions" needed to be asked about why the investigation was launched, a hint at the Merc's suspicions that enemies in Washington had pushed for the probe.

Jack Sandner, elected chairman of the Merc that January, was most defiant. "We never believed we had gone wrong," he stated emphatically. In cocktail conversation later in the evening, Leo Melamed laughed aloud over the fact that his nemesis from the yen trial, defense lawyer Thomas Durkin, who had requested copies of Melamed's trading records, had secured a separate trial for broker Sam Cali. On a motion joined by trader Ray Pace, Durkin claimed Cali could not get a fair trial because his defense—claiming the alleged actions were standard "custom and practice" on the trading floor and endorsed by everyone from Melamed on down—was at odds with the outright denials offered by the other traders. Melamed knew Durkin would have a tough time matching the success of the lawyers in the yen trial. "That's malpractice," Melamed chortled.

For the government, the yen verdict was quite a comedown from the heady days of early September, when the yen and soybean trials had first gotten underway. There seemed little room for jurors with multiple defendants, the lawyers, spectators, and audio and video equipment jamming the courtrooms. The trials had looked like easy winners as the government meticulously laid out its cases. But after the opening arguments, the trials had quickly bogged down with trade-by-trade explorations of each charge. Agent Dietrich Volk had spent 22 long days on the stand in the yen trial, constantly referring to his book of FBI Form 302 documents to refresh his memory. The yen trial often seemed to bog down, with the prosecutors themselves appearing to be confused by some of the nuances of trading. After the singularly lackluster closing arguments, the yen verdict would not be much of a shock.

The afternoon the yen verdict came in, U.S. Attorney Foreman held a meeting of his top aides to map their future strategy. Their most powerful weapon was the 101 counts remaining against the yen traders, including racketeering charges against four of them. What's more, there was a distinct pattern to the results. Many of the no-verdict counts were concentrated toward the end of the investigation, a time when FBI agent Volk's understanding of the pits had peaked. For example, the jury had returned no verdict on five trades in mid-

December, in which Volk participated as defendants Baker, Michael Sidel, Gary Wright, and Joseph O'Malley allegedly passed large sums to one another by filling wash trades. The tallies on the deals ranged as high as $3,125; there were no $12.50 rip-offs like those that had received so much negative attention in the press and had scarcely struck jurors as criminal.

The feds also saw promise in early reports about the jury's deliberations. The panel had voted 10–2 in favor of conviction on most of the hung counts. Two jurors had decided late in the deliberations to dismiss every count in the trial. One even read a magazine as the others deliberated the charges count by count, looking up from her reading only to vote "not guilty" on every poll. "They didn't offer a rational reason," lamented juror Martin Feuer. "They just fell back on the 'reasonable doubt' phrase. The same people were voting innocent right down the line."

The yen jury's deliberations had apparently followed the pattern set the previous summer by the Swiss franc jury. There, too, a mixed verdict had resulted largely from a refusal by an individual juror to accept the government's case. Although the prosecutors had vowed to retry all of the hung counts in that case, they quietly and quickly settled charges against Robert Mosky and local traders David Zatz and Danny Scheck days after the yen verdict came in. Mosky pleaded guilty to just one commodity-law violation and had all remaining counts, including the racketeering charge, dismissed.

Despite the yen result, the feds remained convinced that a jury could understand the charges and would even accept weeks of mind-numbing testimony about the trades from the FBI agent and traders cooperating with the government. They felt the soybean convictions had proved that point. But ironically, what had once been considered the strongest part of the government's case—the audiotapes recorded by undercover agents—in fact had proved to be the weakest element. The audio fidelity was poor. Often, background trading noises drowned out the allegedly illegal discussions taking place, and defendants were able to present their own transcripts of the tapes that often seemed exculpatory. More ominously for the government, jurors seemed to distrust the tapes as evidence. Although the soybean jurors had accepted them as fair, some yen jurors criticized the FBI agent's ability to switch the recorder on and off as fitted his needs. "The tape recorder should have kept going," jury foreman Christopher Cumberbatch said.

For former traders who had cut their deals with the government as far back as January 18, 1989, the trials had ground on slowly. Yen traders Brian and James Sledz, Aric March, and Thomas Braniff; soybean traders David Skrodzki, John Eggum, and James Nowak, and Swiss franc traders Mark Fuhrman and William Walsh found testifying at trial a lengthy ordeal. Their service as government witnesses was expected to substantially lighten their punishment, but the traders would not be sentenced until after the government had completed its cases and sentenced any traders convicted with the help of the cooperators' testimony. Even then, in addition to the fines they would pay and the remote chance of brief jail sentences, they also would be barred from all commodities trading for three years by the Commodity Futures Trading Commission. And they would never again be allowed to set foot on the floor of an exchange. Even for those who pleaded guilty but were not on call to testify for the government, life was hard. Barred from the trading floors, they found getting jobs a challenge. Treasury-bond trader Melanie Kosar went to work in her father's dry cleaning store.

Ironically, the exchange sanctions were not nearly as severe against traders convicted at trial as against those who cooperated with the investigation. Convicted Swiss franc trader Robert Mosky, for example, was suspended from the Merc floor for four months, but after being credited with the time he was away from the trading floor after the trial, he was free to return immediately.

Those who defended themselves found that a fair trial did not come free. Yen trader Joseph O'Malley sold his house and briefly moved in with his in-laws in order to pay his lawyer. But some traders, like yen local Robert Bailin, were able to maintain apartments at the Presidential Towers complex. Virtually all the accused traders continued going to the pits to trade in the mornings before coming to court, although the exchanges asked the brokers not to handle any customer orders. John Baker, thinner, his hair gradually returning to its natural white as he quit dying it, toiled in the pits by morning and defended his reputation by afternoon, becoming almost a folk hero among certain traders. Defense lawyer Mike Shanahan said all the yen defendants were heroes. "Everybody on the exchange owes these fellas a debt of gratitude for standing up to these charges," he said.

The government had now had one clear (soybean) victory, one (yen) defeat, and one (Swiss franc) wash. Operation Sourmash and Operation Hedgeclipper were at a crossroads. U.S. Attorney Foreman issued a stiff-upper-lip statement endorsing the ongoing investigations, and insisting the government intended to retry all the hung counts against the yen defendants. "The serious criminal activity uncovered by this investigation deepens our commitment to vigorously prosecute the insidious crime of fraud in the exchanges," Foreman said.

The yen verdict was an occasion for reappraisal, but not for capitulation by the government. The record assembled before the yen verdict had been impressive indeed: 20 guilty pleas among the four targeted pits, one no contest plea, even racketeering convictions against eight traders. The feds made no effort to squelch talk that new indictments would be forthcoming, and that charges might even be brought in the Standard & Poor's 500 trading pit.

Defense lawyers, however, saw Foreman's promise to press forward as little more than opening bluster in what were expected to become long and tedious settlement negotiations. They speculated that the government would settle most charges against the yen traders and retry only those counts it considered certain winners against some of the most notable defendants, focusing particular attention on the racketeering charges against four yen brokers. "I expect only the cases that are overwhelming in the degree of proof to be brought," reasoned Jeffrey Steinback, a lawyer who represented several traders who knew they were targets of the investigation but hoped to avoid indictment.

For their part, the exchanges would continue to snipe at the government's efforts and offer precious little support. After the prosecution's soybean sweep, the Board of Trade had reasoned that the convicted traders in the bean case represented less than one percent of its members. And now the Merc seemed poised to gear up its powerful publicity machine to portray the investigation as a complete bust. Never mind the weeks of testimony, from traders as well as the government agents, about hair-raising customer rip-offs and dirty inside deals. "These trials that took six months at untold cost could have been handled internally in a matter of hours," Merc lawyer Jerrold Salzman said.

Of course, it is true that the exchanges' self-regulatory structures could have handled the problems uncovered by the investigation and prosecuted in the trials. That was just the point. The exchanges had not done so. For up to two years, four traders in their pits wantonly broke every relevant exchange rule and federal law. Still, when the investigation had gone public in January of 1989, the exchanges were taken completely by surprise. Self-regulation had not worked; somebody else had to step in.

□ □ □

FOR THE EXCHANGES, life had proceeded almost as normal during the 18 months between the August 2, 1989, indictment of 45 traders and a clerk and the conclusion of the trials in early 1991. In the executive suites of the exchanges, life went on. The charged atmosphere of the early days quickly faded, and the Board of Trade and Chicago Mercantile Exchange returned to running their businesses as normal. Just as they had done in the aftermath of the 1987 stock market crash, the two exchanges put together an image rehabilitation campaign that persuaded investors and regulators that the exchanges were well-run, customer-friendly institutions. But behind the facade, the exchanges held their course, though not always with the same cast of leaders at the helm.

A changing of the guard occurred at the Board. Karsten Mahlmann, who became only the second chairman to resign in the history of the Board of Trade, left Chicago, his reputation tarnished by the collapse of Stotler. Facing years of interminable Stotler lawsuits, he was hired in late 1990 by his former political adversary, Leslie Rosenthal, to represent the Rosenthal Collins Group trading firm in its London office. Mahlmann's successor as Board of Trade chairman, veteran trader Billy O'Connor, was elected to a full term in January 1991. The soft-spoken O'Connor, who is driven to work in a kelly green Rolls Royce limousine, defeated Patrick Arbor, the former exchange vice-chairman whose trades had once been abused by bean broker David Skrodzki. Thomas Donovan, ever the polished politician, remained as president of the Board.

At the Merc, there was no changing of the guard. Rather, there was another game of musical chairs. At the end of 1990, Leo Melamed officially stepped down as chairman of the executive committee and resigned his title as special counsel to the board of governors. But his power remained virtually absolute. He remained chairman of the Merc's Globex computerized trading project. And when the Board's O'Connor suggested the Merc and the Board of Trade discuss the possibility of merging certain noncompetitive functions like trade checking and clearing, Melamed was named chairman of the joint Merc-Board task force.

Melamed also was the apparent power behind the surprise return of Jack Sandner as chairman of the Merc. To uninformed outsiders, the race to succeed two-term chairman John Geldermann had appeared to be no race at all. Steven Wollack, vice-chairman of the exchange, had announced his intentions to run and looked to many people like a winner. But such a view did not account for Sandner. Despite the negative publicity over hiring First Commodity Corp. of Boston salespeople and the salary he received from ABS Partners while sitting on the Merc's blue ribbon committee, Sandner decided to take the chairmanship for a third time in late January of 1991. Luckily for Sandner, the chairman was chosen only by the Melamed-dominated board of governors. In his race for a spot on the board—an election in which rank-and-file floor traders had a vote—Sandner was the second-lowest vote-getter among successful candidates, topping only trader Gerald Ordman. To smooth any bruised feelings, Wollack was handed a sop, Sandner's former $150,000-per-year position of legislative liaison for the Merc.

As Melamed headed toward retirement, the Merc appeared to be just where he would like it. A CFTC administrative law judge did find Brian Monieson guilty of a failure to supervise affairs at GNP Commodities. But Melamed's old bridge partner still was running day-to-day operations of his former firm even after the purchase by E.D. & F. Mann International. William Brodsky, the president of the exchange, was being groomed as a potential successor to Melamed in the role of front man for the exchange at national and international industry events. And clearly, Melamed was pleased to have helped return Sandner to the chairmanship, a move Sandner apparently considered his first step toward laying claim to the mantle that Leo might one day lay down.

Melamed would not go gently into his good retirement. At least two extravagant parties were thrown, the second one, at Merc expense, costing upwards of $500,000. The first party was thrown by Thomas Dittmer, the legendary chairman of Refco Inc. Held at Dittmer's lavish North Shore home in June 1990, as the Swiss franc jury was in the midst of its deliberations against three Merc traders, the party was the kind that has made Dittmer famous over the years. Each table was decorated with Melamed memorabilia that included a copy of his unsuccessful science fiction novel, *The Tenth Planet*. Telephones on the tables were interconnected. And a display of computer terminals and quote machines were set up to look like a trading room. Across the screens scrolled an authorized version of Melamed's biography. During the evening's program, each of Melamed's close friends stood to reminisce about their times with Leo over the years.

The Dittmer party would be topped only by Melamed's second retirement bash. The gala event at the Hyatt Regency Chicago to which 2,000 people were invited originally had been planned for the fall, before Melamed's semiofficial retirement date. It was folded into the Merc's annual members' dinner after some members complained about the expense of hosting two such lavish events. Exchange executives, traders, and economists from around the world flew in for the event. Republican chairman Clayton Yeutter spoke, as did economist Milton Friedman. But not everyone in the industry attended. "I've heard Leo's retirement speech two times already," a Board of Trade official said. "I don't think I could handle it again."

□ □ □

FOR THE EXCHANGES THEMSELVES, the investigation led to a series of press conferences about wide-ranging reforms, and then a series of backtracking moves. The strategy seemed designed to do just enough to generate favorable publicity, but not enough to affect the way the floor operated. Even though traders on the floor apparently followed the straight-and-narrow after the massive publicity generated by Operation Sourmash and Operation Hedgeclipper, the long-term nature of the changes appeared uncertain, particularly given the equivocating example set by the exchanges' elders.

After scrambling to fight off the deluge of bad publicity that surrounded news of the investigations, the exchanges publicly relaxed after the indictments were handed down. They seemed to feel the trading floors were safer than ever because the "dishonest few" had been identified and were facing justice. In an interview just before the second anniversary of the government's knock on the door of the industry, the Merc's Melamed chalked up the whole investigation to the egos of a few U.S. prosecutors competing with Rudolph Giuliani, then the headline-grabbing U.S. Attorney for the Southern District of New York. The Chicago lawyers wanted a taste of the limelight in the wake of the highly publicized insider trading cases in New York, Melamed figured.

"The press made a much bigger deal out of the whole thing than it was," Melamed claimed. He said the Merc had already been doing the best job in the industry of screening out abuses on the trading floor. "Our record on disciplinary actions was outstanding. We did a study [after the FBI investigation], and our record is still outstanding."

The record certainly improved, briefly, after the investigation. In 1989, the Merc expelled six members, levied fines of $3.4 million, and sanctioned 120 members altogether—far more aggressive than the two expulsions and $1.1 million in fines in 1988 among the 207 disciplinary actions. But by 1990, fines had fallen to $1.2 million, and expulsions had dropped to four members among the 187 total sanctions.

The Merc's complacency showed. Most of the Merc's reforms were more cosmetic than substantive. Formation of the blue ribbon reform committee was a masterstroke of public relations, but it wound up being a weak swipe at wrongdoing on the exchange. Two trading practices that became notorious because of the publicity that followed disclosure of the investigation—dual trading and curb trading—received kid gloves treatment in the end. After Merc floor traders protested the proposed dual-trading restrictions in the rump session attended by Merc chairman John Geldermann, the exchange's governors backed down. The Merc moved to ban dual trading on all contracts in which the exchange auditing of trades failed to meet a minimum 90 percent standard of accuracy, a standard the CFTC had set three years earlier but that the Merc and the Board had not yet met. The exchange also required all dual traders to manually record trades to the nearest minute, again a long-held standard that was never achieved by the Chicago exchanges. Recording trades by hand, of course, is exactly how traders had broken the rules in the first place. Cutting the time brackets from 30 minutes down to one, while making cheating less convenient, was not likely to eliminate it altogether.

The investigation exposed curb trading as one of the areas most fraught with corruption. Both the Merc and the Board acknowledged that curb trading existed and allowed it to continue. But they changed the rules in an effort to stop the profit skimming that had characterized the after-hours market before the investigation. The reform, which allows a brief after-hours session during which traders may buy or sell only at the day's settlement price, enables customers to enter or exit positions at the end of the trading day.

A pledge to place nonmembers on Merc disciplinary committees fell short when it became apparent that all the appointees would be retired members or nonmember executives of clearing firms that owned seats on the exchange. The exchange's boast that it planned to double its surveillance staff proved less than impressive, considering that the staff at the time was fewer than ten people, responsible for monitoring the activity of some 3,000 Merc members.

The Merc also required all members to attend ethics classes taught by Loyola University's ethics center. The classes—attended by pit brokers, clearing firm executives, and managers of bank trading desks—witnessed some interesting debates about the relative privileges and responsibilities of floor traders. But they seemed to do little to dent the prevailing attitude that being on the trading floor entitled a trader to an "edge" over the customer. The Merc at least tried to make certain its members, reform-resistant as they may have been, would take the classes seriously. In November 1989, the exchange actually fined two traders for arriving at an ethics class "under the influence of alcohol" and "engaging in loud, disruptive, and vexatious conduct."

In a new effort to screen out undesirables—and known FBI agents—the Merc required new applicants to submit photographs with their financial data and stipulated that all its members, not just brokers, must belong to the National Futures Association and undergo an FBI fingerprint background check. Although the Merc's special committee attempted to tighten rules governing trades between members of organized broker groups, the effort failed after the exchange's most influential broker groups protested.

To a floor trader or broker, the Merc's most meaningful changes in response to the investigation were subtle shifts in rule interpretations. In the past, the rules said that the customer was always right and should always get the benefit from an order fill. Under new, more liberal rule interpretations, the Merc allowed brokers to share windfall profits with customers if the customers consented. This created a more level playing field, according to veteran Merc brokers, and so reduced a broker's ability to rationalize theft from customers.

The Board of Trade's approach focused primarily on improvements to its trade-auditing system and a closer monitoring of the activities of broker groups, which had not even been required to register with the exchange before the investigation.

To bolster the audit trail process, the Board of Trade invested an extra $1 million in its Computerized Trade Reconstruction system. The money bought programming that allowed exchange surveillance staff to do a detailed analysis of trading patterns between specific traders and brokers, and to manipulate data more precisely to monitor individual trades. The Board also added 33 employees in surveillance and compliance capacities. Rules were rewritten to increase the size of fines and the length of suspensions Board committees can dole out for trade practice violations.

To complement the CTR enhancements, the Board added new rules that were so obvious it is surprising they had not been written before. Traders and brokers, for instance, were required to record their trades in ink rather than pencil. Clearing firms were required to turn in trading cards to the clearinghouse within one hour after they were collected from the trading floor. These actions limited the amount of time for a crooked trader to fabricate trades.

An important potential tool for detecting trading fraud, a tight audit trail to track every trade, remained as elusive two years after the investigation as it had been the day the FBI agents first visited the floor. A Government Accounting Office study released in late 1989 found that weaknesses in controls over floor trading continued to provide dishonest floor participants with the opportunity to cheat customers through noncompetitive execution of orders, and to conceal this cheating by manipulating the recorded price and time of trades. The study concluded that "most of the types of abuses alleged in the Justice Department indictments could also have been detected and documented with independent, precise, and complete timing of trades." Alas, such standards were never implemented.

While both the Merc and the Board invested millions in the development of CTR, neither exchange had bothered to regulate a most important element in the surveillance loop: the time clocks on each trading desk. By early 1991, the Board would finally synchronize all the trading floor time clocks to a master clock to assure that the individual clocks could not be manipulated. However, two years after the first publicity of the probe, the Merc had not even initiated such a project. In December 1990, a casual tour of the trading floor found trading desk time clocks registering as much as two minutes difference from the exchange's master clock. Many of the time-stamp machines sat with keys at the ready, making it possible for clerks who wanted to doctor the record of a trade to turn back the time register. Merc disciplinary records show that one clerk was fined for manipulating his clock to "improve" a trade just weeks before the FBI investigation became public. There is no way to know how often this happens undetected.

Merc officials say that synchronizing the clocks would be expensive and would not eliminate fraud. A trader or clerk who wishes to trade after the closing bell, for example, can easily time-stamp a blank order form before the close and hold it to log a post-market trade. Once submitted to the back office of the clearing firm, a trade with an after-market time stamp would likely be "edited" to show a legal time as the keypunch operator logged the trade into the Merc's computer. Even handwritten alterations to time stamps have been known to pass through keypunch processing.

Perhaps recognizing that a perfect audit trail is not possible so long as any human factor remains in the trade execution loop, the Merc and the Board became more aggressive in their attempts to develop high-tech trading enhancements after the FBI sting. Working together, the two exchanges engaged electronics vendors to develop hand-held computers that could record trades electronically and reduce traders' ability to alter trades after they have been made. The machines would eliminate the need for time clocks and trading cards and seek to make some varieties of bagmen obsolete. The audit machines were expected to be in place by late 1991.

The Merc's Leo Melamed pegged his hopes for trading reform on the concept of a computerized global trading system, which would eliminate paper orders, pencils, and even floor traders. Globex had been scheduled to go on-line in late 1989. However, technical and security problems repeatedly delayed the Globex launch, which was last scheduled for late 1991.

Globex once was just a Merc project, and the Board briefly considered a Nintendo-style computerized trading system of its own, dubbed Aurora. But when that concept appeared destined for problems with regulators concerned about pre-arranged trading, the Board abandoned Aurora and signed on with the Merc's Globex system. The Globex agreement was evidence of an increasingly close working relationship between the two exchanges. By October 1990, they had announced that they were exploring areas of mutual interest in which they may cooperate in order to contain costs and insure that Chicago would continue to retain its role as the center of worldwide futures trading.

As they work toward a shared future, the Merc and the Board apparently will continue to survive, and even thrive. The rash of bad publicity never dented the volume of business at the Chicago exchanges. While the prolonged trials occasionally captured the interest of the city, they failed to sour the giant brokerage houses and their customers on futures trading. The scandalous episode simply seemed to add another shade to the already off-color public perception of the futures markets. Combined volume at the Merc and the Board of Trade reached 243 million contracts in 1989, compared to 221 million the year before the investigation. At the end of 1990, annual volume for the two exchanges had risen to 258 million. Much of that volume came from trading in the Swiss franc, yen, soybean, and Treasury-bond pits, the direct targets of the FBI moles.

□ □ □

THE FBI INVESTIGATION, designed as it was to clean up the futures markets, first created a mess for the industry's regulators. Both the Commodity Futures Trading Commission and the National Futures Association suffered from the widely held perception that the wrong-doing exposed by the investigation had occurred under the not-so-watchful eyes of the two agencies. With the concept of self-regulation called into question in Congress and among investors, the two agencies had much to lose, and turf to defend.

In late 1990, the National Futures Association agreed to create a clearinghouse to provide public customers with complete information about the disciplinary histories of traders and brokers. The NFA will keep in its computerized files records of the disciplinary actions of each futures exchange, the CFTC, and the NFA. Customers for the first time will be able to access that information with a single telephone call.

After studying the results of the FBI investigation, the CFTC required all U.S. futures exchanges to register broker groups and create rules governing their trading behavior. The agency also drafted guidelines against dual trading and mandated that its own surveillance staff spend more time on exchange trading floors.

The CFTC, in its post-investigation reforms, succeeded in tightening the audit trail slightly. The commission required exchange clearing firms to collect trading cards from the floor every half hour and to have special "brackets," or trading periods, for the opening and closing minutes of each session. This reduced the amount of time traders hold their cards and the potential time available to alter the record of a trade. The agency now also requires that traders keep better records of how they resolve trading errors. Settling outtrades had been done haphazardly and often resulted in pre-arranged trades, informal settlement between brokers and traders, and more customer abuse in the pits.

The CFTC also wrote rules that bar traders with significant disciplinary histories from serving on exchange judicial committees or on the governing boards of industry self-regulatory organizations. One of the first people to be affected by the new rule was Larry Williams, the National Futures Association director elected while under investigation by the NFA. He resigned after losing his NFA case and subsequent appeal.

CFTC chairman Wendy Gramm continued her crusade to expand business overseas for U.S. futures markets. In an address to the Futures Industry Association meeting in Florida in March 1990, she passed over the Chicago embarrassment with a brief comment. "Remember, trading abuses did occur in these markets," she reminded industry leaders. "Reforms must be made. The reforms won't be costless, but they are essential." But Gramm was in a weak political position from which to push the issue much further, and thereby alienate the industry. The FBI investigation had become a convenient political hook for critics of the CFTC, and SEC chairman Richard Breeden, together with Treasury Secretary Nicholas Brady, was conducting an aggressive campaign to gut the CFTC by wresting control of stock index futures away from the commission.

The investigations had made the CFTC more vulnerable than ever to congressional criticism, but the exchanges again rode to the rescue. The 1990 CFTC reauthorization kicked off with attacks by the White House–backed team of Breeden and Brady, but ended with the Chicago exchanges winning the day. The exchanges vigorously lobbied members of the Senate banking and agriculture committees throughout the spring of 1990 to keep the CFTC intact. Even in the wake of the FBI investigation, the exchanges maintained enough clout on Capitol Hill to hold their own against the White House initiative. The Brady reform initiative was never brought to the Senate floor for consideration because its supporters lacked the votes to see it pass.

Still, the CFTC's reauthorization process remained captive to the Senate agriculture committee as 1990 drew to a close. Each attempt to bring a reauthorization bill onto the Senate floor was blocked by Washington Republican Slade Gorton, Jr., who persisted in attaching a proviso that would shift stock-index jurisdiction to the SEC. Compromise legislation was torpedoed by Senator Alan Dixon, the Illinois Democrat and close friend of the Merc. After beating back the initial White House–led onslaught, the exchanges were in no mood to compromise. The CFTC received a boost in its 1991 budget authorization to $44.52 million, all of which could be covered by a transaction tax proposed by President Bush early in 1991. Even so, reauthorization remained in limbo as the 102nd Congress opened its proceedings.

□ □ □

THE CLEAREST WINNERS from Operation Sourmash and Operation Hedgeclipper were the people responsible for orchestrating the investigation.

The role of former U.S. Attorney Dan K. Webb in initiating the investigation has not been known publicly until now. And it's not surprising that Webb never went out of his way to claim credit. As the person who helped originate the probe, Webb put himself in an awkward position by helping the Board formulate its RICO defense strategy and then by taking on Treasury-bond trader Howard Goberstein as a client. Whether Webb's role in initiating the investigation influenced his willingness to allow Goberstein to be the first indicted trader to plead guilty to racketeering charges is not known.

U.S. Attorney Anton Valukas, after taking bows at the press conference announcing the indictments, would not participate meaningfully in the prosecutorial effort again. By December 1989, after nearly five years in office, Valukas had resigned as U.S. Attorney to take a job at his former law firm, Jenner & Block. For Valukas, it was a no-lose proposition. If the cases succeeded, he was credited with initiating the investigation. If they failed, he was no longer around to take the heat.

Valukas's successor, former Lake County, Illinois, prosecutor Fred Foreman, also was in an enviable position, assuming oversight of an investigation that he could either feed or starve depending on its results at trials. For Valukas's assistants who worked on the case, the investigation also proved to be a boon. Ira Raphaelson, though he took considerable heat for his commando tactics on January 18 and 19, led the successful soybean prosecution. As the jury deliberated the verdict, Raphaelson was preparing to leave the U.S. Attorney's office to become the head of a newly organized Savings & Loan fraud task force based in Washington, D.C. Thomas Durkin, who assisted in the soybean case, was named Foreman's First Assistant U.S. Attorney. The other lawyers who led the investigations and the trials—Daniel Gillogly, James Fleissner, Mark Rotert, Mark Pollack, Dean Polales, and Lisa Huestis—gained the experience of a sophisticated and complex undercover investigation.

At the FBI, case agent Jeffrey Frank was transferred to Milwaukee after losing out on a chance to be named to the head of a new squad of agents formed during the middle of the investigation. Ernest G. Locker, Jr., remained in the office as a special agent who heads some of the bureau's toughest white-collar crime cases. The undercover agents—Richard Ostrom, Michael Bassett, Dietrich Volk, and Randall

Jannett—were still busy babysitting the trials of their cases. Their next assignments were not known.

For defense lawyers, the cases proved to be a particular boon. With many charging about $300 per hour during trials, and trials on the cases running for a minimum of 12 weeks, the lawyers stood to net a minimum of $150,000 each for their trial time alone. With the background research, negotiating time, and non-trial court appearances, the lawyers' fees were at least double that amount. A very rough estimate puts the legal fees upwards of $8 million just for lawyers' time. Add to that the fees for the time legal aides spent transcribing tapes and assembling documents, and the figure pops well above $11 million split among the 25 lawyers whose clients went to trial. Whoever first called the investigation the Defense Lawyers Relief Act of 1989 had it right.

Dwayne Andreas of Archer Daniels Midland benefited, too. A long-time critic of the Board of Trade, he was handed an opportunity to put the government to work carrying out a personal, deep-seated grudge against the futures markets. ADM's alleged manipulation of the soybean oil market in 1985 at the same time the firm was training Richard Ostrom to trade in the pits was the height of recklessness, and an indication of the firm's respect for market integrity.

□ □ □

THERE'S ONE LAST GROUP TO MENTION: customers. At the outset, the investigation was designed to make the markets safe for customers wanting to do business in the futures markets. Whether that in fact happens remains at issue.

Certainly, the investigations at first had a salutary effect. In the days after the probes first went public, floor brokers rearranged their decks of orders in a way that no longer facilitated matching customers' buy and sell orders against each other. Brokers and locals began writing checks to each other for outtrades. The curb market slowed down, at least until the exchanges re-created it in their reform efforts.

Only with time will we know whether the customers—from farmers to individual investors to pension funds to insurance companies to even national governments—truly benefited from the investigation or not. But this much, at least, is clear: The customers apparently did not care. Except for the wild days after the investigation first became known, volume at the exchanges did not dip at all. Rather than expressing concern or outrage about being ripped off, dozens of customers sent letters to the exchanges asking for the continuation of dual trading and extolling the honesty of their brokers.

This may have been one case where the people who stood to gain the most from the government's efforts, the customers who send their billions to the trading floors each day, cared the least. Apparently, those folks were not ready for, or interested in, reform.

□ The Verdicts to Date □

NOTE: "CEA Violations" are violations of the Commodity Exchange Act.

The Soybean Pit

Scott Anixter: Pleaded guilty to 4 CEA violations.

Bradley Ashman: Guilty of RICO conspiracy, 2 counts of wire fraud, 17 CEA violations. Not guilty of 1 count of mail fraud, 2 CEA violations.

William A. Barcal III: Guilty of 12 counts of mail fraud, 19 CEA violations. Not guilty of RICO conspiracy, 1 CEA violation.

Charles Bergstrom: Guilty of RICO, RICO conspiracy, 7 counts of mail fraud, 5 counts of wire fraud, 34 CEA violations. Not guilty of 2 counts of mail fraud, 4 counts of wire fraud, 5 CEA violations.

Edward Cox III: Guilty of RICO conspiracy, 13 counts of mail fraud, 5 counts of wire fraud, 37 CEA violations. Not guilty of 2 counts of mail fraud, 3 CEA violations.

Martin J. Dempsey: Guilty of RICO, RICO conspiracy, 21 counts of mail fraud, 1 count of wire fraud, 37 CEA violations. Not guilty of 2 counts of mail fraud, 1 count of wire fraud, 1 CEA violation.

John N. Eggum: Pleaded guilty to 2 counts of mail fraud.

Joel J. Fetchenhier: Guilty of RICO conspiracy, 2 counts of wire fraud, 4 CEA violations. Not guilty of 1 count of wire fraud.

Kenneth Gillen: Pleaded guilty to 1 CEA violation.

Thomas P. Kenney: Guilty of RICO conspiracy, 4 counts of mail fraud, 1 count of wire fraud, 13 CEA violations. Not guilty of 6 counts of mail fraud, 1 count of wire fraud, 5 CEA violations.

Craig LaCrosse: Pleaded guilty to 2 CEA violations.

Bruce W. Mittelstadt: Pleaded guilty to 1 count of mail fraud, 1 CEA violation.

James D. Nowak: Pleaded guilty to RICO conspiracy, 1 count of filing a false income tax return.

Harry O. Patten III: Pleaded guilty to 2 CEA violations.

John Ryan: Guilty of 1 count of wire fraud, 4 CEA violations. Not guilty of 2 counts of mail fraud, 1 count of wire fraud.

Sheldon Schneider: Guilty of RICO conspiracy, 11 counts of mail fraud, 24 CEA violations. Not guilty of 2 counts of mail fraud, 3 counts of wire fraud, 3 CEA violations.

David J. Skrodzki: Pleaded guilty to 1 count of mail fraud, 1 CEA violation.

John A. Vercillo: Guilty of RICO conspiracy, 1 count of mail fraud, 3 counts of wire fraud, 6 CEA violations. Not guilty of 1 count of wire fraud.

Michael Weiser: Pleaded guilty to 3 CEA violations, 1 count of failing to file a federal income tax return.

The Treasury Bond Pit

Howard Goberstein: Pleaded guilty to RICO conspiracy.

Melanie Kosar: Pleaded guilty to 1 count of mail fraud, 1 CEA violation.

John Myskowski: Pleaded guilty to 1 count of mail fraud, 1 CEA violation.

The Swiss Franc Pit

Mark E. Fuhrman: Pleaded guilty to 1 count of wire fraud, 1 CEA violation.

Robert D. Mosky: Guilty of 7 CEA violations. Not guilty of 14 CEA violations, 6 counts of fraud. Jury hung on RICO conspiracy, 25 counts of mail or wire fraud, and 30 CEA violations. Mosky later pleaded guilty to 1 count of wire fraud; government dropped all other unresolved charges.

Danny Scheck: Guilty of 1 CEA violation. Jury hung on 8 counts of mail or wire fraud, 11 CEA violations. Later, Scheck pleaded guilty to 2 CEA violations; government dropped all other unresolved charges.

William A. Walsh: Pleaded guilty to 1 count of wire fraud, 1 CEA violation.

David Zatz: Not guilty of 1 count wire fraud, 1 CEA violation. Jury hung on 5 counts of mail or wire fraud, 7 CEA violations.

The Japanese Yen Pit

Robert H. Bailin: Not guilty of 1 count of mail fraud, 2 counts of wire fraud, 12 CEA violations. Jury hung on 1 count of mail fraud, 4 counts of wire fraud, 9 CEA violations.

John M. Baker, Jr.: Not guilty of 4 counts of mail fraud, 7 counts of wire fraud, 14 CEA violations. Jury hung on RICO conspiracy, 3 counts of mail fraud, 1 count of wire fraud, 11 CEA violations.

Thomas M. Braniff: Pleaded guilty to 1 count of mail fraud, 1 count of wire fraud.

Sam A. Cali: Severed from main yen trial. Faces prosecution on charges of RICO, RICO conspiracy, 7 counts of mail fraud, 32 counts of wire fraud, 56 CEA violations.

Donald E. Callahan: Pleaded guilty to 1 count of mail fraud.

Michael J. Christ: Not guilty of 1 count of mail fraud, 2 counts of wire fraud, 4 CEA violations. Jury hung on 1 count of wire fraud, 2 CEA violations.

Thomas A. Crouch: Not guilty of 2 counts of mail fraud, 2 counts of wire fraud, 6 CEA violations. Jury hung on RICO conspiracy, 11 counts of mail fraud, 3 counts of wire fraud, 15 CEA violations.

Michael I. Greenfield: Not guilty of 1 count of mail fraud, 1 count of wire fraud, 7 CEA violations. Jury hung on 1 count of mail fraud, 2 CEA violations.

Aric H. March: Pleaded guilty to 1 count of mail fraud, 1 CEA violation.

James M. Marren: Not guilty of 5 counts of mail fraud, 1 count of wire fraud, 12 CEA violations. Jury hung on RICO conspiracy, 3 counts of mail fraud, 4 CEA violations.

Kenneth M. Maslak: Not guilty of 3 counts of mail fraud, 6 CEA violations.

Matthew A. Newberger: Not guilty of 2 counts of mail fraud, 5 CEA violations.

Joseph P. O'Malley: Not guilty of 1 count of mail fraud, 1 count of wire fraud, 3 CEA violations. Jury hung on 1 count of mail fraud, 1 count of wire fraud, 3 CEA violations.

Ray Pace: Severed from main yen trial. Faces prosecution on RICO conspiracy, 8 counts of mail fraud, 33 counts of wire fraud, 77 CEA violations.

Daniel Parz: Pleaded guilty to 1 count of wire fraud, 1 CEA violation.

Martin J. Riley: Pleaded no contest to 1 count of mail fraud, 2 CEA violations.

Michael Sidel: Not guilty of 1 count of mail fraud, 1 count of wire fraud, 2 CEA violations. Jury hung on 1 count of mail fraud, 5 CEA violations.

Brian E. Sledz: Pleaded guilty to 1 count of wire fraud, 1 CEA violation.

James G. Sledz: Pleaded guilty to 1 count of mail fraud, 1 CEA violation.

Michael D. Smith: Not guilty of 5 counts of mail fraud, 4 counts of wire fraud, 12 CEA violations. Jury hung on RICO conspiracy, 3 counts of wire fraud, 7 CEA violations.

Gary A. Wright: Not guilty of 5 CEA violations. Jury hung on 2 counts of mail fraud, 4 CEA violations.

———————————— □□□ ————————————

CHAPTER SIXTEEN

Epilogue: What Should Be Done?

PERHAPS PAUL JENKINS, the FBI agent who ran the boiler-room stings of the early 1980s, put it best. "What's wrong with this picture?"

Consider: Leo Melamed, the father of the futures industry, is also the father of futures regulation, serving on the industry's self-regulatory agency until his resignation early in 1990. Meanwhile, traders call Melamed "Adjustment Leo" because of persistent floor-broker complaints, which Melamed denies, that he frequently asks for price changes on orders that are not filled to his satisfaction.

Karsten "Cash" Mahlmann, at the very time he is testifying on Capitol Hill about the dangers of overregulation, is locked in a losing battle for control of his own trading firm. With Mahlmann forced out of power at Stotler & Co. and preoccupied with his responsibilities as chairman of the Chicago Board of Trade, Stotler fraudulently transfers customer funds to help keep its corporate parent from drowning in red ink. Despite holding a seat on the board of the National Futures Association, which is responsible for protecting customer funds against fraud, Mahlmann never breathes a word of Stotler's troubles.

The NFA, headed by former Board of Trade president Robert Wilmouth, builds an impressive record against two-bit hustlers but lets larger fraud cases, such as the rip-offs perpetrated by First Commodity Corp. of Boston, run wild for years. Meanwhile, NFA members with records of rules violations and blatant conflicts of interest serve on the agency's board of directors.

The Commodity Futures Trading Commission, permanently preoccupied with earning a new lease on life from Congress, fails to take the necessary steps to root out corruption in the Chicago markets. A former CFTC chairman takes a post on the board of the Chicago Mercantile Exchange within weeks of resigning from the commission. And members of Congress responsible for making the CFTC strong enough to effectively regulate the futures markets continue to receive healthy speaking fees and PAC money from the industry they regulate.

Brokers depend on local traders for liquidity, and locals need brokers for a piece of the action. Expediency prompts them to create a ritualized system of "busting" trades, accepting losing trades in return for winners later, pre-arranging trades and trading after the closing bell—all in the name of making the markets work. Even when traders like Anthony Castellano are caught breaking rules again and again, they stay in business on the floor. And so comfortable are floor traders in the belief that they are beyond the reach of the law, that when rumors spread that Rick Carlson is an undercover FBI agent, traders continue to make illegal trades with him.

Broker groups control the flow of trading on the Merc, and increasingly at the Board, so much so that many traders consider them a dangerous, anticompetitive influence. Even as a Merc blue ribbon committee ponders the fate of broker groups, Jack Sandner, who sits on the panel, makes a joke of its supposed vigilance by accepting a paycheck from a broker group of which he is part owner.

What's wrong with this picture? Indeed. The list goes on and on. But unlike the federal prosecutors who cluttered their indictments with some truly meaningless charges, we won't throw in every single indiscretion we can find. That would cheapen the endemic problems by lumping them in with a crowd of minor irritants, much as the government's case in the commodities investigations was tarnished by including petty curb-trading rip-offs of as little as $12.50 along with $25,000 fictitious trades. This confused the juries, not to mention the general public, and made the government look like an overly zealous prosecutorial behemoth. As we present our case for fixing the futures markets, the last thing we want to do is confuse the jury.

In his closing arguments in the Swiss franc trial of Robert Mosky, Danny Scheck, and David Zatz in July 1990, Assistant U.S. Attorney James Fleissner summarized the ten major strains running through the defense arguments. The most colorful, and the most accurate, that Fleissner identified was the "Wizard of Oz" defense—an allusion to the little man behind the curtain who is unveiled by the dog Toto. Frantically working the levers and pedals that maintain the illusion of the Wizard's invincibility, he booms into the microphone, "Pay no attention to that man behind the curtain," as if the reverberations will convince Dorothy and friends that what they are seeing is not true. "The mighty and powerful Oz has spoken."

Much like that vain and vulnerable man, the futures industry has depended too long on its deft use of razzle-dazzle and sleight of hand. Working the levers in Congress and promoting a public sense of mystery about its inner workings, the industry has conjured an aura of invincibility. The ragtag group of immigrants and streetfighters that has built one of the world's great financial communities has grown defensive with success. They remind us frequently about the exchanges' long history of growth in both volume and international stature and warn that any change risks losing it all. They have painted their business as something, in the words of prosecutor Fleissner, "too complex for mere mortals to understand." By locking up loyalty among regulators, legislators, and even customers, they have created their own small Land of Oz, where the streets are paved with gold. They consider all powerful outsiders as dangerous to them as wicked witches of the West.

Whatever their shortcomings, and there are some, Operations Sourmash and Hedgeclipper have at least pulled back the curtain on this enchanted land. Where once we saw the power of raw market forces at work, we now see corrupt influences rubbing a market raw. Where once we might have believed the industry is managed best by those who know it best, we now know that such knowledge often plays to the public's worst advantage. Where we once believed that the open outcry system offered the customer the best price in the most liquid market possible, now we're not so certain. Open outcry is crying out for change.

Marketplaces are built on the concept of change—changes in prices, in risk levels, in the weather, in politics. However, unless the leaders of those markets are willing to act, the futures marketplaces will fall victim to their own inability to change. A potential catalyst for reform, the government sting instead has been taken as a threat to survival that must be defeated. Pay no attention to that blue-ribbon reform committee that sat behind the Merc's closed doors. Preservation of the status quo was its top objective. Blinded by their streetfighter's instinct for self-preservation, the leaders of the futures exchanges could not recognize Operations Sourmash and Hedgeclipper as the antiseptic doses they were: chances to eradicate the virus infecting the markets before the whole system becomes feverish with corrupt dealings and dirty politics—and dies.

There are no simple prescriptions for survival and success. Despite the patently self-serving logic of the exchanges' "Hands Off!" warnings, there is a modicum of truth to what they say. Market mechanisms *are* delicate. And there is no lack of competitors—in New York, London, Tokyo, to name a few—who would like to reproduce the success the Chicago exchanges have created. Even so, the resistance to reform is itself a threat to the very existence of the markets. Certainly, trading volume remains robust. Customers still flock to the markets. But the corruption revealed on the floor, the conflicts in the executive suites, the soft touch bought and paid for in Washington: Together they draw a picture of a system on the verge of breakdown.

This is the time to redraw that picture. We recommend a total overhaul of the concept of self-regulation. Former Senator Thomas Eagleton (D-Missouri), when quitting the Merc's board in a self-righteous huff, called self-regulation "the Chicago mirage," and he was right. As Eagleton noted, "self-regulation" and "nonregulation" have become synonymous. While we suggest certain specific changes, our recommendations fall into four groups. The first involves opening the exchange governing processes to outsiders. The second involves the free flow of information. The third involves regulation. And the fourth, modernization. These four principles are the ground on which the future of futures trading should be based.

☐ Invite more outsiders onto exchange boards.

Current CFTC rules mandate that each exchange have a token number of "public directors" from outside the industry. A token few is not enough, particularly given the Wizard of Oz mysticism that the market insiders so expertly use to cow the outsiders. Boards of the exchanges should be composed of a majority of directors from outside the industry, with a large minority still coming from the group of member firms, individual traders, and staff that today dominate exchange politics. Outsiders should also be placed on the exchanges' executive committees, where most policy is made.

If the insider group is correct in its positions, even a majority of outside directors can be swayed. But only a majority of true outsiders— not industry shills chosen for their conciliatory views—can muster the diverse range of expertise and political clout necessary to outgun the clubby rule of the market men. It is telling that, in the wake of the investigation, the reform most actively promoted by certain Merc officials would ease the floor broker's responsibility to repay customers for mistakes and allow brokers to share the profits of mistakes that work in their customers' favor. Such insider thinking would never fly on a board filled with outsiders.

□ Let members vote on all salaried officers who are not exchange staff.

The Merc's Leo Melamed earned $500,000, but Melamed had not been elected to a Merc office in years. Jack Sandner in 1988 was appointed to the redundant post of special adviser at a salary of $150,000. Leo may have been worth the money, but Sandner's salary seems to be largely Melamed's personal thanks for loyalty over the years. Members should not have to pay for such an expression of gratitude. Besides, they should have a chance to say whether Melamed, or some future Melamed, is worth the money. A referendum in May of 1990, suggesting just such a vote, failed to win a majority at the Merc by a narrow margin. Melamed put his full weight against the proposal. While top policy-setting posts should be elective, permanent staff members, such as exchange presidents and lawyers, rightfully are not elected. Some jobs simply cannot be done by elected officers: witness Congress.

□ Make exchange officers put their brokerage firm assets into blind trusts during their terms of office and take leaves from positions at their brokerage firms.

The concept works for U.S. presidents and top government officials; it should be good enough for market officials. Blind trusts would not eliminate conflicts of interest entirely, but they would be a strong step toward reducing the direct cause-and-effect distractions that currently must influence every exchange policy decision. Required leaves of absence might scare away a few potential officeholders, but most firms would gladly allow employees leaves in return for the prestige value of having a major exchange officeholder aboard.

□ Recompose disciplinary committees to include more outsiders, including regulatory officials.

The same benefits brought by outsiders to the boards—diverse viewpoints, more critical thinking, fewer conflicts of interest—also apply in the committee system. By adding at least one staffer from the Commodity Futures Trading Commission to each disciplinary committee, the exchanges would guarantee that regulators are aware of all the dirty laundry, not just the scraps that are hung out in public. In addition to improving the flow of information, a vital concern as evidenced by the Stotler affair, such exposure would help reduce suspicions that the disciplinary processes at the two exchanges are rigged games. To avoid undue government influence, the CFTC representative could be a nonvoting member. Even the business conduct committees of the exchanges, the most influential panel on both boards, should have CFTC representation.

☐ Reconstruct the National Futures Association board with customer advocates.

Just as conflicts of interest can plague an exchange, they also tarnish the quasi-regulatory NFA. In fact, the conflict here is worse because the NFA was created for the sole purpose of regulation. Instead, it now serves simply as a marketing tool that gives customers a false sense of regulatory security. Karsten Mahlmann's conflict alone is reason enough to rebuild the NFA board so that its directors cannot come from the leadership of one of the exchanges.

☐ Improve the flow of information by publishing details of all disciplinary actions.

In most cases, only the most cursory explanations of events are described when exchanges, following CFTC rules, publicly post fines and suspensions. If full details were published, even to the point of including victims' names where applicable, then members, regulators, and the public could judge for themselves whether exchange justice is meted out fairly. Exchanges also should be required to send notice of fines directly to media outlets, something done voluntarily but not uniformly today. Victims' names would give outside parties a chance to poll those most directly affected by transgressions to see if they feel exchange justice is blind.

☐ Forward all disciplinary records to the NFA and the CFTC.

Currently, the CFTC keeps on hand records of exchange fines and suspensions, but nothing more. Often, the agency is not even aware of the details of a given incident. Rap sheets, which include both proven and unproven charges in a person's record, are useful to cops on the street; so would a list of all exchange actions help regulators discern a pattern of activity. Certainly, if favoritism is present in the disciplinary process, a comprehensive list of both proven and unproven allegations would be helpful. The NFA does not even receive reports on exchange findings of guilt. That must change. What's more, the agencies should actively cross-check new filings to keep tabs on repeat offenders.

☐ Register all traders, both locals and brokers, with the NFA.

Currently, locals do not have to register with the agency. A broker whose CFTC registration is revoked can become a local and continue to abet corruption. Ample testimony in the trials shows that it takes two, a local and a broker, to steal. By forcing even local traders to register with the NFA, regulators would have the power to revoke registration, thereby booting unsavory characters off the exchange.

☐ Make brokerage firms send lists of the disciplinary histories of all floor brokers they employ to their customers.

Every firm thinks it deals only with the best brokers. There might be a few dishonest creeps on the floor, but they always fill orders for some *other* customer, or so the thinking goes. If the firms know that their customers will be looking over their shoulders on broker selection, they'll be more inclined to choose carefully. An added benefit: Brokers who know that improprieties will cost them business will think twice about the funny stuff.

☐ To strengthen the CFTC, double the agency's budget and staff.

At a time when the challenges to regulation are becoming ever more sophisticated, the CFTC is woefully underfunded to combat crime. The 518-person staff and $34.7 million 1989 budget were barely a notch above the level of 1979, while the industry's daily trading volume of 260 million contracts was more than triple 1979 levels. Budget balancers should look to the example set by the Securities and Exchange Commission. Thanks to an aggressive enforcement department, the SEC is one of the few federal agencies that actually turns a profit.

☐ Give the CFTC permanent authorization.

The quadrennial minuet among the exchanges, regulators, and legislators is a three-step to disaster. Unlike the SEC, which exists indefinitely, the CFTC must go begging to Congress every four years for a new life. The upshot: The agency depends on supportive legislators, who in turn accept financial support from the exchanges. A regulator that angers the exchanges just might anger the lawmakers, and invite disaster. The system is a recipe for "Just Do Whatever You Want" regulation. And reauthorization now has become a permanent process, a mini-industry on Capitol Hill. The CFTC's weak position also plays to the advantage of the SEC, which is seeking to undermine the CFTC's clout in the financial markets. The CFTC's perpetual reauthorization process gives the SEC, which already has home-court advantage among the old money and power sets in Washington and New York, too many free swipes at its rival agency.

☐ Don't give the CFTC authority for covert operations.

Face it, the CFTC is not the FBI. It does not have the resources, much less the apparatus and experience, to conduct undercover stings. Besides, the CFTC's regrettable enforcement record shows that the agency has enough trouble flexing its overt power, never mind the covert variety. If nothing else, Sourmash and Hedgeclipper demonstrate that the CFTC can turn to the experts if it thinks a covert investigation will uncover what dutiful overt work cannot. If adequately funded, the CFTC could help finance such work. The idea of allowing those stiff CFTC suits who watch the markets each day to play Joe G-man makes us shiver.

☐ To modernize the markets, introduce computerized trading during nighttime, and during the day.

If open outcry really is the best system in the world, as the exchanges claim, it should be able to go head to head with black boxes. The exchanges control the modernization timetable because they know nobody can force them to computerize: The Commodity Futures Trading Act gives them a monopoly on futures trading. They should be forced to earn that privilege by putting their system of shouts and hand signals up against bits and bytes. We're willing to give open outcry the benefit of the doubt; perhaps it would win. Most certainly it would be improved by the competition. Delaying the introduction of computers will only delay improvements in open outcry, which means when computers make their inevitable appearance, open outcry already may be dead.

☐ Give small investors a break by using computers to match retail orders.

If the trials made one thing clear it was this: The small trades, the one- and two-lots, are easy prey for unscrupulous traders. What's more, they're at a disadvantage in the market anyway, because many traders do not want to be bothered with them. At the Chicago Board Options Exchange, the Retail Automated Execution System, dubbed

RAES, automatically matches retail orders, assigning buys and sells to floor traders who sign up for the system each day. With no need for alteration, such a system would work well in the futures pits.

That's enough for starters. We do not claim that our prescription will automatically rout corruption on the commodity exchanges. If we've learned anything sitting through trials and interviewing traders, lawyers, and government officials, we've found that the incentive to steal far outweighs the ingenuity of those who would stamp out theft. It is time to strengthen the disincentive against crime.

Chapter Notes

CHAPTER ONE: *The Knock at the Door*

Pp. 14–17. Testimony of James Sledz, Brian Sledz, Dietrich Volk, and others during hearing held by U.S. District Court Judge William T. Hart on January 30, 1990.

Pp. 18–20. Interviews with participants.

Pp. 20–25. Testimony of John Baker, Sally Baker, Dietrich Volk, and others in suppression hearing held January 29, 1990. Also, interviews with Baker's lawyers and with Chicago Mercantile Exchange traders.

Pp. 25–28. Interviews with William Crawford, Christopher Drew, William Neikirk, and others.

Pp. 28–31. Interviews with numerous traders and clerks on January 19, 1989. Also, various press accounts, particularly from Knight-Ridder Financial News. Observations of authors.

Pp. 32–33. Interviews with numerous defense lawyers.

Pp. 33–36. Interviews with participants.

Pp. 36–38. Interviews with Andrew Yemma, John Geldermann, Jerrold Salzman, William Crawford, Jr., and others. Observations by the authors.

CHAPTER TWO: *Manias, Bucket Shops, and Corners*

Pp. 42–43. J. Duncan LaPlante, "Growth and Organization of Commodity Markets," in Perry J. Kaufman, editor, *Handbook of Futures Markets: Commodity, Financial, Stock Index, and Options* (New York: John Wiley & Sons, 1984).

Pg. 44. Tulipomania information from Charles Mackay, *Extraordinary Popular Delusions and the Madness of Crowds* (Boston: L.C. Page, 1932).

Pp. 45–50. We used several helpful sources for early Board of Trade history: Charles H. Taylor, *History of the Board of Trade of the City of Chicago, Volume I* (Chicago: Robert O. Law Co., 1917).

Legal and legislative developments, particularly regarding bucket shops and populists: Jonathan Lurie, *The Chicago Board of Trade 1859–1905: The Dynamics of Self-Regulation* (Urbana, Ill.: University of Illinois Press, 1979). Also, Leon T. Kendall, "The Chicago Board of Trade and the Federal Government: A Study of Their Interrelationship, 1848 to 1952," a doctoral dissertation for the Indiana University School of Business, 1956.

Economic interpretation: Thomas A. Hieronymus, *Economics of Futures Trading For Commercial and Personal Profit* (New York: Commodity Research Bureau, 1971).

A comprehensive and readable history: William G. Ferris, *The Grain Traders: The Story of the Chicago Board of Trade* (East Lansing, Mich.: Michigan State University Press, 1988).

Pp. 50–53.   Leiter corner information from several sources. Edward Jerome Dies, *The Plunger: A Tale of the Wheat Pit* (New York: Covici-Friede, 1929).

Paul Gilbert and Charles Lee Bryson *Chicago and Its Makers*, (Chicago: Felix Mendelsohn, 1929).

Irwin Ross, "The Wheat Pit's Wildest Ride Ever." *Commodities*, August 1978.

George Horace Lorimer, "The Man Who Could Not Be Cornered." *Chicago Magazine*, Spring 1966.

William G. Ferris, "The Great Corner." *The Farm Quarterly*, Spring 1966.

Chicago Daily Tribune, January 2, 1898.

Pp. 53–54.   James A. Patten with Boyden Sparkes, *In the Wheat Pit* (New York: The Curtis Publishing Co., 1927), a reprint of a series of articles originally published by the *Saturday Evening Post*. Also, *Worker's Magazine*, April 18, 1890. *Harper's Weekly*, May 1, 1909, and extensive coverage in *Chicago Daily Tribune*.

Pp. 55–56.   John H. Stassen, "Propaganda as Positive Law—Section 3 of the Commodity Exchange Act. (A Case Study of How Economic Facts Can be Changed by Act of Congress)." *Chicago Kent Law Review*, Vol. 8, No. 3, 1982.

Pp. 56–57.   Cutten testimony before Business Conduct Committee, Chicago Board of Trade archives, April 21, 1927. Also, April 9, 1927 copies of the *Chicago Daily Tribune* and Chicago *Herald-American*; April 20, 1927 issue of *The Price Current-Grain Reporter*. Cutten tax information from *Chicago Daily Tribune*.

CHAPTER THREE: *Stumbling Toward Reform*

Pp. 58–59.   Sources for Crawford information include *The New York Times*, July 25, 1933 and August 13, 1933. Also, hearings before the U.S. House Committee on Agriculture, February 5, 7, 8, 1935, transcript from Chicago Board of Trade archives.

Pp. 59–60.   Spats incident from *The New York Times*, December 28, 1933.

Pp. 60–62.   Report of the Special Committee of the Board of Trade, March 28, 1938, Chicago Board of Trade archives. *The New York Times*, December 2, 1937 and March 26, 1938. Also, Dan Morgan, *Merchants of Grain* (New York: Viking Press, 1979).

Pg. 63.   Letter of Daniel F. Rice to the Chicago Board of Trade's directors, December 7, 1959, from Chicago Board of Trade archives.

Pp. 64–65.   *The New York Times*, December 6 and 24, 1963. Report of Chicago Board of Trade special committee, February 20, 1964, Chicago Board of Trade archives.

Pg. 66.   *Chicago Tribune*, October 13, 1973, March 4, 1974.

Pp. 67–69.   The best account of the Hunt episode is: Stephen Fay, *Beyond Greed* (New York: Viking Press, 1982).

Pp. 71–72.   Sanders case received extensive coverage, the best of which was *Barron's*, February 22, 1988.

Pg. 71.   Judge Aspen's remarks from transcript of trial, U.S. vs. Sanders et al., November 3, 1988.

CHAPTER FOUR: *Scrappy Survivor: The Early Years of the Merc*

Pp. 73–75.   Early history of the Merc comes from documents in the Chicago Mercantile Exchange archives, including annual reports for the years 1922–1935 published in the *Dairy Produce Yearbook*, copies of the 1898 Chicago Butter and Egg Board certificate of intention, and the 1915 articles of incorporation.

Pp. 73–76.   Harold Speer Irwin, *Evolution of Futures Trading*, 1954.

Pg. 76.   Edwin Nourse, *The Chicago Produce Market*, 1918.

Pp. 80–85.   Interview with Everette B. Harris, May 1990.

Pp. 80–85.   Chicago Mercantile Exchange archives, interview with Everette B. Harris, November 1989.

Pp. 83–85.   Interview with Glenn Andersen, May 1990.

Pp. 84–85.   Interview with Leo Melamed, June 1990.

Pp. 80–82.   Information on the onion market incident from *The Chicago Daily Tribune*, June 23, 1956; *The New York Times*, October 9, 1956, *The New York Times*, August 30, 1958; *Chicago Tribune*, November 11, 1959, and a later *Barron's* article by Holbrook Working, February 4, 1963. Also, interviews with Chicago Mercantile Exchange members.

Pg. 83.   Information on G. H. Miller and Co.'s license revocation in relation to the Merc's egg market is from *The New York Times*, September 27, 1956.

Pg. 85.   National Cattlemen's Association poll, 1986.

CHAPTER FIVE: *Years of Plenty: The Young Turks Take Charge*

Pp. 87–96.   Historical and statistical information from International Monetary Market yearbooks, 1974–1980; Chicago Mercantile Exchange annual reports 1983–1986, and from an unpublished history of CME products and volume, Chicago Mercantile Exchange department of statistics.

Pp. 87–92.   Account of Leo Melamed's early years as Merc chairman from interview with Melamed, June 1990.

Pp. 94–95.   Gold volume from Merc and COMEX statistics departments.

Pp. 96–97.   Discussion of the Harold Brady Mexican peso tax case taken from court documents, including: In the matter of The Siegel Trading Company, Inc., United States of America before the Commodity Futures Trading Commission, CFTC docket No. 77-1, judgment recorded May 26, 1978; Testimony of Maury A. Kravitz, August 18, 1977, In the matter of The Siegel Trading Co., before a CFTC administrative law judge; United States of America vs. Joseph Siegel and Alvin Winograd, No. 78 CR606 before Judge James B. Moran, Government's pre-trial brief docketed February 6, 1980 and transcripts of court proceedings February–April 1980.

Pp. 96–97.   For a general discussion of tax straddles and commodities trading see *The Wall Street Journal*, June 6, 1978, p. 1.

Pp. 99–100.   Discussion of conditions on the Merc trading floor from interviews with floor traders.

Pp. 101–102.   Information regarding broker groups from interviews with floor traders and Chicago Mercantile Exchange special executive reports regarding dual trading and broker groups, 1987.

CHAPTER SIX: *Leo & Co.: The Merc Today*

Pp. 106–107.   *Chicago Sun-Times*, January 9, 1967. Margaret Laws, "Vanguard of the Futures: That's Where Leo Melamed Has Put the Merc." *Barron's*, March 29, 1982. Leo Melamed as told to Barbara Marsh, "I'm Alive! That Entitles Me to a Commercial Motivation." *Crain's Chicago Business*, June 7, 1988. Ginger Szala, "Leo Melamed. Father of Financial Futures Builds Exchange and Industry." *Futures*, July 1988.

Also, interview with Leo Melamed, October 19, 1990.

Pg. 108.   "Intermarket Interview: Leo Melamed." *Intermarket*, July 1986. Speech by Leo Melamed, Boca Raton, Florida, March 8, 1990. Conversation with John Conheeny, Boca Raton, Florida, March 8, 1990.

Congressional incidents: *The Wall Street Journal*, December 3, 1984. Also, interviews with congressional staffers.

Pg. 109.   *Chicago Sun-Times*, December 16, 1987.

Pp. 109–110.   *Chicago Sun-Times*, December 19, 1988.

Pg. 111.   Referendum letter by Emmett Whealan, Douglas Bragan, May 1990. Interviews with Bragan, others.

Pp. 112–113.   Anonymously circulated memos to Merc members, dated June 18, 1990, June 21, 1990. Also, yen trader Sam A. Cali's Oct. 1, 1990 court memorandum in support of his "custom and practice" defense strategy.

Pg. 114.   Interview with Brian Monieson. October 4, 1990.

"Intermarket Interview: Brian Monieson." *Intermarket*, January 1985.

Pg. 115. *The Wall Street Journal.* October 27, 1989. Also, Merc disciplinary action of August 8, 1986, interviews with Merc staffers, and Monieson interview.

Pp. 115–116. GNP information from CFTC administrative hearing In Re: GNP Commodities, et al. November 1989. CFTC Docket No. 89-1.

Pg. 117. Account of Yeutter and Melamed testimony in Chicago.

Pp. 117–125. Interview with John F. "Jack" Sandner, January 1991; interview with Maury Kravitz, November 1990. Particularly useful were *Chicago Sun-Times*, January 22, 1987 and January 18, 1980; "A Maverick at the Merc," *Forbes*, February 1, 1982. The Congressional Witch Trial; *Intermarket*, August 1988, and March and April 1986; *The Wall Street Journal*, April 7, 1980.

Pp. 117–118. The Herrings' experience with RB&H was taken from *Chicago Tribune*, February 29, 1989.

Pg. 122. Chicago Mercantile Exchange pamphlet of Sandner's speeches to the membership.

Pp. 122–123. Information on Sandner's committee appointments come from the Merc's committee listings for 1986, and on Merc disciplinary records.

Pg. 124. *The Wall Street Journal*, October 2, 1989.

Pp. 124–125. *The Wall Street Journal*, February 10 and 14, 1989.

Pg. 125. CFTC sanctions against RB&H noted in CFTC press release dated September 28, 1987.

Pp. 125–133. Information on Maury Kravitz, ABS Partners and broker group comes in part from interview with Kravitz, November 1990.

Pp. 125–126. *Chicago Tribune*, November 24, 1987.

Pg. 127. Discussion of broker groups comes from interviews with clearing firm managers and Chicago Mercantile Exchange floor traders. Also see *Chicago Tribune*, January 30, 1989.

Pp. 128–129. From interviews with ABS Partners customers and ABS Partners marketing brochure issued in 1990.

Pg. 129. Background on members of the ABS Partners group from National Futures Association registration documents and interviews with Chicago Mercantile Exchange traders.

Pg. 129. National Futures Association and the Chicago Crime Commission. *The Wall Street Journal*, May 10, 1989; *Chicago Tribune*, June 24, 1986.

Pg. 130. *Chicago Tribune*, November 30, 1989.

Pg. 130. Information on Lewis Borsellino comes from ABS Partners marketing brochure, Merc disciplinary records, interviews with floor traders, and *Chicago Tribune*, January 11, 1988.

Pg. 132. Interrelationships between floor broker groups can be seen in unpublished CFTC computer printout—"CME registration of broker associations." Also, Ginger Szala and Susan Abbott, "Broker Groups: The Good, and Bad and the Ugly," *Futures*, February 1990.

Pg. 132. Merc disciplinary records.

CHAPTER SEVEN: *Inside the Board of Trade*

Pp. 135–136.   Ginger Szala, "Karsten 'Cash' Mahlmann: Chairman's Teamwork Approach Sparks CBOT Developments." *Futures*, July 1988. *Chicago Tribune*, January 9, 1987. Also, interviews.

Pg. 137.   *The Wall Street Journal*, January 5, 1988.

Pg. 137.   Testimony before the Senate Committee on Agriculture, Nutrition and Forestry, May 17, 1989. Stotler's hiring of Michael Kolb: *The Wall Street Journal*, February 13, 1989. Information on Stotler's hiring of introducing brokers from National Futures Association registration records. Stotler's public offering information from Securities and Exchange Commission filings and various newspaper reports. Also, David Greising, "This Trader's Future Looks Bearish." *Business Week*, August 6, 1990.

Pg. 138.   Best account of Egan's rise at Stotler is *Chicago Tribune*, August 19, 1990. Information on SEC and CFTC roles in Stotler affair from interviews by authors.

Stotler financial information from Stotler's SEC filings, Stotler's public statements of July 15, 24, and 25, 1990, various newspaper stories and interviews. Also, CFTC U.S. District Court lawsuit against Stotler Group filed in Chicago, July 31, 1990.

Pp. 140–141.   Interview with Donovan, September 27, 1990. Various newspaper stories about Donovan, particularly *Chicago Sun-Times*, August 10, 1964 and September 7, 1974. Bill Granger and Lori Granger. *Lords of the Last Machine* (New York: Random House, 1987).

Pg. 143.   Interview with Leslie Rosenthal, December 1989. CFTC settlement with Rosenthal & Co., Leslie Rosenthal and others, November 13, 1986. Also, CFTC order of June 8, 1984, regarding CFTC Docket 77-10.

Chicago Tribune, November 26, 1980 and November 26, 1981. Information about election abnormalities from: *Chicago Tribune*, January 12, 1982. David Greising, "A Blast from the Past for the Chicago Board of Trade?" *Business Week*, December 25, 1989. Information about Rosenthal's actions as chairman from various newspaper accounts, interviews with past board members and CBOT files.

CHAPTER EIGHT: *Friends in High Places*

Pp. 146–149.   Chicago Mercantile Exchange disciplinary actions regarding Anthony Castellano were issued September 26, 1983; October 29, 1985; April 3, 1987; and November 18, 1989. Also, In the matter of Anthony Castellano before the Commodity Futures Trading Commission, George H. Painter, administrative law judge, CFTC docket no. SD-88-1. Decision November 23, 1988.

Pp. 149–150.   Knight-Ridder Financial News, February 6, 1989.

Pg. 152.   Testimony of Richard L. Fogel, Assistant Comptroller General, General Government Programs, before the Senate Committee on Agriculture, Nutrition, and Forestry, February 23, 1989.

Pp. 152–156. All political action committee data are from the Federal Election Commission.

Pg. 152. "Money to Burn," *Common Cause Magazine*. January/February 1985.

Pg. 155. From AMPAC records and CFPF annual report to members, CFPF newsletter, 1988.

Pg. 156. Interview with Thomas Donovan, October 1988.

Pg. 157. Interview with Jack Sandner, October 1988. Knight-Ridder Financial News, October 13 and 19, 1988. *The Wall Street Journal*, October 20, 1987 and February 2, 1989; "Interview," *Intermarket*, March 1986.

Pg. 158. *Chicago Sun-Times*, September 23, 1988.

Pg. 159. Interview with Warren Lebeck, June 1990.

Pg. 159. Historical budget figures from the CFTC and the SEC.

Pp. 160–163. Interview with Robert Wilmouth, October 1990.

Pp. 160–161. NFA Rulebook.

Pg. 161. Schallaci information from NFA disciplinary decision, July 1, 1988, also Merc disciplinary actions dated December 8, 1980; April 12, 1983; February 8, 1985; and May 23, 1988.

Pg. 163. *The Wall Street Journal*, Oct. 16, 1990.

CHAPTER NINE: *From Abscam to Hedgeclipper*

Pp. 168–171. The authoritative source on Operation Greylord is: James Tuohy and Rob Warden. *Greylord: Justice, Chicago Style* (New York: G. Putnam's Sons, 1989). Useful information on history of undercover stings came from: Fiora Johnson Skelly, "Honeytraps." *Chicago Lawyer*, January 1984 and Rob Warden, "Fake Cases." *Chicago Lawyer*, January 1984. Also, *Chicago Sun-Times*, March 22, 1986; December 16, 1986; March 4, 1987; May 2, 1987.

Pp. 171–173. Incubator information from *Chicago Tribune*, December 25, 1985; January 2, 1986; January 20, 1986, and other dates. Also, interview with Anton Valukas, October 10, 1990. Interview with Thomas M. Burton, September 1989. *Chicago Tribune*, January 24, 1989.

Pp. 173–175. Interviews with Valukas, Stephen Senderowitz, and others. Also, various newspaper stories, particularly useful was: Walter B. Levis and Dan Weir, "The 'Tough Tony' Years: Tackling White Collar Crime." *Chicago Lawyer*, January 1990.

Pg. 175. On Groover case, various newspaper sources, records of proceedings in U.S. v. Richard C. Groover, 77 CR 560.

Pg. 175. *Chicago Tribune*, January 22, 1989.

Pp. 176–178. Information on boiler room operations from interviews with Paul Jenkins and Stephen Senderowitz, various court filings, and numerous newspaper articles. Of particular note: *Chicago Tribune*, October 14, 1979; *Journal of Commerce*, March 26 and March 27, 1980.

CHAPTER TEN: *The Origins of the Sting*

Pp. 179–181. Best sources of Andreas information were: Ronald Henkoff, "Oh, How the Grain Grows at ADM." *Fortune*, October 8, 1990.

Lee Froehlich, "On Top of the Food Chain: Why Dwayne Andreas' Clout Extends Beyond the Farm Belt." *Chicago Enterprise*, July/August 1989. E. J. Kahn, Jr., "Profiles: The Absolute Beginning." *The New Yorker*, February 16, 1987.

Pp. 181–182.   Interview with Dwayne Andreas, August 1990.

Pp. 182–185.   Information on original meetings from various sources at FBI, U.S. Attorney's office, and ADM. Also, certain information was disclosed in testimony of Richard Ostrom in U.S. vs. Dempsey et al. Dan K. Webb did not respond to repeated requests for interviews.

Pp. 185–186.   Information on ADM's March 1985 soybean oil trading from interviews with past Business Conduct Committee members and other Board of Trade sources.

Pp. 187–190.   Interviews with various government sources, exchange records and observation of authors.

CHAPTER ELEVEN: *Life as a Mole*

Pg. 191.   Authors gained access to Richard Ostrom's FBI Form 302 of January 22, 1986, which was not released at trial.

Pg. 192.   Interviews with various government sources. Interview with Daniel Henning, January 1989.

Pg. 193.   NFA filings of Richard Ostrom/"Rick Carlson," Michael Bassett/"Michael McLoughlin," Randall Jannett/"Randy Jackson," and Dietrich Volk/"Peter Vogel." Also, *Chicago Tribune*, January 20, 1989 and February 7, 1989; *Chicago Sun-Times*, January 22, 1989. Knight-Ridder Financial News, January 20, 1989 and January 23, 1989, as well as various testimony at trial.

Unless otherwise noted, information in this chapter comes from testimony of the FBI agent involved, and tape recordings of conversations. Prosecution and defense versions of tapes sometimes differed. We used official transcripts offered at trial.

Pp. 195–196.   Testimony of Richard Ostrom, taped conversation in U.S. vs. Dempsey et al.

Pg. 196.   Interview with Jacob Morowitz, August 1990.

Pp. 197–198.   Testimony of Randall Jannett, taped conversations in U.S. vs. Mosky et al.

Pp. 200–202.   Testimony of Jannett, taped conversation, testimony of Mark Fuhrman in U.S. vs. Mosky et al.

Pg. 202.   Testimony of Dietrich Volk, taped conversation in U.S. vs. Bailin et al.

Pg. 204.   Interview with Jacob Morowitz.

Pg. 207.   Interviews with various government sources.

Pp. 208–209.   Interview with Jacob Morowitz.

Pg. 209.   Testimony of Volk, Thomas Braniff, and taped conversation in U.S. vs. Bailin et al.

Pg. 213.   Interviews with various government sources.

Pg. 214.   FBI Form 302 interview with James Nowak, not disclosed at trial.

CHAPTER TWELVE: *Running for Cover*

Pp. 218–219.　Interviews with Susan Shellenbarger, Scott Mc-Murray, John Koten and others.

Pg. 219.　Interview with Gavin Maliska, personal observations.

Pp. 221–222.　Interview with Greg Burns.

Pp. 222–223.　Interviews with Christopher Drew, William Neikirk, William Crawford, Jr., and others.

Pp. 223–224.　Interview with *New York Times* sources. Eric Berg does not recall the reason for his late appearance.

Pp. 224–227.　Interviews with Celesta Jurkovich, Thomas Donovan, Leo Melamed, Andrew Yemma, and others.

Pg. 226.　CIVN producer Kelly Murphy denies that the network reported that Melamed had been subpoenaed. CIVN did not retain tapes of its broadcast.

Pp. 227–229.　Testimony of William Walsh, U.S. vs. Mosky et al.

Pp. 229–230.　Interviews with Gavin Maliska, Greg Burns, and personal observations.

Pp. 230–233.　Interviews with various government sources.

Pp. 234–235.　*The Wall Street Journal*, January 23, 1989. Interview with Leo Melamed, observations.

Pp. 235–238.　Interviews with William Crawford, Jr., Christopher Drew, and William Neikirk.

Pp. 239–240.　Interviews with Raymond Carmichael, Thomas Donovan, Paul McGuire, and various traders.

Pp. 240–241.　Interviews with Christopher Drew, William Neikirk.

CHAPTER THIRTEEN: *Damage Control*

Pg. 243.　Interviews with Thomas Eagleton, Jerrold Salzman, and other members of the blue ribbon committee.

Pp. 244–245.　Interviews with Christopher Drew and John Troelstrup. "Chicago Tonight with John Callaway." WTTW-TV, Chicago, February 2, 1989.

Pp. 245–246.　Interviews with various traders, newspaper accounts.

Pp. 246–247.　Interview with Thomas M. Burton. *Chicago Tribune*, February 5, 1989.

Pp. 247–248.　Interview with John Koten, copy of *The Wall Street Journal* survey, and various newspaper reports.

Pp. 248–249.　Interviews with various congressional staffers and numerous newspaper articles.

Pp. 249–251.　March 9, 1989 testimony of Wendy Gramm before Senate Committee on Agriculture, Nutrition and Forestry. Also, various newspaper accounts and interviews with Senate staffers.

Pp. 251–252.　Interviews with participants. Jack Sandner and Leo Melamed claim no recollection of the meeting.

Pp. 252–253.　David L. Protess and Rob Warden, "In the Pits." *Chicago Lawyer*, May 19, 1989. Also, interview with James Fox, tape of Jeff Bailey interview with Melanie Kosar.

Pp. 254–255. Interviews with Tim Brennan, John Geldermann, and other traders, newspaper accounts.

Pg. 256. Testimony of David Skrodzki and Pat Arbor in U.S. vs. Dempsey et al. Also, information about telephone threats from FBI Form 302 not revealed at trial.

Pp. 256–257. Interviews with lawyers. Eddie Genson declined comment.

Pp. 258–259. Interviews with Neikirk, Drew, and David Protess. Four articles by David L. Protess, "Commodities Investigation—The Story Behind The Story." *Chicago Lawyer*, March 1989. "Did the Press Play Prosecutor in Covering an FBI Sting?" *Columbia Journalism Review*, July/ August 1989. "Front Page: They Can Dish It Out, But They Can't Take It." *Chicago Times Magazine*, October 1989. "News That Can Wait: Reflections on the Commodities Controversy." *The Business Journalism Review*, January 1990. Also, letters to the editor of the *Columbia Journalism Review* by Christopher Drew, Dean Baquet, Thomas Burton, William Neikirk, and Jeff Bailey.

Pp. 260–261. Interviews with lawyers.

CHAPTER FOURTEEN: *The Reckoning*

Throughout this chapter, for purposes of readability, violations of the Commodity Exchange Act are referred to simply as "trading violations."

Pp. 262–267. Interviews with participants.

Pp. 267–269. Observations, interviews with traders, various newspaper accounts.

Pp. 269–273. Testimony, court filings, evidence, and interviews with defense and prosecution lawyers in U.S. vs. Dempsey et al. Also, interviews with lawyers. Also, National Futures Association registration files, interviews with traders, defense lawyers, August 3, 1989 issues of *Chicago Tribune*, *Chicago Sun-Times*, and *The Wall Street Journal* were used throughout remainder of chapter.

Pp. 273–274. Court filings, interviews in U.S. vs. Goberstein et al.

Pp. 274–276. Testimony, court filings, evidence, and interviews with defense and prosecution lawyers in U.S. vs. Mosky et al.

Pp. 276–279. Testimony, court filings, evidence, and interviews with defense and prosecution lawyers and certain traders in U.S. vs. Bailin et al.

CHAPTER FIFTEEN: *The Aftermath*

Pg. 283. Interview with U.S. Attorney Fred Foreman.

Pg. 286. Interview with Melanie Kosar.

Pg. 290. Interview with Leo Melamed, October 19, 1990.

Pp. 291–292. The Board of Trade discusses its trading reforms in a special report to membership, "Task Force for the Exchange Business Plan," July 18, 1990. Also, notice to members titled "Improvements to the Chicago Board of Trade's Surveillance and Governing Systems, as of September 1990."

Pp. 289–292. The Chicago Mercantile Exchange's special committee recommendations for trade practice revisions are from a report to members released April 19, 1989.

Pg. 292. Merc disciplinary action against Randy Broadwater, January 13, 1989.

Pg. 293. Time stamp discussion from interviews with clearing firm floor managers and officers.

Pg. 294. Volume statistics from the Futures Industry Association.

Pp. 295–296. CFTC proposed rules for requiring registration of broker associations published in Federal Register, Vol. 55, No. 70, April 11, 1990; regarding service on self-regulatory governing committees, Vol. 54, No. 171, September 6, 1989; restricting dual trading by floor brokers, Vol. 55, No. 6, January 11, 1990; and resolving trading errors and unmatched trades, Vol. 54, No. 171, September 6, 1989.

Pg. 298. Interviews with defense lawyers.

Index